THE MIGHTY 'MOX

THE MIGHTY 'MOX:

The 75th Anniversary History
of the People, Stories, and Events that
Made KMOX a Radio Giant

By Sally and Rob Rains

Foreword by Charles Brennan

Diamond Communications, Inc.
South Bend, Indiana

THE MIGHTY 'MOX:

The 75th Anniversary History
of the People, Stories, and Events that Made
KMOX a Radio Giant
Copyright © 2000 by Sally and Rob Rains

10 9 8 7 6 5 4 3 2 1

Manufactured in the United States of America

Diamond Communications, Inc.
Post Office Box 88
South Bend, Indiana 46624-0088
Editorial: 219-299-9278
Orders Only: 800-480-3717
Fax: 219-299-9296
Website: www.diamondbooks.com

Library of Congress Cataloging-in-Publication Data

Rains, Sally Tippett.
   The mighty 'MOX : the 75th anniversary history of the
people, stories, and events that made KMOX a radio giant / by Sally
and Rob Rains ; foreword by Charles Brennan.
   p. cm.
   ISBN 1-888698-35-7
  1. KMOX (Radio station : Saint Louis, Mo.)--History. 2. Radio
broadcasting--Missouri--Saint Louis--History. I. Rains, Rob. II. Title.
PN1991.3.U6 R35 2000
384.54'06'577866--dc21

00-047440

CONTENTS

Authors' Note...vi

Note to Readers...vii

Acknowledgments...viii

Foreword...xi

It Happened One Christmas Eve...xv

Roster

A 1

B 11

C 62

D 113

E 133

F 138

G 146

H 156

J 198

K 206

L 224

M 233

Roster

N 267

O 271

P 279

Q 283

R 289

S 303

T 325

V 330

W 335

Y 362

Z 363

Epilogue...370

Bibliography...372

About the Authors...375

AUTHORS' NOTE

The authors would like to express our appreciation to Jill Langford of Diamond Communications for her interest in publishing this book, and to Karen Carroll and Susan Tatham at KMOX for believing in the project. Frank Absher also provided a great deal of input and helpful information.

We would like to also thank our wonderful family, including sons B.J. and Mike, whom we hope to have 75 years of history to celebrate. In a way, we have KMOX to thank for our relationship. Sally was working at KMOX, covering a Cardinals' game, when we met. Rob was working for United Press International at the time.

We would like to dedicate this book to everyone at The Bob Costas Cancer Center at Cardinal Glennon Children's Hospital and the St. Louis University Radiation/Oncology Department. They perform miracles.

Sally and Rob Rains
September 2000

NOTE TO READERS

This book tells the story of the people and events in the 75 years KMOX has been on the air. The authors chose to let the people themselves tell the stories in their own words, having interviewed more than 120 past or present employees and more than 35 listeners or others with special KMOX memories.

This book is a collection of those stories, intended to be historically accurate but also a fun look at the people and events of the past 75 years. No two people remember stories exactly the same, and that is true in the stories contained in this book.

What is also true is the scores of great people and announcers who have worked at KMOX over the years. Some of them are well known to listeners, others worked behind-the-scenes and may have never had their names mentioned on the air. Still, they were important to the station's success and its heritage.

The authors encourage the readers to read all of the stories contained in this book, even if you may not know the person. You may know his or her stories, or the people he or she is talking about.

The book is not intended to be a listing of everyone who ever worked at KMOX. To do that would be impossible. Also, many of those who worked at KMOX over the years also went on to great careers at other stations or at the network level. The intent of this book is to share their experiences while working at KMOX, not their entire careers. We apologize to anyone we may have accidently left out.

Our goal is that reading a story will let the reader remember his own experiences of listening to KMOX, a very special radio station.

Sally and Rob Rains

ACKNOWLEDGMENTS

Thank you to the following people who have worked or done shows for KMOX and talked to us about their memories regarding KMOX:

Frank Absher, Tom Ackerman, John Amann, Vicki Atlas, Jim Baer, Jim Bafaro, Ron Barber, Shirley Bates, Lisa Bedian, Tony Bello, Joan Beuckman, Bill Bidwill, Jr., Rodger Brand, Charles Brennan, Mike Breitenstein, Dr. Armand Brodeur, Bob Broeg, Carole Buck, Jack Buck, Joe Buck, Tom Barton, Jack Buechner, Bob Canepa, John Carney, Karen Carroll, Mike Claiborne, Yvonne Cole, Larry Conners, Bob Costas, Frank Cusumano, Carol Daniel, Bob Danko, Tom Dehner, Duane Davison, Geri Davison, Tim Dorsey, Peggy (Cohill) Drenkhahn, Dave Dugan, Paul Douglass, Ollie Dowell, Alice English, Stuart Esrock, Barb Felt, Jan (Macchi) Fox, Bill Gainey, Jeanette (Hoag) Grider, Ed Griesedieck, Paul Grundhauser, Bob Hamilton, Harry Hamm, Coach Hammer, Bruce Hayward, Clint Hasse, Bea Higgins, Nancy Higgins, Bob Heil, Jim Holder, Rick Horton, Julius Hunter, Matt Hyland, Charles Jaco, Ron Jacober, Colin Jarrette, Ken Jones, Randy Karraker, Anne Keefe, Brian Kelly, Tom Langmyer, Cindy Lennox, Irv Litvag, Robert R. Lynn, Megan Lynch, Margie Manning, Greg Maracek, Don Marsh, Kent Martin, Susie Mathieu, Bob Mayhall, Emmett McAuliffe, Doug McElvein, Dan McLaughlin, Gene McNary, Jason Merrill, Don Miller, Mike Miller, McGraw Millhaven, Chris Mihill, Scott Mosby, Clarence (C.J.) Nieder, Juli Nieman, Bill Ott, Steve Overby, Mike Owens, Frank Pawloski, Joe Pollack, Rick Powers, Roy Queen, Jay Randolph, Bill Reker, Tinker Reilley, John Rooney, Rudy Ruzicka, Zip Rzeppa, Scott St. James, Tom Schiller, Vince Schoemehl, Rene Servier, Mike Shannon, Joe Sonderman, Elaine Stern, David Strauss, Susan Tatham, Casey Van Allen, Elaine Viets, Jim White, Pat White, Wendy Wiese, Taffy Wilbur, Emil Wilde, Bill Wilkerson, Ken Wilson, Nan Wyatt, and Don Wolff.

Thank you to the following people who helped us either by providing memories or helping us reach someone:

Babe Barham, Gordon Barham, Elaine Bly, Kathy Bosch, Adelle

ACKNOWLEDGMENTS

Burnes, Richard Buthod, Suzanne Corbett, Jim Cullen, Pam Davis, Martha DeGray, Ted Drewes, Brook Dubman, Pam Grant, Re Hardy, Mike Harris, Rena Hasse, Bill Hepper, Charles Hoessle, Kip Ingle, Bob Kuban, John Londoff, Sr., Lil Musial, Stan Musial, Nancy Newton, Earl Roach, Therese Shelton, Jerry Schober, Doug Sleade, Anna Smith, Curt Smith, Elmo Smith, Lemoine "Bud" Stark, Mary Stark, Joan Tabash, Lauri Van Slyke, and Frank Viverito.

An extra special thanks to Margie and Jack Tippett for their enthusiasm and tireless help with this book: reading it, checking for mistakes, offering suggestions, and picking up children when needed. You should get a bigger billing than this for all the help and support you provided.

FOREWORD

Stephen E. Ambrose is a celebrated bestselling author of numerous historical books, and is a frequent guest on KMOX radio. He was on the air one morning a few years ago, beginning the book tour for *Undaunted Courage*.

"Later that night, at 10 o'clock, I was finishing my book-signing appearance at the Missouri Historical Society in Forest Park," Ambrose said. "Suddenly a guy came running and puffing down the museum's long marble hallway.

"He came up to me out of breath and said, 'Thank God I got here in time. Would you sign one more?'"

Ambrose readily agreed, asking him how he had heard about the book signing.

"I was listening to KMOX this morning," the man said.

"I responded kind of casually, 'Well, where were you?'" asked Ambrose, expecting him to say he was driving around St. Louis or a similar reply.

"Actually," the man said, "I was 30,000 feet above St. Louis."

That response wasn't one Ambrose had anticipated. "How did you do that?" Ambrose inquired.

"The man said, 'I'm a pilot. I work for TWA. I always fly over the Missouri River and am enthralled by Lewis and Clark. I heard you on KMOX. I landed in Seattle, hopped immediately on a plane back to St. Louis, got a cab at Lambert and came over here. Now I've got to get back to the airport and back to Seattle to pick up my bird to get flying again tomorrow morning. Don't tell the FAA.'"

That story provided Ambrose with just one proper summation.

"KMOX," he said, "is my favorite radio station in the whole country."

For 75 years, KMOX has been bringing the worlds of news, information, sports, and entertainment to millions of listeners. No one radio station has ever done it better.

In 1998, the head of ABC Radio boasted at a New York radio conference that one of his stations, KGO in San Francisco, had been ranked number one longer than any other radio station in America, "except for KMOX in St. Louis, of course," he said.

What he was saying is something that is generally acknowledged by both executives and listeners alike: There is KMOX, and there is everybody else.

KMOX became the first radio station in the country to rank number one among all listeners for 100 consecutive quarterly ratings books. That is a span covering 25 years.

While the raw numbers are impressive, they don't come close to matching the stories of the people who have worked at KMOX over the past 75 years.

A young guitar player known as "Rhubarb Red" was part of *The International Oil Burner Show* between 4:30 and 7 AM from 1927 to 1930. He later became the famous country and jazz guitarist and inventor Les Paul.

In the summer of 1965 Bill Bradley worked for KMOX as a reporter.

In 1972, KMOX scooped the world that George McGovern had picked Missouri's Tom Eagleton to be his vice-presidential runningmate. KMOX's Bob Hardy was in Eagleton's hotel suite when the Missouri senator took the phone call from McGovern.

Part of the magic of KMOX is its unbelievable range. Washington insider Frank Mankiewicz has climbed to the highest point in Washington DC, the National Cathedral, to pick up KMOX. The late comedian Jerry Clower used to tune in from his home in Yazoo City, Mississippi.

Once, Jim White was telling listeners on his late-night program that he wished he had Charles Kuralt's job. The next call White took was from Kuralt, stuck in three feet of snow in Nebraska. He said he would trade places, taking White's spot in the warm KMOX studio.

Over the last 75 years, KMOX has been constantly changing, keeping up with the times. In 1927, a soprano singer was part of the staff. Years later, KMOX became the first CBS radio station to air editorials and endorse candidates for public office. The station broadcast Dr. Tom Dooley's programs from Southeast Asia. The 1960s brought the debut of talk radio and *At Your Service* programs. At the end of the Cold War, KMOX reporters visited five cities between Berlin and Moscow in five days.

FOREWORD

In 1994, the transcript of an interview with President Bill Clinton was printed verbatim in *The New York Times*. This year, KMOX will raise hundreds of thousands of dollars for charities through its "Outreach St. Louis" program.

The legacy of KMOX could well be the sports announcers who have passed through its studios. Some of the greatest names in broadcasting worked here, including Jack Buck, Dan Kelly, Bob Costas, Dan Dierdorf, Joe Garagiola, Harry Caray, Skip Caray, Bob Starr, Gary Bender, John Rooney, Mike Shannon, Joe Buck, Ron Jacober, Randy Karraker…the list goes on and on.

The most important people to KMOX, however, are the same now as they were 75 years ago, the listeners. They may not even realize how special KMOX is, because what they hear on the air is what they have come to know and expect. And nobody with the privilege and enjoyment of working there would have it any other way.

It is simply, according to people like Ambrose and those not as famous, the best radio station in America. Some things don't change.

Charles Brennan
September 2000

IT HAPPENED ONE CHRISTMAS EVE...

Christmas Eve is always a magical time, when much of the world celebrates the birth of Jesus Christ. It was especially magical for another reason in 1925, when a group of St. Louis businessmen had an additional reason to celebrate and Midwesterners had the beginnings of a "mighty" new friendship.

The group of businessmen had come together a few months earlier with the idea of starting a radio station. Other stations already were on the air in St. Louis at the time, but this group of investors had the idea of making their station the best in town. They called their group the Voice of St. Louis, Incorporated, and applied to the Commerce Department for the call letters KVSL. The request was denied.

The group then asked for the letters KMO, but learned that designation had already been granted to a maritime facility on the West Coast. So the group went back a third time and got its designation approved—KMOX.

The K is the letter designated for stations operating west of the Mississippi River. It was a coincidence that it also was the first letter of Kirkwood, the site of the first transmitting tower. MO is for Missouri and the X stood for Christmas Eve, the night of the first broadcast.

The station's debut was headline news in St. Louis, even if the original broadcast from the 5,000-watt transmitter site in Kirkwood was brief.

The first program broadcast on the station was Christmas music performed by the St. Peter's Episcopal Church choir. Nate Caldwell was the first announcer. After a short organ interlude, a symphony performed "The Star Spangled Banner" and "Hail to the Chief." The first broadcast from the station's lavish studios in the Mayfair Hotel originated the following day, Christmas Day.

Thomas Patrick Convey was the first general manager, and some of the earliest programming on KMOX included music, the market reports from the floor of the Merchants Exchange, musical performances, stories read on the air, and dance tunes.

The immediate response to KMOX's launch was very positive, not only in St. Louis but from listeners in far-flung locations. Telegrams came in from as far away as Saskatchewan, Canada, Oregon, Wyoming, and Colorado.

Mrs. John Noble in Marshfield, Oregon, reported, "Programs very clear. Will listen for your organ tomorrow night."

Even then, people were beginning to plan their days around the times of KMOX broadcasts.

"One of my earliest memories," said Bud Stark of south St. Louis, "is of the man who lived upstairs from us. He had a crystal radio. What a thrill it was to sit and listen to sound coming out of the air!"

In 1925, the population of St. Louis was comprised of a large number of German immigrants and newly assembled Italians, as the Hill had seen a significant growth in the first half of the decade. There was also a sizable Irish American contingent. The black population was on the increase and since 1910 the number of African-Americans in St. Louis and other urban areas of Missouri had increased by 30 percent. The state's Constitution mandated that schools were to be segregated. Though it was not Missouri law, most restaurants, hotels, hospitals, theaters, and athletic fields in St. Louis were segregated.

Prohibition continued to be a problem. Anheuser-Busch pressed forward and stayed in business by selling soft drinks made of corn sugar, malt syrup, and yeast.

Streetcars carried people where they wanted to go, along with buses and cars. People were becoming interested in balloons, dirigibles, and airplanes. Lambert Field was starting to be developed, and short flights between St. Louis and Chicago were increasing. A young man named Charles Lindbergh was flying the mail between the two cities. It was 18 months before his famous May 27, 1927 flight to Paris.

Freed-Eismann was advertising radio sets for sale in the *Globe-Democrat* for $145. "Know the joy of owning a radio," the advertisement read. "Have this Freed-Eismann radio installed in your home before New Year's Eve. Brings in distant stations with splendid success—and is simple to operate."

Roast at Thomas Market was 15 cents a pound. Vandervoorts was selling men's overcoats for $27.75. At Barney's, located at 10th and Washington, $1.25 percolators were on sale for 49 cents. C.E. Williams Show Store at 6th and Franklin was giving out double eagle stamps on Mondays. Famous Barr was selling bedroom chairs, normally $15, for $5.95.

Playing at the New St. Louis Theatre was *Gus Edward's Juvenile Frolic* and tickets for the night performances cost 65 cents. Playing at the Missouri Theater was James M. Barrie's *A Kiss for Cinderella*.

The first voice and musical broadcast had been in 1906, so when the licensed stations began to come on the air, they were already using music. In 1916 the great music composer W.C. Handy was heard on a Memphis experimental radio station. That was considered by many to be the first live musical broadcast.

Sports also was becoming an important part of radio, as it was also becoming increasing important in the lives of Americans who were following the exploits of heroes such as Babe Ruth and Jack Dempsey. Dempsey's heavyweight title bout against Billy Miske was the first prize fight broadcast on radio. The World Series also was carried on the radio, and baseball games were being broadcast over the telephone or by re-creation, giving the information after it had been received over the Western Union ticker.

The Cardinals won their first National League pennant in KMOX's first year on the air, 1926. There was no broadcast of games during the regular season, but KMOX carried the World Series. The headline in the *Globe-Democrat* on Tuesday morning, October 5, read: "KMOX to Broadcast Game Here Today Play by Play."

The story read:

Today's World Series game at Sportsman's Park will be broadcast by KMOX, "The Voice of St. Louis," starting at 1:30 PM with Porter Brown announcing. Through the courtesy of the Associated Press and the *Globe-Democrat*, the story of the game will be a running description of each pitched ball.

This service will be continued tomorrow and Thursday, and when the series goes back to New York for the final clash, the Associated Press wire, direct from the Yankee Stadium press box, will furnish the St. Louis fans, via KMOX, the play-by-play account of the game.

The score will be prominently announced in all parts of the city where there are radio receiving sets. No scores will be given out by the *Globe-Democrat* by telephone because of the congestion resulting from this practice.

The first regular-season broadcasts of Cardinals games came the following year, in 1927, with Garnett Marks the announcer. He broadcast the home games for both the Cardinals and Browns and did re-creations from the studio for the away games.

KMOX also gave extensive coverage to Lindbergh's historic flight. On an exhibition fly-over tour, Lindbergh came through St. Louis shortly after his historical flight to Paris.

"I was lucky enough to be able to see him," said Bud Stark, who was in grade school at the time. "They took all of the school children and put us on streetcars and took us downtown. We got to sit on the cobblestones by the Mississippi River. Lindbergh flew by, up and down the river for a while. How excited we were!"

By 1929, KMOX was growing. The station was authorized to increase its power from 5,000 to 50,000 watts and given clear-channel status. A year earlier the station had become one of the 16 original United Independent Broadcasters stations, a group that was to become the CBS network. The network agreed to provide each station with 10 hours of programming a week, paying the stations $50 an hour to carry the programming. The first major network advertiser was the Congress Cigar Co., led by a 25-year-old businessman named William S. Paley. He bought 26 weeks of advertising in the hope that it would increase sales. It was a huge success, and Paley became an investor in the network and later bought the network and renamed it CBS. The network became a "substantial" owner of the station in 1929 and took over management of the station in 1932.

KMOX was looking for new talent for local programming at the same time the network programming was being organized. A 16-year-old named Roy Queen heard about the auditions and hopped a train to St. Louis to try out. He was hired by Katherine McEntire, who was called the "manager" of the station.

Queen was a guitar-playing singer who could yodel. During his tryout, McEntire was in another room, but could hear the auditions. She came in and asked, "Who was that making that sound?" When told it was Queen, she said, "I like it, I think I can sell it."

In 1929 France Laux joined KMOX as another announcer. He originally was brought in from Oklahoma for a 30-day trial. He ended up staying until 1953.

Laux, who became famous for doing the Cardinals and Browns games, was the announcer on the music show and Queen was one of the performers. Queen worked on and off for KMOX over the next 25 years, with the *Uncle Dick Slack Show* in the 1940s being the most popular of his broadcasts.

The 1930s started what is commonly referred to as the "Golden Age" of Radio. The CBS network provided KMOX with much of its network programming, including the popular soap operas. The Cardinals' and the Browns' broadcasts were not regulated and could be heard on several radio stations including KMOX, KWK, and WIL with different announcers calling the games.

"I used to listen to France Laux," said Bing Devine, a longtime baseball executive. "What he said was what most people thought. He was very factual. In those days, it was fairly raw. Nobody came up with the idea of being a 'personality' on the radio. They just told you what was happening. The advent of television brought about all of these announcers with colorful personalities."

"I used to listen to France Laux every day there was a ballgame, or else I went to the games," said Martha DeGray. "I would come home from school about 3 o'clock and turn on the games and hear France Laux. Other days I'd grab a snack, then run over to the ballpark. I was part of the 'knot hole gang' when I was nine, so was Peanuts [Jim Zagarri, her good friend]. You had to talk to your teacher about it and they would give you a pass. You didn't have to pay; you could get in on your pass. The boys got to sit down the third-base line in what is now loge, but there weren't many girls and we had to sit up higher. I was nuts about Joe Medwick. I could see him from where I sat really well."

Devine, who eventually became general manager of both the St. Louis baseball and football Cardinals, worked as a runner at Sportsman's Park when Sam Breadon owned the team. It was one of his first jobs.

"My job was to go to the guy who was taking tickets and he would write down on a piece of paper the attendance, and then I'd take it up to the pressbox," Devine said. "You had to take it out to show Sam Breadon. Many times he would change the attendance number. I remember one day when the Browns had played a day game and the Cardinals were playing a little later in the same day. [They would often have two games at Sportsman's Park.]

"The Browns had played to 22,000 people and when the ticket manager gave me the paper, it said the Cardinals' attendance was 17,000. I took it out to Mr. Breadon and he said, 'What did the Browns do?' So he told me to change it to 24,000. I got another piece of paper and changed it, then I took it up to J. Roy Stockton, [of the *Post-Dispatch*] who said, 'Who are you trying to fool?' I said, 'That's what I was given.' Well, I could tell J. Roy was going to write something about them changing the attendance, so I went to Mr. Breadon's nephew. I said, 'It looks like we've got a problem. J. Roy doesn't like the attendance. He wrote the game story and put something in about it.' So the nephew went to Mr. Breadon and they changed it back to 17,000. Stockton wrote something like: 'The Cardinals originally announced 24,000 in attendance, but after re-examining their information they realized it was only 17,000.' Actually, it was fairly common to change the attendance in that day."

In the 1930s KMOX went through several general managers and each turned out to be so successful they were moved on to WBBM in Chicago. J.L. Van Volkenberg was named sales manager in 1932 and promoted to general manager a year later. Shortly before he took over, the station moved into new studios in the Mart Building, having outgrown the studios in the Mayfair Hotel.

The move to the Mart Building came in December 1931, where the new facility was three times the size of the old studios. There were seven studios in the new building, including the famous Studio B, which was two stories high to house a bi-level stage and featured a seating capacity of 400. That was the studio used for *The Land We Live In* broadcasts.

"You'd walk up one of two flights of curving stairs from the building lobby to the second floor, and there was a huge map of the United States on the wall with a light for each city in which CBS had a radio station," said Irv Litvag, a writer at KMOX in the 1950s. "St. Louis was the brightest light. The reception room was so large that you could fit one of today's radio stations inside of it. The large speaker on the wall had seven lights under it—one for each studio, and you could tell by glancing at them which studio was originating the show you were hearing. Then you went down a long hallway, and you could look through a plate glass window into the studios."

James Shouse succeeded Van Volkenburg as GM and served until

1937, when Merle Jones replaced him. Jones was involved in many of the significant developments in KMOX's history. Under his leadership, KMOX grew to 120 employees in 1938, making it the largest radio station in St. Louis.

"Merle Jones was an important general manager for KMOX," said Litvag. "He was one of the really great ones. KMOX became a great radio station under Merle Jones. In addition to doing a lot of sports broadcasting, they started producing local programs.

"They had a studio orchestra, quiz shows, and variety shows. This was before television, so the idea of a local radio show doing a quiz show would not be that unusual."

The most famous show that Jones was responsible for was *The Land We Live In*. It was a 30-minute weekly show, broadcast on Sunday nights, and sponsored by the Union Electric Co.

"It was a dramatic show featuring some facet of St. Louis history each week," said Litvag. "It was on from 6:30 to 7 PM."

In addition to listening to *The Land We Live In*, people were tuning in to KMOX to hear such entertainers as Tommy Dorsey, Benny Goodman, Wayne King, Guy Lombardo, and Glenn Miller.

Another popular show was the Santa Claus show. Children from all over the area would send their Christmas lists to KMOX and a Santa Claus, complete with "ho, ho, ho," would read the lists. Children loved to listen to be sure Santa got their lists. The Santa shows ran every evening for 15 minutes starting the day after Thanksgiving and running until December 23rd.

"We didn't have a radio until 1930," said Martha DeGray. "It just wasn't one of the necessities of life, so you didn't have one. I remember I used to run up to the neighbors' house to listen to Santa Claus. I would write letters each year and I'd rush up to the neighbor's to hear if Santa Claus would read my letter."

By 1933, CBS was producing its own shows, including *Jack Armstrong, the All-American Boy*.

One of the most exciting and popular shows of that era was *Amos 'n' Andy*. Next came Bing Crosby, Kate Smith, Eddie Cantor, Burns and Allen, Ed Wynn, Rudy Vallee, and the ventriloquist Edgar Bergen with his dummy, Charlie McCarthy.

The importance of radio was evident when H.G. Wells' book, *The War of the Worlds* was broadcast nationally in 1938 and despite three warnings that it was a fictional broadcast, many people who heard the program but not the advisory panicked. It was a terrifying night for many listeners.

"I'll never forget the day they broadcast that the world was coming to an end. [*The War of The Worlds* broadcast]," said Babe Barham. "Boy it scared everyone. Gordon [her husband] was listening with me."

"It was so real," her husband said. "We didn't know what to do. We really thought the world was coming to an end; it was terrible."

"We called the kids up we were so scared," said Babe.

People became so involved with the radio programs that they planned their schedules for the day around the broadcasts. According to the *Globe-Democrat* in a February 14, 1949 article: "Telephone switchboards at KMOX, the *St. Louis Globe-Democrat*, and the police headquarters were jammed by thousands of callers when a broken cable caused listeners to miss the entire 'Jack Benny Program' and the 'Amos 'n Andy Show,' the last ten minutes of 'The Spike Jones Show,' and the first ten minutes of 'The Adventures of Sam Spade.' According to Wendell Campbell, KMOX's general manager, 'It couldn't have happened at a worse time—Benny's show is one of the more popular on the air."

"When I was a teenager, KMOX had soap operas on," said Mary Stark, who used to listen to them in the 1930s and 1940s. "They used to list the shows every day in the newspapers. The soap operas were usually 15 minutes long and my favorite was *Ma Perkins*.

"I believe Oxydol owned *Ma Perkins*. When I got married, I was home all day and I listened to *Ma Perkins* every day. I'll never forget one day I went downtown and suddenly I remembered *Ma Perkins* was in this terrible position—a cliffhanger. I got so upset I was going to miss it! That was when I found out you could go for a week and they'd drag those things out."

"My mother liked *Ma Perkins*, too," said Martha DeGray. "My father worked at Proctor and Gamble, so maybe it was because it was sponsored by Oxydol."

Stark also remembered programs like *Little Theatre on Times Square* and *Lux Radio Theatre*. "They were half-hour shows," she said. "*Lux*

Theatre was Cecil B. DeMille. It was the movies on radio. He was the announcer. On *Little Theatre in Times Square* I remember an actor named Les Tremaine."

The Lux Radio Theater was one of the more popular shows on KMOX at the time. DeMille was the host, and each program was a condensed version of movies, often times featuring the original stars. DeMille was the biggest name in Hollywood.

"Soap operas on radio were a big part of our lives," said Gordon Barham, a great-grandfather and longtime listener of KMOX. "Mondays were always wash days in our house. They were wash days because my mother said they should be, and she came over to help my wife, Babe, and I."

"Back in those days people were more regimented about when they did things," said Babe Barham, "like Monday was wash day, Tuesdays we did the mending, like that. Anyway, we would do the wash in the basement and we would be listening to the radio. We liked to listen to *Our Gal Sunday* and *Helen Trent.*"

Our Gal Sunday was about a girl from the Appalachian Mountains who married an English nobleman, and her adaptations to the new life of royalty. It was very popular and came on right before the news.

"One day my mom got her arm stuck in the ringer on the washer," said Barham. "I didn't know how to stop it, so I reversed it."

The radio was on the whole time.

"The funny thing about those days was how everybody would gather around and 'watch' the radio," said Babe Barham. "It was like a television set, even though you couldn't see anything, people would just sit around the radio. It was a big part of our lives back then."

"I remember we lived on a farm [near what is now Florissant]," said Anna Smith of south St. Louis County. "When *Our Gal Sunday* would come on, my sister Mary would call my mother and she stopped whatever she was doing to come in and listen. If she was out in the fields, she would still come in and pull her stool up to the radio. We had an upright, cabinet type radio in the dining room and that's where everybody would be."

The city of St. Louis was growing. In 1935 it was decided to build

a new park area along the downtown riverfront. The Jefferson National Expansion Memorial was established by an executive order signed by President Franklin Roosevelt. Demolition of the buildings on what is now the Arch grounds began in 1939, even though it would be more than 25 years before the Gateway Arch was completed.

Then and now, listeners were brought to their radios not only because of feature programming but also because of major news announcements. Such was the case when it was announced on December 7, 1941 that the Japanese had bombed Pearl Harbor.

Nearly everyone who heard that broadcast remembers where he or she was or exactly what he or she was doing at that moment.

"I'll never forget hearing the announcement of the bombing of Pearl Harbor on the radio," said Elmo Smith, a resident of South County.

President Roosevelt began using the radio for his "fireside chats." It was a way to come into Americans' homes and talk to them.

During the war, Americans stayed near their radios to be informed on what was happening with the troops and to find relief from war worries with their favorite entertainers. Stars such as Bob Hope, Fibber McGee and Molly, Red Skelton, Arthur Godfrey, and Frank Sinatra all became famous during the 1940s.

"We got married in 1941," said Elmo Smith. "One of the gifts we got for our wedding was a portable radio. The table models were starting to become popular around this time. We still have it. It was a square black plastic radio."

"We listened to Arthur Godfrey all the time," said Martha DeGray, longtime resident of St. Louis. "I remember Tony Marvin was an announcer on the *Arthur Godfrey Show*. He had the most exotic, sexy voice and I always wondered what he looked like. When it went to television, I got to see him and he was just as good looking as his voice sounded."

Nineteen forty-one saw the last frequency change in the station's history, moving from 1110 to 1120 on the dial, one of 24 clear channel stations in the United States.

In 1944 Jones left KMOX as general manager and was replaced by Frank Falknor. He was succeeded a year later by Wendell Campbell.

Even in the 1940s KMOX was a civic-minded station, and one of the things they participated in was a day when the Boy Scouts took over the town.

"I remember coming to KMOX and meeting Wendell Campbell," said Doug Sleade, who got to be "KMOX General Manager For A Day" going along with the Boy Scouts special day. "They were doing a live western show that day and I got to meet the host, who was a musician. I remember he had this beautiful Gibson Guitar. They were playing the music live in the studio. Everyone was very nice to me, and as "GM for a Day" I remember several employees asked me for a raise."

Also in 1948 the winner of a nationwide search for an architect to design the Arch grounds with a $50,000 prize was announced. The winner was Eero Saarinen, a young architect of Finnish decent.

One of the people Campbell brought to the station was Rex Davis, who moved to St. Louis in 1946 after working in Cincinnati. Davis quickly became the top personality on KMOX.

"Rex was held in very high regard by the CBS network," said Irv Litvag. "The network often brought Rex in to help at national political conventions. He helped the network with their coverage."

Davis had the highest rated program in St. Louis with his noon news. It was a 15-minute newscast. His 8 AM newscast was the second highest rated show, and Davis' news broadcast at 7:15 AM was the third highest.

Campbell's four years as GM ended in 1949, when Erwin Shomo took over for a year. He handed the job over to John Akerman. Akerman served as GM until 1952, then Gene Wilkey occupied the position until 1955, when Robert Hyland was named to the job.

In the 1950s the advent of television forced radio to make some changes. Program directors had to think of their listeners and how they were changing. They were no longer just appealing to the family huddled around the radio; they were playing to the motorist in his car, the housewife doing her daily work, and a vacationing worker sunning on the beach with a transistor radio.

One of the most popular programs at the time was baseball broadcasts. Several stations, including KMOX, had been carrying the games for years. After the Cardinals won the World Series in 1946, however, owner Sam Breadon decided to regulate the broadcast rights. He only

wanted one station carrying the games, with one set of announcers, and he picked the team of Harry Caray and Gabby Street on WTMV instead of Laux and KMOX.

Breadon's theory was that even though KMOX was a bigger station, he thought Caray was a better showman and would do a better job of promoting the games and thus increase attendance. Even after Breadon sold the Cardinals, those contracts continued, with the broadcasts moving to KXOK, even after Anheuser Busch bought the Cardinals in 1953.

The broadcasts had been sponsored by Griesedieck Brothers, a rival of Anheuser-Busch, and Busch had to be convinced that Caray could sell his beer as well as he was selling the Cardinals and Griesedieck's beer. He also told his advertising executives, however, that he wanted another announcer, which led to the hiring of Jack Buck and Milo Hamilton.

Those three broadcast the games on KXOK in 1954, but the relationship between the Cardinals and KMOX was about to be renewed, thanks to Hyland's elevation to general manager.

Hyland was a big baseball fan. He had played in college, and his father, Dr. Robert F. Hyland, was the Cardinals' team doctor and had been called the "surgeon general of baseball." Hyland had gone into radio after college, working first at WTAD in Quincy, Illinois, before working at WEW in St. Louis. He moved to WBBM in Chicago to join CBS, then the network moved him back to St. Louis in 1952 as assistant sales manager at KMOX. One of his first decisions as GM was to acquire the rights to broadcast the Cardinals' games.

"He approached New York [CBS network] with a proposal," said Clarence Nieder, a longtime engineer. "Now you have to realize baseball was not always popular for radio stations to want to carry because most games were in the day and that was when the soap operas were. It would interrupt their programming.

"Hyland's proposal was 'if you'll allow me to tape the daytime programming so I can run it at night, I can run baseball during the day, and I'll get you higher ratings.' They said, 'If it works, you're in; if it doesn't, you're out.'"

"Everything started to revolve around baseball," Buck said. "He knew how big baseball was in St. Louis and he was aware what a rallying point it would be for the station."

As was the case with most of Hyland's decisions, he was correct, proving the baseball games could co-exist with the news and sports broadcasts and both local and network entertainment shows, such as *Art Linkletter's Houseparty*.

Hyland also decided in 1958 to begin broadcasting editorials and to endorse candidates for public office. It was the first station in St. Louis to run editorials, and the first CBS-owned station to take a stance on the issues of the day.

Hyland also led the successful campaign to make KMOX the first radio station to gain access to the Missouri legislature. KMOX broadcast an entire session, and followed that by broadcasting a Board of Aldermen's meeting.

The KMOX studios remained in the Mart Building until 1957, when the building's latest owner, the U.S. Government, needed the space for its biggest tenant, the U.S. Army Support Center. Temporary studios were built in Soulard, before a new building was constructed at the corner of Hampton and Wise Avenues. KMOX moved to that building in 1959.

Television was becoming more popular all the time, and CBS was interested in acquiring a St. Louis station. The network applied for Channel 11, but the local owners of Channel 4 wanted to sell and sold the station to CBS. Ted Koplar then bought Channel 11.

"Many people from KMOX radio went to the television station at this time," said Nieder. 'Lots of people from KXOK came over to work for KMOX radio. We joked that if you were a former KXOK person, you could get a job at KMOX.'

Some of the people who came to KMOX at this time were Shirley Jacoby, Charlie Scott, Rudy Ruzicka, Nieder, Bob Gotsch, Laurent Torno, and J. Roy McCarthy.

On June 23, 1959, construction began on the Gateway Arch.

It was that same year that on another radio station, KXOK, a broadcaster named Roger Bell did an hour-long show that was mostly talk. Hyland found out about it and came up with the idea of beginning talk programs on KMOX. He talked to others about his idea, including Buck and Bob Broeg, and the almost universal opinion was this time Hyland was wrong. The idea wouldn't work. He decided to go ahead anyway.

Hyland hired Bell, who changed his name back to his real name, J. Roy McCarthy. Hyland decided to call the programs *At Your Service*, and he even gave away KMOX's entire music library. He didn't want to be tempted to go back to carrying music; he was so convinced his idea was going to be successful.

Buck and McCarthy were the co-hosts of the first *At Your Service* program, broadcast on February 29, 1960. Hyland came on the air to introduce the concept, and then Buck began the interview with the first guest, Mayor Raymond Tucker. The broadcast ran for two hours.

Alice English was the program director at the time.

"Talk radio was very different than it is today," she said. "Mr. Hyland's intent was to educate and inform people. We tried to stay away from controversy."

The guests were given a list of questions ahead of time, allowing them a chance to prepare for the show. The hosts were also provided with questions and background information so they could present the topic in an informed way.

"Jack Buck crossed the lines," said English. "He could do the baseball games and host sports call-in programs, but he also came in in the afternoon and did general interest topics."

One of the most famous interviews on KMOX was when First Lady Eleanor Roosevelt came into the KMOX studio and was interviewed by Buck on *At Your Service*.

Those special broadcasts, of course, produced a big audience and generated many telephone calls. There were other days, however, when the programs were not as popular. Some KMOX employees would go to another part of the office and make a call into the studio so it appeared listeners were calling. The programs aired between noon and 7 PM Monday through Friday.

Only when a select group of topics was refined, including programs such as *Ask the Vet*, *Ask the Gardener*, *Ask the Doctor*, and *Ask the Lawyer*, did the concept really begin to succeed.

"I'll never forget the first time I went on KMOX," said Dr. Armand Brodeur, who now has been on KMOX for more than 40 years. "I was to be on the show with J. Roy McCarthy. They asked me to submit a list of questions I would like him to ask me. I did that and within three minutes of starting the show, Mr. Hyland showed up in the studio and at the commercial break he asked me if I would like to work for KMOX."

Other hosts of *At Your Service* shows in those days included Davis, Jim Butler, and Bob Hardy, who came to work at KMOX in 1960. They all became integral parts of KMOX's growth over the next several years.

Butler did anything ever asked of him over the 40-plus years he spent at KMOX. He even did color on the St. Louis Hawks' basketball games and St. Louis football Cardinals' games, even though he claimed not to know much about sports.

Hardy joined Davis on the morning drive program, and it quickly became the highest rated program on virtually any station in the country. Hardy was involved in almost all of the key news stories in St. Louis for more than 30 years.

The November day in 1963 when President Kennedy was assassinated in Dallas was a monumental day at KMOX. All who were there that day remember how the employees jumped into action, and laid the foundation for countless episodes like it in the future.

"I remember I was eating french fries at the Parkmoor," said English. "It used to be an outdoor drive-in. I had my radio on, and as soon as I heard Rex Davis announce it, I headed back for the station. They had already sprung into action."

Davis was so stunned when he read the bulletin after it was handed to him, that he had to pause for a moment before he could read it. Hardy began anchoring the station's programming and remained on the air from 1 PM until the following morning.

In 1965, when two Fontbonne College nuns went to Selma, Alabama, to lead a civil rights march, they accepted Hyland's offer to explain their mission and answer questions on KMOX. A record 20,000 calls swamped the telephone lines during the five hours they were on the air.

KMOX also provided extensive coverage of the construction of the Gateway Arch. Those who worked at the station had a bird's eye view of the project after KMOX moved from Hampton Avenue to their new, and present day, studios on Memorial Drive on the riverfront.

In 1968, when the keystone was put in the top, KMOX was there reporting it all. Hardy had done three broadcasts, at least one with Jim Butler, from a platform called a Creeper Derrick that ascended up the Arch as it was being built.

"The day they put the keystone in was a big day," said Rita Hardy, Bob Hardy's widow. "We took the kids out of school so they could see it."

Hardy was feeling the effects of a heavy workload, so he went to Hyland in 1969 to ask him to hire an additional *At Your Service* host. Hyland told him to find somebody, and Hardy brought in an announcer he had heard on KDKA in Pittsburgh—Jim White.

White was an all-purpose announcer who could do anything and was willing to do anything for the good of the station. Hyland put him on nights, switched him to days, and then asked him to work a split day-night shift.

He finally settled on the late-night shift and became known as the "Big Bumper" because he would talk to the "creatures of the night" (the listeners) and would talk about "things that go bump in the night." According to John McGuire of The *Post-Dispatch*, the phrase came from a Scottish prayer: "From ghosties and ghoulies, and long-legged beasties, dear Lord protect us from things that go bump in the night."

"When we first started advertising with Jim White it was in 1970," said Ted Drewes, the owner of Ted Drewes Frozen Custard, "the rates were only about $50 for a commercial back then, but that was getting in on it at the beginning. As I remember it, you could get a discount, maybe $25 a commercial, if it was after midnight."

"There was some sales information about it," said Bill Ott, an engineer at the station. "When Jim White first came, we really didn't even have advertisers in that time slot. People did not want to advertise because they didn't think anyone was listening, but some sponsors came on board, and Carol House Furniture was one of the big success stories."

Soon the rates went up and White was attracting all kinds of listeners and advertisers.

"We were just a little ice cream joint at the time," said Drewes. "We couldn't afford an ad budget. We started with a few ads on another station and our sales went up 10 percent. I told my wife, Dottie, 10 percent is a pretty significant raise in sales, and she agreed. We bought some time on KMOX on Jim White's show and our sales went up 15 percent, so that's when we got into advertising."

Besides the local advertising, Drewes said the 50,000 watts of KMOX blasting all over the United States at night did something else for his ice cream stands.

"It sort of made us a tourist attraction," said Drewes. "I can't tell you how many people have said, 'When we come to St. Louis, one of the first things we want to do is get a Ted Drewes.' People who have moved away often still listen to KMOX at night. They hear about Ted Drewes and it reminds them about it, so when they are passing through or coming home, they remember it and come.

"I remember once I was in Nova Scotia for our Christmas tree business and I turned on the radio and could pick up KMOX and it was 1,700 miles away!"

In 1970, another important broadcaster was introduced to the KMOX audience. Anne Keefe, who had been on her way from Rochester, New York, to a television job in Kansas City when Hyland intercepted her and changed her plans, joined the station.

"I was a good editor and writer," said Keefe. "At the time, I didn't have any great ambitions, I just needed a job and wanted to provide for my children."

Keefe became very popular, and was both loved and respected by the St. Louis audiences as she informed and entertained them each afternoon.

"Anne Keefe and Bob Hardy were exceptional on-air personalities," said Jeanette [Hoag] Grider, a producer. "Their background, preparation, and on-air professionalism set them apart from so many broadcasters. There was literally no topic they could not cover in an interview or call-in setting. Regardless of their own opinions, which did sometimes leak through a little, they were always willing to let others express an opinion. In any crisis, they could stay on the air as long as necessary to adequately cover the story and never had the attitude of 'My shift's over, gotta go home.'"

Hyland had now put together a formidable group of news broadcasters and hosts of *At Your Service* programming with Davis, Hardy,

White, and Keefe. He had sports covered with Buck, and Dan Kelly, who had come in 1968, the second year of the Blues' existence, to be their play-by-play announcer.

What he still had a need for, however, was a major personality to become the host of the station's morning show. That person arrived in 1971—Jack Carney.

"Carney was a comedian who happened to be articulate," Buck said. "He knew a lot about a lot of things. He knew a lot of people. He was made for radio."

His show became the most popular program on St. Louis radio. Advertisers were waiting in line for an opening so Carney could begin selling their products or services. His comedic skits and programs made listeners laugh so hard they sometimes almost had to pull off the highway for fear of having an accident.

Carney ruled the 9 AM until noontime slot for 13 years, and Hyland expected that to continue far into the future. That plan came to a tragic halt, however, when Carney died of a heart attack after taking a scuba diving lesson in 1984. He was 52 years old.

Many hosts were tried and it wasn't until 1990 that some level of normalcy returned to the morning program when Charles Brennan took over, working with a variety of co-hosts.

Through the strength of the programming in the 1970s and the changes in the 1980s, a constant for the station was the strength and reputation of the news department.

John Angelides was the news director, and KMOX became recognized as the station to turn on when an emergency or disaster was happening. If a national story broke, Angelides had his newsroom assembled and covered the story from all angles.

"If there was a big story, you could call anywhere and get anybody on the air," said newsman Mike Owens. "Mr. Hyland didn't mind if you tried, at least you tried. There was a saying around there: 'There is no such thing as a sin of co-mission, but there was a sin of o-mission.'"

The KMOX newsroom is small in comparison to many television stations, but the mentality among the reporters was that they were competing against those stations, as well as the city's two daily newspapers. In the 1970s newswriters typed their stories on typewriters. The words "rip and read" were almost non-existent unless there was a breaking story.

Newswriters could be found in the newsroom making calls, doing research, listening to tape-recorded interviews or getting ready to go on the air or out for a story. One constant today is the huge picture window, which looks directly toward the Gateway Arch and the riverfront.

"You're sitting in front of the Arch every morning," said Stuart Esrock, a newsman who came to KMOX in 1979. "You see the sunrise between the legs. The view is so beautiful."

The station became known for news coverage that extended beyond the breaking stories and political coverage. KMOX became involved in a cutting-edge broadcast that included hook-ups with a station and listeners in Moscow. This took the *At Your Service* concept to another scale, allowing listeners in Moscow to ask questions to the listeners in the United States and vice-versa.

"It was typical of Hardy and Robert Hyland," said Don Corrigan, a journalism professor at Webster University who was involved in the broadcasts as an observer through an educational grant. "These two men had so much energy for those experiments. It was part of that pioneer spirit that Hyland and Hardy both had to always keep KMOX on the cutting edge. This was the first time anything like this had ever been done in the U.S. It really says something about KMOX because St. Louis was like the 20th city in the country. The people in Moscow could very well have gone with a station in New York or Los Angeles, but they chose St. Louis because of KMOX and Bob Hardy."

Just as important to the growth and success of the station was its sports coverage, where one of the KMOX mottos was to call itself "The Sports Voice of America."

In addition to the Cardinals and Blues, KMOX at one time was the home of broadcasts of the football Cardinals, the St. Louis Hawks of the NBA, the University of Missouri football and basketball games, St. Louis Steamers indoor soccer, and the Saint Louis University basketball games.

"Growing up in Peoria, Illinois, I could pick up KMOX," said former Cardinals public relations director Kip Ingle. "We still had a stand-up radio. My dad and I would go downstairs and listen every night to Jack Buck and the Cardinal games until one or both of us would fall asleep.

"I remember when I was in Boy Scouts, one night I was on a camp out. I had brought my little transistor radio so I could listen to the games in my tent. I'll never forget being in my sleeping bag vividly listening to Bob Gibson's no-hitter against the Pirates. What a thrill."

The Missouri broadcasts also were popular. Harry Caray did the football games for years and his son Skip worked as a producer. John Rooney, Bill Wilkerson, Bob Starr, and Bob Costas also were some of the announcers who spent time as the play-by-play announcers.

Baseball was still the principle sport at the station, however, which meant that when the players staged a lengthy strike in 1981, the station had to scramble for substitute programming.

Never to be beaten, even by Major League Baseball, KMOX came up with an innovative idea. It was decided the station would broadcast games even though none were being played. Old games were re-created. With the use of *The Sporting News*, Buck and Mike Shannon were able to re-create several games and broadcast them as if they were live.

"I remember getting the box scores and as much information about the games as we could from *The Sporting News* and old clips from the newspaper," said a sports assistant at the time. "To make it even more realistic we found out what the weather actually was by contacting the weather service and we found out what songs were popular that week. That way they were able to say, 'It's a beautiful, sunny day, temperatures are in the upper 70s,' and songs played in the background along with the sound effects of crowd noise made the listener feel as if he or she was listening on that day's game."

Winning the World Series in 1982 and reaching the fall classic again in 1985 and 1987 only increased the Cardinals' popularity and the broadcasts on KMOX.

"You could really get the scope of KMOX on the Cardinal Caravans," said Ingle. "You could go to Springfield, Missouri; Columbia, Missouri; or Bloomington, Illinois, and everybody would know KMOX. It's the same way now with my job with baseball memorabilia. There are so many Cardinal fans all over the country and it is because they listen to the games on KMOX. When I'm driving in southern Georgia, KMOX comes in clearer than the Braves network."

"I used to be able to pick it up as I traveled," said Bing Devine. "In 1979-80 we were living in Montreal. Because of the time change, the Cardinal games would be a little later, so after the game in Montreal was over, I'd be driving back to my hotel and I'd drive a route so I could pick up the Cardinals. Often I wouldn't even go back, I'd just keep driving around just so I could hear KMOX."

The *Sports Open Lines* also became very successful on KMOX. Different hosts, including J. Roy Stockton, the sports editor of the *Post-Dispatch*, and Bob Burnes, the sports editor of the *Globe-Democrat*, took turns as hosts of the programs. Wilkerson, Costas, and Dan Dierdorf also filled that role, and, in later years, Ron Jacober and Randy Karraker have moved into that assignment.

"I remember when Ed was on with Bob Costas," said Jean Wilks, widow of the *Post-Dispatch* sports editor Ed Wilks. "Ed had a lot of opinions and he would say whatever he wanted. Once he was on with Bob and they were talking about baseball salaries. Ed was of the old guard and thought baseball should stay the way it was. Someone called up and started complaining that the Cardinals wouldn't pay more to a player. Bob asked Ed, 'Well, what do you think he should be making?' Ed said, 'About $65,000.' The phone lights lit up like crazy!"

"KMOX became known for their baseball," said Hall-of-Famer Stan Musial. "Bob Hyland loved St. Louis, he loved baseball, and he loved the Cardinals. It became their feature programming over the years."

When a baseball game is scheduled and it is delayed or postponed by rain, that sometimes can create interesting programming. Such was the case one day when rain interrupted a game in Atlanta. It so happened nobody was working in the sports office, so when Buck and Shannon gave the broadcast back to the local stations, there was nobody at KMOX to go on the air.

After the news, Hyland called and told the engineers to send the game back to Atlanta and let Buck and Shannon fill from there. When the engineer made the call, however, he found out the broadcasters had left the booth because of a lightning storm.

The only option left was to read news, which Bob Hamilton did, for one hour and 45 minutes, perhaps the longest newscast ever on KMOX.

"We had news from Mozambique, from other obscure countries, from everywhere," said Hamilton.

When the games were being played, one future Hall-of-Famer who was listening as a boy growing up in Louisiana was Lou Brock. Brock mentioned those days in his Hall-of-Fame induction speech in 1985.

"I sat in my room at night down in Louisiana listening to KMOX, a big city station carrying the word back to the sticks," Brock said. "I knew what I wanted to do. I knew that Jim Crow was a foe I would have to combat and beat. Jim Crow was a barrier to society. I knew I had to overcome it.

"Those KMOX broadcasts made my spirits soar. They gave me the courage to react to my inner feelings. They fed me a fantasy. I was the one who had to take the step, to force myself to cross the railroad tracks and let me enjoy the fantasy I thrilled to in those radio broadcasts."

Another sign of respect for KMOX was the knowledge that many of their personalities were being sought by the networks to do various news and sports broadcasts. Buck and Kelly did many national broadcasts, and another broadcaster whose star quickly rose to the national level was that of Bob Costas.

Costas first went to CBS and then moved to NBC, but because of his loyalty to Robert Hyland, he kept close ties to KMOX. Wilkerson also moved out of sports to become part of the morning drive team when Davis retired, working with Hardy.

In 1986, Wendy Wiese joined Hardy and Wilkerson and the trio quickly developed into a very popular team, allowing KMOX to continue to dominance of the important morning news block which it had built with Davis and Hardy.

"I was so young when I started," said Wiese. "It was just a thrill to be there, and Bob and Bill were so helpful to me."

Hyland was pleased with the success of his key performers, and his personality let them move into the limelight and receive the bulk of attention and credit for the station's success.

"He wanted us all to be viewed as 'stars,'" said Keefe. "Yet he would let us do silly things which let people know we were approachable."

One such event was when Keefe, Costas, and Dierdorf "covered" a wrestling match featuring Hulk Hogan at Kiel Auditorium. Keefe was in an evening gown and Costas and Dierdorf wore tuxedos.

"One silly thing we did one day was a fashion show," said Rodger Brand, the current traffic reporter. "Even though it was radio, we did this fashion show. We really were wearing these clothes. I had a tux on and a white scarf. I was really wearing it and it looked really nice. I don't remember why we did it, but we did."

"That was part of Hyland's genius," said Keefe. "He knew how to do it. By going on the air doing these crazy things, it made the difference in meeting someone who says, 'Nice to meet you, Ms. Keefe,' and someone who comes up to you and gives you a hug and says, 'Nice to meet you, Anne!'"

Other stunts that went on KMOX included Costas and Dierdorf with their "Friday Frank Forecasts," grading hot dogs from around the country, and Jay Randolph providing the play-by-play one year of fireworks on the riverfront on the Fourth of July. Hyland wanted his people to be seen as professionals, yet he liked it when people saw another side of them.

"Some people were intimidated by Robert Hyland," said Brand. "Once I got to know him, I wasn't intimidated by him. He was such a nice man."

The employees were used to Hyland and understood the way he ran the station and the way he wanted things done. His style might have been different than other executives, but there was no questioning its success.

People knew Hyland could not live forever, but nobody was prepared when he became ill with cancer and died in 1992.

"I'll never forget the day he died [March 4, 1992]," said Wiese. "We were about to go on and Bob [Hardy] was sitting there with tears in his eyes, 'I can't do this,' he said, 'I can't go on [the air], I can't do this.' I looked at him and said, 'Yes you can, Bob, yes you can.'"

The interim general manager after Hyland's death was Cathy Gamble, who had been the financial controller. According to those who worked there, several days later some executives from CBS network were seen in what had been Hyland's office. For so long, CBS had let KMOX run itself. Hyland had power that no other general manager in the CBS system possessed. After he was promoted to senior vice president of CBS, he was the only network executive who

oversaw the station. If Hyland's death had not convinced them a change was coming, they knew it when the network executives began to arrive on the scene.

The network brought in Rod Zimmerman from Detroit to become the next general manager, giving him the unenviable task of following in Hyland's footsteps. He came in with orders from the network to make changes, and that's what he did.

For years Hyland had been paying people who often came on the station as experts or special guests. His strategy was that if they were being paid by KMOX, they couldn't work for any other station in town. This list included athletes, coaches, team executives, and anybody else he wanted on KMOX. Zimmerman got rid of all of those people.

"The phantom payroll was legendary," said Jim White. "When I was program director, I sent my secretary over to get an employee list for something I was doing. She came back with the list and I saw all these strange names on it. With that someone came flying through the door and said, 'You've got the wrong list!' and switched lists with me."

The station was hit with another loss two years later when Hardy collapsed and died from a heart attack.

Two years later, in 1996, several key employees, including Wilkerson, Wiese, and Kevin Horrigan, left KMOX to join former boss Tim Dorsey at a new station he had acquired in Belleville, WIBV.

"It was a sad day to see everybody leave," said Casey Van Allen, former production manager at KMOX. "It was like the family was divorcing. It was a bad time for this radio station. This station is so legendary and even though it may appear dysfunctional to some people, we really are a close family. It was just real sad to see everybody go.

"I'm very happy they're doing so well at KTRS [they eventually switched to KTRS under the same ownership]. It's made St. Louis a better market. We have very high quality talk radio in this town, so out of the bad came the good."

One of the replacements was Nan Wyatt, a former employee who had been working for WBBM in Chicago.

"Tom Langmyer called me and said, 'We've had a bit of a problem,'" said Wyatt. "He wanted to know if I would come back and do morning drive. I had just had my son and it seemed like a good move for my husband, my son, and I, so we came back."

The employees who stayed at KMOX and the new ones who joined the station realized that Zimmerman was acting on orders from his bosses. Their goal remained the same as it had been under Hyland's regime—to be the best radio station they could be. Zimmerman was later named general manager of WBBM in Chicago, and after CBS sold its radio division to Westinghouse, Karen Carroll, a veteran radio executive in St. Louis, was brought in as the new general manager.

Matt Hyland, the son of Robert Hyland who had started at KMOX then left to work for the St. Louis Blues, returned to the station. He was part of the second generation of KMOX staff members that included John Kelly, Joe Buck, and John Carney.

"Coming back to KMOX was comfortable," Hyland said. "Being around those people was like going home. But then KMOX is like that for many St. Louisians. People have moved back or are making the trip to St. Louis from wherever. They may be driving in the middle of the night, but when their radio can pick up KMOX, they know they are home."

KMOX recently set a record by winning the local Arbitron ratings for more than 30 consecutive years. The faces have changed, with current program hosts such as Carol Daniel, Doug McKelvin, and McGraw Milhaven, but the success and impact of the station continues.

"I've spent a lot of money on that station," said Johnny Londoff, who has advertised his Johnny Londoff Chevrolet for more than 40 years on KMOX. "If you wanted your message heard, you had to be on KMOX."

"The stories go on and on about the quality of work that was achieved over so many years at KMOX," said Jeanette Grider, who was a producer at KMOX. "I think each of us who worked there at any time value the opportunity we had to learn about radio in such a remarkable environment. To be part of an operation that started its journey when radio was a new and untried entity and to be a part of historical success as well as the day-to-day job of providing groundbreaking and meaningful news and information programs is something every employee—past or present, happy or disgruntled—can't help but value."

It didn't take Carroll long to realize the importance of KMOX.

"It is the lifeline of St. Louis, Carroll said. "It's the Arch. It's Highway 40. That's what I learned when I got here that I didn't know. It's been that way for 75 years, and I don't see that changing."

BEN ABELL

The KMOX weather station actually could be found in one room in a two-story white metal building at the St. Louis Downtown-Parks Airport in Cahokia, Illinois. That was where meteorologist Ben Abell reviewed the charts and other weather information beginning at 4 AM before going on the air to forecast the weather for the day.

Like all forecasters, there were times when Abell didn't get the prediction quite right.

One January weekend in 1982, he and other local forecasters called for rain. The prediction then changed to light snow, with accumulations of up to four inches. By the time the snow stopped falling a day later, between 20 and 24 inches were on the ground around the metropolitan area.

"It just kept coming down," Abell said in a 1992 interview with the *Belleville News-Democrat*. "I felt like going outside and waving a stick with a white flag, but I was afraid I'd get hit by a bolt of lightning if I did."

Abell's full-time job was teaching classes on weather, hydrology, severe storms, and air pollution at Parks College, a career he began in 1962. He received his master's degree from Saint Louis University, which at the time was one of only 11 schools which had programs in meteorology. He also did on-air forecasts for public radio station KWMU and for the Radio Information Service for the blind. Abell was on KMOX during morning and evening drive.

FRANK ABSHER

Frank Absher was a news reporter from the late 1970s to early 1980s. His best memories are of three particular incidents.

"On Christmas of 1980, Bob Costas and I were handling the 'Bermuda Triangle,' the 4-6 PM." said Absher. "There was nothing planned, so we flew by the seats of our pants. Bob suggested we bring in my son, Jeff, who was seven at the time. He was interviewed live, giving a kid's view of Christmas, and because of Bob's total professionalism, it was great radio.

"When President Reagan was shot, I dashed into Mr. Hyland's office to tell him. His immediate reaction was, 'You're in charge of our coverage. Drop all commercials. I don't care how much it costs. Do it.' With Bob Hardy at the microphone we ended up scooping the network on several major developments in the story.

"In 1982, the Cardinals were in the playoffs, but three of the divisions went down to the final regular-season game one Saturday afternoon. With Paul Grundhauser handling the board and Mr. Hyland calling the shots via phone from his home, we managed to broadcast three games live simultaneously without any glitches.

"We had so much pride in our work in those days and we were proud to say we worked for KMOX. The spirit of camaraderie and loyalty to the station was so great that everyone pitched in when needed, allowing even the second-stringers like me to turn out a top broadcast product."

TOM ACKERMAN

A native of St. Louis, Tom Ackerman joined the KMOX sports department in 1997 as a producer and is now a reporter and weekend host of *Sports Open Line*.

Ackerman spent his college years at Indiana University doing play-by-play for the IU basketball, football, and baseball teams. He also hosted a sports talk show.

"I used to call *Sports Open Line* when I was a young sports fan," he said. "When my parents thought I was doing my homework, I was

actually in my room dialing 436-7900. I loved KMOX and wanted to get involved working at the station."

He started producing the Sunday morning show with Ron Jacober and Bill Reker. Later he was brought on as a sports reporter and did intermission reports on Blues broadcasts.

"There isn't a day that goes by that I don't think about how lucky and happy I am to be in this position at 25 years old," said Ackerman. "It motivates me to do things, top-notch, KMOX quality. There have been many late nights when I've stayed in the studio and recorded something 30 times because it's not absolutely perfect. The tradition and history of KMOX deserve nothing less."

Ackerman was surprised that even though he got to work at the place he held in a high esteem, the people are down to earth.

"They are as humble and down to earth as anyone you'll find," he said. "When I met Jack Buck for the first time, he shook my hand, picked up the phone, and asked, 'What kind of pizza do you like?'"

LEE ADAMS

Lee Adams was the host of the *Housewives Protective League Show*. It was a show owned by the network, but done by local talent. They were sent a packet and Adams was able to pick and choose whatever he wanted to use.

"He was a great talent," said Bob Canepa, the salesman who sold the show. "The thing I remember about Lee was that he had Belgere Chevrolet as a sponsor. It was across from Sportsman's Park. Because of that, Lee Adams got the very first Corvette in St. Louis."

"It was in 1953," said Tony Bello, a salesman at the time. "Lee wanted to drive it out to Los Angeles to visit his family and then proceed up the coast to Carmel by the Sea, California. Gene Wilkey and Bob Hyland asked me to accompany Lee out to Los Angeles, then fly back home afterward to make sure he made it in one piece! So with the Corvette's convertible top down and plenty of suntan lotion and zinc oxide on our noses, we started our long trek down the highway [with no seat belts in those days].

"On the second day we were cruising along the six-lane highway

outside of Flagstaff, Arizona, doing about 85 MPH when Lee yelled over, 'Tony, ole friend, I'm going to open her up and see what she can do!' I replied back, 'Lee, ole buddy, St. Christopher jumped out about 10 miles back when you hit 80 MPH!' Lee pressed on the accelerator and when we hit 100 the car dropped into a low gear and ripped the transmission into a mass of metal! We were locked up and started to spin sideways down the highway until Lee was able to stop it. The good Lord was watching over us that day and kept us inside the car and no injuries. We were towed into Flagstaff to the Chevy dealer for major transmission repairs. So one of my first assignments was almost one of my last!"

JOHN AMANN

John Amann, who is currently a professor of law at Saint Louis University, started at KMOX in 1978 as an intern.

"I was 19 years old and got to do the morning drive with Ava Erlich and Barry Birr," said Amann. "We wrote and helped prepare for Rex Davis and Bob Hardy. I worked from 4:00 in the morning until noon. A few times they had to call me because I overslept. I was not used to getting up and eating breakfast at 2:30 in the morning."

Besides writing the news, Amann started doing on-air reports and he even got to read the sports on the Jack Carney show a few times.

"My biggest memory was the day Congressman Gephardt came into the station," said Amann. "He had just been elected congressman and he came in to KMOX. There were no reporters available so John Angelides said to me, 'Go in the studio and interview Congressman Gephardt.' I was petrified. I wasn't prepared; I'd only been working there for two weeks. I said, 'Congressman, what do you want to talk about? And it all worked out fine, he was promoting a bill and had a lot he wanted to talk about."

Another intimidating time for Amann was when he was an intern and it was his job to distribute The *Globe-Democrat* newspaper as soon as it came out at 3 or 4:00 in the morning.

"I was told to take three into Mr. Hyland's office and I did," said Amann. "The first time I did it, I went into Mr. Hyland's office expect-

4

ing it to be dark, but there he was at his desk eating a package of crackers and drinking a glass of water in his suit and tie and it was 4:00 in the morning! I didn't know he worked those hours, but I sure found out."

OTTIS ANDERSON

Ottis Anderson was the star runningback for the St. Louis Cardinals in the 1970s. *The Ottis and Theotis Show*, co-hosted by runningback Theotis Brown, was broadcast each Monday night during the NFL season. The show featured interviews with guests from around the NFL. They had a signature signoff for each show. "This is Ottis Anderson, and I'm Theotis Brown, reminding you" and then they would both say at the same time, "If you can't be a good sport, don't play."

"Ottis was a shy, bashful kind of guy," said Jim Holder, who put the show together. "He was a genuinely nice person who kind of kept to himself. Once Theotis would get in there he would bring out the humor in O.J."

JOHN ANGELIDES

John Angelides had been the city editor of the *St. Louis Globe-Democrat* before being named news director at KMOX in January of 1974. He was promoted to executive news director in 1978 and held that position until he retired in 1995. He had his office at the front of the newsroom where he could see everyone and everyone could see him. Angelides was a very respected and a hard newsman. Under his reign, KMOX grew to be a news source that even the CBS network looked to for help on breaking national stories.

When Krakow, Missouri, resident Rocky Sickmann was taken hostage with the other hostages in Iran in 1979, KMOX covered the story from every angle.

"During the ordeal, we interviewed his friends and family," said Angelides. "We covered all sides of the story when he was a hostage and then when he was released, we had Rocky on the radio. We asked him what was it like to be a captive. KMOX even hired him to work there for a while."

THE MIGHTY 'MOX

When President Ronald Reagan was shot in 1982, Angelides put everyone on the story—news department and sports as well. A sports reporter was calling the Denver library to find the last books checked out by John Hinckley. A news reporter was calling restaurants asking if Hinckley had frequented them. Soon the network reporters were calling KMOX for information.

On New Year's Eve in 1980 an ice storm hit St. Louis. Angelides had not planned to be working that night, but as often happened, his plans abruptly changed.

"It was a huge ice storm," said Joan Beuckman, who was on the news desk at the time. The calls coming in were overwhelming and I was the only one there besides the engineer. The police were calling us telling us this road was closed or that road was closed and 100,000 people were without electricity. I was just getting swamped. Suddenly I looked up and in walked Mr. Hyland in a trench coat and a pair of boots. 'Thought you'd probably need some help,' he said and he got on the phone helping take the calls.

"Somehow we knew John Angelides was at Musial and Biggie's for New Year's Eve so I called him there. He immediately came in and helped us find Mark McDonough [another reporter] and soon it was a little more under control."

Said Angelides, "It was one of those storms that just came on us. A little bad weather was predicted, but the extent was totally unexpected. It was a big ice storm. We did surveys and focus groups and found out that whenever there was a catastrophe of any kind, like a snowstorm, plane crash, major highway accident, people turned to KMOX to get their information. We became the 'emergency' radio station for everybody."

A plane crash in 1976 stands out in Angelides' memory of big events at KMOX. Jerry Litton was killed in the crash, the night he won the Democratic primary for the U.S. Senate. He was leaving on a small plane from his home in Chillicothe to fly to a victory party in Kansas City when the plane crashed.

"I had sent Joyce Mitchell to cover Litton's election," said Angelides. "She was in Kansas City, and ended up driving to Chillicothe. We ended up getting the mood at campaign headquarters when they heard about

6

the crash, then when they found out he was dead, the reaction from his hometown and the officials at the crash. It was a fluke that we had her up there. We were the only St. Louis station to have that kind of coverage of Litton's death."

During the big flood of 1993, KMOX had five or six reporters covering different aspects of the story.

"We were constantly doing updates," said Angelides. "I had reporters in boats with the fire department making tours of the area. Some reporters were sent to towns up by Hannibal or down by Ste. Genevieve. We did 24-hour coverage."

Angelides added, "When I worked at KMOX, I truly felt it was the golden age of radio. I felt in the days of Bob Hyland, KMOX was at its zenith. Bill Paley used to say that—that KMOX was the jewel in CBS's crown. They used to pull ratings of 23 on the AM and with the FM combo they'd have about 30. Now things are different. You have different things to contend with. There are so many morning television shows. People may watch television while getting ready for work and then pop a CD on in their car. There are just so many choices today."

"John Angelides was a great boss," said Bill Bidwill, Jr., who worked at KMOX in the summer between 1978 and 1980. "He treated everyone the same. He treated them as an equal to him."

"He was an incredible mentor and teacher and he was also a lot of fun," said Stu Esrock. "And he was the most well-connected person I've ever met. I guess it was from his days at the *Globe*. He knew everybody from the city government, he had the 'ins' with the Board of Aldermen, that was why he was news director, he knew everybody and always came up with stories."

"John Angelides was under a lot of pressure to win awards," said newsman Mike Owens. "It meant a lot to Robert Hyland to have an award-winning station, and John Angelides had two reporters who won Peabody Awards for stories they did on dioxin.

"We used to joke around with John and call him 'Jack Angel-Ides.' We would say it to his face; he was a good boss. Very knowledgeable. He let you do what you wanted to do. He would say to you, 'What do you want to do?' and then let you do it. Now you had to follow through and work hard, but he let you do what you wanted."

7

One time Owens asked if he could do a series that was timely to an event going on in the news and Angelides was very supportive.

"A woman named Janet Cook had won the Pulitzer Prize on a story she'd done on a young child addicted to heroin," said Owens. "It turned out to be a fabricated story and we were talking about it. I said, 'John, could I do a series on Journalistic Ethics?' and he said yes. It turned out to be a 15-part series on Journalistic ethics. I spent four or five days on interviewing media critics, college professors, Dennis Riggs from Channel 4, and others in that field."

After leaving KMOX, Angelides teamed with former KMOX news reporter Jeff Rainford to open a public relations company, Rainford-Angelides.

BOB ANTHONY

Bob Anthony started on the air at KMOX as a staff announcer in 1958. His full name was Robert Anthony La Fata, but he chose to use his middle name as his last name on the air.

"They would turn off the big transmitter to clean it up on Sunday nights," said Anthony's wife, Tinker Reilley, who also worked at KMOX. "They went to a smaller wattage. He did a show from 10 PM until 3 or 4 in the morning. I remember meeting him for breakfast at 5:00. He played records and did the kind of show that John McCormick did.

"I remember once Mr. Hyland came to Bob and said, 'Do you have any plans for the week of such and such?' Bob said no and Mr. Hyland said, 'Well, you better go to the library because you're going to do the live coverage of the Hambletonian.' Bob said, "I don't know anything about trotting,' and Mr. Hyland said, ' Well, you've got two weeks to learn.' So he boned up on horseracing."

Anthony was interested in flying because he had been a pilot in World War II. Chris Sarros, who was an engineer at the station, was a pilot and had several planes. Sarros once took Anthony, Reilley, and Bob Hardy up in one of his planes.

"It was a real pretty day outside," said Reilley. "Bob Hardy was off and we all decided to meet and go flying. We met at Creve Coeur airfield which was where Chris Sarros parked his planes. Chris had this plane called a WACO and it had an open cockpit. There was just

this wide strap that went across your legs. That was it and you were out in the open. The pilot flew in the back. So Chris was in the back and Bob Hardy and I were in the front. Bob [Anthony] was in the plane behind us."

They stopped in Alton to have lunch. While they were having lunch, Reilley wondered why the men kept trying to get her to eat more.

"Here have a little more salad, Tinker. Want some more bread?' they were saying," said Reilley. "I couldn't figure it out until Chris started doing barrell rolls with that plane. They were trying to get me sick. I didn't get sick, but when we got back, Hardy barely made it to the shed. He lost about three pounds I think!"

Anthony was one of the first hosts of *At Your Service* programming and worked at KMOX until 1970. After leaving the station, he and his wife formed an advertising agency. He died in 1998 at the age of 75.

CHARLES ASHMAN

Charles Ashman was a short-lived host of evening *At Your Service* programs in 1973, but his four months at KMOX were quite newsworthy.

He had visited St. Louis in October 1972, while on a tour promoting his new book, a biography of Henry Kissinger titled *Kissinger: The Adventures of Super-Kraut*. Robert Hyland was impressed with Ashman, and hired him to become the host of the evening programs.

Ashman went on the air in February 1973, and his show featured nationally known guests and was a major success. While looking into his background for a feature story, the *St. Louis Globe-Democrat* learned, however, that Ashman also was misrepresenting several facts about himself.

Three days before the newspaper published a very negative article about his past, Ashman resigned from KMOX.

VICKI ATLAS

Vicki Atlas has been the co-host of *Total Information AM* on Saturdays and works as a fill-in host on other programs.

"One of the funniest shows we did was Bill Reker and I talking about Thanksgiving," said Atlas. "We asked the callers how they made their turkeys. We got the craziest responses. One woman said she put popcorn in the turkey and the turkey bottom exploded! Another caller said a guy had shot a turkey and didn't take off the neck and he served it that way. He said everyone refused to eat it. One caller set the turkey out and the dog ate it, and another said they cooked the turkey all night only to realize they forgot to turn on the oven! They went out for burgers."

Atlas owns Atlas Communications and does video work, free-lance broadcasting, and gives seminars to corporations.

JIM BAER

Jim Baer was KMOX's resident expert on high school sports for 18 years. He started in 1974 when he was the sports editor for the *Suburban Journals*.

"I had a hint that Robert Hyland was looking to expand local coverage so I called him," Baer said. "I said, 'Mr. Hyland, you do a great job of covering sports on your station, but you could use some help with high school sports.' He said, 'You know, Jim you're right. We could have you write it and Bob Costas could read it, but you wouldn't want to do that would you?' He thought about it and as luck would have it, the *Globe-Democrat* and *Post-Dispatch* had a newspaper strike 30 days later. KMOX was calling me every hour to give reports. It was right in the middle of the prep football season."

The first night Baer went into the studio to do his report he was scared to death and those around him knew it.

"I remember [John] Toler [the engineer] saying, 'Ah, don't be getting nervous, there are only 25,000 listeners out there.' I almost started to cry, my heart was in my stomach! The guys behind the glass [producer and engineer] were doing 'the sign of the cross' saying, 'You can do it, you can do it.'"

Baer had a big white Dodge that he drove that the *Journals* gave him. Hyland had put a two-way radio in it so he could do reports for the station. One day before a high school football game he had driven

the car down to the track at Vianney so he could do some radio reports before the game. When he went to move the car, he found he was stuck.

"I was stuck in the cinders on the track and it was a half an hour before Vianney's football game was to start!" said Baer. "Don Heeb, the longtime coach there, sent the whole football team over to my car. '1,2,3, Lift!' and they lifted it up and moved it."

Another memory for Baer concerned a Kirkwood football player, Alvin Miller. Miller was a three-sport star, excelling in football, basketball, and track. In his senior year the St. Louis media were trying to find out where he planned to go to college.

"On the day before the National Signing Day he still hadn't told anyone," said Baer. "Everyone was clamoring to find out what college he was going to. I ran into him at Omni Sports in Kirkwood. They had Magic Johnson in there signing autographs and the line was clear out to Webster. Alvin and his friends were at the back of the line and when he saw me, he asked, 'Can you help us get up to the front of the line?' Well, I knew Tom Holley who owned Omni Sports so I said sure, and got them up to the front.

"Then I got Alvin in the store room and said, 'I got you in this place, now where are you going to school?' He said, 'I'm not saying, but I will tell you it starts with an "N" and ends with a "D." I went on the radio and announced, 'Alvin Miller is going to Notre Dame.' Well unbeknownst to me, Lou Holtz, the Notre Dame coach, was in Chicago driving in his car and was listening to KMOX. He hears me say Alvin Miller, who was a Parade All American, was going to Notre Dame and he veered off the road!"

One of Baer's embarrassing moments on KMOX came after he had had some trouble recording his report.

"I didn't get it right the first time so I did it again and said, 'Take two on the high school report in 3,2,1,' and did it again. We would always do the '3,2,1' countdown so the person recording it would know when to start. Well, the guy who was recording it didn't listen to the tape and didn't realize I'd done it twice, so as I'm driving home from the station, I hear my taped report. The announcer says, 'Now here's Jim Baer with the high school report,' and you hear, 'Take two on the high school report in 3,2,1.' I couldn't believe it!"

Baer currently is the public relations director for the Bowling Hall of Fame.

JIM BAFARO

Jim Bafaro was a news reporter from 1984 until 1989, and one night stands out above all others in his memory.

"I was the guy who told Robert Hyland that Jack Carney had died," said Bafaro. "I had been at the station for 10 months. Man, what an assignment that was for a 24-year-old kid! I had been hired in February of 1984. Flash forward to November.

"I had just come back from getting a quick bite to eat when I sat down at my desk in the newsroom. There had just been another development in the then-ongoing saga of whether the Big Red were going to leave St. Louis, and I was getting ready to make a phone call to one of the principals in the story. I had plugged my tape recorder into the phone and I was just getting ready to make a call when the phone rang. It was Dr. Stephen Ayers, who did some on-air work at the station, so the name was familiar. He also was Jack Carney's personal physician.

"The phone conversation, literally, went something like this.

Jim Bafaro: Radio News, may we help you?

Stephen Ayers: Hi, this is Dr. Steven Ayers, who's this?

JB: This is Jim Bafaro...

SA: (somewhat cheerily): Oh, hi Jim! Say, I don't think we've met. Y'know, I've met most of the people down at the station, but I haven't met you yet. Next time I'm down there, why don't you come over and introduce yourself?

JB: OK, I'll do that.

SA (rather matter-of-factly): Say Jim, Jack Carney died tonight."

Bafaro was obviously overcome by shock, but composed himself enough to ask the necessary questions. Ayers went on to explain a little about how Carney died, of a heart attack after taking a scuba diving lesson. The next part of the conversation showed just how people feared giving Hyland bad news:

SA: Jim, here's what I want you to do. I want you to call Mr. Hyland

and tell him Jack has died, then give him my number and have him call me...

JB: Tell you what, Doctor, why don't YOU call Hyland and tell him and leave me outta this!

SA: No, I like my way better."

Bafaro got off the phone and started to call Mr. Hyland. "I remember I had to stop about midway through the dialing process to let all of this sink in," Bafaro said. "Geez, I'm 24—just a kid from South St. Louis basically fresh out of J-School with a year of radio experience under my belt and I'm telling possibly the most powerful radio mogul in America that his million-dollar morning talent has just died unexpectedly!

"I composed myself and decided to just keep talking. He answered. I told him. He shouted, 'What?' I just kept talking. I gave him Dr. Ayers' number. He hung up.

"A minute later he called back, and told me I was an idiot for giving him the wrong number.

"So I gave it to him again [he had taken it down wrong] and the next thing you know, all hell broke loose.

"The Blues were playing in Vancouver that night, and news anchor Bill Reker broke in on the air with the news. After that, the flood of phone calls began. It was close to 10 PM, and all of the TV folks were calling for confirmation. My college roomie Vince McDonough was an editor at the *Belleville News Democrat* and he called, so I told him. Calls started coming in from all over the country.

"I remember after the game ended, we did a whole big special, with listener phone calls. Several of the station's personalities came in. [News anchor] Ron Barber was particularly broken up because he had worked alongside Carney for a time.

"I remember going to the Denny's on Hampton with [producer] Fred Bodimer and [reporter] Steve Houston after all the dust had settled, about 3 AM. Over a few burgers we all wondered what the station would do now. And as you know, they never were able to find anyone to come close to filling Carney's shoes in that time slot."

14

RON BARBER

After working at KSD for years, Ron Barber came to KMOX in September of 1980. He added comedy to the news. His stern, deliberate delivery of the news gave him authority, but his chatty personality let the listeners see his funny side. He often remained on the air after the newscast, talking with the hosts. Those who worked with Barber considered him one of the funniest guys around.

"He and I used to come in in the late afternoon when Carney was doing his afternoon show," said Bob Costas. "Carney would pose us those questions from the *Ellery Queen Minute Mysteries.* It was a syndicated thing. Barber and I would try to figure out the mysteries. Even if you were real good, your ratio for solving the mysteries was about one in three or four.

"Jack Carney would pick on Ron so bad," said Lisa Bedian who worked with Barber. "One time I was talking to both of them about the leisure suits that my dad wore. My mom and I were trying to get him to throw them out. Carney told me to bring one in, and we wrapped it up and gave it to Ron. He put the thing on, he was so funny.

"Another thing I remember about Barber," she said, "was how much he liked hot sauce. We were always getting fast food for dinner, and I remember he actually sucked hot sauce from Naugles through a straw!"

"Ron Barber was a hellion—with a capital 'H,'" said Dr. Armand Brodeur, longtime KMOX medical expert. "One time when Jack Carney was on the air, Ron went in and pulled his trousers down about six or eight inches, right there when Carney was on the air! That was one of the few things Jack couldn't exploit on the air. He just played it straight and went on with the show."

One memorable moment for him was when he was working the evening shift and he had the unwelcome task of reading a story about a colleague. KMOX-TV newsman Steve Trenkman was driving home with his family. His wife was in the car behind him with their children. He was killed in a car accident, and when it came across the UPI wires, Barber was very upset. Professionalism took over as he got on the air and announced the devastating story.

"We had not been that close," said Barber, "but it was just so awful

that it happened and with his family there. We had heard about the accident and then the news started to trickle up from KMOX-TV [which was downstairs] that it might be Steve. Finally Herb Humphreys verified it and I went on the air with it."

Barber and Hyland had a strained relationship, and Barber felt that Jack Carney was his lifeline to Hyland.

"Carney convinced him to let me stay on the air during his shift," said Barber. The day after Carney died Barber's shift was changed.

"Jack was a big backer of mine, but after he died there was nothing he could do," said Barber. "Hyland moved me to the 11:00 PM to 4:00 AM shift. I decided I was not going to just give up or quit. I went at it 100 percent going to every fire I could and covering as many events as I could. I'd go off in the middle of the night to cover a homicide. It was very unnerving to be driving in North St. Louis in that rickety old KMOX newscar.

"I once did a report from a fire where there were people stuck inside because of the bars on the windows. I did a story from the firefighters' point of view. I was really pleased when at the Monday morning staff meeting Mr. Hyland said, 'Barber did a hell of a job.'"

He covered many other stories, including trials and the story of a radical group known as the Covenant, Sword, and the Arm of the Lord (CSA).

"We broke into Cardinal baseball when a Missouri police officer was killed by the CSA around 1985," said Barber. "I had some great memories working there. There were some great times."

Barber owns Take Off Careers For The 21st Century" Video Company and, along with Don Marsh, he owns "In The Line Of Duty" Video Production company which sells training tapes to Police and Fire Departments nationwide.

TOM BARTON

Tom Barton was the engineer for the Cardinal baseball broadcasts. He had worked for the Padres in 1969 at the team's inception. The unique thing about Barton was he produced and did the engineering.

Other teams including the Cardinals used a producer (the Cardinals longtime producer for baseball was Bernie Fox) and an engineer.

"I had a union card and a degree in economics," said Barton. "I convinced the Padres I could do both functions. I became helpful to the visiting clubs because I'd go in and visit both clubhouses and get the information on the lineups. I'd sit down with Lindsey Nelson or Vin Scully or whoever. I had a lot to offer and I got information from them that we could use. On the first day of the trip the broadcasters would sit down with me and we would exchange information."

One day Jack Buck came to Barton.

"If you ever think of leaving San Diego, I'd appreciate it if you'd come to St. Louis and meet with Bob Hyland," said Buck.

In those days the Anheuser Busch Brewery had an agency, Gardner Advertising, that handled the Cardinal broadcast, and the decisions were made in conjunction with the agency.

"I came in with the Padres later in the season and met with Mr. Hyland on a Saturday morning," said Barton. "We got along famously. I wasn't really looking but the concept intrigued me. Bill Fisher, from Gardner, came out to San Diego after that and we met at the Polo Lounge at the Beverly Hills Hotel. He brought the contract and I signed it. They were very generous; they shipped everything including my car. I moved to St. Louis in February of 1974."

One day after Barton had been working there for two years he wanted a raise.

"I went in to Mr. Hyland and said, 'I want a raise.' He asked, 'How much do you want?' I said, '$3,272.' He looked at me and said, 'Where did you come up with that number, $3,272?' I said, 'I just had my backyard tiered in railroad ties and that's how much it cost.' Mr. Hyland said, 'If you didn't have the money, why did you put the railroad ties in?' I said, 'Mr. Hyland, I just couldn't watch my poor wife push that mower up that hill one more time!' He got a good laugh out of that and gave me the raise."

Barton got along very well with Hyland and enjoyed his time with the Cardinals.

"I even got a World Series ring in 1982 just like the players," he said.

He left to go to the brewery when Anheuser-Busch decided to take steps to gain more control of the Cardinal broadcasts. They decided to go in-house rather than use an advertising agency.

When Barton went to Anheuser-Busch, Bud Sports was started.

"When I worked for Anheuser-Busch, I had many meetings with Robert Hyland because we were dealing with the baseball rights. I went to work very early, and Mr. Hyland went to work very early. We got along well, but we had some heated meetings at times. At one time he asked me if I would like to come back to work at KMOX. It was after I had been at AB for about six years."

The offer would have put Barton in a very high position, however he declined.

"I thought Bob Hyland was an incredible power and a power for good. He was not just a general manager of a radio station," described Barton, "he was a political figure and a focal point for the community on different levels. He was involved in so many activities around town it would confound many people."

Barton now runs his own company, Marz, which is an internet company. They also do television production and webcasting.

"We do television production for networks like TNN and ESPN. We did a webcast for Congressman Richard Gephardt's Tech 2000 Summit at the Science Center."

SHIRLEY JACOBY BATES

In 2000, Shirley Bates celebrated her 40th anniversary at KMOX. As the traffic director, Bates was involved in almost everything happening at the station. Traffic director has nothing to do with the traffic reports—those are left up to the traffic reporters. Bates' job involved working with the sales department and coordinating all of the traffic within the radio station, the commercials, etc. Bates has always been a very necessary person at the station.

"She is really good at her job," said Bob Hamilton of the newsroom.

When she started, she had 10 years of traffic experience at other stations, including WEW and KXOK. She was hired as secretary to the

controller. After finding out how KMOX did its traffic coordination she saw that KMOX was behind the times.

"I told Mr. Hyland they should use the Flexolite system [which is not used anymore, but at the time was the state of the art]. He listened and then got me in touch with [producer] Bernie Fox who said, 'KMOX is very complex and the Flexolite system won't work for us.' I kept saying, 'I've worked with it and I know it. I know it would be better than the antiquated system they were using. I kept trying, but finally it was determined that 'it won't work.' Mr. Hyland looked at me and said, 'You still think it will work, don't you?' and I said, 'yes.' He said, 'Do it.' And I've been the traffic coordinator ever since [almost 40 years]."

Bates has been a longtime and trusted employee at KMOX.

"When she had one of her children back in the '60s," said Jan Fox who worked with her, "she found out how necessary she was to that station. She had the child on a Friday and Mr. Hyland called her on Monday to see if she could come in."

"She was nice and funny," said Tinker Reilley who worked with her in the 1960s. "But she could wiggle those commercials around. She could make openings where there were no openings. The salesmen would say, 'Shirl, could you get me in at 7:30 in the morning?' and somehow she would be able to do it."

Mr. Hyland enjoyed her.

"One of the times he enjoyed was when I'd throw one of my fits," Bates said. "If we would get oversold [too many commercials for the allotted time] and then I was told I had to fit something in, I'd go crazy. I had a very messy desk, just piles all over it. I knew I couldn't throw anything or I'd lose it, so I would just pick up a pile and slam it down and cuss, and then pick up another pile. This one particular day I was doing that and I noticed it was awfully quiet around me. I looked up and there was Mr. Hyland standing there. 'Are you upset?' he asked me. 'Yes I am!' I said. He just walked out of my office and told someone down the hall, 'Shirley's upstairs having one of her fits.'"

Bates attributes her 40 years of KMOX and no ulcers to the ability to let her feelings out.

"Another story involving Shirley and Mr. Hyland," revealed Fox,

"was he had this beautiful and very expensive collection of Steuben Crystal on shelves all along the side of his office. One day Shirley brought in one of her kids. Somehow he got away from her when she was doing something and when she caught up with him, he was in Mr. Hyland's office playing with some of the Steubenware. This is thousands and thousands of dollars worth of crystal and her son is playing with it. What was worse was Mr. Hyland came in just then."

DAVE BAUM

Dave Baum was brought in from Chicago to co-host the afternoon block of *At Your Service* programming in 1977. He was on the air for about five months before the hosts of those shows were changed.

LISA BEDIAN

Lisa Bedian worked at KMOX in the early days of women in sports. She did general reporting, interviewing, sportswriting, and producing. Bedian worked under Jim Holder and he gave her many responsibilities.

"Randy Karraker was my intern," she said. "KMOX then hired him; he replaced me when I left.

"I'll never forget the Great Blizzard of 1982 and how we spent it at KMOX," said Bedian. "We were snowed-in downtown. Whoever was there was there and we only had the one pair of clothes we came to work in. Mr. Hyland put us up at the Marriott downtown, and I finally bought a shirt at the gift shop because I could not stand wearing the same thing for the third day.

"I remember Bill Wilkerson bought everyone dinner one night at the hotel. When he went to turn in the expenses, Mr. Hyland said he would not pay for the alcohol bill."

One of Bedian's jobs was to produce *Sports Open Line*. She was in charge of getting the guests, taking the calls and screening them before putting them on the air, and running the commercials at the appropriate time.

"Here is a story about the quintessential KMOX experience," she

said. "It was March of 1982 and Mizzou was really good at basketball that year. They had Steve Stipanovich, Jon Sundvold, and those guys. The NCAA Regionals were being played in St. Louis.

"Bill Hazen was the on-air talent and the first few calls he took were all about basketball. Suddenly the bat phone rang and it was Mr. Hyland. He said, 'I'm sick of basketball and it's baseball season, no more basketball calls.'"

After Hyland hung up, Bedian quickly called her father. "I said, 'Dad, you're going to be the next caller on KMOX. Talk about the Garry Templeton-Ozzie Smith deal. He called in and it was like Pavlov's dog. Everybody started calling and talking about baseball."

After leaving KMOX, Bedian went to KMOV-TV and then on to the CBS Radio Network in New York as a producer.

"When I was at Channel 4, I was the first woman producer in the CBS television network," she said. Bedian has stayed in the media, moving back to St. Louis to work in the public relations department at KSDK-TV.

TONY BELLO

Tony Bello worked at KMOX from 1953 to 1960. He started as an account executive, then went on to become the local sales manager, national sales manager, and the general sales manager.

Before going to KMOX, Bello had started at KSD television in 1947. After that he worked at KWK as a newscaster, commercial announcer, and had various other duties.

"The seven years I worked at KMOX were especially delightful and I enjoy reminiscing about them now," said Bello. "I was hired as an account executive by Robert Hyland, who was general sales manager in 1953. At the time, Gene Wilkey was general manager. Bob Hyland was the most dedicated and hard working broadcaster I've ever had the pleasure of working with and a very classy gentleman."

One of the shows that Bello sold advertising time for was *The House-wives Protective League.*

"The HPL director or host on KMOX was Lee Adams. Before an ad-

vertiser could be accepted on these HPL shows, their product or services had to be submitted and approved by a select group of local women in each market," Said Bello. "It was broadcasting's *Good Housekeeping* seal of approval type of thing and it was very effective. Advertisers were waiting in line to buy into the HPL Shows!"

Bello left KMOX to go back to KSD-TV in 1960 and worked there until 1985 in sales and became vice president–director of sales. He is retired and living in St. Louis.

GARY BENDER

Gary Bender worked in the sports department in the 1970s and '80s. He was one of the many who got his "start" at KMOX and then moved on to the national scene. Besides doing the morning sportscasts, Bender also did the play-by-play for the football Cardinals.

Jack Carney always got a kick out of teasing Bender as he would come into his studio to read the sports. Carney always called him, "Young, handsome Gary Bender," which embarrassed Bender.

"I thought Carney and Bender were the best," said Frank Cusumano, who has his own talk show on KFNS, and started as an intern at KMOX. "The best single bit of radio on KMOX was the 10:00 AM sports when Bender would go into Carney's studio. Bender always called Carney 'Jackson' and Carney would call him 'Young, handsome Gary Bender.' I always saw Gary Bender when we worked on the Rams and we always talked about Jack Carney. Bender always talks about what a comic genius Jack Carney was."

"Jack could bring out the best in people," said Frank Pawloski. "Gary Bender, by nature is not a real funny guy doing the sports. Gary's an angel. He would come in there so straight-laced and then Jack would get him going. He would try to get Gary to look funny and Gary would just play it so straight, it was hilarious. Gary would come in and give a sportscast. Then he'd say something like, 'The Cardinals made a trade...' Then Jack would try to put him on the spot by saying something like, 'So Gary, what do you think of it? Did we get gypped?'"

Bender left St. Louis to do play-by-play assignments for various

teams, returning to town as the voice of the Rams in 1995. He kept that job for four seasons before moving on to become the radio voice of the Chicago Bears.

JERRY BERGER

Jerry Berger, the columnist for the *St. Louis Post-Dispatch*, worked for Robert Hyland at KMOX in the 1970s.

"Jerry Berger did public relations for them," said *Post-Dispatch* writer John McGuire. "He also worked for the Muny at that time. He wrote press releases for KMOX. Jerry helped me with an article I did on Robert Hyland. He gave me suggestions about people to call. He was very instrumental in getting me going on the article because I got a little discouraged because Hyland was so difficult to talk to. He really didn't want to talk about himself. Berger would call me and say, 'Why don't you talk to this person?' He was a help."

JOAN BEUCKMAN

Joan Beuckman started in 1975 as a newswriter/producer responsible for writing documentaries. She later spent several years as the night news editor, leaving in 1996 to become news director at KTRS radio.

Her job included writing news stories for the following morning's broadcasts, as well as sending reporters to cover stories during the overnight hours.

"I will never forget the night Bob Costas was supposed to be the in-studio talent, but there was a baseball game going on so he went ahead and took an earlier flight since he was due to go out of town that night," said Beuckman. "Well, it ended up that there was a rain-out at the ballpark and there was no one at the studio except me and the engineer, Juan Najera. I was on the phone with Bob Hyland. 'Have you ever produced a show?' he asked me. 'No,' I answered and he said, 'Well you're going to learn!' So we called one of the sports guys at home and he filled in from his living room, while Jim White rushed down to the

station. I don't think we played a single commercial during that time. I had no idea how to do the commercials."

Beuckman won awards for the station with her documentaries.

"They were designed to win awards for KMOX," she said.

Documentaries on child welfare and child labor laws or foster care can be very interesting and winning awards like the Sidney Hillman Award given by the International Garment Industry or her National Headliners Award given by the New Jersey Press Club can be very gratifying, but nothing can compare to working in the newsroom when a major news event occurs.

The day President Ronald Reagan was shot the KMOX newsroom went into full-scale attack. With news director John Angelides at the helm, staffers from the newsroom to the sports office to the producers were all given jobs. The networks were calling KMOX to get information.

"It took a while before people really realized the president was shot too," said Beuckman, who was working the news desk that day. "The AP ran a story that James Brady had actually died; it was chaos. I was getting the news department to find local angles for the story. I was standing over the wire, in those days we still had the wires."

Nowadays at a radio station, reporters can get their information through computers, but before the desktop computers, there were big cumbersome machines sputtering out rolls and rolls of paper with typed information. KMOX had both the AP (Associated Press) and UPI (United Press International) wires.

"And then there was the day the Pope [Pope John Paul II] was shot," she said. "I was routinely pulling things off the wire when I saw that the Pope had been shot. I ran to the studio where Jack Carney was doing his show. I started waving my arm outside the door and he was doing a live commercial. He looked up at me annoyed that I was interrupting him. I opened the door and went inside and I could see his face was growing red that I was doing this. As I noticed he was going to read another live commercial, I pulled the copy out of his hand and gave him the wire story. He started to read the copy cold, 'This just in, the Pope, oh my God!' he said and he continued reading it. He had started off with an edge in his voice because I had just barged into his show, but

actually he knew I would never have done it if it wasn't really important, and he was glad in the end, but that's how it is with live radio."

Another experience she had with live radio involved her own children's school. Beuckman, who was divorced from car dealer Bo Beuckman, lived in Collinsville and their children attended the Collinsville schools.

"There was a big strike in the Collinsville School District and my kids were in there," she said. "The strike was settled, but the school district announced the kids would have to go extra during the Christmas holidays so the students stayed out of school to protest this decision. I was up at the school and called in to tell them about this. I was at a pay phone at a high school, surrounded by a mob of kids, and they decide back at the station I should go on the air live with a report. I wasn't normally an on-air person, but when Bob Hardy said he wanted a live report, I did it as best I could. Then he says, 'OK, Joanie, we know how Joan the reporter feels, that was a nice report, but how does Joan the mother of students in the district feel?'"

Another time she found out how nerve-wracking it can be in live radio was during a tornado. There was a tornado spotted in Edwardsville, and the power was out so she went to a pay phone in Maryville, Illinois.

"I did my live report and then hung up," she said. "As soon as I hung up, the pay phone rang and a voice said, 'I just heard your report and I can see you.' I hung up and ran to my car!"

BILL BIDWILL, JR.

The son of the owner of the Arizona Cardinals, Bill Bidwill, Jr., who is now an executive with the team, worked at KMOX for three summers when he was in high school. He mainly listened to interviews and broke them down by quotes, typing them up for use in the newscasts.

"He worked mostly in news, but he did some in sports," said Jim Holder of the sports department (at that time). "I remember I had him call someone for an interview. It was some NFL star. I remember thinking, this is sure something, the son of an NFL team owner is calling this football star and doing an interview with him."

One of Bidwill's most memorable days was "when the guy parachuted under the Arch," he said. "I was ticked because I was in the newsroom at the time and I missed it. KMOX has this great big glass window and you have a perfect view of the Arch. Here this guy landed on the Arch and was going to jump off again, maybe with a second parachute. Well, he landed on the Arch, but he slid down one of the legs and died."

People began calling the station and the reporters thought it was a hoax, but then they realized it was for real and sent a reporter to cover the story.

"He was doing it for that television show, *That's Incredible*," said Bidwill. "I remember it was early on a Saturday morning, and there we were right across the street from it with a perfect view and we missed it."

Even though Bidwill's father was Bill Bidwill, the owner of the St. Louis football Cardinals, he did not receive any special treatment.

"I was the low man on the totem pole," said Bidwill. "I remember two times the KMOX news car got a flat tire and I had to go out and change the tire!"

He had another memory of the news car. The news cars were just regular cars with white cards with "KMOX NEWS" in big black letters printed on them. For some reason it was always exciting for news or sports assistants to get to ride in the "news car" rather than their own car. It seemed more "official."

"Once I got sent on a bank robbery with Anne Keefe because there was no one else there to cover it," said Bidwill. "I remember I drove the KMOX news car. Anne did reports from the two-way radio in the car because we didn't have a cell phone back then. She called in to Bob Hardy, but she could not hear his questions so we would have to turn the car radio up real loud to hear the questions, then real quick turn it down so there would be no feedback when Anne did her report."

"I remember going to cover that bank robbery," said Keefe. "We were scared to death not knowing where we were going. We stopped at a gas station and got directions. I loved working with Billy Bidwill. He was so smart. He was only in high school at the time, but he could hold his own with me in a discussion. I remember telling his mom that. He was so smart he could always give me a good solid argument."

Bidwill always liked Jack Carney and he would listen to his show.

"A group of us interns and assistants would go back to the studio right behind Jack Carney's studio when he was doing his show just to listen," said Bidwill. "We went back there, first of all, to hide, and also just to watch Carney do his show. He was magnificent. He used to adlib and was just so amazing to watch, he was just an all-round fun guy.

"I have great memories of my days at KMOX. There were a lot of big-named personalities working there, but they didn't have big-name personalities egos. They treated everyone the same."

KEN BILLUPS

Ken Billups was at KMOX in the late 1960s. He was a musician and music director at one of the area high schools and he worked part-time at KMOX, doing big band shows on the weekends.

BARRY BIRR

Barry Birr worked in the newsroom in the '70s as an on-air reporter. He worked on the morning drive show.

"He was there when I was an intern," said Stuart Esrock, who worked at KMOX for four years. "Barry Birr was a really solid newsman. He would go over stories with me when I was in the newsroom. He was so helpful, one of those people who took an interest in the interns and wanted to help them."

BUDDY BLATTNER

The play-by-play announcer for the St. Louis Browns from 1950-1953, Buddy Blattner also broadcast Cardinal games for two years, 1960-61, but spent most of his St. Louis career providing the play-by-play of the St. Louis Hawks in the NBA.

"He was the best basketball announcer I ever heard," said Jack Buck.

Ed Macauley, who played with the Hawks and later coached the team, said many of the players considered Blattner a grandfather-type even though he wasn't that old.

"He was well respected both by players and management," Macauley said. "He was a very professional broadcaster. He had a lot of impact in town, because he made up nicknames for all the guys. Bob Pettit was 'Big Blue' because of a big blue overcoat that he wore. He called Cliff Hagen 'Little Abner'; he called me 'Easy Ed.' He had names for everybody.

"When we went around the city, people would call us by the nicknames that Buddy had given us. He did a great job for the Hawks."

Blattner's impact on attendance for the Hawks wasn't as great as the baseball announcers, because of the difference between the basketball and baseball schedules. Fans couldn't come in from Oklahoma or Arkansas for the weekend for one basketball game the way they did for baseball games.

Buck said he did not believe owner Ben Kerner would have moved the Hawks to St. Louis from Milwaukee if he had not been able to have the games broadcast on KMOX.

"It has always been a boon to any team to have its games on the station," Buck said.

During the two years Macauley coached the Hawks, he became closer with Blattner.

"We would go out after the games and talk," Macauley said. "In those days we didn't have any assistant coaches so he was a great help to me personally. It helped that the things we talked about didn't go any farther than that."

Blattner also broadcast baseball for the California Angels and Kansas City Royals, as well as network *Game of the Week* telecasts with Dizzy Dean. He is now retired and lives in Lake Ozark, Missouri.

MIRIAM BLUE

Miriam Blue, or "Miss Blue" as Jack Carney and his fans everywhere referred to her, was a cleaning lady. She was 61 years old, and very wise and motherly. As she cleaned, she would talk to anyone and always made people feel good. Carney recognized the wisdom and charm of this older woman who was living with her daughter and two grandchildren. He just happened to bring her on his show once and

she was so well received that any time she would walk by his studio, he would call her in.

"She would be cleaning and would stop in and talk to Jack," said Carney's producer Frank Pawloski. "Jack really enjoyed her. One day she was in there during the news and he just asked her to stay. She was so upbeat and she would always say, 'Well, Jackie, ALL'S WELL!' That became her trademark."

One day Miss Blue forgot to say "All is Well" and the listeners started calling in.

Miss Blue, who would take the bus to work each day from East St. Louis, became so popular that Carney used to write her into some of the show's comedy bits. He had a skit where she played an Indian maiden. He also put her in one with Bob Starr. He called it "As the Stomach Turns." It was a little three-minute soap opera.

Miriam Blue became almost a cult figure, and media around the country became interested in her. *Sunday Pictures* magazine, *People* magazine, and CBS-TV interviewed her. She even flew to New York to appear on *To Tell The Truth*. She stumped everyone on the show except Kitty Carlisle.

At one time, Carney had her giving advice to the lovelorn. One caller asked, 'Is it OK to burn my bra?' Without missing a beat, Miss Blue replied, 'Sure, but be sure to take it off first!'

Though she was heard on Carney's show, she was not given plum hours because of her "celebrity" status.

"She still cleaned the offices," said Robert R. Lynn, who worked in the news department. "I loved Miss Blue. She came in on Saturdays and cleaned the place up. I would always talk to her. Miriam was just a wonderful gal. One time when I was at work, she got word of an emergency at home and she needed to get to her home in East St. Louis quickly. She always used public transportation so she would have had to take the bus. I gave her a ride home, and she was always so appreciative of that."

John McGuire of the *Post-Dispatch* did a feature article on Miss Blue for *People* magazine. When the magazine found out about this "cleaning woman" who was giving advice to the lovelorn, they wanted a feature on her.

"They [KMOX] sent me a bunch of tapes of her appearances," he

said. "I had heard her a few times, but usually when she was on was when I was at work. After I heard the shows I was amazed at how it was all orchestrated by Carney. If you listen to the tapes, you could see he set her up. He would hear her say 'all is well' and then pick up on that and say 'give us an ALL's WELL' and that's how he got her to do that."

That is what many found to be the genius in Jack Carney. He saw the possibility in Miriam Blue and the goodness in her and brought it out.

"Another thing I thought was interesting was when I was talking to her, she mentioned how much she used to like to ride the street car over to St. Louis and look in the windows," said McGuire. "She never mentioned going in the stores. It was always just to 'look in the windows.' I asked someone about it and they pointed out that it was when she was a young woman in the 1950s and St. Louis was segregated. Blacks could not go in certain department stores. She wasn't bitter about it when she talked. She just said it very matter of factly, 'I took the street car and I loved going around and looking in windows in the stores,' she would say."

FRED BODIMER

Fred Bodimer is the religion editor for KMOX. He did the bulk of the work on the coverage of the Pope and Billy Graham visits to St. Louis. Among other things, Bodimer does a weekly show called *The World of Religion*. It had originally been produced by the CBS Radio Network.

"At one time when CBS was cutting back, they decided to drop *The World of Religion*," said Bob Hamilton of the newsroom. "Robert Hyland said, 'If they're not going to do it, we will,' and to this day Fred Bodimer has been doing it. He does it for the CBS network and for the Voice of America."

Bodimer also serves as the producer for *Total Information PM*.

"Fred Bodimer is by far the brightest, most talented person I've ever worked with," said Carol Daniel, one of the hosts of the afternoon drive show. "He has really helped me. He makes me want to do better on the air, and he helps me to be so prepared and relaxed. He is a confidant and a friend. Having people like Fred makes difficult days easier to handle."

BILL BRADLEY

After he graduated from Princeton, and before going off to Oxford as a Rhodes Scholar, former U.S. senator Bill Bradley worked in the news room at KMOX as a reporter and essayist.

"My first assignment was to interview the governor of Missouri on his new budget," said Bradley, a native of Crystal City, Missouri. "I got on a small plane bound for Jefferson City and met the governor at a barbecue. I took out my UHER tape recorder and with my hand-held mike plugged into my tape recorder, I began to ask the governor about the budget.

"At the conclusion of the interview, I felt I had some good quotes, and boarded the small plane back to St. Louis. As soon as I arrived back at the office, I headed straight for the editing room—took out the tape and reeled it to a master tape only to find that nothing had been recorded. I had inadvertently placed my index finger on the erase button during the interview."

Luckily, Bradley's bosses were understanding. He even continued to work for the station while at Oxford. He had the designation of being the station's European Correspondent.

"My second most memorable experience with KMOX was when I was assigned as their European Correspondent when I was at Oxford," Bradley said. "I was given the plum assignment of interviewing Richard Burton, Elizabeth Taylor, Lord Harlech [a friend of John Kennedy's], upon the third anniversary of the assassination of Kennedy, and Mary Quant, the original designer of the mini skirt, to name a few. All of these interviews were pleasurable and extremely informative. I again used my UHER, and this time kept my finger off the erase button."

BRUCE BRADLEY

Bruce Bradley, who, as a teenager, taught himself not to stutter by talking repeatedly into a tape recorder, came to KMOX in 1992 after 37 years of radio experience. Robert Hyland had had several different people in for tryouts. Bob Osborne was the program director at the

time and when he first heard Bradley there was nothing that set him apart from the others.

"I heard him and thought he was so funny," said Barb Felt who worked with Osborne, "But for some reason Bob Osborne didn't immediately take to him. I told him I had been listening to Bruce Bradley in my car and had to pull over he was just so funny. Well, the next day I was at the gynecologist's office and as I sat waiting for my name to be called, what do I hear all the ladies talking about? 'Did you hear that Bruce Bradley? Wasn't he great? Wasn't he funny?' I went back and told that to Osborne and Mr. Hyland and they'd gotten a lot of those similar remarks. He was hired."

"I never saw anybody who was funnier faster than Bruce Bradley," said his producer, Rene Servier. "He could be funny for 10 seconds if you needed him to be. You could say, 'you need to fill 45 seconds,' and he would."

Bradley's career wasn't always funny, however. Despite having worked in other major markets, he had been out of radio for five months when he came to work for KMOX. He arrived in town with $50 in his pocket.

In a December 1988 interview with *St. Louis* magazine, Bradley also recalled a day on the air which was no fun. It was the radio host's nightmare when he was receiving no telephone calls and had no idea what he was going to talk about.

"I had about 40 minutes left to go before I was finished, and hardly any commercials to use as crutches, and I had about a minute and a half of material left, no ideas, because when you start to panic, your mind closes, and I thought, 'My Lord, I'm dying on the radio. No one is calling. No one will ever call.'

"And I tossed out some subject—in desperation—I asked a question about race, or about sex, or about religion, one of those things that you grab at, and you think, 'Well, they'll call about this.' And this woman called up and I thought, 'Thank God a phone is ringing.' And I put her on the air and she said, 'You just put that subject out because it's inflammatory and you're not getting any telephone calls.' I thought, 'Oh my Lord, it's like being naked in public.' For some reason or other, people started calling, and they ignored her call, but I admitted it on the air. I said, 'You're right...' That was the worst, as bad as any moment I've ever had in my life."

Bradley was popular by himself, but the listeners really enjoyed it when he was teamed with Anne Keefe. His shows with Keefe were among the most popular on KMOX at that time. Both Bradley and Keefe started their careers in Rochester, New York, but did not meet until they came to KMOX.

"Bruce Bradley was the funniest person I ever worked with," said Keefe. "I enjoyed working with Bruce, we could have differing opinions, but we respected each other and kidded in a gentle way."

"Every day I was bowled over with how entertaining Bruce Bradley and Anne Keefe were," said Nan Wyatt. He really impressed me with his quick wit."

Wyatt remembered breaking onto his show once when she first started at KMOX.

"We had an unconfirmed report of a tornado touching down on 270," she said. "John Angelides [news director] said we had to break in and warn the people. He jotted something down and handed it to me. I ran into the studio and Bruce was on the air. He didn't know I was coming, but he was just so calm it was as if he expected me. I got in there and he said, 'Here's Nan Wyatt with a bulletin.' I looked down at the paper and I could not read the chicken scratches John had written! Finally, I found the words to say, 'We have an unconfirmed report of a tornado touching down along Highway 270; everybody is urged to take cover.' Luckily more information was coming through and they brought me some typed pages. Bruce was an expert at handling things that were unexpected."

One of the unexpected things that happened on his shift did not have to do with a news story.

"Bruce Bradley was on the air doing an interview and a pipe burst in the ceiling above the console," said Jeanette Grider. "With the water starting to rush down, he picked up his prep materials and kept on talking until a reasonable moment where he could take a commercial break. He then headed down the hall to the back-up studio and picked up where he left off."

"I'll never forget the Gulf War [Desert Storm] started on Bruce's shift," said Servier. "We knew it was coming down, and Mr. Hyland

said once the war started there would be no commercials so we real quick took a break and put in as many commercials as we could."

KMOX did not run any commercials for several days as per Hyland's mandate.

"You really could not say, 'Now here's the shooting report brought to you by so and so,'" said Servier. "Bruce Bradley was doing his drive time and after that would be the sports. He ended up staying very late that night. Suddenly when the war started it was like 'ok, our war coverage is starting in 5,4,3,2, 1, go!' and the whole place went wild. Senators were calling us to give us their input, I was calling the governor, congressmen, senators to get them to go on with Bruce. I'd say, 'Hello Senator, this is Rene from KMOX, would you go on with Bruce Bradley' and they did."

Bradley was getting all of his information from the newsroom and Servier.

"I was there watching CNN, as well as two other television networks, the wire services and a laptop computer on my lap, and, of course, we had our own sources we were talking to. They told the sports guys not to come in so he worked their shift. The next show was *Ask the Gardener*, so Bruce worked through that time slot also. I was on the board until 11:00 and Bruce stayed longer than that. I don't think either of us ate that night."

Some of the memories of Bradley are personal.

"I'll never forget when Bruce Bradley announced pregnancy updates about me," said Wendy Wiese. "I was pregnant with my daughter Maggie. To set the stage, that morning after we got off the air, Bob Hardy asked if I wanted to get some breakfast. I said I was feeling kind of funny so I went home and got on the heating pad. My water broke and the first call I made (before I even called the doctor or my husband) was Mr. Hyland because I figured I wouldn't be in tomorrow if I was having the baby. He said, 'I'm proud of you honey, good luck, tell Chris (my husband) to call us.' Well, he had a friend with connections at St. Luke's, so Mr. Hyland kept getting updates and then Bruce would broadcast them."

Meanwhile, Wiese's in-laws were driving to St. Louis when they heard the news, and as soon as they could pick up KMOX, they began to hear Bradley's updates.

"'They've given her the epidural,' Bruce told everyone." said Wiese. "Maggie was born around 4:17, right in the middle of afternoon drive and Bruce got to announce it!"

Bradley resigned from the station, but came back at Robert Hyland's request, shortly before Hyland's death. His second stint was short-lived, however. In 2000, he returned to the airwaves in St. Louis, moving back from Arizona to host a show on KTRS.

JIM BRADY

Jim Brady worked for 18 years in broadcasting and spent 21 years with the St. Louis County Police Department. Brady worked in the KMOX newsroom before leaving to become the news director at KTVI-TV.

RODGER BRAND

Rodger Brand is a traffic reporter for KMOX, flying in Jet Copter One. He generally takes the area of Highway 40 and north where Megan Lynch (who is in Airborne One, an airplane) covers the area south of 40. Because of air restrictions near Lambert it is easier to get the helicopter into the airspace than the airplane so that was part of the consideration when dividing the metropolitan area.

"Rodger has covered hostage situations, people in the river, so many things," said Megan Lynch. "On a daily basis we see so many things up there. We are constantly reporting back to the station or talking about a situation on the air and then they follow up on it. He's been there for a while and has seen a lot."

Before the airplane was added, Brand covered the entire metropolitan area himself.

"He probably could have been resentful because he gave me half of his territory," said Lynch, "But he was so helpful. He has always treated me as an equal. He said, "When I first started, he said, 'Don't stress out too much, you'll learn it.'"

Brand has often been on the radio with morning talk show host Charles Brennan. After he parks the helicopter, he will often come on the show for discussion of topics that don't always include the traffic reports.

CHARLES BRENNAN

The co-host of *The Morning Meeting* for the last 10 years, Charles Brennan has been involved in many memorable moments. He has seen a guest arrested by federal agents just after finishing an interview; he has had a guest, Marie Osmond, read a tornado warning because no one else was in the studio; and he has conducted a 30-minute interview with President Clinton which was reprinted word-for-word in *The New York Times*.

Brennan had been working at a station near Boston when he got the offer from KMOX and joined the staff in 1988. His first job was to host the nighttime hours of *At Your Service*, as well as weekend daytime hours, and to fill in for other hosts whenever necessary.

"When I first got here, Bruce Bradley shook my hand and said, 'Congratulations, you're now working seven days a week.' Most of the time he was right," Brennan said.

Brennan said he once worked 62 consecutive days, and often would get off the air at 3 AM and have to be back on the air at 9 AM. In those situations, Robert Hyland arranged for him to get a room at the Marriott.

He became one of the co-hosts of the morning program in 1990, joined by Art Fleming and Kevin Horrigan. Fleming had been hosting the show with Mary Phelan. That trio stayed together for a year, before Fleming left the show and Brennan and Horrigan remained.

"We had a lot of fun, and sometimes it was at Fleming's expense," Brennan said. "He didn't really prepare too well, and we decided to play a joke on him one day. We had Debby Boone here, and she went along with it. We hid her in another studio, and pretended she was an oceanographer from Massachusetts who had written a book. We told Art we had not received the book, but had some facts about it. Kevin had actually typed the list up.

"I played like I was sick, and Kevin left supposedly because he had been called into Mr. Hyland's office. That left Art to do the interview, and he was really getting flustered. Debby Boone kept giving him yes

and no answers and disagreeing with the things he was saying. Finally we sprung it on him."

The Marie Osmond episode occurred when she said she would like to host the show, and didn't need Brennan or Horrigan. Both got up and walked out, leaving her alone in the studio. When the tornado warning bulletin came through, there was no one else there to read it.

Once when he was hosting an evening show, the guest was someone who had developed a get-rich-quick scheme. Brennan didn't know there was a warrant out for the man's arrest, but as soon as the show was over, federal marshals came in and arrested him.

"I guess the moral to that story is not to come do an interview on a 50,000-watt radio station when there is a warrant for your arrest," Brennan said.

Shortly after St. Louis' rapid transit system, MetroLink, opened, Brennan got into a discussion about whether someone could drive his or her car from the airport to America's Center faster than you could get there on MetroLink. That led to an on-air race.

Driving the car was Walt Glatthaar and Rodger Brand, with two nuns. They won.

Brennan is a history buff, and has come to learn and appreciate the history of downtown St. Louis and KMOX. He is the co-author of a book called " Walking Historic Downtown St Louis" from Virginia Publishing Company, and has been instrumental in placing plaques at locations where historical events occurred.

He spearheaded the successful drive to allow street musicians and find vendors throughout downtown.

Nancy Newton and her husband, Neal, consider themselves "regulars" to his broadcasts and Nancy keeps the radio to KMOX all morning as she goes about her daily routines.

"I have three radios and they're all going," she said. "That way I don't have to turn it on as I go from room to room. I really enjoy Charles Brennan. He's so intelligent and he really does his homework. He knows a lot of things and if he has a guest who has written a book, you know he's read the book.

"I especially liked the show from Powell Hall. He had the maestro, Hans Vonk, on. There was a woman who sang and she had a beautiful

voice, she was wonderful."

Newton likes the way Brennan makes his listeners feel like they know him.

"We go to a lot of his events and now he knows us," said Newton. "Once he told us we don't even have to make reservations, just go ahead and come since we're regulars."

One time she was at a show and introduced herself and said she had seen him out with his wife, Beth and their son, Charlie D.

"I told him I'd seen them walking at Tilles Park. He was so nice he started talking to me about it. He said, 'We went around five times,' and he told me that his little boy gets tired of being in his stroller so sometimes he has to carry him. That's one thing about Charlie: he doesn't talk about his family too much, but you know he is married and has a son, and whenever he mentions his wife, it is always something real nice."

There was one show that Nancy Newton especially liked.

"It was the one with James Bradley, who wrote the book *Flags of Our Fathers*. His father was one of the men who raised the flag at Iwo Jima. Neal [her husband] went right out and bought the book after hearing that show," Nancy Newton said. "James Bradley said his dad didn't talk about that episode or the war at all, but after he died they found some papers and he decided to write the book. Neal was just fascinated about it. Charlie always gets such interesting guests. He really goes out there and looks for great guests whether they are show people, authors, government people, anybody, if they are interesting, Charles Brennan will find them."

Charlie Hoessle, the director of the St. Louis Zoo, is a frequent guest on Brennan's show.

"Charlie calls me occasionally and I sometimes bring animals down to the studio," said Hoessle. "Anytime Charlie calls me or anybody from KMOX, for that matter, I have told my PR staff to be sure I am always available for them. I like to do the interviews on KMOX myself."

Brennan's program also has gone out of town, broadcasting from Washington, DC, New York, Cleveland, Chicago, Cardinals' spring training, and other cities. He reported live from Germany in 1998.

Guests on his program have included Dr. Billy Graham, former

President Jimmy Carter, Jay Leno, David Letterman, James Michener, Neil Diamond, Michael J. Fox, Al Gore, John Goodman, and Henry Kissinger.

Brennan often has authors on his show, and he has literally made author Stephen Ambrose a household name in St. Louis. Ambrose appears frequently on his show.

"Stephen Ambrose was a college professor, historian, author," said Richard Buthod of Unique Books and formerly of the Booksource. "KMOX and Charles Brennan has enabled listeners to hear him and he is so knowledgeable and is a very good storyteller. Charles Brennan really does his homework as far as reading the books of the authors he has on. If he doesn't, he sure fakes it better than anyone I know. He is a great person to have interview an author because he always seems to know so much about the subject.

"St. Louis is fortunate in being an absolute 'must-stop' on national book tours and that is largely because of KMOX. An interview on KMOX almost has to happen for a book to succeed. What begins as a publicity stop ends as an eye-opening discussion that increases the intellectual level in St. Louis because of the opportunity given by KMOX with hosts like Charles Brennan. With the combination of knowledgeable hosts on KMOX, the fascinating authors they get on, and the carefully screened callers, listening to an author interview on that station is time well spent."

Brennan has a cast of characters who occasionally appear on his show. John Ferarra, of The Pasta House Co., is a frequent guest, as is Gus Torregrossa of Gus's Fashions. Another is Jasper Giardina of Jasper's Tropical Gifts and Fruit Baskets.

"I listen to Charles every day," said Giardina. "He's on when we are here making our fruit basket orders. I've actually been associated with KMOX for 30 years. I used to bring baskets in and leave them at the desk, and then Robert Hyland saw me in the hall one day. He said, 'What are you doing?' I said, 'I just brought in a basket.' He said, 'Well, why don't you bring the basket in and hand it to the guest yourself?' I said, 'Mr. Hyland, I can't speak well. I don't want to do that.' And he said, 'Young man, you just go in and be yourself.' He went in with me."

He has brought many baskets in for Brennan's guests.

"Nobody sponsors me," he said. "I just do it. I like it because when you hand somebody a fruit basket you get their attention. They want to know where it's from and who sent it."

Giardina has pictures of many stars he has given the baskets to.

"They're not just publicity shots," he said. "I am in the pictures with these people. I've got Geraldo, Richard Simmons, Chuck Woolery, Jay Leno. Many of the movie stars actually write me letters when they get home to thank me for the baskets. I've got letters from Anne Baxter, Phyllis Diller, Marie Osmond. I just do it because I like to do it."

DR. ARMAND BRODEUR

Dr. Armand Brodeur has been a part of KMOX since its days on Hampton Avenue. It all started because of a visit from his next-door neighbor.

"I lived next door to Ed Bonner, a real popular disc jockey on KXOK at the time," said Brodeur. "His wife, Jeanne, worked for KMOX. One day she called and asked if I would be on the *J. Roy McCarthy Show*. I was really excited. I thought wow, they have such great people like Rex Davis, who also lived by me in Kirkwood. Rex Davis was really a big star there and I felt flattered that they wanted me to go on.

"For the first interview she told me to bring five medical questions with me so he would know what to ask me. I got there and gave him the questions. Three minutes into the broadcast Roy went to a commercial break. Robert Hyland walked in and pointed to me and said, 'You, I want to hire you.'

Soon Brodeur went from guest to host and had a program called *Ask The Doctor* where people would call up about their aches and pains and Dr. Brodeur would talk to them about it. He wanted to expand the show and he didn't really like that title, so he changed it to *Doctor to Doctor* and brought in other doctors to work with him.

"I thought, wouldn't it be nice if you could listen in on a conversation between two doctors," said Brodeur, "as if you were in the waiting room and they had left the door open."

Peggy Cohill Drenkhahn was his producer.

"He is one I think so highly of," said Drenkhahn. "He has done

such tremendous things for the community through the broadcasting. He was such a pleasure to work with."

Brodeur has served as KMOX's expert doctor for more than 40 years and continues to do medical features that run on Saturdays and Sundays. This prominent pediatric radiologist, who was instrumental in the start of Cardinal Glennon Children's Hospital, was often used for his expertise whenever needed. He has had such a successful broadcasting career besides his medical career, he started the National Association of Medical Communicators.

"It was because of my association with the famous radio station, KMOX, that I gained a great deal of credibility within the American Medical Association," said Brodeur, who has 79 plaques and awards and not enough wall or shelf space to display them all. "When the AMA found out I was a regular on KMOX, which was widely known because of its far-reaching signal, they took notice of me and wanted me to be a teacher."

Brodeur became one of only 10 physicians (out of the 55,000 membership in the United States) selected as faculty to do teaching on radio/TV/platform. He has remained in that capacity ever since. Brodeur has his own credentials, but he feels that his regular appearances on KMOX have contributed to his national recognition. He has been on *The David Letterman Show* twice, has appeared on *Tomorrow with Tom Snyder*, and others.

Due to Brodeur's pushing, the corridors of Cardinal Glennon Children's Hospitals were painted with murals so the facility would be more child-friendly.

"We didn't want it to look like a hospital," said the affable Brodeur, who is also an accomplished magician and used to put on magic shows for the children at the hospital. "People found out about the decorating of the walls, and the national media wanted to interview me."

Charles Kuralt came to St. Louis to do a feature story on Brodeur.

"I remember I took the telephone call in the hall," said Brodeur. "It was Charles Kuralt himself. He was so charming and gracious. When he talked about coming to St. Louis to do the interview, I said, 'Why don't you drive to my house and bring your producers and have dinner at my house?' About that time I heard a pan drop in the kitchen! He

came and was terrific. In fact, he turned to my wife, Gloria, and said, 'We've been all over the world and never have we had a dinner we enjoyed more than this."

Doing a medical show can be a bit interesting at times. People call up and ask whatever they want to ask.

"Once I had an expert on about bronchitis and asthma," said Brodeur. "We were just talking about bronchitis and asthma, and the producer screened the calls so they would all be about the subject. All of a sudden a woman gets on and starts talking about her tapeworm! Those are the kinds of things you have to deal with."

Brodeur was instrumental in forming the national organization which is now known as NAMC, the National Association of Medical Communicators, and was the first president.

"There are two things I always say when I speak to groups," said Brodeur. "One is you want to have an interesting subject and speak in layman's language, don't use big medical terms. The other thing I say (and this can be applied to everyone, not just medical communicators): 'If you want to make an impression, you don't have to talk long you just have to talk strong.' If you can't say something in 70 seconds you probably need 70 minutes!"

BOB BROEG

"And this is Bob Broeg for Fred Broeg," or "this is Bob Broeg for Sam Cavato." That is how Bob Broeg would begin and end his weekend radio commentaries. Each week the former *Post-Dispatch* sports editor broadcast a three-minute program about the topic of his choice. Broeg was also a frequent guest on *Sports Open Line* for years during his newspaper career.

The octogenarian has been around sports since his days in the Knot Hole Gang at Sportsmen's Park. He has remained active in writing and doing his radio vignettes, and has written at least 18 books, including one on his experiences as a sportswriter.

In recent years, Broeg has been known to talk about the "good old days of baseball"—the days of Frankie Frisch, Pepper Martin, his favorite, Stan Musial, and another favorite, the old redhead, Red Schoendienst.

Broeg lives in St. Louis and enjoys being involved with the local chapter of the Baseball Writers Association of America. He is a Hall-of-Famer, having been inducted in the Writers' Wing of the Baseball Hall of Fame in Cooperstown and The National Baseball Congress Hall of Fame.

CHARLES BROWN

One of Charlie Brown's jobs at KMOX was to work with Dan Dierdorf for the afternoon drive program.

"It seemed Mr. Hyland could never find anyone for the afternoon drive slot," said former KMOX newsman Kent Martin. "He tried many people there, and Charlie Brown and Dan Dierdorf were one pair. I remember Charlie played the straight man to Dan. Dan would run in the newsroom typing all kinds of jokes, trying to crack Charlie up. He was always joking with him, they really got along great."

Brown left the station to go on a missionary visit to Guam, where he is reported to be happy and doing more radio work.

MIKE BROWN

Mike Brown hosts *The Money Show* on Saturday afternoons. He offers advice on investments, the economy, and talks about the latest trends. A former reporter for KMOV-TV, Brown is now a licensed investment broker and works for Prudential Securities.

THEOTIS BROWN

Theotis Brown was a runningback with the St. Louis Cardinals and was the co-host of a weekly show with runningback Ottis Anderson. *The Ottis and Theotis Show* ran each Monday night during the football season, prior to *Monday Night Football*.

"Theotis would bring out the humor in the show," said Jim Holder who first recorded the show and then had portions of it broadcast on *Monday Night Football*. "He would humor O.J. Theotis was the one who kind of quarterbacked the show."

CAROLE BUCK

She isn't on the radio as much as her husband or son, but Carole Buck's voice also is familiar to KMOX listeners.

With her family, Carole hosts the traditional "Christmas at the Buck's" program each Christmas morning. The Bucks invite hundreds of friends to their house, play and sing Christmas carols, and enjoy the spirit of the morning. It is annually one of the most popular programs on the station.

The Bucks used to host the program at the KMOX studios, but decided to move the broadcast to their home when children Joe and Julie were little.

"When we were still down at the studio, Julie was about four years old and she wouldn't talk," Jack Buck said. "I kept saying, 'Julie, say something.' Finally she said, 'The Arch is falling.'"

Joe and Julie also were on the air as young children when Harry Fender, playing Santa Claus, called them on the telephone.

"Julie told him, 'Don't give Joe Buck anything because he said you're not the real Santa Claus,'" Buck said. Fender asked Julie to get her brother to the telephone, and when Joe took the call, Fender said, "This is Santa Claus and you're not getting anything for Christmas." Joe said, "I believe, I believe."

On other programs, Carole has hosted discussions with wives of Cardinal players, getting their perspective on the team and their famous husbands.

"She's lived basically the same life we have," said Lauri Van Slyke, the wife of former Cardinal and Pirates outfielder Andy Van Slyke.

Buck would gather several players' wives in her condo in Florida during spring training and have a round-table discussion with them on the air. In 1984, she gathered Kim Herr, Denise Smith, Merle Ramsey, and Van Slyke.

"I remember looking around and thinking, 'I'm in pretty good company; what am I doing here?'" said Van Slyke, whose husband had just joined the team. "Tom Herr, Ozzie Smith, and Mike Ramsey were all established players and she asked me on the show."

Of course, Andy Van Slyke went on to become an All-Star and Gold Glove winner.

"We just talked about spring training," said Lauri Van Slyke, "what it was like for all of us. We talked about the wife angle. Carole is easy to talk to. Of course I've known her for years. Her daughter, Julie, babysat our son, A.J., all the time. Julie was probably watching all of the kids while we were on the air. Now Julie has twin sons of her own, and our kids are the ages they could babysit for her."

Carole also is an entertainer. She played in *How to Succeed in Business Without Really Trying* on Broadway, and also has performed in that production at The Muny. She recalled being reminded of how much power Robert Hyland carried when it came to The Muny.

"Someone called him from New York and said they were bringing *How to Succeed* to St. Louis to appear at The Muny," Carole Buck said. "He replied that that was great, and then said they, meaning the St. Louis people, already had someone to play the role I had played on Broadway. He wanted me to do it. The guy in New York said they had somebody for that role. Hyland insisted, and when the guy wouldn't budge, Hyland said, 'then don't come.' I think they canceled the show."

Her husband was out of town when Carole also got a lesson in Hyland's importance and power. Her father was traveling on one of the cruise ships down the Mississippi River and had become ill. They were near Cairo, Illinois.

Carole called Hyland and explained that her father was having a problem.

"Before you knew it, he had the local police, the Illinois State Police, the Missouri Highway Patrol, the Red Cross, he had everybody there," Jack Buck said. "That's the kind of guy he was. He would do anything for you."

JACK BUCK

As well known as he is as a sportscaster on a national level, Jack Buck is much more than that to St. Louisians.

He is a friend. He is the premier master of ceremonies at dinners and banquets. He is a tireless worker for charity. People who don't

care about sports or know nothing about sports still know all about Jack Buck.

"Jack Buck is a great, great broadcaster," said Bob Costas. "Though he is known nationally, he is better appreciated by the people in St. Louis because KMOX has given him the opportunity to be on the air in other ways besides just sportscasting. People feel as if they really know him in St. Louis. Nationally he is known as one of the best broadcasters but in St. Louis, he is known as the best. Over the years here they've gotten the full range of his ability and personality."

Buck moved to St. Louis in 1954 to join the Cardinals' broadcast team with Harry Caray and Milo Hamilton. The games were being carried by KXOK. The next year, Robert Hyland acquired the broadcast rights for KMOX and thus began Buck's long tenure with the station.

Over the years, he has broadcast practically every sport imaginable. He also was one of the first hosts of *At Your Service* programming, anchoring the opening broadcast on February 29, 1960. Mayor Raymond Tucker was his first guest.

"Hyland called and told me what he was going to do," Buck said. "I told him I didn't think it would work. I didn't think our audience would respond to that kind of programming. He went ahead and did it anyway, giving away almost the entire music library so there wasn't any way he could reverse the decision."

The *At Your Service* programs opened up a whole different world of guests for Buck, including people like Eleanor Roosevelt, and helped make him a better interviewer, skills he used when doing his sports broadcasts.

"It increased my education tenfold," Buck said. "We really changed the way radio was perceived…We educated the public about things that were going on in this country."

One of Buck's jobs in his early days at KMOX was a program at Musial and Biggie's Restaurant, which ran after the Cardinals' game. He would conduct interviews and also play records.

He was doing the program one Tuesday night, and there was nothing special going on. He remembers it being a light night in the restaurant, with not many people there. At that moment, Jimmy Durante

entered the restaurant. He had come to St. Louis for a private corpora-
tion function, and not many people knew he was in town and he certainly had not been scheduled to come to the restaurant.

Buck put him on the air: "It wasn't really an interview, he just
started talking. Fifteen minutes later, you couldn't find a place in the
parking lot. The restaurant was packed, it was a memorable night."

Another KMOX-originated programs in those days was the *House-
wives Protective League*, usually hosted by Grant Williams. One day
Williams failed to show up, and Buck was recruited to fill in.

"They handed me a script and said, 'you're on,'" Buck said. "I had
not read it ahead of time, and when I came to the word 'organism,' I
pronounced it 'orgasm.' The engineer disappeared below the desk."

Buck didn't make many mistakes, however, as he began to earn the
respect of sports fans around the country. He moved to the national
stage, but he always kept his roots at KMOX and in St. Louis.

He is certain Hyland was one of the people who influenced network executives to hire him as the voice of *Monday Night Football* on
CBS Radio.

"Hyland liked personalities," Buck said. "He didn't care if people
were more popular than he was or made more money than he did. He
let me and Bob Costas and Dan Kelly work those national games."

Working those national broadcasts helped Buck earn selection to
the Broadcasters' Wing of the Baseball Hall of Fame, and also to earn
the Pete Rozelle Award and be inducted into the Football Hall of Fame.

Buck appeared at the Smithsonian Institute in Washington, DC, in
1993 to be honored as one of baseball's 12 greatest play-by-play men as
featured in author Curt Smith's book *Voices of The Game*. Buck was the
featured guest at the event held at the National History Museum.

"He came to the seminar and it was the night before he left for
Ireland and the Irish Derby," said Curt Smith. "I remember he said he
was looking forward to going out of the country. I've always liked Jack
Buck because he broadcast a year in the 1950s in my hometown of Rochester. He is a great student of the game. I enjoyed his understanding of
St. Louis and why it is the baseball capital of the country. He has a
grasp of Cardinal history. He's seen so much in Cardinal history."

Buck is also featured in Smith's other book, *The Storytellers*.

When a new employee goes to work at KMOX, one of the first questions he or she is often asked by relatives and friends is if they have had a chance to meet Jack Buck.

"I've gotten to know Jack Buck since I started working at KMOX," said Brian Kelly, who grew up idolizing Buck. "There is nothing like being in the sports office when Jack Buck is telling stories. I love to listen to him; he is the best storyteller there is."

"The first time I met Jack Buck," said John Amann who worked in the newsroom, "he came in carrying a big box of candy. He went around and shared it with everyone. Someone probably gave it to him."

"Jack Buck is just a class act," said Stuart Esrock, who worked in the newsroom in the early 1980s. "One time I was on a date. This was in 1983 just after we'd won the World Series in 1982. We were going to the Esquire Theater and had stopped at Jack's or Better restaurant to eat. It was my second time out with this young woman. Jack Buck walked in. My date says, 'Look, it's Jack Buck!' I said, 'I know him.' She goes, 'Do you really? Do you work with him?' I thought I was really impressing my date at this point. I said, 'I work with him on the *To Your Health* features I write for him.'

"At this point he sees me and calls out, 'Hi Stuart.' I say, 'Hi Jack.' He comes over and just starts chatting. 'What are you doing? Going to a movie? Aren't you going to introduce me?' And I introduced my date to Jack Buck and now I'm like a god to her. A few minutes after he left, the waiter shows up with some drinks; I said, 'I'm sorry, we didn't order these,' and he said, 'Mr. Buck sent them over.' Then he sent some appetizers over. He is just so classy. Here I was just a little peon and he treated me like an equal."

A group of Boy Scouts taking a tour of KMOX one day got to meet Buck when Hyland asked him to lead the tour group.

"When we got back to his office, I turned to his fabulous collection of Steubenware and told the Scouts, 'Now each of you can select a piece of glassware as a souvenir.' Hyland came flying out of his chair, 'No, no,' he was saying. He didn't want to laugh when he was at work."

The rich and famous, as well as the anonymous radio listener, all have positive things to say about Buck.

"You can't say enough about Jack Buck," said Gene McNary. "I was

the chairman of the Athletic Committee for the Missouri Athletic Club when we started the Sports Personality of the Year award. I remember Jack, Lou Brock, and I were on the cover of their publication, the *Cherry Diamond,* that year."

"The MAC holds Jack in high regard (they even have a restaurant named after him, The Jack Buck Grille). Jack is the best emcee with his repertoire of jokes, and he can make things so funny just impromptu. He has always had a quick wit. When I came back from Washington, DC, after working as the head of Immigration, I went to KMOX to do an interview. I saw Jack and he said, 'Hi, welcome back. Did you like the job?' I said, 'Yes, I did,' and he said, 'Well, you let all those Mexicans come in!' He was just kidding me. That's just how he is, always witty. Jack Buck has meant a lot to St. Louis over the years."

"Jack Buck is one of the best read people I have ever seen," said Richard Buthod of Unique Books, a company which distributes books to libraries all over the United States. "He has read so much and it showed in his autobiography. That book taught me about his interest in subjects that were non-sports figures."

Buck's charity work has also been an important aspect of his career. "Jack was always a big supporter and friend of the Variety Club," said Therese Shelton, the executive director of the Variety Club Telethon until 1993. "He personally gave us large contributions. I invited him to be on the telethon one time. We called the station and were told 'Bob Hyland doesn't like television. No one from KMOX can be on TV.' So we figured that was that. Sunday afternoon we looked up and there was Jack Buck! He emceed and introduced the stars. I said, 'What is Bob Hyland going to think of this?' And he said, 'Bob Hyland never watches television. If he says anything, I'll just say what were you doing watching television?'"

Buck's charity did not stop with the non-profit events. He was always known for helping people and KFNS president Greg Maracek knows firsthand how generous he can be. Maracek owned SNI Sports Network, which owned the rights to the University of Missouri sports broadcasts from until 1982.

"When I was just starting out, I went to Jack with an idea," said Maracek. "It was for the *Base Burglar Show* with Lou Brock. We coined the phrase 'base burglar' with that show. I told him the idea and he took me in to see Robert Hyland. He said, 'This young guy wants to get started in business and I'm gonna help him. I'll do the voice on this show and Lou Brock will be featured. I got to sell four spots [commercials] for every show. Mr. Hyland ended up giving me the network list and said, 'Call all these stations, maybe they'll buy it.'

"It was so successful we did a show with Jim Bakken called *The Point After* that Costas did. Bakken was leading the NFL in scoring. We broadcast the shows on KMOX and then made tapes and mailed them to the network radio stations. The Lou Brock show was what started it. Buck just did it to be nice, to help me. Lou got a little recognition out of it. Jack introduced me to Hyland and I ended up knowing him very well and having to talk to him very often for the next four years."

"One of the best things about working at KMOX was being able even to be in the same building with Jack Buck," said Joe Sonderman, who, among other duties, did the weather. "I grew up in St. Louis and am still thrilled every time I go into the press box at Busch or the KMOX booth. I was only nine years old when Bob Gibson threw his no-hitter in Pittsburgh, but I can still remember every word as Jack set the scene perfectly. 'And Gibson is one strike away from the no-hitter. He takes off his cap, he mops his brow…he looks in and gets the sign and it's a STRIKE THREE CALLED! A no-hitter for Gibson…Simmons roars to the mound.'"

"Jack Buck and I have a great relationship," said Casey Van Allen of KMOX. "When he comes in to the station he comes to my studio. He's Mr. Friendly. He's KMOX's daddy. He's everybody's father in the radio station."

Shortly after Jack Carney died, KMOX began selling Jack Buck as a spokesman for commercials. He had done a lot of the commercials with the Cardinals, but Carney had done the majority of commercials. Casey Van Allen produced all of the commercials and he has worked with Buck for many years.

"Jack Buck records everything with me," he said. "Other than Jack Buck, I've been on the air the longest at KMOX so we go way back. Jack would come into the studio after being on the road for the

ballgames and we would record a lot of commercials at once. He'd look at the stack of about 60 commercials he had to read and say, 'Well, you got a little time?'

"We'd go through and read all 60 commercials and it got to be a real thrill. He would never miss a word and all 60 commercials would time out exactly 60 seconds each. He could read and look at the clock. He was from the old school of radio where you look at the clock and when it hits 50 seconds, his eyes will jump to the end of the copy and he'll wrap it up exactly. It's a real talent he has, he's good at it."

Buck very rarely made mistakes or required two takes to record a commercial, but Van Allen remembers one slip up.

"We were doing a spot for Eucalypta-Mint. It was that rub-on stuff for your joints," said Van Allen. "They'd asked for Jack to do the commercials. For the first and only time, Jack could not say 'Eucalypta-Mint.' They had it four times in the commercial! He tried it a few times, then I finally had him say 'Eucalypta-Mint' one time and I spliced it in. That was in the days of tape and I had to copy it several times and then cut and splice the tape, that was before digitals. That was the only time I ever saw him miss a beat, and it worked out just fine the way we did it."

Van Allen remembers another story involving Buck, this one demonstrating Buck's kindness.

"One of my interns was a student at Lindenwood College on the baseball team; he was All-Conference in the state of Missouri as a pitcher," said Van Allen. "Jack started talking to him one day. He will talk to anyone and draw things out of you. He started talking about baseball and then he went to his drawer and got out a baseball and said, 'Let's see how you can pitch.' They went out on the roof and he played catch with the kid. Jack Buck playing catch with an intern. Then he said, 'When you get done here, I want you to come over to Busch Stadium and I'll introduce you to the pitching coach.' The kid was so excited he almost started crying."

As it turned out, Dennis Magraine, the ex-intern did not pitch for the Cardinals, but he did become a sports reporter at a station in Nashville, Tennessee.

"I wouldn't be surprised if it was from being inspired by Jack Buck," said Van Allen. "I've never met anyone like Jack. He refuses to look at the negative of a situation. If you say something negative to him, he

will not respond. You could never bad-mouth a person to him. He would never get into that. He is a very positive person. He can come in and sit down with you and it's such an uplifting spirit that came in."

One time after a trip to Europe, Buck went in to Van Allen with a poem he had written.

"I've just got back from Europe," Buck told Van Allen. "We walked down near the cemetery at Normandy and I wrote a poem. Do you want to hear it?"

"I said, 'It's great, let's go record it.' So he recorded this heart-wrenching poem about D-day, about Normandy. We put music behind it and the station plays it every year on D-Day."

In the spring of 2000, Stan Musial had a total knee replacement and was laid up for several weeks.

"Jack Buck was so sweet to Stan," said Musial's wife, Lil. "While he was recuperating from his operation, Jack would come by every day and bring him ice cream or he'd bring him pizza from his restaurant, J. Buck's. He'd walk in and say, 'Well, we're gonna play gin rummy today!' He brought magazines for him to read. He loves Stan and Stan loves him. You know everyone tells you how wonderful the operation is, but they don't tell you how painful it is. It just took him so long to recover, but Jack was there for him."

"Jack's got a big heart," said Stan Musial. "He never says no to anything. He's involved in so many charities around town. He is quite a guy."

JOE BUCK

Carole Buck remembers the day that she received a cassette tape in the mail of a home run call from her son, Joe Buck, who was broadcasting minor league games in Louisville, Kentucky.

She took the tape down to KMOX and played it for Robert Hyland.

"There's the gift," Hyland told Carole Buck.

"What he heard was that Joe had the gift which Jack has," Carole Buck said. "He had the gift of being a great broadcaster."

There is no doubt in Joe Buck's mind that being Jack Buck's son helped launch his career in broadcasting, but he also knows he has had to earn his advancements to the network level on his own.

He has learned many of the do's and don'ts from his dad, but he also has seen first-hand the skills necessary to be considered one of the best broadcasters in the country before he was 30 years old.

"He is the best young sportscaster I've heard in 20 years," said Bob Costas.

Joe was always hanging around the broadcast booth with his dad when he was growing up, and got his actual start calling the games on his 18th birthday, a gift from his dad.

The Cardinals were playing the Mets at Shea Stadium in New York, and in the middle of the game, Jack Buck said, "And here to bring you the play-by-play of the seventh inning is Joe Buck." He and partner Mike Shannon then got up and left the booth, leaving Joe Buck no choice but to go on the air.

"I would never have done it if I had any question that Joe would not have been able to do it," Jack Buck said. "But I knew he could do it. He had no choice. Mike and I left. He was happy it turned out to be a one-two-three inning."

"I was scared to death," said Buck. "I had been doing the game into a tape recorder. Luckily, I got through it and there were no ejections or brawls. God was with me even if my dad wasn't."

Joe decided at an early age that he wanted to follow his father into the broadcast booth. In addition to hanging out at the ballpark as much as possible growing up, Joe got his start doing the sports on the college station at Missouri-St. Louis when he was still in high school.

"He would get himself up every morning and go out to UMSL and read the sports on the station," Jack Buck said. "He really worked at it."

"Joe Buck is great," said Joe Sonderman who worked with him at KMOX. "We were spoiled growing up because we heard the best announcers in the country and we still do. You really notice it when you go to another market. No one can touch Jack, Joe, and Mike.

"I had an autographed ball from the 1987 World Series. I left it somewhere and it was stolen. When Joe Buck was doing sports on the FM, I told him. He went into the clubhouse and got a ball for me signed by Whitey [Herzog], Ozzie [Smith], and the rest. I will never forget that."

When Buck was a youngster, he would come to the Fourth of July rooftop parties at the station. In the first few years, Hyland would invite selected employees, usually just the big name on-air talent. They could bring their families and enjoy a picnic while watching the fireworks from the party. It was a great view; the best in St. Louis. At one of the parties, a young Joe Buck left the party and wandered into the sports office where he chatted with an intern, one of the few people working in the station on the holiday.

"Why don't you come out to the party?" Buck asked.

"I have to work," said the intern.

"You could just go and get some food." Buck said.

"Well, I don't think they would like that," the intern said. "I am not invited, but thanks anyway."

With that, Joe Buck went outside and filled up a plate of food and brought it inside along with his own food and sat in the sports office eating barbecue with the interns.

Joe Buck continues in his concern for others. He has spoken at many schools, including being the host of *Jeopardy* at Sperreng Middle School in the Lindbergh School District in 2000 and appears at many charitable events throughout the year.

JOEL BUCHSBAUM

Joel Buchsbaum had the distinction of never having had his name pronounced correctly on KMOX. The first person who had the football expert on called him Joel "Bush-bomb" and from then on Joel "Bux-bomb" became Joel "Bush-bomb" to the KMOX listening audience.

"I always knew if I turned on KMOX on Sunday nights I would hear Joel Buchsbaum," said KSDK television's Frank Cusumano. "I always listened."

"The thing about Joel Buchsbaum was everybody wanted to meet him," said Bob Costas. "They wanted to know what sort of an individual was behind the manic 'know everything about everybody' with the stacks of books from floor to ceiling, and the squeaky voice people liked to imitate. I was the same way. I wanted to meet him, so when I moved to New York, I called him several times and he kept putting me off. 'I'd love to but I have so much work to do. I'm up to my eyeballs in

work.' I've had the same amount of audiences with Joel Buchsbaum as I have had with the Pope, and that's none."

One time Joe Buck was hosting a *Sports Open Line.*

"Joel Buchsbaum was on the show and I was listening," said Costas. "I wanted to tell Joe something so I called him on the private line during a commercial. While I was talking to him, I started joking around and using a Joel Buchsbaum voice. I was saying things like, 'You're on with the sup-ah wide receiv-ah with good hands and speed. He can't be overlooked, could go high in the draft.' Joe called me back and told me the lines were crossed and Joel had heard the whole thing! Then I had to call him back and apologize. He actually could not have been nicer. He said, 'Don't worry about it, Bob!' Joel Buchsbaum has an amazing knowledge of the most obscure information imaginable. I don't know anyone who knows as much about any one topic as he does."

JACK BUECHNER

Jack Buechner, the former congressman from Missouri's Second District, had a weekly show on KMOX discussing politics when he was a member of the state legislature.

"Harriett Woods and I did a program from Jefferson City for four years after the end of each week's session," said Buechner, now a corporate lawyer and international lobbyist in Washington, DC. "From 1974-79 we did a program on Thursdays after the legislative session from January through May. It was in the afternoon with Anne Keefe as the host."

"Jack Buechner and Harriet Woods were great together," said Anne Keefe. "The show was when they were in the state legislature. You got to hear two points of view, but they had a good chemistry. It was like 'I can tease you without hurting you.' They were very candid about what was going on."

Said Buechner, "We also did a few shows with Jim White at night. Those night time shows were a hoot since it was not your regular 'newshound' listeners. One night a caller started in about aliens and Jim White started pointing outside. We couldn't figure out what he was doing until we saw the full moon. All the weirdos come out with the full moon. The programs lasted an hour. We each gave a wrap-up of our respective chambers and then took questions.

"Some of the other members were so jealous and they would have people call the station and argue that we were 'too opinionated, too liberal, too suburban…' you name it. The hope was that they'd can us (we did it for free) and then they'd get a shot. Ultimately, Harriett ran for either senator or lieutenant governor and they made her quit— 'equal time' and they never could find another senator they would let on the air for an hour."

BOB BURNES

Bob Burnes was well known in St. Louis as the sports editor of the *Globe-Democrat* and for his column, The Benchwarmer, when he added sportscasting at KMOX to his duties.

"Bob Burnes did a nightly 15-minute *Sports Commentary* sponsored by Texaco," remembered Irv Litvag, who worked at KMOX at the time. "That's how he got started in radio. He would come in every afternoon to the newsroom about 4:30 or 5 to write his show."

"He worked there for 42 years," said Adelle, Burnes' widow. "Bob Hyland's father was Dr. Hyland, the team doctor for the St. Louis Cardinals, and Bob [Burnes] knew him because he covered the Cardinals for the *Globe*. He [Bob Hyland] was so pleased when he called Bob to ask him if he wanted to host a show and he said yes."

Doing the nightly sports show led to Burnes hosting the early days of *Sports Open Line* when KMOX changed its programming to talk radio in 1960.

"I thought Mr. Hyland was terrific," said Adelle Burnes. "I know some people did not like him or were scared of him, but I thought he was just terrific. I think people just did not know him because he did not particularly socialize with the employees. He was usually in the office."

Burnes had covered both the St. Louis Browns and the Cardinals at different times and had traveled with the team.

"He loved baseball, but he did cover other sports," said Adelle. "He broadcast the Missouri University football games for about three years, during the Al Onofrio days. For many years, Bob was on the radio five

nights a week and on Saturday and Sunday mornings. He would go straight from the *Globe* so he could be on at 6:15 and just grab something out of the vending machine for dinner. After that he would go back to the office or to the baseball game."

One of the funny stories regarding Burnes involved a near-fire in the studio. He was smoking his ever-present cigar one day. In those days you could smoke in the office, even cigars. Burnes was reading the paper, and smoking a cigar. A caller on the phone was asking him a question, and, as he was prone to do sometimes, he shut his eyes for better concentration to hear the caller, and the cigar touched the newspaper. Soon the paper was on fire. Once he saw he had a flaming paper in his hand, Bill Wilkerson, who was on the air with Burnes, tried to put out the fire without knowing what had happened.

"I had forgotten that story," said Adelle Burnes, "But once you mention it, I remember it. That was funny. They went right on and no one knew there was a fire in the studio."

Besides doing the football on the air, Burnes covered Blues hockey and Saint Louis University (his alma mater). He was interested in all sports and kept current even into his later years. In his later years at KMOX he broadcast only one day a week, Sundays, and during the budget cuts under Rod Zimmerman, Burnes was one of the many who got their pink slips.

"Bob Burnes was like a father figure," said Emmett McAuliffe, talk-show host on KMOX. "There was a certain dignity about him. He didn't quibble. Even though he was old, he was one of those stable forces in your life that you think will always be there. His death really affected me. I had called in to the radio station as a kid. I called his show."

"I remember picking Bob Burnes up on Sunday mornings," said Kip Ingle, former public relations director for the Cardinals. "I lived in Peoria, Illinois, and you could hear KMOX. I would listen to the Sunday morning show to hear the general manager's report and other information about the team. I even heard Jim Toomey [Cardinals public relations director at the time]. I didn't know that one day I would end up working for him!"

All of those who worked with Burnes at KMOX and at the *Globe-Democrat* have their favorite stories about him.

"There would be piles on his desk four feet high, but he could find anything," said Joe Pollack. "It was always a wonder the pile didn't fall on the floor while he was digging in there to pull out whatever it was he was looking for.

"He was always great with the callers, and even if he didn't know the answer, he would make something up."

It was a call to Burnes on *Sports Open Line* one night that prompted Hyland to install a delay switch, so whatever the caller said didn't go out on KMOX live.

"A guy called up and said, 'Is this Bob Burnes?'" recalled Jack Buck. "When he said yes, the guy said a bad word and hung up. We had the delay installed the next day."

JIM BUTLER

Jim Butler was a jack-of-all-trades at KMOX. In the 1950s he had an overnight show from 11:30-5 AM called *All Night Frolic*, earning him the honorary title as the Night Mayor of St. Louis. Parts of the show resembled the infomercials of today. He was the first executive producer of *At Your Service* in 1960. Butler joined with Bob Hardy to do broadcasts from the Gateway Arch at various stages of its construction. They climbed ladders to the platforms at the various stages of completion. He was the original host of *The Trading Station* in 1968. Butler did many commercials and was a studio newscaster. He was even named chief engineer at one time before he retired from his long and distinguished career.

"Jim Butler ended up being chief engineer for a while," said Bill Ott, engineer at KMOX. "He didn't know how to change fuses, but he did all the paper work. He had been doing announcing, but they needed someone to help with the paperwork and he did it."

Part of Butler's success and ability to do such a variety of tasks was due to the fact he listened to what other people had to say and was genuinely interested in a variety of topics.

"Jim Butler was nice to do interviews with," said Jerry Schober, superintendent of the Arch grounds. "He would never try to steer you somewhere in an interview you did not want to go. He was nice to talk to."

Butler knew that the management at KMOX counted on him to be flexible in his duties, but nothing could have prepared him for what happened one day in 1957 when he walked by Mr. Hyland's office at the wrong time.

"I was getting ready to go do a remote for the Hawks," said Clarence Nieder, an engineer who was preparing to go to a small town in Illinois where the St. Louis Hawks basketball team was playing a pre-season game. "I was in the office packing up to get ready. Jim Butler had just gotten off his shift. This was when the studios were at 9th and Sidney, and you had to pass Mr. Hyland's office when you left. It was by the back door. So Jim is leaving and Mr. Hyland was on the phone. He puts the phone down and says, 'Come in here.' It turned out he was talking to Ben Kerner, the owner of the Hawks.

"Kerner was asking him who he had decided on as the color commentator for the Hawks. Since the game was that night, and Hyland hadn't thought about it, he saw Butler walking by and decided he would be doing it. So Jim walked back to me and said, 'Can I ride down there? I've got to do this.' Then he asks me if I know anything about sports. 'Not a thing,' I said.

"When we got to the little town, he went around and bought every newspaper he could find and then went to the high school where the game was going to be played and started asking people about the team. He got one of those yellow legal pads and wrote everything down and he literally read everything he wrote word for word. He ended up being the Hawks' color commentator along with Bud Blattner the entire year."

Butler learned to like sports over the years. From 1961 to 1965 he did the color commentary for the St. Louis football Cardinals and then came back in 1969 to work with Ray Geracy, who did the play-by-play.

Nieder said Butler used that same technique of writing everything down on another assignment.

"He was supposed to do the radio commentary on the Veiled Prophet Parade," said Nieder. "Well, what can you say on radio during a parade, so he did a lot of research and wrote everything down and read it word for word as each float went by. He wrote it all out, he was very professional."

"He had the night shift before John McCormick," said Bob Canepa, former sales manager of KMOX. " I had to take signs advertising him out to record stores all around Missouri and Illinois promoting his program."

Butler left the station in 1989 after 39 years of service.

JOHN BUTLER

John Butler is the current news director, succeeding longtime news director, John Angelides. Butler, who has both a television and radio background, came to St. Louis from Syracuse in 1995.

He was brought to St. Louis by Tom Langmyer, who had worked with Butler at the New York station before moving to KMOX.

"He has done a great job of building a wonderful solid news team," Langmyer said. "He also has worked to develop partnerships with KMOV-TV, the *St. Louis Business-Journal*, the Suburban Journals and create projects with the *St. Louis Post-Dispatch*."

Langmyer wanted to hire a news director who would build the kind of staff that would consistently break stories, not simply react to stories that they were picking up from other sources.

"If there is any change in the way KMOX does the news now compared to years ago, it would be that there are more sound bites," said Bob Hamilton. "It's more current with more use of sound."

"It's just natural that things are going to change over the years," said Larry Conners, KMOV television anchor who occasionally fills in on KMOX. "John Butler is running a different show."

Butler is known as a hard worker and at an employee party he was voted the employee who needed to "lighten up." He seemed pleased with the honor.

The KMOX phone system allows for a person to make one message and forward it on to many numbers. He likes to call and leave voice mails about all the awards that KMOX wins.

"KMOX wins a lot of awards," said Vicki Atlas, who has had a talk show and has done news for KMOX. "They do a lot of documentaries for that purpose."

"John Butler has a similar background to mine," said Don Marsh,

who fills in on KMOX when needed. "He was in television and then went into radio. He's a very nice guy, good to work for."

"He's great to work for," said Brian Kelly, who works in the newsroom. "He gets excited when things are happening. When something's breaking, he gets pumped up. He senses the importance of KMOX and how important it is to the community."

BILL CALDER

Bill Calder had been a disc jockey at KSD, moved to KMOX briefly in 1969, returned to KSD, then left St. Louis to take a job in New York. He returned to KMOX to host *At Your Service* programming in 1974.

"I'll never forget the time he locked himself in the studio," said Jim White. "Mr. Hyland had put out an edict, 'No more coffee in the Studio.' So Bill Calder locked himself in the studio one time when he was on the air to protest. He put chairs up in front of the doors. When Mr. Hyland found out about it, he ran in there. He finally changed his mind, so Bill Calder is responsible for the re-introduction of coffee in the studio."

HELEN CAMPBELL

Helen Campbell was the human resources director for many years, responsible for new employees as well as many other tasks. Though small in stature, she was involved in many operations at the station.

WENDELL CAMPBELL

Wendell Campbell was the general manager from 1945 until 1949—except for one day in 1948. That was a day KMOX participated in a Boy Scout program in which scouts took over and ran the city of St. Louis for a day.

"I was assigned to be the general manager of KMOX," said Doug Sleade, who was 13 at the time. He now lives in Decatur, Illinois. "I got to meet Wendell Campbell and other administrative people and news people. We were shown around the station and I got to meet Rex Davis and talk to him. Wendell Campbell and the others from KMOX gave us great treatment and a great tour. One thing I remember as being the 'general manager' was that one employee asked me for a raise!

"On that tour I also got to see a live country music show they were doing and I got to meet a country western singer, but since it was 52 years ago, I don't remember his name. The thing I remember about him was he had a beautiful Gibson guitar. I was really appreciative of Campbell and everyone there that day because I learned a lot and they were really nice to me. It was very civic-minded of KMOX to give young boys a chance to meet some well-known people and learn how a radio station works."

BOB CANEPA

Bob Canepa was a salesman in the 1950s. He was promoted to sales manager, but he liked being able to have more accounts as a general salesman; so after four years as sales manager, he went back to being a salesman.

"I had been in the grocery business in 1952," said Canepa. "We manufactured salad dressings and distributed other types of groceries. I got tired of making salad dressings and was about to take a job at KXOK when their salesman, John White, went to KMOX. I got a call and John White was in Robert Hyland's office and they asked me to come down."

Hyland had worked with John White when he was at KXOK. After leaving St. Louis and working at WBBM, Hyland came to KMOX and he hired White away from KXOK. When they were looking for a merchandise manager, White thought of Canepa.

"As merchandise manager, I would work with the stores to be sure the promotions that KMOX was doing were in the stores. One of the programs I promoted was the HPL Program. Lee Adams was the host

of the *Housewives Protective League Show.* It was to radio what *Good Housekeeping* was to magazines. It was a show with topics of interest to women, but men listened also."

Canepa once went to 100 record stores in Illinois and Missouri to set up signs that said, "Listen to Jim Butler on KMOX...The Night Mayor of KMOX."

One of the shows Canepa sold was the *Teen O'Clock Time Show* in the 1960s.

"I sold the show to Coca-Cola," said Canepa. "We would have different high schools come down to the Chase on a Saturday morning. We'd give them a free coke and they got to see whatever big name talent was performing at the Chase. It was a big thrill for them. The Stan Daughtery Band would perform.

"KMOX was an interesting station. You would be walking down the hall and not be surprised to see anyone. One time I saw Mr. Hyland talking to Lowell Thomas. Another time I looked outside Mr. Hyland's office and there he was talking to Arthur Godfrey. They got in all the big stars. Milton Berle came to KMOX, so did Ginger Rogers and Joan Crawford. Mr. Hyland and Harold Koplar of the Chase [and Channel 11] cooperated very much. All the big stars who were at the Chase wound up on KMOX."

"One time Bob Canepa tried to get the Chevy dealers to sign on as Cardinal sponsors," remembered Johnny Londoff of Johnny Londoff Chevrolet. "The dealers as a whole weren't too keen on the idea. Mr. Hyland called me a few times. I persuaded the Chevy dealers to do it. Then the Cardinals lost seven or eight games. The Chevy dealers came back and said, 'Why'd we do that?' It wasn't looking too good. Well, that was the year they came from behind and won the pennant! Mr. Hyland ended up calling me and saying, 'See I told you you should do it!'"

Chris Canepa, Bob's son, worked at KMOX for five years. Canepa is now retired.

"I am enjoying the fruits of my labors, I do a lot of dishes, gardening, play golf, and run the grandkids around," he said. "I also watch the stockmarket."

HARRY CARAY

After listening to Cardinal baseball broadcasts for years, Harry Caray was convinced he could do a better job. In 1942, he mailed a letter to KMOX general manager Merle Jones asking for the job. He marked the letter personal and mailed it to Jones' home.

Jones thought enough of Caray's ingenuity that he gave him the audition—and Caray was terrible. He was disappointed, and getting ready to leave the studio, when he remembered Jones had said he would personally listen to the audition. Caray made that an issue, got another audition and did much better.

There were no openings on the Cardinals' broadcasts until 1945, however, when Caray finally landed a job on WTMV, a tiny station from East St. Louis that broadcast the home games. He got the job in much the same way he had pursued Merle Jones of KMOX. He went in to personally see the president of Griesedieck Brothers brewery, which owned the broadcasting rights, and convinced him he could do a better job—despite the fact he had no baseball play-by-play experience.

In those years, any station willing to broadcast the games was allowed to do so, as long as they had a sponsor. There were three broadcasting teams doing the Cardinals games in 1945 and 1946, France Laux, Dizzy Dean, and Caray.

After the 1946 season, however, Cardinals owner Sam Breadon decided to award exclusive rights to his broadcasts, and he picked the Griesedieck team of Caray and Gabby Street despite the fact they were on weaker stations. Breadon thought Caray and Street did the best job of selling the Cardinals of any of the broadcasters. He thought if Caray was the only broadcaster calling the games, fans would have to listen to him and then the audience would grow.

In 1953, Anheuser Busch bought the Cardinals and Caray had to campaign again for his job, convincing owner August Busch, Jr., that he could do just as good a job of selling Budweiser and the Cardinals as he had for Griesedieck Brothers. Busch agreed to give him a chance, and it turned out to be a great move.

After the broadcasts moved to KMOX in 1955—one of Robert

Hyland's first moves as general manager was to acquire the rights from KXOK—Caray's popularity soared.

Bea Higgins worked at an advertising agency and she worked closely with Caray, first at the agency and for years as his personal secretary.

"At the agency I worked with Harry Caray, Stretch Miller, Gabby Street, and then Jack Buck," Higgins said. "When I got married, I wanted to raise my family, so I just worked for Harry, doing his fan mail."

She went to his house every day to go through the mail.

"There were stacks of mail," she said. "Some of the most remarkable mail was what he would get from blind people. One I remember and I wish I'd kept it, it said, 'I can almost see what's happening' when he did the broadcast."

While at the agency, her job involved helping on the broadcast of the away games.

"They did not travel with the teams like they do now," she said. "Harry's office was in the Paul Brown Building. I remember sometimes it was just me, Harry, and the engineer. He would be sitting by the ticker tape machine and it would come out saying, 'ball one, ball two,' etc. and then it would say there was a home run. Harry would be leaning back in his chair saying, 'It might be, it could be, it is! A home run!' I found those broadcasts so interesting."

Higgins had always been a sports fan, and it was lucky because she constantly listened to the games.

"I had to listen to hear what he said," she continued. "I always liked baseball and was one of the Knot Hole gang, so I'm a fan, but I listened because if he said something, I'd think, 'Oh, we're gonna get letters about that.' Harry loved the fans. He went over every letter. We would discuss what he should write. Sometimes I would disagree with him and say, 'you don't want to say that, it would be better if you'd say this...' He might agree or he might not and we'd discuss it some more. He signed every one of his letters.

"I really liked working for Harry; well, I liked working for all those guys," she said. "Harry announced all of my children's births on the radio. It was great working for him. People thought it was great and used to ask me all about him. Shortly before he died I saw him. I had

not seen him since he left town, so it was a great reunion to get together with him."

Even if people never met Caray, they considered him their friend because of all the time they spent listening to him on the radio. He helped make heroes out of the Cardinal players as well, not only to St. Louis listeners but to thousands of people around the Midwest on the Cardinals broadcasting network, which included more than 100 stations in Illinois, Arkansas, Kansas, Oklahoma, Iowa, Kentucky, and other states.

"Harry was on KMOX for a long time," said Stan Musial. "He always sang my praises all those years."

"I loved to listen to Harry Caray and his sidekick, Gabby Street," said listener Doug Sleade, of Decatur, Illinois. "Harry got me to idolize and try to emulate Enos Slaughter, Stan Musial, and players back then."

"Harry was the greatest," said engineer C.J. Nieder. "He did the Missouri University football games and I engineered them. He would get there early to prepare for them. There would be times he was sick, so sick he would have pills sitting in front of him and he would look like death warmed over, but he was so enthusiastic and so pumped up for the games that you would never know he didn't feel good. He was a real showman."

"Some of my fondest memories of KMOX involve Harry Caray and my grandfather," said Elaine Viets. "I remember my grandfather sitting in his recliner on Sunday afternoons with a beer in his hand arguing with Harry Caray. 'Oh Harry, you're full of it!' he'd yell. My grandmother would say, 'If he aggravates ya that much, why do ya listen?' But Sunday afternoons in the recliner with the beer and listening to Harry Caray, it was a ritual. A sacred ritual."

"Harry Caray made the game more interesting than it really was," said Gene McNary, former County Executive and director of the U.S. Immigration and Naturalization Department. "He was a great play-by-play man. He wasn't the community leader that Jack Buck is, but he sure made the games exciting."

"I used to listen to the Cardinal games at night when I was a kid," said McNary, who grew up in Muncie, Indiana. "My dad was a Cardinal fan, so we listened to KMOX."

Harry Caray was present for, and had recorded for a KMOX broadcast, the last words of Cardinal executive Branch Rickey.

"Harry and I were in Columbia to see Branch Rickey be inducted into the Missouri Sports Hall of Fame," said Nieder. "We were not broadcasting it live, but Harry was there and we had it recorded to run it later. As it turned out Branch Rickey was very ill. He was in a hospital in Columbia and, against his doctor's orders, he got out of his hospital bed to come and accept his award."

After they introduced him, Rickey got up to the podium and started to deliver a very motivational speech.

"His theme was 'they paid the price,'" said Nieder. "I was right there next to Branch Rickey with my microphone up to his mouth so we could get the whole thing. He talked about people who paid the price for what they did. He named different athletes. One guy he talked about had a very bad injury on his left side of the thigh. He'd had surgery and was never supposed to play in a game, but as he sat on the bench the team got into a situation where they really needed him to hit. He got a hit and as he rounded third toward home the play was so close that he had to slide and he slid on that side and endured all that pain, and Branch Rickey said, 'He paid the price.'

"Suddenly he says, 'I don't believe I'm going to be able to continue' and he slumps down, and falls onto the floor. All heck breaks loose and people are yelling, 'Is there a doctor in the house?' He went into a coma and lingered a few days, but died soon after. We had that on tape, him telling that inspirational story and then saying, 'I don't believe I'm going to be able to continue,' but we never used it on the radio. It gives you chills to think that Branch Rickey had gotten himself out of his sick bed and he had 'paid the price' to give that inspirational speech, and it was his last."

In a much-publicized accident, Caray was hit by a car as he was crossing Kingshighway and suffered a broken leg. He wound up in Queeny Towers in a full body cast. The hospital had never seen a more flamboyant patient.

If one story that made the rounds at KMOX was true, Caray had his dinners brought in every night by Peanuts Wahlem. Hack Ullrich, the maître d' at the Chase, would come by from the Chase later and bring him more food. He would drink martinis in his hospital bed and read the boxes of mail that would come in to him.

Caray was fired from the Cardinals after the 1969 season, but that only led to him becoming even more nationally known during his years doing the Chicago Cubs broadcasts on WGN-TV.

He never changed the style of broadcasting he developed in St. Louis, as he explained to Curt Smith in *Voices of The Game*.

"My whole philosophy has always been to broadcast the way a fan would broadcast," Caray said. "I'm so tough on my guys because I want them to win so much. I've often thought that if you give the microphone to a fan, he'd sound a lot like me. The disappointment, the hurt, the anger, the bitterness—the love, the ecstasy, they'd all be there."

Even after leaving St. Louis, Caray's many fans remained.

"Harry moved to Palm Springs," said Bob Canepa. "I used to visit him every year when we went there to play golf. On the week he died, I was out there. I talked to him on Wednesday and we were trying to figure when we could get together. It didn't work out for us, and he died on Friday. I had gone to that restaurant where he died just that week."

SKIP CARAY

Skip Caray started as a producer on KMOX in 1969. He went on to do some play-by-play on KMOX and eventually got the Hawks' basketball job when the team moved to Atlanta. Caray produced the Mizzou football games. Skip Caray is now the play-by-play voice of the Atlanta Braves.

Harry Caray and Skip Caray were one of the many father-sons to come out of KMOX. Joe Buck followed his famous father, Jack; John Carney became a talk show host like his father, Jack; Dan Kelly, Jr., and his brother John became announcers after hearing their father, Dan Kelly; and Matt Hyland, son of Robert Hyland, now works as the sports marketing director.

JACK CARNEY

He was nominated for the Radio Hall of Fame in 2000, but if St. Louisians were doing the voting, Jack Carney would have been a landslide winner years ago.

"Jack Carney was as recognizable in St. Louis as anybody on television, maybe more so," said former St. Louis mayor Vince Schoemehl. "He was the definition of excellence on KMOX."

Harry Fender, one of Carney's closest friends, called him "the greatest radio man ever in St. Louis" and few would disagree.

Carney occupied the 9 AM until noon shift on KMOX for 13 years, and when he died of a heart attack at the age of 52 in 1984, it left a tremendous void at the station. He dominated the market in terms of bringing in important guests, in terms of advertisers and revenue and in terms of listeners. Nobody produced more laughs, and nobody enjoyed doing it more than Carney.

No matter who you talk to, if they were listening to St. Louis radio during the years Carney graced KMOX, they have a favorite story about him or something they remember from his show.

"The great thing about Jack Carney," said former producer Frank Pawloski, "was that he was not the one who always had to get the laugh. He would set others up on his show to get laughs. As long as people would hear it on his show, they'd say, 'Did you hear that on the Carney show?' He didn't have to be the one who always got the laughs."

"Jack always liked to have fun," said Fred Zielonko, who worked for Carney, putting together his comedy shows and the celebrity specials. When he began working for him, Carney was living on the 17th floor of the Chase in a two-story apartment overlooking Forest Park. After Carney was married, he moved into a home on Lindell, and Zielonko used the carriage house in the back as a studio. For about six months, Zielonko lived in the other side of the studio.

"One morning Jack called me," said Zielonko. "He said, 'You have breakfast yet?' And I said, 'No.' He said, 'Come on down, I'm makin' pancakes.' Jack was an excellent cook. He would put sour cream in the dough of his pancakes and they were great. They would stay with you all day."

So Zielonko walked up to Carney's house and sat in the kitchen eating pancakes while Carney bustled around.

"I asked him, 'Where's Jody?' referring to Carney's wife. He said 'Oh, I don't know,' and went out the door of the kitchen," said Zielonko. "Pretty soon the other door swings open and I look up expecting to see

Jody. In walks Phyllis Diller! She was a house guest and I didn't even know it. She says, 'Hi, I'm Phyllis Diller,' and I'm like, "Hi, I'm Fred Zielonko.' Jack comes back in the kitchen and goes, 'Oh, I see you met Phyllis. She was in town and she was supposed to stay at a hotel, but I said, 'Why don't you just stay with us?' My mouth was hanging open. That was the stuff I encountered all the time with Jack. He loved to have his fun. We had a lot of fun."

Over the years Carney brought the most famous people onto his show. If they were starring at the Muny Opera, they would stop by his show. Actors, authors, politicians, anybody who was anybody came on the *Jack Carney Show.* Bing Crosby, Alan Alda, Richard Simmons were all guests. Diller was on many times. Diller, who was from St. Louis and came back from time to time, was very good friends with Carney.

One time when Diller was on the show, Carney decided to call their good mutual friend, Stan Kann, the organist. Kann, who had played the Fox Theater in St. Louis, was living in California at the time. The conversation went something like this:

Jack Carney: We have Phyllis Diller here in the studio; hey, Phyllis, let's call our friend Stan Kann.

(As he is fumbling for Kann's phone number, you hear something in the background.)

JC: What are you doing?

PD: I'm fixing my hair!

(They get him on the line)

Stan Kann: Hello?

JC (in a southern accent): Mr. Kann, you don't know me, but I'm here with my wife, Sheryl Lee, and we got your number off the Hollywood Map of Stars.

SK: I'm on the map of Hollywood Stars?

PD: Hello, Mr. Kann, this is Sheryl Lee, would it be all right if we came over to your house?

SK: Well, uh…

JC: We just want to stop by for a few minutes and meet you.

PD: I just want to kiss you on the lips! Can we come?

SK: I'm sorry, I can't. I have a commercial meeting here in a few minutes.

JC: Oh we just want to come over for a few minutes, get down doggie.

PD: We brought our dog, do you hear him? Ruff! Ruff!

JC: Do you like parrots?

SK: I think this is somebody I know.

PD: I heard you have a parrot and you gave it to that dumb blonde Phyllis Diller!

SK: Oh my gosh! Phyllis!

PD: I'm here with Jack Carney.

SK: Phyllis Diller's in St. Louis with Jack Carney! What a wonderful surprise! I almost fell for this!

After they chatted for a few minutes, they let Kann go because he had that commercial meeting and then Diller and Carney ad libbed about Kann and mused about his really being on the Hollywood Map of Stars. Diller told this elaborate story about Stan Kann being on the map.

"One night Stan got so drunk he couldn't find his way home, so he asked someone to help him find his house on the map," said Diller. "They thought he was Don Knotts, so they showed him the way to Don Knott's house. The next morning Stan Kann woke up in bed between Don Knotts and his wife!"

Another big star Carney had on his show was magician Doug Hening. Carney knew KMOX colleague Dr. Armand Brodeur was very interested in magic and was very good at it, so he invited Brodeur to sit in during the interview.

"He said, 'Don't you say a word, Brodeur. If you open your mouth, I'm closing it,'" said Brodeur. "He didn't want me to start asking questions, 'How did you do that? How do you do this?' Carney was at the top of the pack as an interviewer and as a broadcaster. He could even make opening mail interesting. On a Tuesday morning he might be opening his mail and just start reading it to himself. He could keep the listeners fascinated just opening his mail!"

"I'll never forget the time he had Mickey Mantle on the show," said Jim Holder. "They had to send down to Fando's [the restaurant/bar downstairs] to get three or four beers for Mickey Mantle. Here it was in the morning and Mantle is sipping some of the Anheuser-Busch products."

One of the special things about Carney's shows were the radio skits. He made Miss Blue a star, and also involved Bob Costas and others at the station.

"Jack wrote those radio plays himself," said Costas. "Phyllis Diller was in town once and wrote one of the scripts. Very often visiting actors would play a part, people in town at the Muny or something. I remember one time Shirley Jones came in and he had written her into one of the plays. It was obvious she had no interest in doing this and was totally above it and totally annoyed by it. Carney passed the script out and though she didn't want to do it, she reluctantly went along. Instead of getting into it, she read it like a phone book with an air of disdain. Unless everyone plays along and understands, it's just a silly melodrama, it doesn't work. We went through with it and Jack realized what was going on, but he tried to be gracious to her because he knew she was going to be on his show for the whole hour. Those Tiki Jack and Rob Roy things were genuinely funny. They still hold up when they play them back more than 20 years later."

Carney had worked in St. Louis before joining KMOX, spinning records as a rock-and-roll disc jockey at WIL. He left St. Louis to go to New York, then moved to San Francisco before he was lured back to St. Louis and KMOX.

"I was instrumental in bringing Jack Carney in," said Bob Canepa who sold his show. "Jack wanted to come back to St. Louis after being in California. Mr. Hyland called me into his office and said, 'I got Carney who wants to come back. You sold against him when he was at WIL, what do you think?' I said, 'If you want to get him, I'll sell him.' He called Jack and said, 'Come on in.' I had 24 accounts on his show."

"I was moonlighting at the Stadium Club at the front desk," said former KMOX salesperson Barb Felt. "Mr. Hyland called me and said, 'Miss Felt! Jack Carney is going to be my guest, make a guest reservation under my name.' I was so excited at the prospect of seeing Jack Carney as he had been a big star to me when he was on WIL. Suddenly this guy bounds in the double doors at the Stadium Club. He had on a short-sleeved shirt, had not shaved, was disheveled and a bit slumped over. I thought he was a bum and I was about to call security to have him thrown out when he smiled at me and said, 'Hi, I'm Jack Carney!'

I said, 'Oh hi, Mr. Carney, we've been expecting you. Come on back with me and I'll help you find a coat to wear.'"

She got him to his table. He came back periodically and joked around with her. Later Carney came up to Felt's desk, 'I've lost my glasses! Can you help me find my glasses? If I don't have those glasses, I can't see to do the show tomorrow, I can't see the copy.' Since he had been kidding around with her, she thought he was kidding about the glasses just to get her to come out and help look for them, so she dismissed him even though he persisted. After he left, a waitress came up to her.

"I just found these glasses," she said. "Do you know who they could belong to?"

"I went, 'Oh my gosh, he was telling the truth! These were Jack Carney's glasses! And I thought, 'Now he's not going to be able to do the show and it was his first day on KMOX.' So I called KMOX and got hold of a security person. I said I had these glasses and I was going to bring them over and I wanted to be sure they got to Jack Carney before he went on the air. I listened the next day and he sounded great, so I supposed he'd gotten the glasses. He was so happy he called and asked me to dinner to show his appreciation."

Carney was the best pitchman KMOX has ever had. Advertisers lined up for the opportunity to have Carney talk about their restaurant or food or clothing item. If Carney told his listeners the food at a restaurant was good, there would be a line waiting to get in.

"I think I probably got more free advertising out of Jack Carney than anything else," said Ted Drewes, owner of Ted Drewes. "Bob Costas, who was broken in on Carney's show and went to NBC, became friends with Willard Scott. One time Willard Scott was in St. Louis and being driven around by a limo driver who has driven Bob. He said, 'Take me some place Costas likes,' and he took him to Ted Drewes.

"Once Leonard Slatkin was on and he mentioned that he was almost 40 and had never had a Ted Drewes. Tim Dorsey called me and we rushed some custard to KMOX for Slatkin. Jack Carney spoon-fed Leonard Slatkin Ted Drewes and the rest is history. When he left St. Louis, he said one thing he would miss was Ted Drewes."

Drewes knew Carney mentioned his product because he liked it himself.

"Carney was being sponsored by Velvet Freeze," said Drewes, "yet he would still mention Ted Drewes. I didn't want to crowd in on him when he already had an ice cream company as an advertiser. Once Jack Carney said, 'I'll know I'm in Heaven when I have a Ted Drewes Butterscotch Concrete in one hand and a Lemmons Lemon Pie in the other.' Wouldn't it be nice if you could somehow ship a concrete up to Heaven?"

The Carney Show was always sold out and there were always 50 or more advertisers waiting to sign up if a spot opened up. At that time the limit on commercials was 18 minutes an hour, and Carney could have filled many more spots.

"The money he brought in from those live commercials was unbelievable," said Pawloski. "He was always booked up."

According to published reports, advertisers paid $230 per minute for Carney's show and had to commit to three spots a week for 13 weeks, a total of almost $9,000. He brought KMOX approximately $3.1 million a year.

"He was the ultimate broadcaster and ultimate pitchman," said news reporter Kent Martin. "He also was an overgrown kid, but this endeared him to his loyal listeners. He never sounded anything less than totally in control and professional on the air and made everyone who came through his studio at once lively, interesting, and engaging.

"One day I was sitting in the news production booth and into Jack's studio next door walked Lauren Bacall. Great show, great talk, a fabulous guest. I asked Jack later what it was like, how did he feel talking with a legend like her. Jack had interviewed the greatest, but he said when Bacall walked in, he was petrified. He never let it show on the air."

Carney had a lot of interests and his listeners knew all about them. He was fond of the arts and enjoyed going to shows. He also collected classic cars, and liked to ride his horse. Old-time radio was a hobby and interest for him as well as part of his profession. His home was filled from floor to ceiling with books. When people went to visit, as they rang the doorbell they would be treated to one of 50 tunes the doorbell played.

His listeners knew about his wife, Jody, also. They met at a Valentine's party and he took her out only once after that before they saw each other a year later and began dating.

"You don't love and trust people very often in your life the way I feel about my wife," he told *St. Louis Magazine* in April of 1981. She's a rare individual."

Carney also liked to talk about his son, John. John (who is now a talk-show host on KMOX) was in high school at CBC and he played the drums. Carney was divorced from John's mother, who had lived in California. Before John moved to St. Louis, he lived with his mother and stayed with Carney in the summer or for holidays. When asked about his son, he would say he talked about him on the air not to commercialize him, but because he was important to him. The father and son went to Africa for a month in 1971 when John was seven.

Carney was paid $100,000 a year when he came to KMOX, and was earning $300,000 around the time of his death, a very good paycheck for a radio personality in the 1980s.

"I wrote the commercials for the Victorian House, who sponsored Jack's show," said Therese Shelton. "When you write commercials, you have to try to write in the person's voice who will read it. Jack did a lot of ad libbing on his commercials, but I was always proud that most of the time he read my commercials word for word. I had found a way to do them the way he would do them. The thing about Jack was he was loyal. He bought a lot of clothes at the Victorian House. He was great at doing commercials. He could make you so hungry doing a commercial after he ate at the restaurant."

Carney claimed he never had an argument with Robert Hyland because they shared similar tastes, including how dedicated they were to their particular jobs. Though he was extremely funny on his shows, he took each show very seriously. While he was on the air, all calls were directed to his secretaries, first Marie D'Sa, then Joan Kelly, and later Katie Slade. He trusted them to talk to his guests and advertisers so he could go about the business of doing the shows.

Peggy Cohill Drenkhahn started producing the show and then Pawloski took over. Zielonko and Dave Hill served as his home producers. He had a vast music library at his home and they would put together old radio shows to be used for the *Saturday Morning Comedy Show* or for specials.

"If something happened in the news," said Pawloski, "like if CBS

news announced a famous singer had died, he would call either Dave Hill or Fred and say something like, 'Could you bring tape 482 down here and pull some stuff on so and so?' Twenty minutes later he'd be doing a radio special about someone who'd died a half an hour ago. He had an incredible library. He would do the same thing if it was someone's birthday, like Frank Sinatra's."

The *Saturday Morning Comedy Show* was one of his favorites, because of his love for old-time radio. Traffic director Shirley (Jacoby) Bates would have the log ready for Saturday morning with the commercials he was to use.

"Jack always taped the *Comedy Show* at 1 o'clock on Fridays," said Pawloski. Carney would always take us to lunch after his show, but we had to be right back up there by 1 to get started."

The group went to Fando's Restaurant for lunch, which was downstairs. There was a cafeteria and also a bar.

"Sometimes we would see a lot of Channel 4 people there," said Pawloski. "Jack always liked it when he ran into Julius Hunter. Julius was one of his favorites. Jack always took me, Clarence Nieder [his engineer], and then Colin Jarrette when he started working on the show, Katie Slade [or his other secretaries], Dave Hill, or Fred Zielonko and anyone else who he might choose to invite. If Jack Buck was around, he'd say, 'Hey Jack, why don't you join us for lunch?'"

After lunch they would begin the taping.

"Now as great of a guy as Jack was," said Pawloski, "when we taped these shows he could be demanding. You couldn't fool around. When he was in the studio doing the *Comedy Show* he locked the door because he didn't want anyone disturbing us. I won't say it was intense because it was just so funny, but he did want you to do your job so the show would turn out."

There would be several shows chosen ahead of time and Carney knew what he would be doing for the "live" commercials. He would introduce the shows.

"Now let's go to Fibber McGee and Molly and Fibber McGee is trying to build something."

Carney's quick wit made his shows the success they were. He was one of the most popular radio stars the city has ever known.

"I'll never forget his bits with the laugh box," said Vince Schoemehl.

"You know what a laugh box is, well he was telling a story with a laugh box. I was driving down Hanley Road in Clayton. Carney started telling this story and started using this laugh box in only the way Carney would do it. I got to laughing so hard I literally had to pull off the road. I was afraid I was going to have an accident. It was just Jack Carney and that laugh box, it was so hilarious. He had a sense of humor unequaled."

Another person who almost had to pull over while driving was Lil Musial, the wife of Stan Musial.

"I used to love to listen to Jack Carney," she said. "I listened to him quite a bit. He was always so funny. I remember one time he was talking to this guy and he was from Pittsburgh. [Musial is from Donora, Pennsylvania.] Jack Carney turned it into a joke, something about, 'I've heard of all kinds of hamburgers, but have you ever heard of a Pittsburgher?' It was just so funny I almost went off the road!"

Carney told jokes often on his show. He would tell new jokes or just take an old standard joke and tell it. One he was fond of telling was about a snail.

The story began when the snail bought a new car. He told the dealer he wanted a big "S" painted on the side. The dealer asked the snail why he wanted an "S" painted on the side, and the snail said, "That way when I'm driving down the highway, people will see me and say, look at that S car go!"

"Listeners to this day," said John Carney, "continue to send me his recipes or articles about him that were in the paper, and they send me tapes of his show. 'This was when Jack had on Max Morath' or 'This was when he had on Arnold Schwartzenegger'. These people had their little portable cassette recorders and set it next to their radio, so not only would I get these Jack Carney tapes but I would hear the garbage disposal going in the background and the dog barking and they're doing the dishes. It was just amazing to me how many people taped his shows."

Carney could even get elected officials in on his act. He would get police chief Eugene Camp to go along with his jokes. Example: Carney reported that a strange looking art object known as a Rarie had been tipped over in Forest Park by a culprit who turned out to be from Australia. Carney called the police chief for comment and Camp said: 'It's

a long way to tip a Rarie!"

"I got to know Carney when he was a rock jock on WIL," said former Congressman Jack Buechner, who is now a Washington attorney. "He was broadcasting from the hotel that is across from the SLU Law school [it's now a dorm]…I would come by after CBC and he'd let me spin records and talk."

Carney did a program one time with Calvin Trillen, the Kansas City-raised food editor for *The New Yorker* magazine. He liked to add Arthur Bryant's Rib place in Kansas City as one of his best restaurants in the USA. The conversation was about favorite food/cuisines. Buechner remembered it this way.

"Trillen and Carney agreed that 'kosher Romanian' was their favorite. [Carney was half-Jewish.] They spoke of the spiciness. When Carney said, 'Kosher Romanian is SOOOOO spicey that it's killed more Jews than Hitler!' I almost drove off the Forest Park Expressway when I heard that!"

On a more serious note regarding authors, Carney was very well-read and enjoyed having authors on his show.

"The *Jack Carney Show* was very important to writers or authors," said Richard Buthod of Unique Books, and formerly of the Booksource. "He was gone before I moved to St. Louis, but the stories are legendary of the books that became best sellers because the author was on Carney's show."

"Oh yes," said Zielonko. "There were New York publicists who knew that if the book got on Jack's show, it would sell. He loved to read. If he talked about a book on the air, it would sell a ton. He had this incredible intellectual curiosity that lasted for about 15 minutes at a time, that was why he was such a great radio host. He would get real interested in something, that was why he was such a great interviewer. If he read a book and talked about it, thousands of copies would be sold."

One time Carney had William Least Heat Moon, the author of *Blue Highways*, on his show. Carney loved the book.

"They got to be friends," said Zielonko. "Jack took him to lunch one day and I was with them. We walked by a bookstore and Moon saw his book in the window. He said 'I'm always happy to see my book in the window, let's go in.' So he went in and introduced himself and

offered to sign the books. Walking back, Jack said, 'That was really nice of you to do that.' William Least Heat Moon said, 'Oh, I like to do that, because once you sign the books, they can't return them!'"

Nearly every KMOX listener can come up with a Carney story or remember something involving a Carney show. Mary Stark, a KMOX listener since she was a child in the 1930s, remembered one.

"I saw Bob Costas at a charity event," she said, "and I went up to him and talked to him about it. I asked him 'do you still keep your socks in a ball?' Jack Carney used to always say 'here comes little Bobby Costas' and I always pictured this little kid riding up on his bicycle. One day he and Bob Costas were talking about socks. They would talk about anything.

"Bob Costas said he keeps his socks rolled up in little balls like I do. Jack Carney was really making fun of him for it. When I asked him about it at the fundraiser, he said, 'Yes, I do, of course it makes them stretched out but it keeps the drawers nice and organized.

"Another thing I remember about the Carney show was when my son was on it. Jack Carney used to have people call up and do things on the air. My son called up and played the kazoo through a washing machine hose with a funnel on the end. That was the kind of things Jack Carney would do."

The segment was called "Stairway to Stardom." Clarence Nieder would play a musical fanfare and then Carney would open the phone lines to anyone with a strange talent. On one show, a caller played "Sewanee River" on his head using his knuckles.

Carney had the knack of putting others in the spotlight. He took Miriam Blue, a cleaning lady at KMOX, and turned her into a household name.

"Miss Blue really was a cleaning lady," said Pawloski. "If Jack was having a bad day, he would call her in and she would always cheer him up and say, 'Well Jackie, ALL'S WELL'. He started putting her on the air and the people really liked her."

"Carney had such wonderful versatility," said John McGuire of the *Post-Dispatch* who wrote several articles about him. "I remember listening to him when a guest had cancelled and he could just pick up and go on. His ad lib was incredible."

Since all of Carney's listeners felt like they knew him personally, it was fitting that he asked them to be in his parade. He decided to have a parade called "The Jack Carney I've Always Wanted To Be In A Parade But Nobody's Asked Me Parade." He threw the idea out on the airwaves and waited to see what would happen. The people from the promotions department got in gear and helped out as well as other employees and interns. The day of the parade in Forest Park Carney may have even surprised himself with its success.

"The way the parades got started," said Colin Jarrette, Carney's engineer at the time, "was Frank Pawloski and I were sitting with Jack one day and Jack mentioned how he had not been asked to be in some of the parades in St. Louis. We would always come up with crazy ideas when we were sitting around talking. Frank said 'why doesn't Jack just put on a parade?' I thought it was a good idea. We started talking about it and he put it out on the air and everyone was so excited. He had certain friends that were well connnected and that's how it happened."

All did not go as smoothly for Jarrette and Carney regarding that first parade, however.

"Jack said he wanted to get a lot of publicity for the parade so he would get some elephants," said Jarrette. "If you have elephants you need the people walking behind with the shovels. He wanted me to carry a shovel and I said 'no way'. So the day came that a photographer was to come and take some publicity pictures with these new shovels Jack had bought, I said, 'I'm not going to do it. It's the first parade I've ever been in and I'm not going to do it.' He kept insisting and I said, 'It's beneath my dignity.' Jack said, 'If you don't do it, you're out of the parade.' I said, 'Fine, I'm out of the parade.' When the fellow came up to take the pictures and I would not do it, Jack said, 'You're out of the parade.'

"He came back a little later and said, 'I'll tell you what, you're back in the parade if you will ride a motor bike. You can be a marshal.' So we were back in business. I rode throughout the parade, passing out candy to kids, smiling, waving, and doing public relations. Zielonko was another marshal. We had three parades and I was in all three of them."

"Colin was always very dignified," said former producer Rene Sevier. "He was very conscious of 'this is my space, this is my deal.' He was

very polite."

"I'll never forget those parades," said Mary Stark. "I remember the 'drill team.' It was a bunch of people dressed in uniforms acting very serious and carrying Black and Decker drills! Anybody could be in the parades. They could just pull their kids in a wagon if they wanted to."

"They started out with six or eight floats and Jack's friends with a couple of horses," said Jarrette. "By the third parade we had them lined up for a mile at the beginning of the parade."

"Jack would always invite us over to his house before the parade," said Therese Shelton. "He lived in this wonderful old house across from Forest Park. He had a large book collection in his library. He would invite us over before the parade, then he would have a big picnic afterwards. Jack would lead the parade each year. One year he rode a horse, one year he was in a carriage. He could get a bigger turnout than the president. If Jack promoted something on his show, you would get results. We'd have people waiting in line if he promoted something."

"When we moved here in 1982," said Frank Viverito, president of the St. Louis Sports Commission, "more than anything else or anybody else, it was Jack Carney who introduced St. Louis to me. Especially in those first few months. I listened religiously and enjoyed every minute of it."

Jerry Schober, who was the superintendent of the Arch grounds, worked in the Old Courthouse just a block from KMOX. One day just as Schober was walking outside, he was surprised to look up and see an airplane flying between the legs of the Arch. That is against the law and is something Schober and his associates always feared because of the harm that could cause to the pilot and also to those visitors to the Arch grounds underneath. At the same time he'd seen it, Carney had seen it from his studio at KMOX.

"The next day I got so many calls in the office," said Schober. "People were saying, 'He shouldn't have said that!' 'What was he doing saying that on the air?' I didn't know what was going on, so I asked someone and evidently Jack Carney had gone on the air hoping the guy who had flown between the legs of the Arch was listening. He asked him to call the Carney show and said, 'We won't say your name on the air, we just want to talk to you.' He didn't mean any harm, but if people started

doing this to get on the radio, it could be very dangerous.

"I called Bob Hyland on his private number. He said, 'You want to go on the air with Jack?' I said, 'No, I don't want to have a problem with Jack. I just wanted to let you know how dangerous it could be.' The next thing I know Jack comes on the line and we're live, 'Hey, we've got Jerry Schober on the line,' he said. I said, 'We've got the guy's number,' so no one would be tempted to try it. We didn't have his number yet, but I didn't want others trying it. Jack Carney was just so smooth, he wasn't upset. He said, 'Well, I flew through the legs of the Arch once myself, and that was just on two martinis!' and that was how we ended it."

Charlie Hoessle, the St. Louis Zoo director, became a household name because of Carney.

"I would bring animals every time I went down there," said Hoessle. "Jack really didn't like snakes, but he never said I couldn't bring them so sometimes I brought snakes on his show. Even though it was radio and you couldn't see the animals, Jack would talk about the animals and ask questions about them so bringing them added a lot to the program."

Carney announced the Zoo's Parent Program on his show.

"We talked about how you could adopt an animal and pay the food bill," said Hoessle, "leaving the other money available for research and other things."

For a while there was a kiosk when you entered the Zoo at the south end. Visitors could push a button and hear Carney welcome them to the zoo and direct them to points of interest.

"Jack Carney had a great deal of information in his head," said Hoessle. "He read a lot and could talk about anything. When we first started doing this, he didn't know as much about animals or conservation, but he read and learned a lot and after a while he actually became an advocate for Conservation and Preservation of endangered species."

Hoessle and his wife became good friends with Jack and his wife, Jody.

"They invited us over for one Thanksgiving," he said. "He also invited his engineer, Colin Jarette, that year, and Colin's wife. There were about 10 of us around the table, and we all didn't know each other, but became friends by the end of the night."

"He would invite anyone from the station who could not go home

to come over for Thanksgiving," said Zielonko. "One time he had these Russian immigrants painting the outside of his house. He said, 'Well I guess you'll be taking off for Thanksgiving,' and they didn't know what Thanksgiving was. He invited them over for Thanksgiving. Jack would cook five or six turkeys."

At the time he was on the Carney show, Hoessle was a general curator. One day Carney overheard Hyland say Hoessle had a good chance of becoming the next director.

"He came to me and said, 'If it happens would you come on the show and announce it, I don't want to read about it in the paper.' He wanted to break the story and we did. When I got the job, I came on his show and he announced it," Hoessle said.

"I got my start on the *Jack Carney Show*," said Harry Hamm, KMOX entertainment editor. "They told me I'd be on with Jack, only trouble was, they didn't tell Jack he had a movie critic. When I went in there, he didn't really like it. He asked me if I could put it on tape. I said, 'With all due respect, Mr. Carney, I've been trying for five years to get on this station, I don't want to tape it.' After a while, he started to like having me on and he called me his 'resident reviewer'. This was in the heyday of his show. Being on his show really helped me a lot."

Newsman Ron Barber became close friends with Carney both on and off the air.

"I first met him shortly after arriving at KMOX," said Barber. "Mr. Hyland decided to split Jack's shift and have him do his morning show and then come back in the afternoon to shore up the ratings at that time. I had listened to him and thought he was a genius before I met him. When we met, I was going in the door to the studio and he was rounding the corner with a mouth full of pencils and papers. We literally 'ran into each other', as he stuck out his hand to shake mine, pens and papers went flying. I was really excited to work with him. He was a character, and, for lack of a better phrase, I just fell in love with him on first sight."

Carney and Barber would pull stunts on each other while on the air. The listeners were aware of some of them, but often they were not.

"Jack loved his time on the air, and when I would be reading the local news and it went a little long, he would come in and tickle me or

gauge me as I read the news to get me to hurry up," said Barber. "One time I was wearing this horrible old tie, which was as wide as my desk. I was reading the weather and he just walked in the studio with a pair of scissors and cut the tie off! I broke up on the air. Whenever I was reading the news and Jack was pulling a stunt on me, I would try to maintain a level of decorum, but it was hard.

"One time I was reading the news from the big studio down the hall and I saw him come in with fire in his eyes. He was about to enter the door and I knew he'd do something so I sped up. 'Partly cloudy, 61, back to Jack,' I said. He realized I'd thrown it back to him and he was not in his studio. He had to run all the way back and he was completely breathless. He didn't bother me after that."

Barber pulled his share of stunts on Carney, too.

"Once when Jack was reading a commercial," said Barber, "I picked up a pitcher of water and gently poured water on his head. I think it was the first time anyone had pulled a stunt on him that broke him up on the air."

"Jack did all sorts of things to Ron Barber," said Zielonko. "He would try to break him up by setting his copy on fire or shoot him with a squirt gun.

"Jack tried to get Costas. He thought Costas was way too serious. I remember one day when Barber was doing the news and Costas was doing the sports, we almost got burned. Jack had this great idea he was going to get Costas so he had me get all these sound effects. I had one ready and when Costas came breezing in two seconds before he was to go on the air, I played this sound effect. It sounded like a guy falling out of an airplane and yelling 'Ahhhhhhhhh!' as he fell.

"We did the sound effect and then Costas read the lead story which had just broke. [Yankees player] Thurman Munson had been killed in a plane crash. It was terrible! We couldn't believe it! We had no way of knowing what Costas was going to say. Of course, the bat phone rang and it was Mr. Hyland. I was scared to answer it because I'd done the sound effect, but he knew who was behind it. 'Tell him to come into my office now!'" Well they were on the air, but Jack had to get up and go in there!"

Carney was always pulling pranks on people.

"One time Joe Sullivan the GM of the football team was in the hospital," said Zielonko. "He had had a heart attack and was in the intensive care unit. Jack showed up at the hospital in a priest collar. 'Father So and So here to see Brother Sullivan.' They let him in and he leans over Joe in the bed, who then opens his eyes. Sullivan said when he looked up, he knew he hadn't made it through the surgery and he knew he wasn't in Heaven!"

Besides being a prankster, Carney also had a big heart.

"One day Jack pulled up in front of the station in his Jeep Renegade," said Zielonko. "He was walking in and saw a young couple. They asked him directions and then they started chatting. Jack found out they were visiting St. Louis and he said, 'Well how are you getting around?' They said, 'Walking,' and he said, 'Here, take my car.' He actually gave the people the keys to his car. He said, 'Now I get off at noon, so just have it back here by noon.'"

"Jack was a good friend of the Baums' who owned the Victorian House," said Therese Shelton. "The night he died, he was to have dinner with A.W. [Baum]. I had seen him the day before and looking back on it, I remembered he could barely make it up the stairs."

"By then the studio had been moved to the third floor of his house," said Zielonko. "That day he came up to the studio when he got home. He did that a lot and asked me what I was working on. I turned to him and said 'Jack, you look tired.' He said, 'I feel tired.' Then when he was leaving, he winked at me. Jack never winked at me. He walked downstairs and that was the last time I saw him."

Carney was taking a scuba diving course when he suffered a massive heart attack and died.

"He and his wife, Jody, were planning to take a trip," said Pawloski. "They were getting ready to go on a Thanksgiving holiday to the Cayman Islands and they were taking the lessons at Whispering Hills to get ready for the trip."

Later an autopsy revealed that Carney suffered from heart disease and arteriosclerosis (hardening of the arteries). He had gotten out of the pool, complained of dizziness, and collapsed. Creve Coeur Fire Department paramedics tried to revive him, but he died when he got to St. John's Hospital.

"He had actually taken a physical and an EKG before taking the scuba diving class," said Zielonko. "They required it. He didn't take a stress test, though."

Zielonko was having dinner with Harry Fender, Carney's good friend who had become a friend of Zielonko's, when they received the news of Carney's death.

"I was at Harry's house," said Zielonko. "My brother called there and said, 'Jody just called, call her.' I called her and she told me and I told Harry. He was just devastated. I went home and got the call from Robert Hyland."

The word came into KMOX from his physician to reporter Jim Bafaro. It was a daunting experience for a young reporter to have to tell the tragic news to his boss, Robert Hyland. At first Hyland slammed the phone down, then he called back and they came up with a plan. They went immediately to a tribute and as word got out people began calling KMOX. Past employees and local dignitaries and celebrities all wanted to comment on the man they all considered a friend.

"I had just come back from a vacation," said Barber. "I'd had dinner with a friend and was just coming back to work when Bob Mayhall met me in the hall and told me Jack had died. I was stunned. I made the announcement over the air and it was very difficult. It was one of the toughest things I've ever experienced in my life. I remember choking up and having trouble finishing my report. Jerry Berger mentioned that the next day in his column. I stayed in the studio as people started calling in and we were calling people."

Though Zielonko was saddened at the death of his friend, he went into the studio and worked all night putting together an obituary to use the next morning.

"It was so upsetting to hear Jack had died," said Stuart Esrock, who had worked in the newsroom for four years. "I was working at an ad agency, and I heard the news. I just got in the car and drove down to the station to be with everybody."

Carney's friends from all over began calling the radio station as soon as they heard the news. The phone lines were jammed.

Katie Slade, who worked for Jack at the time of his death, was calling people at 1 o'clock in the morning to get them to go on with Jim

White to talk about Carney.

"When Jack Carney died, they called me," said Scott St. James, who had worked with Carney before he left to go to a station in Los Angeles. "They called me to talk about him on the air. Then later Hyland called to ask me to come back to KMOX. It was then I came up with this credo and I told him, 'I never replace a legend, I only replace the guy who replaced the legend.' When you think about it, no one could replace Carney."

John Angelides, the longtime news director, remembered something Hyland said about Carney.

"We had these staff meetings every morning with all the department heads," said Angelides. "Jack Carney had passed away, and they were trying to figure what to do with that time slot. Mr. Hyland said, 'No one is indispensable at this radio station. The station goes on'. He was trying to tell us we had to go on, like if the president dies, the country goes on. Mr. Hyland said, 'I'm not indispensable, Jack Buck's not indispensable (and he thought the world of Jack Buck), and Jack Carney is not indispensable. The station will go on.' Do you know he came up to me months later and said, 'I never thought I'd say this, but Jack Carney was indispensable.'"

"Jack Carney was the Babe Ruth of Radio," said Pawloski to the *Belleville News Democrat* when they called him and interviewed him. The next day the headline read: "The Babe Ruth of Radio is Dead."

JOHN CARNEY

John Carney is used to hearing comparisons with his father, Jack Carney, but he has also now established himself and his own style of show. He is the nightly host from 10 PM until 2 AM.

"I went into the business and I work at KMOX, so I knew it would happen," said Carney, "But the worst time was when I worked at KTRS and some woman actually accused me of being my dad. She goes, 'I can't believe you people would have the audacity to play Jack Carney tapes. He never worked at your station, he was at KMOX. I'm gonna tell the FCC, I'm gonna tell the FAA, I'm gonna tell the NAACP and the NCAA and we're gonna see that you guys get shut down.' I said, 'Well

ma'am, please explain to me how the dead Jack Carney just gave today's weather forecast.' She said, 'Well, you've manipulated something.' Click. I could not talk her out of it."

Being Jack Carney's son as well as succeeding the retired Jim White in his shift were both challenging tasks for Carney.

"Jim White was great," said Carney. "He took me under his wing. He told the callers to be nice to me; that my show followed him. He said, 'Call up John, he's lonely, he wants some callers'. I like Jim a lot. It was a challenge for me to take his place. In fact, I don't even like to call it that, because he created late-night call-in talk radio. He was the first one to do any of that stuff. I didn't want to come in and try to emulate him, yet I didn't want to re-create the wheel, so I was in a really weird spot. At KTRS I thought I had my act and that was celebrity interviews. I didn't take a lot of phone calls; I didn't state my feelings on gun control or abortion. It was celebrity interviews. It wasn't rocket science. I talked to sitcom stars and comedians and I had to change the show because it's tough to get big celebrities at 1 o'clock in the morning. So after a while it came to be a happy medium. It's usually interviews the first two hours then midnight to two, we turn it around, and put the microphones out into space."

One of his favorite programming ideas took a week to do. Being the son of a famous person, John thought it would fun to interview other 'celebrity kids.'

"After coming from the Lucky Sperm Club myself," he said, "it was not only fun to do, but I think it was therapeutic for me and the people involved. It was Joe Buck [son of Jack Buck], John Kelly [Dan Kelly], Jay Randolph, Jr. [Jay Randolph], Vince Bommarito, Jr. [Vince Bommarito, owner of Tony's Restaurant in St. Louis], and Danny David [Russ David, bandleader]. It was a great week."

Counting Carney, three of the "celebrity kids" were on KMOX. Add to that Matt Hyland, son of former general manager Robert Hyland, and the number of father-son acts at KMOX is high.

"I have no idea why that is," said Carney. "I went into it because he told me not to. I think this town [St. Louis] tends to embrace dynasties. He told me not to do it, but unfortunately he died six months after I started in broadcasting, so I wasn't really able to learn any of

this from him."

Though comparisons are inevitable with Carney and his famous dad, he tries to be himself while also cherishing the memory of his father. As a child, John Carney and his father and mother lived in California. Jack had worked in St. Louis and then left for a while, moving to California. When Jack returned to St. Louis, divorced, John and his mother remained on the West Coast. John's mother later passed away, and John moved to St. Louis to be with his father. It was a mixed-up time in the family as Jack was just about to embark on his marriage to Jody Morioka, and it seemed a solution to have John live in an apartment nearby.

"I lived by myself, came and went as I pleased, but I saw my dad a lot, especially when I wanted money," said Carney. "Whenever I wanted money I would go downtown to KMOX, either hitch a ride or take the bus and go into KMOX to ask my dad to give me some. I'd hit him up for money and he would never give me any unless I read the weather. After I read the weather forecast, he gave me the money, so actually I've been on KMOX for a lot longer than it seems."

Even though Carney is a grown man with two children of his own, he still remembers KMOX when he was a child.

"Every single night without exception I'll get off the elevator on the third floor and the smell of KMOX hits me," Carney said. "KMOX has smelled the same for 30 years, everything about it. But it seems much smaller now, probably because hopefully I've stopped growing. It is still very nostalgic. It doesn't matter who you are, you can't help but be caught up in who graced those halls. It still hits me that I'm on the air at the same station that Jack Buck is, and Bob Costas. The people who have come out of that station, the legends! It also reminds me that I am entrusted with something special."

Carney had trouble getting up in the mornings for school so the school secretary Marie Ahner would call him up every morning.

"She was great," Carney said. "I would not have made it through high school if not for her. No one else was keeping track of me. She would call me up and say, 'John please come to school today,' and I went. Those were interesting times."

Being in St. Louis as the son of Jack Carney he went to school with

kids like Bill Bidwill, Jr., and Matt Hyland.

"In gym class one day we were wrestling each other and I gave him [Hyland] a bloody nose," said Carney. "I came home and told my pop and he went ballistic. 'Of all the kids you could give a bloody nose to you gave Bob Hyland's son a bloody nose!' I said, 'I didn't do it on purpose, Dad... we were wrestling!"

Harry Fender, who was a good friend of his father, was reaching retirement age when John moved to St. Louis and he had plenty of time to spend with John. They enjoyed getting together nearly every day.

"Harry kind of adopted me when I first came to town," said Carney. "Dad was busy and Harry took me under his wing. He took me to the zoo. He took me everywhere. We just became running buddies. I've always been around older people. As a kid, I've always been around Dad's friends and I've always kind of held my own so it didn't seem strange for a 14-year-old to be bumming around with a 75-year-old. My friends were always kind of envious of my relationship with Harry because he was 'Captain 11'! [*Captain 11* was a children's television show and Fender played the loveable 'Captain 11' which was shown on channel 11, KPLR in St. Louis, in the 1960s] I didn't know who Captain 11 was! (having grown up in California) I could have understood if it was Mr. Rogers, but it was amazing the amount of people who would say, 'You know Captain 11?'"

There was one incident involving Fender that Carney remembers happening when he was very young. Jack Carney was going to have a surprise birthday party for his friend and he asked John to come up with an idea to get Harry Fender over to his house. The day of the party arrived and John had not come up with an idea, so he just went over to Fender's house to persuade him to come over. The problem was, he didn't want to go anywhere.

"My only job was to get Harry over there," said Carney. "Dad's got 300 people over at the house and I can't get Harry to come. Big party, live band, I got one task: get Harry to come to the party. So I go over to the Chase and I'm talking with him, 'Why don't you come over, Harry?' He says, 'No, I don't really feel like it.' I kept trying to persuade him to come. Now I was visiting from California so I was probably 11 or 12. I did what any other adolescent would do, I began crying. I finally talked

him into it. It took me an hour!"

People who used to listen to Jack Carney knew that Jack was good friends with Harry Fender, so John Carney often was asked about Harry Fender.

"People would always say, 'How's Harry Fender?'" he said. "'Do you ever see Harry Fender?' 'Why don't you have Harry Fender on the show?' And I steered clear because that was Dad's bag. I intentionally tried to stay away from the guests that he was associated with because I get the comparisons enough. I try not to invite extras. Well, one time I decided, 'OK, I'm gonna break down and ask Harry on.' So we get Harry in the studio. It's going pretty well, but his girlfriend is sitting several feet away and saying, 'Hey Harry, tell them about the time when you and Jack Benny lit the house on fire!' The listeners can't hear it, but it's just loud enough to distract me and Harry."

Fender never liked to divulge his age, and Carney had known that. He also knew that some listener was going to ask and Carney knew Fender would play the game and not tell.

"So I said, 'All right I gotta ask, people are going to want to know, let's get this started up again, how old are you Harry?' He looked at me and said '87.' Well, there goes that routine! I guess we won't be doing that joke!"

Carney also is friends with Ronnie Ryan, the owner of Ronnie's Ice Cream. Carney lives near the company, and he occasionally walks up there to get ice cream with his daughters. His favorite is Ronnie's Rocky Mountain drumsticks.

He and Ryan often wind up talking about music. "One of the things we have in common is he loves the Grateful Dead," Ryan said. "He's a Dead Head and I'm a Dead Head. I think he's seen them 25 or 30 times. He really knows his music."

Carney plays the drums and is in two bands. One band is a blues band called St. Steven's Blues, which was touring for a while and he did not go with them. His newer band, a dance band, is the 'Carn Dawgs.' Their first show was at Busch Stadium on the Fourth of July. He learned to play the drums from the best.

"Bob Kuban was my teacher," said Carney.

"John Carney is a talented guy," said Kuban. "He's doing well on

92

the show and he's a good drummer. I used to go to his house every Saturday for his lessons starting back when he was 11 or 12 and was in town in the summers. It was at Jack Carney's house. We'd do the lessons down in his basement."

Carney started playing in bands when he was in high school and has always enjoyed it. Once he realized his dad had not seen him play, he invited him.

"I was in college, it was 1982," said Carney. "I was playing in a club called 'Fourth and Pine' downtown. And I said to my dad, 'Look, I've been playing music since I was nine, and you have never come to see me play. I'm not looking for *Courtship of Eddie's Father* [a TV show in the early '70s] here, but how about a little support?' So he comes down to the Fourth and Pine gig and he brings Mitch Miller! So here comes Dad and MITCH MILLER! So during the break the band's backstage and I'm saying, 'Mitch Miller's out there! We gotta do something for Mitch.' So we quickly re-worked some music and made those sing-a-longs. Here's Mitch Miller standing on stage with the band and we're doing sing-a-longs to The Allman Brothers and Tom Petty! He didn't know the words; I think he just nodded his head and waved his hands."

Now Carney is the father of two girls, Jaede and Joerdan. They like watching their dad play.

"Once I was out playing a show last summer, and my oldest daughter, who is four, climbed up on my shoulders, and I actually played an entire song on percussion with a four-year-old on my shoulders!"

As the years have passed, many of John Carney's listeners are young enough that they did not know his dad, and many of John Carney's listeners who did know his dad now know John's style and appreciate his uniqueness. He does not worry anymore about guests that remind people of his dad. He still keeps in touch with Phyllis Diller, who was a very good friend to Jack.

"I talk to her at least once a year," said John. "And I've had her on the show. The one friend of Dad's that I really keep in touch with is Gary Owens from *Laugh-In*, who is here at WIL. I also talk to Frankie Laine on occasion."

"The great thing about John Carney is he can cook," said Suzanne Corbett, cooking expert and author of *Pushcarts and Stalls, The Soulard*

Market Cookbook (Palmerston and Reed Publishing). "I've known John a long time. He likes food, and God knows I like food, and we both like to cook. We see each other at community events involving cooking, like at last year's 'Cookin' For Kids Event' for the St. Vincent's Home for Children. He was the chairman of the event. They had restaurants that brought food and then celebrities served it. He does a lot of work for charity. We've been stirring pots and dishing food for charity for a long time."

"I really do like to cook," said Carney. "I've taught a class at Dierbergs. I would like to do that some day, be a chef."

Corbett was on Carney's show talking about *Push Carts and Stalls*.

"I went down to the studio and brought food with me," she said. "Then he started giving me the business on the air."

John Carney: Why is this apple crumb tart so dry?

Suzanne Corbett: It's a crumb tart, CRUMB tart. Crumbs are dry.

John: How come my nice quote that I gave you didn't make the cover of the book?'

Suzanne: You made the bookmark.

John: What do you mean the bookmark?

Suzanne: It's a collector's item bookmark.

John: I've never seen any bookmark.

Suzanne: They're out there. Lots of people have them.

John: If anyone has a bookmark with my quote on it, call us here at the station.

(As Suzanne tells it, then it pops up on the screen, "I got the bookmark." Suddenly others called in.)

"Wouldn't you know it," said Suzanne "the one call they took turned out to be my crummy brother! I said, 'that's what brothers are for.'"

Carney loves his late-night spot.

"I love it," said Carney, whose producer, Steve Schrader, screens the calls. "I get that taste of 44 states at night, KMOX at night blankets the country. More than half of my calls come from other cities, and it's just intoxicating. It's just amazing how many people call me from Boston, and Kansas, and Denver and Florida. These people are not from St. Louis. I can understand when someone moves away, it's hard to

keep in touch, picking up the hometown newspaper. It's amazing how many people swear by KMOX at night. Now you could understand it if it was the baseball game, but I'm talking about all the people that are listening to me, to my show."

When asked what was his strangest call, he said, "Just wait every 15 minutes and you'll get the next strangest call." He has had celebrities call.

"John Goodman has called several times," said Carney. "He's listening at night. Once he was in town and he showed up here with an Imo's pizza. John and I got to know each other when I was working at KTRS, he's one of the investors, he was actually my boss, but we've gotten to be better friends since I've left."

Working from 10 PM to 2 AM can be a lonely shift at KMOX. In the past, there were engineers, producers, and news people wandering around. Now that there are not as many engineers, there are not many people hanging around the station at that hour.

"In the newsroom there may be Bill Reker or Bob Hamilton at the news desk," said Carney. "Up until midnight there might be a reporter, but after that, it's just me and my producer."

In 1999, John Carney became a part of the news, not just someone who might report it.

"Probably the most national publicity that KMOX ever got," he said, "was when I was in China adopting my second daughter, Joerdan. The NATO forces accidentally bombed the Chinese Embassy in Yugoslavia and I was behind, well, I won't say 'enemy lines,' but our hotel was right next to one of the U.S. embassies that was being protested. We're three days away from leaving and there are 100,000 angry Chinese people outside the hotel. As soon as it hit the fan I called KMOX to file a little report. Bill Reker was on with Vicki Atlas. I gave KMOX a couple of feeds. They fed it to CBS New York. Not only do I have the *Post* and all the TV stations calling, but I have stations all over the world. When we got to Los Angeles, we were surprised to see how big this thing had gotten when we were met by a mob of people and got cameras stuck in our faces. I had to call KMOX and say, 'I know this sounds crazy, but I'm gonna need a police escort when we get back'".

KAREN CARROLL

Even though she had been involved in management of radio stations in St. Louis for 20 years, Karen Carroll learned a lesson about the importance of KMOX soon after taking over as the station's general manager.

"I had been raising money and working in this city for 20 years, and after I came to KMOX, one of the leaders in the city asked me, 'Now where did you move in from?' That told me the only station he knew was KMOX.

"What I didn't get until I got here was how important the radio station is to every leader in the community."

Carroll is not the same type of general manager as either Robert Hyland or Rod Zimmerman. She has a different style, and has made changes she believes will put KMOX in a better position to remain an industry leader for years to come. She is very active in charity circles, and her main focus is called Outreach St. Louis. She sees part of KMOX's future as increasing its involvement in various community matters.

"She is a very driven leader," said Tom Langmyer. "She has incredible amounts of energy. She doesn't settle for anything less than full dedication from her people. She is a very challenging person who is never willing to accept the status quo. She does a lot of inspecting to make sure things are operating the way they should be. She asks a lot of questions. She is always wanting to know if there is a better way to do things."

Carroll said she tries to listen to what others are saying and ask questions rather than always try to dictate what KMOX should be doing.

"I think I share my opinions more as a listener than as a boss," she said. "What did I need to know? What did I miss? We have to make sure we are breaking news, not simply reacting to it. We don't take a position on the issues, either for or against. We want to give the listeners the information and let them make their own decisions."

Her style also is try to make sure the station keeps up with the changes in society, and keeps providing the type of information the listeners want, with the quality they have come to expect from KMOX.

"Karen Carroll is a highly creative individual who is leading the current generation of KMOX listeners into the next era," said general

sales manager Clinton Hasse. "Her open-mindedness to new ideas is what is helping the station continue to grow."

She doesn't want anyone at the station working in fear, or being afraid of disagreeing with her on an issue. She tries to be as open and available to everyone as possible. Once a year she hosts a summer pool party for the employees.

"She opens her house to the KMOX staff," said Bob Hamilton. "Her mom is there. It breaks the ice and lets everyone have fun. She is very accessible."

"Her house is beautifully decorated with lots of artwork," said Vicki Atlas who has worked at KMOX for the last two years. "The thing that really stunned me was when you walk into her house, the first thing you see is this wonderful, relaxing fountain. She is such a high energy person and she has this calming fountain."

The parties are not stiff, formal corporate parties. Carroll has been known to host the parties in a relaxed atmosphere. She has also welcomed staff members to her home at other times of the year, cooking dinner for them.

"She has really done a lot to brighten up the station," said Emmett McAuliffe who does the overnights on Friday nights. "The KMOX office looks a little nicer since she came. She didn't do a whole color scheme change or anything, she just made it brighter, opened up the executive office suite, changed the curtains, moved the hosts offices to the third floor where the studios are. They had been on the fourth floor for a while and it was more inconvenient for them. She also fixed the coffee area and improved the lunch room."

One decision Carroll made was to move the annual Holiday Radio Show to the Sheldon Theater.

"It is so much of a homey environment in the Sheldon," said Tom Schiller, the sales manager. "Karen Carroll has really embraced the Holiday Show. The KMOX listeners were really treated to something spectacular. There are a lot of things she has embraced and several she has blazed the trail on; the holiday auction is one of them."

In recent years, KMOX's Outreach St. Louis has organized radio-a-thons, but in 1999 Carroll came up with the idea to have a live-radio auction instead.

"It was really a success," said Schiller. "The auction raised a lot of money for charity."

The station held the auctions for a week with many unique prizes, including a trip to the All-Star Game and a trip to Holland.

"Karen Carroll has done a lot for this station," said Schiller, "She has opened up a lot of doors. People feel they can talk to the general manager and tell her how they feel. It's a very collaborative atmosphere where people can really have input."

Carroll tells her employees she wants to be "customer focused." She has instigated marketing meetings once a week to discuss customer focus.

"One of the big impacts she has made is her community interest," said *Total Information AM* host Nan Wyatt. "She is a native of St. Louis and she is very plugged in to the community, like Robert Hyland was. She knows the community. Rather than have specific charities she is involved with, Karen Carroll is interested in the total community. She has a big interest in women and women's issues, such as with the American Cancer Society and breast cancer research. She is also interested in the Urban League. It's the focus on the fabric of the community that is important to her."

BOB CHASE

Bob Chase was better known in St. Louis for his work on television than on KMOX, except for one night. He was supposed to be working, but had left the station during a *Monday Night Football* broadcast.

"The line went dead between KMOX and CBS," said news reporter Ron Barber. "Bob had left the studio and there was no one on the air. Total silence."

Chase worked for 16 years at KSDK-TV, where he became the news anchor of the first 5 PM news broadcast in the country. He twice ran for Congress. Chase died in 1999 at the age of 72.

PAPPY CHESHIRE

Pappy Cheshire was the first announcer on the *Uncle Dick Slack's*

Barn Dance Show. He worked at KMOX before going to Hollywood to work as a character actor in several movies.

"On the *Uncle Dick Slack Show* Pappy Cheshire was a character like Buddy Ebson was on the *Beverly Hillbillies,*" said Martha DeGray. "He went into the movies. If you watch AMC, you'll see some of his movies every once in a while."

"Mr. Hyland called me in Texas about the show with Pappy," said Roy Queen, who took over as emcee after Cheshire left. "He said, 'We're going to build a show around you and Pappy Cheshire.' I was real excited and I knew Pappy. He was in vaudeville."

MIKE CLAIBORNE

Mike Claiborne worked as both a guest and host of *Sports Open Line* programs in the 1980s when he moved back to his hometown of St. Louis after college in Nashville, Tennessee.

"I was doing some work for the *St. Louis American,*" said Claiborne. "Some sportswriting. Jim Holder got to know me and he had me on his show. Once I got hired at KMOX I was doing sales during the day. I think I'm the only guy he [Robert Hyland] allowed to do that. It worked out really well.

"It was a great time to work there. It was a blast because people like Robert Hyland don't exist in today's world as far as getting things done. There were no contracts, everything was done by a handshake. I think if Robert Hyland were alive today, the Rams would not be here. We would have gotten an expansion team. He was the only one who could have galvanized it."

Claiborne worked at KMOX until 1990, when he moved to an all-sports station, KASP.

"When I think of Mike Claiborne, I'll never forget the day he got coldcocked with a foul ball at the baseball game," said Mike Harris, who worked at WIL and now is with CBS network in New York. "The little gate behind homeplate where they hand the balls out to the umpires for some reason was open that night. I remember seeing it and thinking, wow, I wonder what the odds are that a ball could get through

that opening, and believe it or not just as I was thinking that, boom! It went straight for Mike's head.

"I remember it was a left-hand hitter, I think it was Steve Braun. He fouled the ball off and it hit Mike right in the middle of the forehead. He went down like he'd been shot. I thought that was the last of him; I really thought he was dead, but he was so lucky. They took him out on a stretcher and he ended up having a concussion, but he was OK. It was unbelievable the ball could just happen to go through that opening and hit him! It would have taken real skill to aim it to make it go through there."

Claiborne is now the program director and host of the afternoon drive program on KFNS radio, which succeeded KASP as St. Louis' all-sports station.

YVONNE COLE

Yvonne Cole was the director of the KMOX Little Red Line, the children cheerleaders for the St. Louis football Cardinals. The Dallas Cowboys and other teams had cheerleaders and Robert Hyland and public relations director Jeannie Whitworth came up with the idea for the Big Red Line as well as the Little Red Line because no other team had children cheerleaders.

"Mr. Hyland came up with the idea," said Cole, who is the Pom Sponsor at Lindbergh High School and teaches science. The Lindbergh Flyerettes have won numerous awards under the direction of Cole and she had been chosen by the Cardinals' public affairs director, Adele Harris, to put on halftime shows once a year using girls from the MO Pom Association.

"I guess it was from those halftime shows that Mr. Hyland knew of me," said Cole. "I had gotten a lot of attention when the television show *Real People* came to town and filmed a group of Poms that I directed from the MO Pom Association. In 1979 when I was six months pregnant with my second child they called me and asked me if I'd be interested in directing this group of kids they were going to call the 'Little Red Line.' [There were the older girls already performing in the Big Red Line.]

"We held auditions through advertisements with the local dancing schools. The girls were 8-10 years of age and wore little jumpers with bibs in the front. They were white with skirts that had the football Cardinal logo on them. They were very 'pom'-oriented, not dance-oriented and I made sure they were little girls doing little girl routines."

BILL CONNERLY

Bill Connerly started working in the sports office in the early 1980s. He was a sports producer, working most frequently with Jack Buck as the producer on Cardinals baseball games.

"Bill Connerly was smooth as silk," said Lisa Bedian, who worked with Connerly in the sports office. "Nothing rattles the guy. He is somewhat quiet with a very dry sense of humor. A good, good person, great guy to work with."

"He had a very laid back way about him," said Joan Tabash, an intern who worked under him. "He was easy going, but was a workaholic. I helped him with the tapes. We were sometimes there until 2 or 3 in the morning. He was very much of a perfectionist."

Connerly advanced out of the broadcast booth to work at Bud Sports.

LARRY CONNERS

Even though he is much better known for his work on television, as news anchor on KMOV, Larry Conners has been a part of KMOX since the 1980s. He does fill-in work for Nan Wyatt or Doug McElvein on *Total Information AM,* and he also has two syndicated programs which air on KMOX, *American Fact or Fiction,* a trivia show which runs on Saturday and Sunday mornings, and *American Story,* a short show with two different stories about raising children and pets.

Though he has been a part of KMOX for many years he never hosted a show even though he discussed it with Robert Hyland.

"Mr. Hyland contacted me," said Conners. "There had been initial contacts and I knew he was interested in having me do some work for

him. This was while I was working at Channel 2 [KTVI, at the time, the ABC affiliate in St. Louis].

"Mr. Hyland wanted to talk to me, but he didn't want anyone else to find out about it," Conners said. "He came up with this clandestine meeting where no one would see us. We met at the zoo, in one of the administrative offices."

It was a good meeting, but somehow Pete Rahn, the media columnist for the *St. Louis Globe-Democrat* who also wrote for *Variety* magazine, learned of the Conners-Hyland Meeting. At that time Julius Hunter, who now works with Conners at KMOV (the CBS afffiliate) and was an anchor with KMOV at the time, was doing a radio show on KMOX on Sunday nights. Rahn wrote in *Variety* magazine that the CBS radio station was firing the CBS television anchor to hire someone from the ABC affiliate. Hunter was not fired, having decided to leave KMOX. Conners and Hyland knew it would make everyone look bad because that was not the way it had really happened and they decided to abandon the idea.

When Rod Zimmerman took over, he and program director Tom Langmyer hired Conners.

"This was over eight years ago," said Conners. "I filled in for Wendy [Wiese] and Bill [Willkerson]. I did a lot of sub work and now with John Butler as news director I still do subbing there. I am honored that they call me, but with the hours I have it's hard to work many days at KMOX. After I do the 10 PM news at KMOV, by the time I get home and get my head on the pillow it's 1 AM. That's a quick turnaround to get back to KMOX to fill in in the mornings."

The mornings are very regimented and there is not much time for diversion, however Conners did get to go into more detail when filling in for Charles Jaco in the afternoon.

"I remember one very direct interview I did with Kit Bond on Charles Jaco's show in the afternoon," said Conners. "It was right around the time that Boeing had announced they would pick up and move. I raised the question to Bond as to whether he was grandstanding. He did not appreciate that question. At the same time he was proposing a bill about a new rating on movies. I was able to go into depth with that topic also."

In his role as anchor on television he is not afforded the luxury of long in-depth interviews with follow up questions such as the one with Senator Bond.

"The television station has never had a problem with me going on KMOX," said Conners. "I am still doing the reporting, even if it is on KMOX, and they realize it. It is a win-win situation for both stations, it is only a positive. KMOV has been very supportive."

Conners said he liked Hyland even though it did not work out for him to work at KMOX the first time they discussed it.

"I once sent him a Christmas card that said something like, 'I've heard some bad things about you, but I can't believe they were true,'" he said.

"Everyone always compares KMOX today to then [the KMOX under Robert Hyland]," said Conners. "It's a different era and times change. Many times when I've been on KMOX, I'll get letters or calls and people will compare me to Bob Hardy. That's a very fine compliment."

THOMAS PATRICK CONVEY

Thomas Patrick Convey was the original general manager at KMOX when the station went on the air in 1925, but became better known later as a sports broadcaster. He left KMOX after only a few months because of a conflict with an investor.

Convey pawned a watch to get enough money to put a deposit down on another station, which received the call letters KWK. He was involved in a legal battle against KMOX that became intense.

In one incident, a news event that both KMOX and KWK were broadcasting, a KMOX employee allegedly cut the KWK cable, knocking the station off the air. Convey had the man arrested, lawsuits followed, and the out-of-court settlement gave KWK the rights to also broadcast baseball games the following year.

It was in baseball that Convey earned his greatest acclaim. He broadcast under his first and middle name, as Thomas Patrick, and became known for his sad line when the Cardinals were losing, "The score .... Ohhh, that score."

When owner Sam Breadon temporarily banned radio broadcasts

in 1934, believing it was hurting attendance, Convey tried to bootleg the games by climbing a ladder on top of the YMCA building, which was across the street from center field, and watching through binoculars. Breadon quickly put a stop to that as well.

JOHN COOPER

John Cooper was a sports producer during the 1980s. Under the direction of Cooper's booking of guests and planning of shows, the sports department thrived. Cooper worked long and hard hours, more than most people would have worked.

Twice paramedics had to be called to the station because co-workers were worried that Cooper was having a heart attack.

Cooper later worked for a time at KTRS radio and now works as a stockbroker.

J.C. CORCORAN

J.C. Corcoran was on KMOX for a brief time as host of the afternoon show in the early 1990s. Robert Hyland saw him as a popular disc jockey on a competing station and hired him, but the move was not successful and Corcoran quickly moved on to another station.

BOB COSTAS

The fact that Bob Costas began his broadcasting career at KMOX as the play-by-play man for the Spirits of St. Louis basketball team can be attributed to his college friend.

Yes, he was hired by Robert Hyland on the strength of a tape he submitted to the station. He did so, however, after a friend, working for the team in the American Basketball Association, tipped Costas the team was looking for a broadcaster.

Costas, still a student at Syracuse University, had broadcast only 10 basketball games in his life but had enough material that he doctored a tape into sounding as if it was all from the same game. He sent

the tape to Bernie Fox, coordinator of the sports department, and the rest is history.

He was 22 years old when he came to St. Louis in 1974, and nobody then could have predicted how big a star Costas would become in the next 25 years, rising to the top of his profession.

He did so through hard work, incredible knowledge, outstanding wit, and, he will admit, a lot of luck.

The Spirits' games, along with hosting *Sports Open Line* and *At Your Service* programs and appearances as young Rob on the Tiki Jack skits on the Jack Carney show, gave Costas his start and provided him with much of his comedic material.

His stories about Marvin Barnes and Fly Williams became legendary. One of the most wildly told stories about Costas' days with the Spirits concerned a game in Memphis, when Costas missed his flight from St. Louis and arrived late, getting to the game after it had started.

Working in the studio, Bill Wilkerson had covered for Costas, claiming technical difficulties prevented them from putting on the game until Costas arrived. After the game, out with several of the players, he was lamenting his fate and predicted that he might be fired when Barnes told him not to fret.

"Don't worry, Bro," Costas repeated Barnes as saying. "I've been looking for a short little white dude to drive my Rolls."

Luckily for Costas, Hyland was understanding and he didn't have to accept the backup job offer.

"I loved listening to Bob Costas on the Spirits of St. Louis basketball games," said listener Bill Hepper. "He made you want to go to the games. I remember going one night and they were throwing out those little basketballs with the Spirits logo on them. That would really be a collector's item to have today. I wish I would have gotten one. "

By the time the Spirits folded, Costas had entrenched himself enough in KMOX and St. Louis that he just picked up other assignments, eventually leading him to the network level, where he first worked for CBS before moving to NBC.

He was extremely popular as the host of *Sports Open Line*, and became involved in numerous pranks and comedic acts at the station, including the night he decided to take Anne Keefe to the wrestling matches in a limousine.

"Dan Dierdorf and I got on a wrestling kick for a while," said Costas. "It was before wrestling was like it is today. It was more fun-loving. I got a kick out of it then. I think we were the only radio station talking about wrestling at the time.

"There was going to be a wrestling match at the Arena between Hulk Hogan and 'Mr. Wonderful,' Paul Orndorf. Dan Dierdorf, Anne Keefe, and I went to the wrestling match in a limo. Dan and I had tuxes on and Anne had on an evening gown. We interviewed people from the wrestling match, and then broadcast the match itself. Afterward we went out with the wrestlers and did reports from the limo. As people found out where we were, they started showing up at each location. We wound up at White Castle on Vandeventer and Choteau about 2:30 in the morning."

One of the people listening later wound up working at KMOX, reporter Brian Kelly.

"To me, that was some of the best radio I ever heard," Kelly said. "It was hilarious. Between Costas and Dierdorf and Anne Keefe, it was so good."

"It was Mr. Hyland's idea," said Keefe. "There we were—they were in dinner jackets and I'm in an evening gown. People were throwing popcorn and beer on us. I was doing my best 'My friend Irma'. I was saying things like, 'Oh, Bobby, he's hitting the referee, is that permissible?'"

Keefe remembered when they went off in their limo at the end of the night, they got a call from Hulk Hogan's limo.

"It was his agent who was big in wrestling circles back then. We were on the air with Jim White. Hogan's agent said, 'Did you find a black bag in your limo? It was put in the wrong limo. We didn't have the bag, but they were sure worried about it. We never found out what was in it or what happened to it."

Costas also mastered his ability to ad lib while at KMOX, a skill that has increased his success when anchoring events such as the Olympics.

"He could ad lib incredibly," said Rick Powers, who was an intern in 1979 and is now the sports director of KDNL-TV in St. Louis. "He

would be doing the midnight sports and he would just rip the tape off the sports ticker and from that he would ad lib his sportscasts just as if it had been written in front of him. He never stopped or paused, the listener would have just assumed he had it all written down, but really all it would be were the scores, winning and losing pitchers, home runs, and maybe another highlight. He was amazing."

Workers around the station enjoyed it when Costas came in because he would always light up the room. He talked to everybody from the youngest intern to the men who worked in the mailroom. Many nights he would rush in at the last minute, but on the nights that he arrived with plenty of time to spare, he could clown around.

One night after having watched the old James Cagney movie, *Yankee Doodle Dandy*, Costas spontaneously hopped up on a newsroom desk and broke into his best George M. Cohan imitation doing a tap dance. "I will never forget that," said newswoman Joan Beuckman. "I was there."

After doing the midnight sportscast one night, Costas was sitting around talking with sports assistant Steve Overby. They decided to go out and get something to eat.

"We walked out the front door of the building and there was this new Jim Meagher Cheverolet with no tires on it," said Overby. "Somebody had stolen the tires and left the car up on blocks. Bob went upstairs and called Jim Meagher at home. It was about 1 in the morning. He said, 'The car you gave me doesn't have any tires on it.' They sent another car out for him."

Costas was a very popular host on *Sports Open Line*. One of his favorite callers was Jim Hill, a name listeners will recognize. Whenever Hill called, Costas instantly recognized his voice.

"One night I was listening to Jim White and I hear Jim Hill talking to Jim White," Costas said. "He was hysterically funny, very entertaining. Then I noticed he would call a lot. I thought he was a delightful person and I wanted to meet him, so I called him up. We went to two baseball games together. He knew a lot about baseball and the old Negro Leagues.

"He was a funny guy. He told me he was a widower and that when his wife died, he collected some on the insurance. I said something like 'So you've got some money,' and he said, 'Oh no Bob, I blew it. Look at

this suit—Famous-Barr, these shoes—Florsheim. And with my wife gone, you know there were some ladies vying for my attention. The money? I blew it, you understand, heh, heh, heh.' These days, Jim is in his mid 80s, he lives in a nursing home and still listens to KMOX."

Ask almost anyone who worked with Costas in those days and they have a favorite story, usually about how he arrived at the studio literally minutes before he was to go on the air.

"Costas always amazed me," said newswriter John Amann. "He could come in 10 minutes before a sportscast and look at the ticker tape. He knew the standings in his head, he could build a whole story around just looking at the line scores. Several times I remember it was two minutes until 12 and he was coming in to do the midnight sports, which would be coming on at maybe eight minutes after midnight. When he wasn't there, I started worrying, but in he always came. He was never under stress, he would just pick up the wire stories and ticker tape and he could edit in his head while he was reading."

Costas' broadcast career was highlighted along with other award-winning broadcasters in Curt Smith's book, *Voices of The Game*; and many of his stories are in Smith's subsequent book, *The Storytellers*.

Smith set up a series of lectures at the Smithsonian Institute's National History Museum in Washington, DC, and Costas was one of the featured speakers.

"It was a nine-part series honoring some of baseball's best play-by-play men," said Smith, 'including Mel Allen, Jack Buck, Al Michaels, Ernie Harwell, Joe Garagiola, Bob Wolff, Jon Miller, and others. Bob's night was sold out. The concept of the series was borrowing from Ralph Edwards' 'This Is Your Life.' I was exceedingly impressed by Bob's command of language, understanding of culture and abiding sense of humor and ability to connect.

"The stories he told, especially the Miss Cheesecake story, brought the house down. Coming from the same generation as he did, I enjoyed the chance to banter about our affection and love for the game. The next day he flew back and called me from St. Louis. 'I want to thank you. That was one of the greatest nights of my life.' We had slides dating back to his Little League days. The Smithsonian has a copy of the slide show."

This is one of the stories included in *The Storytellers*, although it

has been repeated many times.

"In 1986, my wife Randy, and I were expecting our first child," Costas said. "At spring training, we're at lunch with Kirby Puckett and his now-wife, Tonya, and Kirby says, 'Do you know if it's a boy or a girl? We say, 'No.' He says, 'Have you picked a name?' Nope. He says, 'How about Kirby? That works for a boy or a girl.' I say, 'Yeah, fine. Tell ya what. If you're hitting .350 when the kid is born, we'll name him or her after you.' Seemed safe. He'd never hit .300 for a full season.

"Well on due date, Kirby is hitting .397 to lead the majors. He calls and says, 'You got a baby?' I said, 'The baby's late. Actually if the baby holds off for a while and you go into a slump, we can forget the whole thing.' He's still hitting .372 when the child was born. The only way around it was double middle names: The birth certificate reads, 'Keith Michael Kirby Costas.'"

"I always enjoyed Bob Costas," said KMOX medical expert Dr. Armand Brodeur. "I used to invite him to my house for dinner. He would talk to me about Robert Hyland during his early time at KMOX and say, 'What does he do?' 'How can I get his attention?' I told him I'd been there a while and if I wanted to talk to Bob Hyland, I would go in the middle of the night. Bob did that.

"I introduced Bob to Cardinal Glennon," said Brodeur, who was instrumental in starting the hospital and whose picture still hangs in a hall at the children's hospital. "Bob has done a lot for Cardinal Glennon and now they have a cancer wing named after him."

The Bob Costas Center is a beautifully decorated, kid-friendly center for children who have cancer or sickle cell disease. Besides Costas' broadcasting popularity, his involvement in Cardinal Glennon, especially in fundraising efforts, has endeared Costas to the St. Louis community.

Even when he lived in New York, Costas continued to make regular appearances on KMOX and still is active hosting Evening Specials on nights when there are no sports broadcasts.

KATHERYN CRAVENS

Katheryn Cravens came to St. Louis to act in radio plays and be-

came KMOX's expert on the woman's angle in 1933 with her show *Let's Compare Notes*. The show included household hints, fashion, beauty, and style.

She wanted to go into news, but KMOX general manager James Shouse encouraged her to stay with the radio plays. She was finally able to sell him on the idea of her doing news and she started doing an hour-long program.

Cravens encouraged flying before it became popular and as a result the airlines offered free trips. She became known as the flying reporter. CBS bought the show and in 1936 moved her to the network.

FRANK CUSUMANO

When Frank Cusumano was an intern at KMOX in 1983, he could not have known he would one day be a sportscaster for Channel 5 (KSDK) as well as have his own show on the all-sports radio station (KFNS). He was a hard worker and very enthusiastic when he was there, so his co-workers were not surprised at his success.

"I was just in awe and really nervous," said Cusumano from his car phone after doing a radio show, "every step I took while I was around such broadcasting legends. If I looked to my left there was Bob Costas, if I looked to my right, there was Bob Burnes, and then Jack Buck would pop in."

Cusumano said he was a long-time listener of KMOX even before the internship, starting when he was very young.

"I remember being a 10-year-old and listening to Jack Carney," said Cusumano who spent his summers shooting hoops in the gymnasium at Our Lady of the Pillar. "It was my grade school gym and I had a key so I could play basketball. I would bring in my radio and listen to KMOX the whole time. One day Jack Carney was having a contest to win a trip to Dallas to watch the football Cardinals play the Dallas Cowboys. Jack Carney asked a question. It was, 'Who were the first eight members of the National Football League?' I knew the answer, I probably don't know the answer today, but I knew it then and I had a dime in my pocket so I ran to the pay phone and called in. I ended up winning the contest, so I sent my parents to Dallas for their anniversary. They got to take this

big trip on their 10-year-old!"

Cusumano liked the dependability of KMOX.

"My life literally revolved around KMOX," he said. "I know that on Thursdays I could hear Jeff Meyers and Joe Sullivan go toe-to-toe. I knew that during baseball season, Marty Marion would be on. I always called up *Sports Open Line*. I just wanted to be on the air and show off my knowledge or lack of."

Being an intern, Cusumano was the low man on the proverbial totem pole, but he said he never felt that way and he thoroughly enjoyed working there.

"They had this big roll-o-dex," he said. "I remember just spending hours looking at that roll-o-dex and seeing all the famous people's phone numbers. I guess I can admit this since it is many years later, but I remember calling a few of them just to see if they would answer. Once I called Jim Hart and he answered the phone. I was so excited I hung up, and then I told my friends all about it, 'I talked to Jim Hart today.'"

Cusumano actually did talk to many athletes and coaches as he did interviews for the sportscasters and wrote the stories.

"One of the greatest memories for me involved Bob Burnes," said Cusumano. "On Saturday afternoons Bob Burnes would come in and do a show. I would always get there real early and try to come up with three or four nuggets and put them together. I'd type them up, just interesting little stories, and give them to him to use on the air. He always used them and then he would say, 'These were put together by our crack sports intern, Frank Cusumano.' He didn't know it, but I had my friends and family all listening and it was a big thrill to get my name said by Bob Burnes on KMOX. It was just a thrill to have him use my stuff."

Cusumano, who played basketball at DeSmet High School and then at UMSL, was knowledgeable about the high school and college basketball scene and his knowledge came in handy in the sports office.

"I remember I wrote up this page about the recruits and gave it to Bob Costas," said Cusumano. "He delivered it in such a way that it looked like he did it off the top of his head. He was so good. More than being such a good talent, he was so nice, and he was nice to everyone.

"Another big thrill for me was when Bob took me to New York

with him. He had started working at NBC and he and his wife lived in New York. He invited me to New York and I got to stay with him and his wife. I got to go and watch him do the half-time show. Pete Axthelm was with him. NBC picked us up in a limo that morning and drove us to the Meadowlands for an AFC game. That night we went out to dinner: Pete Axthelm, Bob Costas, and Frank Cusumano. Who doesn't fit in that picture?

"Anytime we have an intern, and we have them all the time, I try to always think about the way Bob Costas treated me."

CAROL DANIEL

Carol Daniel has had many different duties at KMOX. She has co-hosted *The Morning Meeting, Total Information PM, At Your Service* shows, and read the news.

"I also worked Sundays with Don Marsh and Saturdays with Bill Reker," she said.

Daniel started at KMOX in April of 1995.

"I was hired by Tom Langmyer who says he heard me on Cape Girardeau station KZIM while he was driving to Memphis," said Daniel. "He called me at the station and said he was interested in seeing if I wanted to come to work for KMOX. I was in the newsroom with other people around and I couldn't talk so all I could say was 'yes,' 'no,' 'sure.'"

Langmyer knew he had caught Daniel off guard, so he told her he would call her back on Monday. When he did, she still seemed surprised.

"Two weeks later, she was on the air on KMOX," Langmyer said. "She was doing a talk show and reading the news, and I really liked her poise and the way she sounded on the air."

When she left KZIM, her fellow employees were sorry to see her go, but excited for her too, so they gave her a going-away party on the air.

"Senator Bond called in to wish me well along with Governor Carnahan," said Daniel. "Rush Limbaugh, who is from Cape Girardeau, even called."

When Daniel first came to KMOX, she joked that she was the station's substitute teacher, filling in for any hosts who missed a day of work.

"Carol is a college friend of mine," said Ollie Dowell, who works in the newsroom. "It's great to come to work and see her face. I get a quick chuckle when recalling the roads in which we've traveled in our personal and professional lives."

"On my first day, John Butler, the news director, described Carol as the cheerleader in the newsroom. I'd say she's that and much more. When the news department reaches a low point, I can always count on Carol to lift my spirits and the spirits of others around me."

Daniel has gotten lifts from callers to the station who have treated her as if she was in their own family.

"When my son, PJ, was born four years ago, a listener sent me a handmade rattle," said Daniel. "It was made of beechwood. When my second son, Marcus, was born he sent me another one. The amazing thing is, the man who made them has a granddaughter who goes to the same daycare as my children and we met one day in the center, not knowing that we had kids there."

Daniel says she gets a lot of letters and calls from her listeners and she takes each one for what they are worth.

"It takes all kinds," she said. "Once there was an angry listener who wrote to management to get that 'creature' off the air. Another woman said on the air if she needed blood, she wouldn't take it from a black person."

She has two favorite guests on her shows.

"I loved [singer] Patti LaBelle," said Daniel. "She was so real in person. It was just like talking to your favorite aunt. We discussed her book, *Don't Block the Blessings*. I found out she is afraid of storms because she had to drive through one on the way to the studio, and she needs absolute darkness to sleep. She also talked about women getting mammograms. She said, 'Girls, check yourself.' Doug was so embarrassed by that that it made me laugh."

Another interview she enjoyed was with Olympian Jackie Joyner-Kersee.

"Jackie was talking about her book and I made her laugh by questioning the cover picture she took," Daniel said. "She had on this black cat suit and her hair was done up and her make-up was just right. She

laughed talking about the photo shoot and how nervous she had been at the time."

Megan Lynch, the traffic reporter who flies in Airborne One and also works in the newsroom, has learned a lot from Daniel.

"I look at Carol Daniel as a mentor," she said. "I look at what she does and how she handles situations. She and Nan Wyatt are good examples for young women in the market."

BOB DANKO

Bob Danko worked at KMOX for 29 years.

"Bobby Danko was the best board operator we ever had," said Bill Ott, an engineer at KMOX. "He ran the console and mixed the commercials. Before we had producers the engineer would sit behind the glass with all the controls. The talent was on the other side of the glass. The engineer played all the tapes. The engineer had to adjust the microphones and all of the levels, and Bobby did a great job."

"I was temporary for six months at the beginning," said Danko. "I worked up until one day before six months. According to union rules, if I'd worked the six months they would have had to hire me. That was in 1968. The chief engineer called me the next year and said they needed someone on staff. He made me a deal, 'If you'll work over Christmas, he'd see what he could do about getting me on staff in 1969 because he knew they'd be hiring another engineer in 1969. I came back a week before Christmas. They hired me on as staff in 1969 and I stayed until 1997.

"One of my biggest memories was I was on the board when man walked on the moon. I think that was on the overnight shift. We had a CBS net alert. When it comes up for a net alert and it is a certain number, you just automatically drop your programming and go to the network. No matter what you're doing, you go to the network. That was how it was when Neil Armstrong walked on the moon. We had a hook-up to Houston to the Command Center."

Danko did remotes and in-studio broadcasts and worked with everyone who worked at KMOX. One time he worked with Bob Costas on a special show.

"At the end of the show," said Danko, "he mentioned everyone on the show who had anything to do with the show and he thanked them, but he forgot to mention me. Later he found out he forgot to mention me and he felt bad about it. He felt so bad he offered my wife and me a free dinner at Dierdorf and Hart's. So for not getting mentioned I got a free dinner at Dierdorf and Hart's."

Danko drives the train at the Zoo several days a week and does audio for KPLR Channel 11 on the weekends.

RICH DAULTON

"Radio Rich" Daulton, as he was later known, got his start in radio as an intern at KMOX. He was hired in 1970 after interning from SIU-Edwardsville. Daulton worked as Jim White's assistant and later wrote the news for John McCormick.

REX DAVIS

Rex Davis was one of KMOX's most beloved broadcasters, spending 35 years as the voice behind the Voice of St. Louis. He was the station's principle newscaster from 1946 until his retirement in 1981 at the age of 71.

For much of that time he was the morning news anchor, working the last dozen years with Bob Hardy in what might have been the most highly rated radio program in the country.

Davis' radio career began in 1931, when he was a 20-year-old student at the University of Cincinnati. His real name was Frank Zwygart. While at station WCKY, the sales manager began to worry about the name Zwygart. He wanted to sell him as a personality but was afraid the listeners would not even be able to spell his name when they wrote to him. He talked to Zwygart and asked, "How about changing your name to Rex, that's a simple name?" As he was trying to think of a good last name, he looked out the window and saw the 'Davis Laundry' truck on the street. From that moment on Frank Zwygart became Rex Davis on the air.

In his career, he reported mine disasters. He edited Edward R.

Murrow's copy. He directed CBS' coverage at political conventions, telling Mike Wallace what to do. In his long and distinguished career, three news events stand out, all of which happened while he was on the air.

Davis reported the glider accident which killed St. Louis mayor William Dee Becker in the early 1940s, the atomic blast that destroyed Hiroshima, and the assassination of President John Kennedy in Dallas in 1963.

When Kennedy was shot, Davis was so shocked after being handed the bulletin that he could not speak for a moment. After a brief pause he said, 'Ladies and Gentleman, I can't believe this, but President Kennedy has been shot.'

"I'll never forget that," said Alice English, who was the program director at KMOX. "I was sitting in my car at the Parkmoor eating some french fries when the news came over the radio. I immediately went back to the station. The newsroom sprang into action. Extra news people came in. Everyone was doing something to help get more information to Rex that he could use on the air."

Shortly after he came to KMOX in 1947 Davis had to cover a mine explosion that killed 111 men in Centralia, Illinois. He had the unpleasant task of going to the high school gym where the bodies were being stored.

He considered his favorite interview of all-time to be *Roots* author, Alex Haley, who was so impressed by Davis' knowledge and questions he said, "You actually read the book."

He said his worst interview was likely one with Earl Butz, the former Secretary of Agriculture, who got so upset with all of the commercial interruptions during the interview that he got up and walked out.

When Davis and Hardy worked together, the two professionals formed a team to get St. Louis up and off to work or school on time. Their show had a definite timetable, and people always were able to judge whether they were on time or late by knowing where they should be when "The Morning March" or Richard Evans' "Thought For the Day" came on the air.

One April Fool's Day, Davis played a practical joke on his listeners by playing "The Morning March" at 6:05 AM, almost an hour early. There was instant panic all over the area.

"One guy threatened to sue us," Davis said. "He said he jumped out of bed, stumbled over the dog and hit his head on the dresser."

Davis' career went a long way from the days his newscasts were sandwiched between *Our Gal Sunday* and *Ma Perkins* soap operas.

"When I did my first show on KMOX," said Dr. Armand Brodeur, a 40-plus year veteran on the station, "It was Rex Davis that had me in awe. I remember thinking, 'I'm going to be on the same radio station Rex Davis is on,' he was a prime talent in the media. He was a big star."

"Rex was Mr. Big on the station as far as the news went," said Lohnny Londoff, Sr., owner of Johnny Londoff Chevrolet, which has advertised for more than 40 years on KMOX. "He was like the Walter Cronkite of St. Louis. I was a good friend of his and I sold him a lot of cars. We would go out to dinner with our wives. Once I really tried to get him to do my advertisements. I said, 'Can you do them for me?' I knew he was limited to doing commercials for Famous Barr at the time, but I wanted him to do mine, also. He said I'd have to talk to Mr. Hyland, so I called him up and asked him to lunch. He said, 'No, I'll take you to lunch.' So we went to this exclusive country club, Bogey Hills, and we sat at this long conference table. He was on one end and I was on the other end. There was no one else there but us and the waiter and chef. I was working him like a yo-yo trying to get him to let Rex do my commercials. At the end of the meal he just said 'no is no,' and I've had my daughters, my sons, and Ozzie Smith doing the commercials."

It was Davis who came up with the idea to announce on the air when schools were closed because of bad weather.

"Rex and Bob worked in the newsroom before being paired up in the morning," said Re Hardy, Bob Hardy's widow. "They were always friends even back when the station was on Hampton. We'd go and have dinner with Rex and Susanne every once in a while. Both Rex and Bob had a great sense of humor. It would just be hilarious when they were out together. Mr. Hyland saw their sense of humor and he saw that they gelled together very well."

"Rex Davis was a very approachable person," said *At Your Service* host Anne Keefe. "Here is a story that was told about him. He was a singer, he used to sing with his church. He had a very nice baritone

voice. One time he was on with Jack Carney and they were talking about his singing. Carney said, 'Have you ever given a concert by yourself?' Rex said, 'No.' Carney said, 'Well, it's time you did,' and he started making phone calls on the air. They called Carnegie Hall to see how much it would cost to rent it out for the concert. Then he called a bus company to see how much it would cost to rent a bus. Carney wondered what it would cost to get scenery and operatic backdrops so they called up companies about that. I don't think they ever really did it, but it was just one of Carney's creative thoughts."

"When I was growing up, transistor radios were the thing," said Bill Hepper, a longtime listener. "I started listening to KMOX every day with Rex Davis and Bob Hardy the day I got my own radio, which was in the sixth grade. Before I got it, there was a contest on KMOX where they were giving away transistor radios. I listened every day and tried so hard to win a radio!"

"Rex and I worked together when Bob Hardy went on vacation," said newsman Emil Wilde. "Rex was very precise. He had certain things he wanted said and written in a certain way. I knew how he liked it and he was easy to write for."

"Rex Davis was the big one I remember on KMOX," said St. Louis bandleader Bob Kuban. "I remember listening to him when I was a kid. He had a show by himself when I was in grade school; it was a talk show. He was good."

Rex Davis and Bob Hardy were such a popular morning team that when Davis hit 65, the CBS mandatory retirement age, Hyland went to New York to pull some strings to keep the team together.

"I always remember being there for Rex's last show," said former sports coordinator Jim Holder. "It was Christmas Day. I came in and did my morning sportscast and I remember thinking, 'Hey, this is an honor to be working with an institution on his last day.' People sent in pastries that day and many people called the station.

"Rex was such a pro. He made everything seem easy, even the day he retired. He might have been a wreck inside, but he probably wasn't. He had his health, and his lovely wife when he retired. He picked a good time to go out. What an institution."

DUANE DAVISON

Duane Davison worked as a sports producer starting in June of 1985. The sports office at that time consisted of Bill Wilkerson, Bob Costas, Nancy Drew, Jim Holder, Charlie Sloes, Dan Kelly, and the baseball broadcast team.

"I did a lot of producing for Bob Costas, who at that time had started working in New York; so much of it was done over the long distance lines," said Davison. "I was really impressed with Costas. Despite all of the fame and attention he was getting at the time, he would take the time to talk to and help people who worked behind the scenes. The first time I met him he looked at me and stopped what he was doing to talk to me. A month later he came back into town and saw me and said, 'Hi Duane.' I was so surprised he remembered my name. I was just a producer, but he was nice to everybody."

Davison, who currently lives in Zionsville, Indiana, and serves on the city council, said one show stands out in his memory.

"Bob [Costas] had the idea to do a 'greatest moments in sports history' show," Davison said. "He said, 'Let's have a show where people call in and ask for their favorite sports events.' We made what we called the 'vault' and got sound effects like the squeaking of a vault being opened. The night before the broadcast we put all the sports moments that we could think of on a cart. [Carts were used for interviews and commercials. They are similar to eight track tapes.] Bob did not have time to do any prepping for the show. He just had me have the carts ready and when the next night came, we just planned to 'wing it.' We had about 50 or 60 carts with the plays on them and then other tapes standing by that we could draw from."

"Randy Karraker and Rob Silverstein were also involved with the broadcast," said Costas. "We produced the *Sports Flashbacks* show so I knew what surrounded these plays."

Listeners were able to call the station and ask for their favorite call. The calls were not screened ahead of time and Costas had no preparation.

"He was incredible. A caller would call and ask for a play and then while I was getting it ready, he started to expound on it," Davison said.

"He had no notes, but he could recall the day of the game, the temperature, the pitcher on the mound, whatever the situation was. A few of the plays were more obscure so it took me a while to find them. No problem, Bob just talked longer on the topic and then I rushed the tape on and it looked like we planned it that way. It was the single greatest show I ever produced on KMOX. We got such a good response I was surprised they did not decide to make it a regular feature."

VIRGINIA DAWES

When Robert Hyland named Virginia Dawes manager of KMOX in 1973, it marked the first time a woman had served as the manager of a CBS-owned and operated station.

For the three previous years Dawes had worked as an assistant to the general manager of both KMOX AM and FM with major responsibilities in general station management. She joined KMOX in 1964 as chief accountant. She also served as station controller and director of administration before being appointed manager.

TOM DEHNER

Tom Dehner was a newswriter at KMOX in the 1970s.

"I'll never forget one Christmas Eve, I was the on-air newsman," Frank Absher said. "Someone had messed up the schedule and John McCormick didn't come in until 2 AM leaving us with a two-hour block to fill beginning after the midnight newscast. We had no music or recorded shows available to us, so I opened up the phone lines after the news for a Christmas open line.

"Tom Dehner was on the news desk. He handled the phones, and it came off beautifully, sounding like it was planned. Neither of us had done it before, but this was the sort of thing our listeners expected, and they responded calling in and talking about their fondest seasonal memories."

BING DEVINE

Bing Devine hosted a show in 1963 and '64 when he was general manager of the Cardinals, then resumed the show in 1968 when he returned to St. Louis.

"I tried to interview personnel from other clubs," Devine said. "I'd make a point of calling them and doing a feature with them. Bernie Fox was my producer. I was glad to do the show because I'd grown up in St. Louis and I'd listened to KMOX since I was eight years old. Whenever I wanted to find out what was going on, I'd turn on the radio."

Devine was very instrumental in bringing Jack Buck to St. Louis.

"He was my broadcaster in Rochester when I was in charge of the Cardinals' Triple-A club there," said Devine. "When Anheuser-Busch bought the team, they wanted Harry Caray, but they also wanted a new voice [that wouldn't be so closely associated to Griesedieck Brothers like he was.] They solicited the minor league teams and asked us if we knew of anyone that was good. I told them about Jack. That was 1954 and I ended up following him to St. Louis in 1955."

DAN DIERDORF

Dan Dierdorf had been a part of KMOX since his playing days with the St. Louis football Cardinals. He did a show with quarterback Jim Hart, and later worked as a host of *Sports Open Lines* and *At Your Service* shows. He also got his start broadcasting football games by working on football Cardinals and Missouri broadcasts.

"One night Dan Dierdorf was hosting a *Sports Open Line* because the Cardinal game was in a rain delay," said Bob Costas. "He called me to help fill in the time."

It was about 6:15 because the Cardinals were in Pittsburgh to play the Pirates.

"When Dierdorf got me on the line, I said, 'If you were any kind of a man, you'd be down at Woofie's, "The Hot Dog With Dignity!" Costas said. He said, 'Well, why don't you meet me at Woofies at 6:45?' All this is on the air. So Dierdorf gets somebody to fill in and he leaves the radio station. He had a car phone, and he's broadcasting from the car. I got to Woofie's first and you should have seen the people. The parking lot is about the size of a postage stamp, yet there were about 500 people there. They all came down to say hello or get on the radio or find out about the 'Hot Dog With Dignity.' The owner of Woofies, the late Charlie Eisen, was in his glory. I got in and manned the drive-

through. When Dan came through, I popped out of the window to take his order. We did the whole broadcast from there, rating the hot dogs at Woofie's."

"Dan Dierdorf is a great guy and a great talent," said Chicago White Sox play-by-play man John Rooney, who worked at KMOX. "I'm good friends with him now, but I got off to a bad start the first time I met him."

Rooney had recently joined KMOX when he first met Dierdorf.

"Our producer said, 'Get hold of Dierdorf and have him interview Roger Staubach," Rooney said. " I could have interviewed him myself, but for some reason the producer told me to get Dan to do it, so I arranged it and told Staubach that Dierdorf would be interviewing him and it was all set up. Well, Dan thought I was going to conduct the interview and interview both him and Roger. So we get on the air and there's a pause and I go, 'OK, take it away Dan.' He's such a professional he went ahead and did the interview. It was a great interview, a nice conversation.

"The next day I'm at the ballpark and I hear Dierdorf talking about me. He's just ripping me because he thought I'd used him to get the interview with Staubach. I went over to him and said, 'Let me introduce myself. I'm John Rooney.' He told me how he felt and then I said, 'You better take this up with the producer.' And then he talked to him and got it all straightened out. What a way to meet Dan Dierdorf!"

Rooney worked with Dierdorf on many occasions, including University of Missouri football.

"One time we were up in the pressbox, on the air, and Mizzou was playing Wisconsin," said Rooney. "This was back when Marlon Adler was the quarterback. Dan says, 'If this guy kicks the field goal to come back and win it, I'll jump out of the booth. He kicked it, and Dan went 'Aaaaaaahhhh!' like he was jumping out."

"I remember he came into the sports office one day," said Joan Tabash, an intern at the time. "He shook my hand and I could not believe how big his hands were!"

"I worked with Dan Dierdorf and Bob Costas when I was at Busch Stadium," said Sports Commission president Frank Viverito. "It was in 1984-85 and they were doing their "Fearless Friday Frank Forecast." They went from stadium to stadium sampling and rating the hot dogs

and then reported on the air. We served Busch Stadium dogs to them on a silver platter and I think we came in second or third nationally, probably behind the Dodger Dogs and maybe Milwaukee's brats."

MICHAEL DIXON

Michael Dixon has been the host of the overnight show, from 2 AM until 5 AM, and many of the people listening in St. Louis and around the country likely don't realize the show originates in Phoenix, where Dixon lives, and not in St. Louis.

"It's funny because he does shows out of Phoenix on KTAR, a station there, and I am a regular on his show," said KMOX electronics expert Bob Heil, "And he does shows out of St. Louis for KMOX and I'm on those shows. There was some talk of Michael coming to St. Louis to get Bob Hardy's job when he retired, but when Bob died, nothing ever came of it. Mr. Hyland used to try to get him to move to St. Louis."

CHARLIE DOMOUROUS

Charlie Domourous was an engineer at KMOX for 28 years, retiring in 1993.

"He was a very generous man," said newsman Bob Hamilton. "Often he would go out and bring back food for everybody at the station. He loved to go to Amighetti's."

Besides the many hours he spent at the station, Domourous was interested in amateur radio. He was an amateur (ham) radio operator for 50 years and communicated with people all over the world.

Once he contacted King Hussein of Jordan, who then sent him a confirmation card lettered in gold and a certificate for contacting all of the Arab countries in a certain time frame.

"He got a lot of us interested in ham radio," said Hamilton. "Jim White is a big ham radio enthusiast and he often talked to Charlie about it. Another engineer, John Toler, got involved and they were always talking about it which got me interested."

"He was a very died-in-the-wool ham radio operator," said Bob Heil. "Charlie was a unique individual. He knew a lot about electron-

ics and a lot about the world. He lived with his sisters all his life. I went with him to a couple of ham conventions."

Domourous was a pro at all times. Though things could get hectic at KMOX, he, as well as all of the engineers, managed to do several jobs at once to insure that the station stayed on the air 24 hours a day.

"One time I was supposed to be on in the 8 o'clock hour," said Dr. Armand Brodeur. "I was there early and there was no engineer. It was getting closer to the time the show was about to start and I was getting worried. At 8 we had CBS news, then at six minutes after the hour, we had the local news, and my show was to start in six minutes. Nowadays it is different, but in those days the engineers worked the board, and no engineer, no show.

"All of a sudden Charlie Domourous came running in with about four seconds to go. Push, push, push, and we were on. It was unbelievable; he was so quick, just boom, boom and he was ready to go, and the listeners knew nothing about it."

Domourous died of a heart attack in 1998.

TIM DORSEY

Tim Dorsey began his career at KMOX as an account executive in 1975, and worked his way up to station manager. He got an indication of what working for Robert Hyland would be like when he was hired for his first job at 5 AM. "It was the only time he had time to see me," Dorsey said.

Years later, when Dorsey's phone rang at 3:30 AM, he knew before he answered who was calling. "His first line was always, 'Did I wake you?' Dorsey said.

Dorsey learned to expect those calls, and to expect the unusual from Hyland, such as the time Hyland called at 3:30 AM and told Dorsey that he was booked on a 6:30 AM flight to Miami to attend a CBS managers' meeting. "He didn't want to go," Dorsey said. "That was the way he did things."

Dorsey spent 16 years at KMOX and spent much of that time working closely with Hyland. His office was in the same area of the building,

and he marveled at the people whom Hyland talked to during an average day.

"His life was spent with his telephone in his ear," Dorsey said. "If he wasn't talking to a senator or a congressman, he was talking to Gussie Busch or Billy Graham. The people he talked to in an average day was just amazing.

"I loved going to work every day. I was the happiest guy in the world because every day brought something different. Watching Hyland operate was like going to the movies. He was a wonderful actor."

Whenever Hyland had an assignment that he didn't want to fulfill, he passed it along to Dorsey. It naturally fell that Dorsey was involved in having to help find the successor to Jack Carney when Carney died.

"We searched the universe," Dorsey said. "One of the first guys we went to was the late Bob Collins, who was the morning guy on WGN in Chicago. He was the king of Chicago. He didn't take the job, but he parlayed it into a big money deal in Chicago."

KMOX ended up hiring Mike Murphy, who had been very popular in Kansas City. "Hyland liked the guy so much he actually went to dinner with him, which was very unusual," Dorsey said.

Murphy lasted on the air for two weeks, being forced to resign after an incident on the air. It was Dorsey's job to take him to dinner at Busch's Grove and tell him he was being let go.

Dorsey had no intention of leaving KMOX, until he received an offer to work for Charter Communications, which at the time was involved in a radio venture. When that didn't work out and Charter chose to stay involved with television properties, Dorsey went back into radio, first taking over WIBV in Belleville and then moving the station to KTRS.

"Tim Dorsey was a big help to me when I was at KMOX," said John Rooney, who went on to the CBS network. "He was heavily involved in sales. If Tim was telling me to do something, I would think, 'It's gotta be right.' He really knew the business. I did the sports updates for the FM, that's how I got to know him."

FRANCES P. DOUGLAS

Frances P. Douglas was the news director at KMOX from 1940 until

1944, joining the station after spending 16 years as the city editor of the *St. Louis Globe-Democrat*.

After his days at KMOX he went back into the newspaper business, serving in various capacities as a reporter and editor with the *Washington Evening Star*. He was a member of the White House Correspondents Association.

He died of a heart attack in 1969 at the age of 71.

PAUL DOUGLASS

Paul Douglass spent many years in the KMOX sales department, and he also appeared on the air as the analyst on the football Cardinals' games when they moved to St. Louis from Chicago.

"He was doing the color on our first exhibition game in 1960," said Joe Pollack. "We were playing the Baltimore Colts in Charleston, South Carolina. We kicked off and it was a squib kick. Douglas was in the background, but he started yelling, 'Fall on the ball, fall on the ball.' He got more excited and said loud enough you could hear it on the air, 'Get that SOB.'"

OLLIE DOWELL

Ollie Dowell started working at KMOX April 1, 1997, the same day Clarence Harmon was elected mayor of St. Louis.

"My first assignment was to cover his victory celebration at Carpenter's Hall on South Hampton," she said. " My reporting of the event and numerous contacts in the city established me as a political reporter. I was eventually assigned to cover City Hall, the Board of Aldermen, and Mayor Harmon. Harmon apparently appreciated my fair coverage because two years later, he offered me a job as his press secretary, but I turned him down."

Dowell is a former television reporter and anchor.

"Among my biggest stories," she said, "President Bill Clinton and the candidates for president, and an RCGA trip to Denver, Colorado. I've watched a dead downtown St. Louis develop into a thriving and energizing place to work and play."

PEGGY COHILL DRENKHAHN

Peggy Cohill Drenkhahn started in 1975 and has been an executive producer for *At Your Service* for nearly 25 years.

"In the early days of *At Your Service* we only had one executive producer," said Drenkhahn. "We only did the programming from 1 o'clock to 3 o'clock in the afternoon so we only needed one. As the years have gone by, we do so many shows that we currently have four executive producers."

One of the programs Drenkhahn produces is the *Newsmakers* show with Charles Jaco.

"It's a good workday," she said. "From the time we start in the morning until it's over. We go like dynamite."

When something happens nationwide or worldwide, KMOX localizes the story as well as tries to get national or international guests on the air.

"I remember the Oklahoma City bombing," Drenkhahn said. "I had a doctor's appointment and when I came back it had all broken lose. Everybody was sitting there trying to book guests. Charles Jaco was the main anchor and everyone was trying to get guests to go on with him."

Another big event she remembers working on was the earthquake in 1989 in San Francisco which took place in the evening during a World Series game.

"We all came in," she said. "It happened at night and I was at the airport picking up my husband. I remember we were waiting for his luggage and we heard about it. My husband went home and I went to the office. When I got there everybody was there.

"They just knew to come. It was really hard to get people on because it was at night and we didn't know people's home phone numbers."

How do they get hold of people at a moment's notice? They have a main index in the newsroom computer and in addition to that everyone has their own set of phone numbers. Some people use notebooks, some use palm pilots.

"Another event I remember was the flood of 1993," said Drenkhahn. "Nan Wyatt was anchoring a talk show. She went out on a boat into

the flood areas. She was talking to the people, seeing what had happened, what their dreams were after the flood. It was live reporting from that boat, she had the microphone right there with the people in the floods.

"We have meetings to plan on what we will do and how to fine-tune the programming. It's a privilege to work with these people. We have an excellent staff of the best talent in the country. I'm honored to work there."

NANCY DREW

To answer the most frequently asked question first—yes, Nancy Drew was her real name.

Drew shared the name with the famous fictional detective but also was known for becoming the first female sportscaster on KMOX and one of the first in the country.

Drew did sportscasts, hosted the *Saturday Sports Showcase* and even did some play-by-play hockey and soccer assignments with the St. Louis Blues and Steamers. She also did locker room interviews for the football Cardinals. She loved golf and covered the local golfers as much as possible.

"I remember a KMOX softball game," said Bob Costas. "The KMOX softball team was playing a team like the St. Louis Police Benevolent Association. So we all go down there. Nancy was there. I was there. At that time there was a separation between KMOX radio and television. Mr. Hyland didn't like his people doing TV, so people generally didn't know what many of the people looked like.

"Nancy was in her 20s, as I was, and she was very poised and professional. Later I was listening to *Sports Open Line* and this guy calls in and he had been to the softball game and had seen Nancy. He said 'This is the sort of woman that men went to war for!' He was on with Bob Burnes, and Burnes played it straight, 'Yes, she's a lovely woman, we're fortunate to have her on our staff.'"

"The thing I remember about Nancy Drew," said Joan Tabash, an intern in the 1980s, "was that the rest of the sports department treated her like one of the guys. She knew a lot about sports."

"She would come in during the newscasts," said newsman Emil Wilde. "I would always throw it to a sports person at the end of my newscast and she was one of them. She was a good person."

"She was a good scout," said Jim Holder who worked with her in the sports department. "I'll never forget this one Big Red football game at Soldier Field in Chicago. It was so cold. Nancy and I flew up together. Steve Piszarkiewicz was the quarterback and Ottis Anderson lost the rushing title that day. It was just so awfully cold and we were there to do the locker room interviews. Nancy was just a good scout about it, never complaining."

One night, Drew was sitting in the KMOX booth during a baseball game at Busch Stadium with the wife of Cardinals' announcer Bob Starr, Brenda, when someone noticed the two women and asked Jim Toomey, the team's public relations director, if he knew who they were.

"Well, you're not going to believe me," Toomey said. "But that's Nancy Drew and Brenda Starr."

Drew was married to football Cardinal Hall-of-Famer Larry Wilson. She worked at KMOX from 1978 until 1986 when she moved with Wilson to Phoenix when the football Cardinals moved to Arizona.

DAVE DUGAN

A journalism professor at the University of Missouri in Columbia, Dave Dugan was a former network correspondent at CBS who became a regular substitute host and newscaster on KMOX.

Dugan came to Missouri to be the founding general manager of public radio station KBIA. The station was used as a lab for journalism students. Dugan started as associate professor and later was promoted to full professor and Chair of the Broadcast News department.

"As part of my job, I visited radio and television stations throughout the state, looking for jobs for graduates of the journalism school," said Dugan. "That led me to Mr. Hyland's office. He said I should work part-time for KMOX while I was at the university, and that it would only be a matter of time before I worked full-time for KMOX. I worked part-time from 1972 to 1986."

When Dugan worked part-time, it was to fill in for somebody, often for Bob Hardy. He enjoyed working with Wendy Wiese, who made him laugh harder one day than he had in 45 years of broadcasting.

"I never laughed so hard as the day Wendy did a dance in the studio," Dugan said. "She contorted herself the way Jim Carrey does and I couldn't stop laughing as I tried to finish the newscast."

Dugan, being a network professional, rarely had trouble keeping his composure.

"The only other time anyone tried to break me up while I was on the air was when Jack Carney mooned me while I was reading a newscast," Dugan said. "Jack was the most talented raconteur I ever heard on the radio, but his mooning didn't have an impact."

Dugan had fun working with Wiese and Bill Wilkerson when he filled in for Hardy.

"Wendy and Bill were hilarious, on just a normal day," he said. "When Bob Hardy was away, I insisted that Bill sit in Bob's chair and set the pace for morning drive. During those times, it was as if Wendy and Bill had a substitute teacher in the classroom. They really cut loose, off the air as well as on."

Dugan's wife had always dreamed of having an ocean-view home in California, so he quit his position at Missouri and KMOX to move there. After Bob Osborne died, Hyland persuaded Dugan to come to St. Louis as the program director, and he stayed for three years.

"Dave Dugan was very smart," said Barb Felt. "He stayed with the university long enough to get tenured. He came back and took over Bob Osborne's spot as program director after Bob died, and stayed with CBS until he was tenured there, too. After that he moved to California and did some free-lance work."

"The most dramatic program I was involved in was an evening call-in program with a Russian broadcaster in Moscow," Dugan said. "This was when the hard-line Communists were attempting to regain control of the government. The broadcaster was Sergei, the broadcaster with whom Bob Hardy had done his monumental broadcasts."

Dugan got to accept a major award for the station while he was there.

"KMOX was named by the NAB (National Association of Broad-

casters) as the winner of the Marconi Award, as the best news-talk station in the country," Dugan said. "When accepting the award, I mentioned that it was really for Robert Hyland. A couple of years later, the NAB named Hyland the executive of the year."

Dugan is now semi-retired, teaching business ethics to corporations in the Kansas City area.

BOB DUNHAM

Bob Dunham was narrator of the live production on KMOX called *The Land We Live In*. He also asked the questions on a number of quiz shows, and served as host for most of the station's other major productions.

ALICE ENGLISH

Alice English was the program director in 1958 when Robert Hyland began running editorials on the station. She wrote the editorials after he gave her his ideas. English was on staff from 1956 to 1969, but after leaving continued to write the editorials until shortly before Hyland's death.

She started out in promotion, writing sales presentations. When the station changed formats to begin talk radio, she worked as a program director and producer for the *At Your Service* programs.

"Things were so different in those days with talk radio," she said. "You had much more control over what was going to be said. A guest would be selected and then questions were written and given to the guest ahead of time so they could be prepared. The host was also given a lot of background information as well as the questions. We tried very hard not to be sensational. We were there to inform, not just for the entertainment of it."

If a congressman were to be on they would talk about what bills were up for consideration.

"One of the most exciting guests we landed on KMOX was Eleanor Roosevelt the first time when she was on with Bob Hardy," said English. "Congressman Tom Curtis, who was very prominent in the Congress in those days was also on, as well as Mayor Tucker and Senator Danforth. There were lots of political figures, but also doctors and scientists. There was just so much emphasis on learning about things that were current, getting more information. The discussions were factual, not sensational."

During the late 1950s and early 1960s there were the racial tensions.

"There was a lot of racial tension in the city," said English. "At one time there were some sit-ins at the banks. Bill Clay, who later became a congressman, was on the Board of Alderman. He was demonstrating against some of the banks on their loan policies. There were lots of civil rights stories like these. We tried very hard to be very sensitive. We tried not to let the discussions escalate into name calling."

When Hyland started doing his editorials, he went straight to English because he liked working with her on the business presentations. He could give her his input and she could write things the way he would have done it.

"We would meet and I'd submit four or five ideas for editorials," she said. "He would always choose the topics. He'd say, 'This is my opinion on this,' or, 'This is what I want to say,' and I researched the facts, looked everything up, and then wrote the editorials.

"The purpose of the editorials was to make KMOX as big a factor as the daily newspapers in St. Louis, to make the radio station a major media in people's minds."

Earlier in her broadcasting career, English had worked as a newscaster on KSD-TV as the first woman newscaster on St. Louis television. Today English lives in Hot Springs, Arkansas, where she is in a local government position, similar to the Board of Aldermen.

"Now I'm on the other side of the microphone," she said.

AVA ERLICH

Ava Erlich, who went on to become a producer at KSDK, was a news reporter at KMOX in 1976 and 1977.

"Ava did a good chunk of the writing for the morning drive show with Rex and Bob," said John Amann. "She wrote many of the series that were on the morning show. Anne Keefe would do the voices along with Bob Hardy."

THE MIGHTY 'MOX

STUART ESROCK

Stuart Esrock started as an intern in 1979, and news director John Angelides was so impressed he told him that KMOX would hire him after his college graduation. Esrock worked for four years at KMOX and then went on to get his masters degree and doctorate. After one year at the University of Kansas, he is now a professor of journalism at the University of Louisville.

"My most memorable story was the day President Reagan got shot," said Esrock. "It was total chaos and confusion. I was sent to the New Cathedral. There was a prayer service that started immediately. It was a real outcry for people. I went there to cover it. You couldn't record inside, but I went in there and listened to the service. I went to the offices in the Archdiocese to use the phone to call in my interviews."

Esrock was also working the day the man parachuted off the Gateway Arch.

"I used to have to work overnights once a week, working with John McCormick on Friday nights," he said. "It was hard to change the sleep schedule, so by 4 in the morning I'd be getting bleary-eyed and be on my seventh cup of coffee, anything to try to keep myself awake. I was sitting there like a zombie, Billy Bidwill was there with me. The phone rang and someone said, 'Did you just see what happened? Someone tried to parachute off the Arch and they slid down.' We were always getting crazy calls, so I thought, 'Yea, right.' Well, we glanced out the window and I said, 'Oh my God!' and I grabbed my tape recorder. There were some security guys there and they'd checked the man and saw he was dead so they covered him with a blanket. I got there before the emergency vehicles. I got the basic facts and called the station. We got it on the air, literally 10 minutes after it happened."

One of the people Esrock interviewed had watched the accident, and he was able to feed the story to the CBS network.

"This guy was driving across the bridge into St. Louis and saw this person parachuting down," Esrock said. "He slowed down as he saw him parachuting, but then watched in horror as he landed on the Arch and slid down. He drove straight to the scene to try to help the guy."

Esrock enjoyed working at KMOX because he loved the camaraderie among the employees.

"We would have these great Uno games up in the lunch room. The regular crowd was Mike Owens, Jan Macchi [Fox], Peggy Cohill [Drenkhahn], Dave St. John, and myself," Esrock said. "We'd be up there playing on our breaks and Jack Carney would stick his head in and roll his eyes at us. A couple of times he'd bring a boat load of food, that he'd gotten from one of his sponsors."

Another major story Esrock covered was the car-bombing which killed George "Sonny" Faheen in the Mansion House garage.

"We all heard the 'boom' in the newsroom when we were working," said Esrock. "I think Joan [Beuckman] took the call. She sent Dave St. John and me over in one of the news cars. I'll never forget when we got there, you could see it was a Volkswagen. It was the first news story I ever covered. Ellen Sherberg had kind of gone over a script with me. She wanted to help me and be sure I repeated the lead after I did my voicer. When we got there, there were tons of cops all around. The car was totally charred, it was still smoldering. We got the details and reported back."

RICHARD EVANS

Richard Evans had one of the most unusual careers in the history of KMOX. Thanks to tape recordings, he continued his "Thought for the Day" messages five mornings a week for 26 years after he was dead.

For most of his adult life, Evans was the voice of *The Spoken Word*, a program broadcast on the CBS network from Temple Square in Salt Lake City. The sermons were so popular that Robert Hyland persuaded Evans to re-record them in short two-minute clips.

Evans did so, eventually putting about 1,900 messages on tape, a seven-year supply. When he died in 1971, the station didn't give any thought to pulling his messages off the air and so they remained, running each day at 6:55 AM, for another 26 years.

Even when listeners learned that the messages were recorded, and that Evans had been dead for years, they didn't want the station to drop him. In 1996, when the *Post-Dispatch* asked in a poll if KMOX should

keep Evans or drop him, the vote was 1,409 to keep him with only 257 voting to drop him.

The topics for the sermons were practical everyday advice dealing with such subjects as love, marriage, raising children, and managing money.

"Most radio stations in America today couldn't get away with doing that because most radio stations don't have the kind of heritage KMOX has," Michael Harrison, editor and publisher of *Talkers Magazine*, a trade publication, told *The Wall Street Journal* in 1997. "People in St. Louis look to that station to give them a certain sense of stability, continuity. It's a station with roots."

Nothing lasts forever, however, and one of the changes general manager Karen Carroll made was to drop Evans. First she moved him to an earlier time slot, and then replaced the messages with other programming.

JACK ETZEL

Jack Etzel was a host of *At Your Service* programs in the 1970s and also worked for a time as the station's public relations director.

FRANK B. FALKNOR

Frank B. Falknor was appointed general manager of KMOX by CBS to succeed Merle Jones in 1944. He was a lieutenant colonel in the Army, and at the time, was serving as an engineer with the Office of Strategic Services in China.

Considered an expert in the field of radio transmission, Falknor served as GM for less than a year before he was replaced by Wendell Campbell.

BARB FELT

Barb Felt started in sales at KMOX-FM in 1973 and then was moved to KMOX-AM shortly thereafter.

"I sold with a unique technique," said Felt. "I would make spec spots (sample commercials) for the accounts I was calling on and bring them in with me. I'd glean the information from the newspapers or other ads. Mr. Hyland had heard about this and had Bob Osborne contact me."

After she began selling for KMOX-FM, Hyland decided he needed a female on the AM sales staff so he transferred her.

"It turned out to be a 'token' job," she said. "I was the only woman, although there had been others including Sue Anderson and Gert Bunches. They gave me the house accounts and it was not a good experience. I asked to be moved and they put me in research and promo-

tions. That was much better. I put together presentations for the sales force and when there was an opening for sales manager of the FM station, Mr. Hyland gave it to me."

Felt left KMOX to run her own recording studio, and is now semi-retired and living in St. Louis.

HARRY FENDER

Harry Fender, who later became known as "Captain 11" on KPLR-TV, and whose voice was heard every night before the Muny productions, worked at KMOX from 1948 until 1969.

Fender had a daily record show in the late 1940s which was broadcast live from his apartment. In the 1950s he was the host of *The Harry Fender Show* from the Steeplechase Room at the Chase Hotel at night.

"You could go to the Chase and watch his show," said Adelle Burnes, widow of *Globe-Democrat* sports editor Bob Burnes. "Harry Fender played records and talked. It was on late at night."

Clarence Nieder produced those shows.

"Harry would do a show from the Steeple Chase from 10:30-1:30 AM," said Nieder. "Then they would have news for about 15 minutes and we would all run up to his apartment on the fourth floor and continue broadcasting the show from there. There was a turntable for records, and he also had some interesting guests.

"One was Christine Jorgenson, the man who turned into the woman. She came to his apartment to do the show. Eddie Howard, the big band leader, also came. Once Eddie Holloran [another big band leader] had an early morning flight to Chicago so he stopped by and was on."

"Harry Fender was very eccentric," said Emil Wilde who did the news for KMOX for nine years. "He would wear things they wear in Europe. I saw him when we would have something extra and he'd be there."

Fender and Jack Carney were good friends. He was like a grandfather to Carney's son, John. Fender enjoyed his time with John Carney when Carney would come to town as a youngster to visit his father. They would hit golf balls, visit the Muny Opera, or hang around the Chase. When Jack Carney died, Fender told the newspaper he considered Jack to be his best friend.

"Before working in St. Louis, Harry had a pretty illustrious Broadway career," said John Carney. "He was in *Ziegfield Follies*. He was their leading man, but Harry had incredible stage fright. He would get physically sick before he went on stage. Here he was their leading man and he had stagefright. Fanny Bryce, Clark Gable, he ran with all those people and he did shows with all those people.

"It got to a point where he would get so physically ill he decided he didn't want to do it anymore. He was probably making 80 grand a week in the 1930s and he just walked away. He didn't want to do it anymore. He came to St. Louis to be a cop. Took like a 900 percent pay cut to leave show business and all those women so that people could shoot at him. Now figure that one out! He got lured back into show business by Robert Hyland. He did that show at the Steeplechase and anyone who was anyone stopped by."

Fender hated to give out his age. One of his frequent replies to that question was to say he was an usher the night Lincoln was shot.

SALLY FITZ

Sally Fitz was a reporter for KMOX in the 1970s. She left KMOX for a television job in Florida, and now is living with her husband and child in Chicago.

ART FLEMING

The original host of the popular television show, *Jeopardy*, Art Fleming became a popular talent on KMOX. Robert Hyland originally had Fleming fly in periodically for day-off relief before he began working on a regular basis and stayed at KMOX for 12 years, from 1980 to 1992.

Fleming was touring the United States hosting the *College Bowl* television show. Bob Costas who was working at KMOX at the time and was a big fan of *Jeopardy*, so he went to Washington University to watch the taping of *College Bowl*.

"I went up to him and met him," said Costas. "I asked him to come on my show, which he did. Mr. Hyland heard the show and came to

me afterward and asked me, 'How do you know Art Fleming?' I said, 'I don't; I just met him and asked him to come on my show.' The next day he hired him to work at KMOX."

"I remember that day, I was walking around the station," said Clarence Nieder, a longtime producer. "I look up and there is this face I recognize from TV. It was Art Fleming. He said, 'Could you make a tape for me?' With all of his credentials Mr. Hyland still made him do a five-minute demo tape."

"I really enjoyed Art Fleming," said KMOX listener Bill Hepper. "He had a gentle manner. He was always so polite to the people who called, and he was knowledgeable. Art Fleming wasn't one of KMOX's big stars, but I really liked listening to him."

"He was a little old-fashioned," said Costas. "He'd say things like, 'Thank you very much friends, we'll see you tomorrow, God willing.'"

"When Art came to KMOX in 1980, they paired us up together," said David Strauss, known on KMOX as Mr. Trivia.

It was a natural, Mr. Trivia and the guy who used to host *Jeopardy*.

"We became a mainstay on Sunday nights," said Strauss. Fleming also worked as the co-host of *Total Information PM*, hosted the morning program with Mary Phelan, and also spent a year as host of *The Morning Meeting*, working with Charles Brennan and Kevin Horrigan.

"He could do things with that voice and a piece of copy that were wonderful," Horrigan said after Fleming died. "He could read a Prairie Farms cottage cheese commercial and make you run out to buy some even if you hated cottage cheese."

Rene Servier remembers a show she did with Fleming that turned out to be a lot harder than it was supposed to be.

"He had an author on, who had written a trivia book," she said. "We had promoted the show as a 'trivia' show. Trivia, *Jeopardy* host, it's a natural, should be a real fun, successful show. Well, Art asked him, 'So who won the Davis Cup in 1984? The guy said, 'I don't know.' Art says, 'Well, it's in your sports section of YOUR book. And the guy goes, 'Well great, so who was it?' So Art says, 'It's on page 84 of your trivia book,' trying to help the guy out. He goes, 'I actually don't know anything about trivia. Trivia by its name is unimportant. This book came around because I had my college kids doing research and these are the things they came up with. My students did all the work.'"

They had only been on the air for four minutes at this point.

"Suddenly the 'bat phone' rang," said Servier. 'Get rid of him!' said Hyland. 'Get rid of who?' I asked him sort of confused. 'I need to talk to Art Fleming.' So he made us pull the guest and here we were with 45 minutes to fill and it's Art Fleming holding a trivia book. I'm certain that whoever booked the guy was told at the Monday morning meeting never to book him again."

CBS sportscaster John Rooney, who worked at KMOX at the same time as Fleming, remembered how thoughtful Art was.

"First of all, I thought meeting Art Fleming was a real thrill," said Rooney. "But I remember one special night in 1980 where everyone thought baseball was headed for a strike. The strike deadline was 2 AM and I'd been working on the story all day and all night.

"Art Fleming comes into the station that night from the theater and he was going to do a short voicer on the show. He sees me working and comes in, 'Hey, can I help you with anything? You've been here all day and you're by yourself, can I write anything for you?' I said, 'Thank you very much, Art, but that's OK.' I was so shocked, here is Art Fleming trying to help some punk kid. I just thought that was so nice. That is the thing I liked about him. I hate people with big egos that let fame go to their heads. Some of the most famous people have egos but they don't let them change their personalities, that's how Art was."

Rudy Ruzicka was the engineer for many of Fleming's shows. "Nothing could upset Art Fleming," he said. "One day he was doing the *At Your Service* at 2 o'clock in the afternoon. Art said, 'Your question or comment.' A fellow called in and somehow got on the air and said, 'I understand Bob Hyland has a bad case of terminal diarrhea.' Art just simply said, 'Thank you for calling sir,' and went on. It wasn't a minute later that the phone rang and it was Mr. Hyland."

"Art Fleming was one of the nicest and classiest men I've ever known," said Costas. "Later on when he lived in Florida, I got together with him when I was down there. He was dying of cancer and in all kinds of pain and discomfort, but he never told me, he never said anything. He disguised it. There was a kind of quiet courage in that. He was a remarkable guy, a really good guy."

Fleming died in 1975 at the age of 70.

PAT FONTAINE

Pat Fontaine was a weather announcer in the late 1960s.

BERNIE FOX

Bernie Fox was a sports producer for KMOX.

"I used to work closely with Bernie," said Alice English, program director in the late 1950s. "The scheduling was hard with the sports broadcasts. There were all sorts of conflicts. We'd work to figure out how to fill the time."

KMOX had regularly scheduled *At Your Service* programming, but if there was a baseball game, for example, the 7 PM to 10:30 PM regular programming would be bumped to broadcast the game. If the game went long, that would go into the programming time, but the bigger problems came when the games were too short.

"If there was a rain delay," said English, "we had to figure out what to get on the air. Bernie was a wonderful sports producer. We had so many great sports experts and he did a great job."

Fox was in charge of the sports programming in the studio, but his most important job was producing the Cardinal baseball games and other sports events.

"Bernie was in charge of all the sports," said sales manager Bob Canepa. "He had this big bulletin board. He would have all the sports teams and pins and people's names on it. That's how he kept it all straight. It was amazing how he managed it all."

Joe Pollack, who worked with Fox on the football Cardinals' broadcasts, never thought Fox received enough credit for all of the work he did at the station.

Fox, like almost everybody else on the KMOX staff, really had only one job—to do whatever Hyland asked him to do.

Frustrated at having to stop at so many traffic lights as he was leaving KMOX, Hyland one time told Fox to find out who the traffic engineer was in St. Louis—and to get him to coordinate the stoplight patterns so he would not have to stop so many times before he got to the highway.

"When Bernie retired," Canepa said, "Mr. Hyland said 'we have to get him some golf clubs,' so he sent me out to get them."

JAN (MACCHI) FOX

Jan Fox had many jobs at KMOX, from executive secretary to director of the KMOX Big Red Line, the football Cardinals' cheerleaders.

One of her responsibilities was to serve as secretary to Jack Buck and help Bob Costas with his fan mail. Costas' fan mail was no easy task.

"He was young, and he was so disorganized in those days," said Fox, who now works at KTRS. "He would get so much fan mail, it was overwhelming for him. But he wanted to answer each letter, so after the letter drawer piled so high and he put them in boxes, about every two months we would answer the letters."

Each sportscaster had a file drawer they could use as their personal drawer (as opposed to having your own desk). Nancy Drew would put her purse in hers. Bob Costas's drawer was so jammed with mail that he could barely get it open to add another letter.

"Bob would box the letters up and have me over to his apartment and we ordered Chinese and went over the letters," said Fox. "We went over every single letter and he answered every one personally. He was a riot. Every letter would start with some sort of a witty anecdote about why it was so late. Some people didn't get replies for a month and a half, but everyone who wrote to Bob Costas got an answer unless it got lost in the mail."

And while on the subject of Bob Costas' mail:

"I remember someone wrote a letter to Hyland in 1976," said Costas. "He gave it to me and said it must be from a fan of mine. The letter said things like, 'All of the people on KMOX are wonderful, like Jack Buck, Bob Hardy, Rex Davis, they're all wonderful except that Bob Costas.' And then the letter went on to say they thought I was 'the most horrible, arrogant, conceited, sarcastic, terrible person KMOX had ever had. He is the worst human being you ever put on KMOX.' I still have that letter and it hangs in a place of honor in my home, in one of my bathrooms. In every place I have lived it's hung over a toilet."

Fox was indispensable for a sports department that had so many stars at the time. Each one of them had many speaking engagements, play-by-play assignments, fan letters, and just generally had many people constantly tugging at them. Fox wore a pleasant smile every day and was always willing to do whatever she was asked.

"That was a really fun sports department," she said. It was the days of Bill Wilkerson and Bob Costas sharing the duties of the *Sports Open Lines*. Gary Bender did the morning sports, Nancy Drew was there, Jim Holder coordinated it, Dan Kelly did the Blues games and came in for *Open Lines*. Jack Buck did the Cardinals and occasionally *Open Lines*. "That was when the sports department was really great."

Jan Fox's duties changed when public relations director Jeannie Whitworth retired. Fox took over as director of the Big Red Line.

"I did it for 10 years," she said. "The Big Red Line was KMOX's. It wasn't like the Dallas Cowboys whose cheerleaders were owned by the team. KMOX lent the Big Red Line to the Cardinals. When they went out for promotions, they represented KMOX."

CATHY GAMBLE

Cathy Gamble was the director of finance for KMOX for many years. She assumed the job of interim general manager after Hyland's death, before Rod Zimmerman was brought in from CBS as the new general manager. She left KMOX to join Fox Sports.

BILL GAINEY

Bill Gainey worked in sales at KMOX from 1973 until 1994. He served as an account executive, general sales manager, and director of sports marketing, which had him selling the baseball Cardinals, Blues and Missouri football games.

"I remember when I first met Dan Kelly," said Gainey. "I introduced myself and he asked me if I was related to Bob Ganey, the hockey player. I told him he was my brother (even though we spelled our last names differently) and he thought it was really neat. About a year later I confessed and he got a kick out of it."

Gainey said the personalities of the station would help the sales people and go on sales calls if it would help get the sale.

"One night after the Cauliflower Ear dinner, I was invited to one of the hotel suites at the Chase Park Plaza," said Gainey. "It was a customer of mine. When I got up there, Jack Buck and Mike Shannon were there as they were friends of his. They had a big card game going on and I watched for a while.

"The next morning I had a sales call with Bob Wamser of Wamser-Firman Outdoor Equipment. Jack Buck was going to meet me there. He had his sunglasses on when he got there. I said, 'Jack, you can take off your sunglasses,' and he said, 'No, I can't, the card game went a bit long last night!' That's how nice all those guys were. No matter how tired they were they would do anything they could to help the sales people."

"One time Bill Gainey wrote a poem," said Casey Van Allen. "It was about baseball memories, about playing baseball with your father as a kid. He read it to Jack Buck. Now it doesn't take much to have him well up, or me either. Here we were both blubbering over listening as Bill read that poem. We recorded Jack reading it, and I produced it with music. It is one of the most requested pieces of Jack's work. Very touching. We play it at the beginning of baseball season or in the middle of the winter sometimes when we're going through baseball withdrawal."

JOE GARAGIOLA

Joe Garagiola was one of the first baseball players to go directly from the field to the broadcast booth, joining Harry Caray and Jack Buck on the Cardinals' games in 1955, the same year the broadcasts moved back to KMOX from KXOK.

"I worked for Joe and for Harry Caray, Gabby Street, Stretch Miller, and Jack Buck when they were on the broadcast team," said Bea Higgins who worked at the advertising agency which had the account for Busch beer.

"Occasionally I would go to the games and I would take my children," she said. "I always got to sit up next to Joe Garagiola's wife. She played the organ for the games."

Garagiola's lack of broadcasting experience showed at times, but he proved to be a quick learner and quickly advanced to prominence as a national broadcaster, working on *The Today Show*, along with his sports assignments.

One of his early shows at KMOX was a preview show before the Missouri football games.

"We had a show called *Pigskin Previews*, which Joe did," said former sales manager Bob Canepa. "It was a 10 minute feature before the Mizzou football game. I sold it with Joe Garagiola. That was the first show he ever got paid to do. It was to help him get used to working with producers, timing, etc."

The show was sponsored by 7-Up. It is sometimes the salesman's job to keep the sponsors happy so when 7-Up wanted Garagiola to come out to their bottling plant and talk to their truck drivers, Canepa got him to do it.

"Joe wasn't too thrilled about doing it at 7 in the morning and neither was I," said Canepa. "But 7-Up was a good sponsor, so we went. After I gave my spiel which they weren't too excited to hear, Joe talked and then took questions. One of the truck drivers tried to corner him into a racial conversation by talking about a play in a game which involved a black ballplayer. It didn't sit well with Joe. He didn't like that guy for trying to put him on the spot so he said, 'For saying a thing like that, I hope you have a flat tire on your truck!' Now that was a big thing to say to a bunch of union truck drivers. Everything turned out fine."

MARINO GARCIA

Marino Garcia was an engineer at KMOX for many years.

RAY GERACY

Ray Geracy was a sportscaster on KMOX. He did the commentary and later the play-by-play for the football Cardinals in the late 1960s.

"Ray Geracy was an interesting guy," said Jim Holder. "He was actually the mayor of a community outside of Chicago [Highland Park]. He was friends with the Bidwill family and he would come to St. Louis to do the games."

"Actually Stormy Bidwill was the one who hired him because he was a friend of Stormy's, who was Bill's brother," said Ron Jacober. "Back then the Bidwill brothers owned the Cardinals together. Stormy lived in the Chicago area and would come in on the weekends. Bill was here throughout the week. Ray Geracy would just come in to do the games."

WALT GLATTHAAR

Walt Glatthaar was the motor sports reporter at KMOX for 33 years, providing reports every Saturday and Sunday from race tracks in the area as well as around the United States and overseas. His reports were carried across the Internet and also on Armed Forces Radio.

"Almost every driver in the country, if not the world, knew Walt," said Ron Jacober.

Glatthaar's long association with KMOX began in 1966. He was hosting a Saturday morning motor sports show on WIBV in Belleville and got into a conversation with Bob Hardy. Hardy helped Glatthaar get an appointment to see Robert Hyland.

Glatthaar's wife, Patti, recalled her husband telling Hyland, "You're the Sports Voice of America, but you don't cover car racing." Hyland asked what event was going on that weekend, and it happened to be a USAC race in Phoenix.

"Mr. Hyland left the room and then came back and handed Walt an airline ticket to Phoenix," Patti Glatthaar said. Glatthaar reported on motor sports for KMOX from that day until June 27, 1999, the day before he died of an apparent heart attack. He was 71.

In addition to his work at KMOX, Glatthaar covered motor sports for ABC for 19 years, was manager of Team Ferrari at the Daytona and Sebring races, was press officer for the 12 hours of Sebring, was the American director of racing for STP, and co-founded the American Indy Car Series.

BOB GODDARD

Bob Goddard was a popular columnist for the *St. Louis Globe-Democrat* and he had a radio program on KMOX on Saturday nights.

"He didn't really pal around with the people from KMOX," said Tinker Reilley, a sales and promotions writer at KMOX when Goddard worked there in the mid-1960s. "He'd have guests on the show, whoever was in town."

Goddard's column in the *Globe* was well-read, called "Around Town" and had tidbits about events happening around St. Louis.

RALPH GRACZAK

Ralph Graczak worked on KMOX in a variety of positions, many times at night.

"His father was Ralph Graczak, who used to do 'Our Own Oddities' in the paper," said Elaine Stern, a producer at the station. "These young people who don't remember Our Own Oddities can't understand me when I try to explain it: 'He would have a picture of a weird looking potato and say it looked like someone.' Ralph the broadcaster is really laid back. You could go to sleep by his voice; I mean that is a compliment. It is an old fashioned, mellow, musical type of voice."

JEANETTE HOAG GRIDER

She was the producer of the morning show with Bob Hardy, Bill Wilkerson, and Wendy Wiese in the 1980s and 1990s. She started as a news intern in 1981 before getting a full-time position. Her primary jobs were booker/producer for Bruce Bradley and later Grant Horton on the 9 AM until noon show, and then *Total Information AM* with Hardy, Wilkerson, and Wiese until 1996.

"She was absolutely wonderful to work with," said KMOX electronics expert Bob Heil. "She screened the calls. She has done a lot of interesting things. Jeanette was very close with Bob Hardy and his wife, Rita."

"Early in my booking experience," said Grider, "there was a mix-up with a prominent military type who had been tentatively scheduled as a guest. As it turned out, the host didn't want to do the topic and I had to call and cancel. The guy was furious and said he was going to call Bob Hyland and have me fired. I was naïve enough to believe it was going to happen but got my courage together and decided to just go in and tell Hyland that the man was going to have me fired if the interview didn't take place. I remember the terror of going in to see him and my shock at his response, which was basically that no one was going to tell him how to run his radio station and that I had no reason to worry about being fired."

Grider worked with many different personalities including Anne Keefe, Jack Buck, and Hardy.

"There were so many stories," she said. "Jack Buck has a tremendous warmth when encountering groups of people. I remember him walking through the lobby as a group of Cub Scouts arrived to take a tour and he bent down and spent time talking with the kids even though he had other things to do. His on-air spontaneity when he hosted shows was terrific. He could almost make the unexpected seem as though he had planned it.

"On another occasion, a children's choir from a local church was going to sing some songs at the annual Christmas meeting and arrived early so we were walking them around for a little tour. Jack was on the air but saw them through the studio window and pulled them in to sing a song on the air."

Grider remembers an incident on April Fool's Day where even Robert Hyland got into the act.

"For all his blustery image, Mr. Hyland loved a great joke and participated in plenty of practical jokes on some of his employees. One April Fool's Day the members of one of the departments put together a fake internal memo telling the department head her private parking space under the building was going to be given to a new salesperson. Since the parking space was a status symbol of sorts and prized for its convenience, she was in a total uproar. When she came in and found the memo on her desk, she hurried into Hyland's office to discuss it. Her officemates called him on his hotline and when she came in, he kept the joke going to the point she really believed her parking space was gone before finally letting her in on the 'April Fool.'

"And then there was the story of the broadcaster who came in to audition for an on-air host position. About an hour before his shift, a huge 'bang!' was heard in the office area. Turns out he didn't realize the doors to the halls leading to the studio didn't swing both ways and he walked into it with such a force it shattered the glass. Hyland had him taken to the emergency room for stitches and then he did his on-air shift. Never got the job, though."

Grider, who continues to work with Wendy Wiese at KTRS, has many funny memories of her.

"One morning Wendy spilled a cup of coffee all over herself," said Grider. "She ended up having to wear somebody's trench coat. I can't remember if it was Mr. Hyland's or Bob Hardy's. We got so many laughs about that. Then there was the time she knocked a coffee onto a console resulting in some engineering rewiring problems. Needless to say, we got her a tippy cup after that."

Grider left KMOX in 1996 and is the executive producer at KTRS, booking guests for George Noory's evening program and she works with the news programs, hosts, and internship program.

ED GRIESEDIECK

Ed Griesedieck is the KMOX legal expert, and has been hosting *Ask the Lawyer* type shows since 1985.

"I was doing some volunteer work for the Bar Association of St. Louis and we were getting some lawyers to 'staff' the *At Your Service* off the air program on the weekends," said Griesedieck. "I got to know the ladies who ran the show pretty well. I acted as their unofficial legal advisor for their weekday stints."

When someone would call and they did not know the answer, they would give Griesedieck a call. For several years he was 'on call' in that capacity and then KMOX asked Griesedieck to try doing a show about law.

"KMOX did not have anyone doing a show like that," he said. "The lawyers they did have were generally for a specific topic. We originally thought the show would be something that they would do once a quarter with a host, but it expanded from that."

Today he usually does the show alone and even runs his own board. Earlier when he was doing the shows with hosts and he was the guest expert, one of his favorites was Anne Keefe.

"She was a favorite of mine because she rarely wanted to talk just about the law," he said. "She wanted to kick around other topics, like current events. It always kept you on your toes."

Griesedieck was a regular on Charles Brennan's shows when Brennan first started on KMOX. He was more of a help to Brennan than just providing him with legal expertise.

"He was new to town and didn't know anyone," said Griesedieck. "My wife introduced him to Beth, his wife, it was a blind date."

KMOX central engineers' board looking into studio, Kirkwood, Missouri (1925).
Courtesy of Media Archives, St. Louis Public Library

Pappy Cheshire and his bunch. *Courtesy of KMOX Radio*

KMOX announcer, France Laux, and Frankie Frisch (1934). *Courtesy of the Cardinals Hall of Fame Museum*

Roy Queen (1930s). *Courtesy of Media Archives, St. Louis Public Library*

KMOX announcer and *Globe-Democrat* columnist, Bob Burnes. Burnes did a sports program every evening starting in the 1950s, and later did *Sports Open Line. Courtesy of Media Archives, St. Louis Public Library*

Harry Caray and Harry Fender on *The Harry Fender Show* at the Chase. *Courtesy of KMOX Radio*

Cardinal broadcast team, Jack Buck, Harry Caray, and Joe Garagiola (1950s).
Courtesy of Media Archives, St. Louis Public Library

Robert Hyland looks on as Harry Fender blows out his birthday candles (1950s).
Courtesy of Media Archives, St. Louis Public Library

Bob Anthony (1960s). *Courtesy of Media Archives, St. Louis Public Library*

Tony Bello, Robert Hyland, Bob Holt, and Jack Buck (getting into a costume) at the Gridiron Dinner (1960s). *Courtesy of KMOX Radio*

Jack Buck does an inteview at the Zoo as Marlin Perkins looks on. *Courtesy of Media Archives, St. Louis Public Library*

Bob Osborne
(1960s). *Courtesy of
Barb Felt*

Don Miller with Copter One (1970s). *Courtesy of KMOX Radio*

Advertisement. *Courtesy of Jim Holder*

Jack Buck, Taffy Wilbur, Jim Butler, and Skip Caray on Old Newsboys Day. *Courtesy of KMOX Radio*

Bob Heil with Bob Hardy in their Shriners' hats.

Rex Davis and Dr. Thomas A. Dooley.

Bob Hardy interviews an official from NASA at McDonnell Douglas.

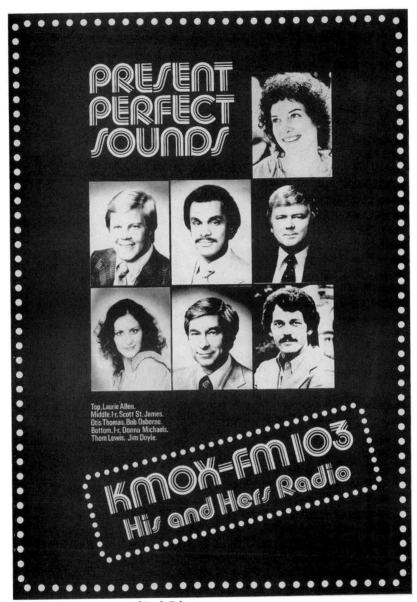

Advertisement. *Courtesy of Barb Felt*

Mary Phelan and Jim White. *Courtesy of the White family*

Bruce Bradley (left) with cleaning expert Don Ashlett. *Courtesy of Jeannette Grider*

Jack Carney and Phyllis Diller interview some children during a live broadcast at the Fox Theatre (1970s). *Courtesy of John Carney*

Jack Carney, Miss Blue, Jim Holder, Kathe Hartley, and Bob Chase on Old Newsboys Day. *Courtesy of KMOX Radio*

Dr. David Hoy with Jim White.

Colin Jarrette and Jack Carney with Carney's secretary, Katie Slade. *Courtesy of Jeannette Grider*

He remembers the days when Robert Hyland ran KMOX.

"In those days," he said, "If you were not taking enough calls during a show, the 'red phone' (also known as the 'bat phone') would ring and Mr. Hyland would tell you about the calls you had received and to speed it up. This could happen no matter what time of day or night."

CHESTER GRUBER

Listeners to KMOX in the 1930s knew Chester Gruber's voice, but they didn't know his name. He was known on the air as Tony Cabooch, and that was the name he used when CBS picked up his show beginning in 1930 and carried it to all of the network stations.

The "Anheuser-Busch Antics" was the first regularly scheduled show to originate from St. Louis. Gruber provided the voices of at least 15 characters. Prior to moving to radio, Gruber had spent 12 years on the stage, refining his acting dialects.

Gruber's show was an immediate success. In his first 14 weeks on the air, he received an estimated 42,000 fan letters.

The show ran on Wednesday and Friday evenings at 6:45 p.m. and was sponsored locally by the F.C. Taylor Fur Co.

PAUL GRUNDHAUSER

Paul Grundhauser was an engineer at KMOX, starting as a temporary worker in 1977.

"In those days, most of the engineers did either production or board operating duties," said Grundhauser. "I was no exception and I did both in those early days. I was laid off shortly after New Years Day in 1978, and was re-hired as a full-time staff engineer in March of 1978."

"He works so hard," said Bob Heil, KMOX electronics expert who, like Grundhauser, is a ham radio operator. "One time after I'd worked there for 30 years I realized I had never seen the KMOX transmitter and I was talking to Jim White who had worked there 20 years and not seen it. Paul took us over to see the new one he had just put up in Granite City, Illinois. He took us out to lunch and then to see the transmitter. I saw all the parts of the old one and other things they were throwing

away. I thought, 'Here's KMOX going into a dumpster'. I saw these wonderful old AMPEX's (tape recorders) and asked what they were going to do with them. Mr. Hyland said, 'I'm going to give them to KDHX or someone, why do you ask, do you want one? I said it would make Jeanette's (Jeanette Hoag, the producer) job easier if we had one of these. The next morning, there is Grundhauser sitting in my driveway with not one but all three of them!"

In 1986 Hyland appointed Grundhauser manager of technical operations (the chief engineer) and he has held that position since.

Grundhauser was an engineer who in 1990 traveled to the Persian Gulf on a plane loaded with military personnel and equipment for Dessert Shield for KMOX. He went with Bob Hardy and Kevin McCarthy as well as Larry Conners, John Martin, and Scott Thomas of KMOV-TV, producing and engineering the KMOX broadcasts. He has worked in all areas of engineering at KMOX including the Cardinal broadcasts.

"In 1990 I went with Bob Hardy to Eastern Europe," said Grundhauser. "We went to five capitals in five days: Berlin, Prague, Budapest, Warsaw, and Moscow. It was Monday through Friday. This was certainly the most complex set of remotes I have ever been involved with. Not only did you have the language barrier, but also the simple logistics of getting set up in a different country every day."

Grundhauser says his job has changed a lot over the years.

"It has changed dramatically over the last five or six years," he said. "A great deal of my time is now taken up with computer issues, and I'm the one they call with questions. I enjoy doing computer work, but it is very time-consuming."

"One of the many times Paul Grundhauser (or any of the engineers) snapped into action was when the delay went out," said former producer Rene Servier. "KMOX is on a six second delay. It's an elaborate system and when the 'delay' is out, you can't take any calls. One night I was producing an open line and the delay went out. Here we were with four hours to fill on 'open line' and no phones. I real quick called Paul and was on the phone with him disconnecting the delay system and running it through the old delay system so we could take calls. He helped me fix it up so that I was actually the delay. I had to sit

and listen to the calls and if I heard anything wrong, I had to real quick slam the pot down. Luckily no one swore on the air that night!"

On one of Doug McElvein's afternoon radio shows, he had Grundhauser take him out to the KMOX transmitter.

"We had Doug go out to the transmitter site and Paul gave us a tour of the transmitter," said Chris Mihill, who was McKelvin's producer. "Paul knows so much about that transmitter. He told us there is so much electricity coming out of it that if you held a fluorescent bulb up to it it would light up, I hope I'm remembering that right. Doug did a segment from the transmitter and you could actually hear the hum and the crackle of the transmitter on the radio."

BOB HAMILTON

Bob Hamilton has been at KMOX for 19 years, working for three general managers. Hamilton's unique voice style and command of the news caused Robert Hyland to hand-pick his hours, anchoring the evening newscasts, and they have remained basically the same for all those years.

"When I first met Mr. Hyland, I was fearful of him," said Hamilton. "I decided that was no good since I had to be on the air, so I decided to turn that fear into respect and I had a great deal of respect for him."

Hamilton respected his boss, but also knew, as did everyone at the station, that Hyland was a hands-on general manager and he had an ear to the radio every minute he was awake.

"I used to try to figure out when he was asleep," said Hamilton. "He worked so hard and for so many hours a day, but I figured he was asleep at 9 o'clock at night, so I knew if I made a mistake in the 9 o'clock news, he would not hear it. One time I made a mistake and 'boom!' there went the phone, it was him."

Hamilton's hours were very long on the days he worked. He worked four days a week, but put in 40 hour weeks.

"I did interviews for him," said Geri Davison, who was an intern. "He said I was one of his best 'men' on the street because I could get anyone for an interview. One time he wanted an interview from Gussie Busch and he sent me over to the stadium to do it. It happened I found

out I was related to him on my mother's side and I had contacted him, so he knew me.

"I'll never forget the day I got to go over and do the interview. The interview went so well, I eventually got invited out to his home at Grant's Farm. I really appreciated Bob Hamilton because he would let me do many things. He was like that with people; he would help you. A very nice man."

HARRY HAMM

Harry Hamm is the entertainment editor on KMOX. Over the years his duties have increased. When he was first hired, he served as critic, attending the Muny and then coming down to the station to report on the show, or going to movies and critiquing them. He started doing celebrity interviews and then took on *At Your Service* duties.

Earl Roach of Roach International Hair Salon cut Hamm's hair and he also cut Robert Hyland's.

"I remember Harry used to come in my salon and ask me when Robert Hyland was coming in," Roach said. "He wanted to meet Bob so he could become the movie critic at KMOX. As it turned out, he did meet Bob in my salon and started working at KMOX."

"That's a true story," said Hamm. "I had had 13 auditions in five years down at KMOX. I would go down there and do sample reviews and submit tapes to Robert Hyland. He would never say yes and he would never say no, so I wanted to get in front of him. I got the idea to call his secretary and I asked where he got his hair cut. She said Earl Roach at Earl's International on Delmar and the Innerbelt. I found out his appointment was at 11:15 every other Saturday."

Hamm started making his appointments for 11:30 in the chair next to Hyland.

"That way he had to see me for 15 minutes every week," said Hamm. "At first he didn't say anything, then he started talking about it and one day I got the call. Earl is as much responsible for me getting the job as anybody, and he gives a good haircut."

Hamm does reports on Monday and Fridays at 5:50 as part of *Total Information PM.* He also fills in open lines and does the *Entertainment and Trivia Show Coast to Coast* on Sunday nights.

"I remember Mr. Hyland was on the board at the Muny, and here I was giving reports about the Muny productions," said Hamm. "One day he called me into his office and said, 'Are you taking it easy on the Muny?' That really caught me off-guard. He said, 'There is only one thing that you have that will define your success and that is your credibility. You don't work for the station, you work for the audience. They will decide if you will stay. You have to be honest and call it like you see it in a respectful, clear way with a little humor. Don't worry what anybody will think, including me.' I think that really taught me a lot."

COACH HAMMER

"I've got a great Bob Hyland story," said Coach Hammer, who had a health and fitness show on KMOX from 1985 until 1990. "I was trying to syndicate this health and fitness show. This guy owned a nationally syndicated broadcasting company here in St. Louis and they had already sold shows from Bob Costas and John Madden to KMOX. He was taking me in to meet Mr. Hyland and to try to talk him into taking the show."

On the way to the station, the syndicator was briefing Hammer about Hyland. "He is very serious; he will only give us about eight minutes of his time if we're lucky. He doesn't like to sign contracts, a handshake is a contract to him. He's a very busy man."

Hammer replied, "But I'm really pumped up about the opportunity to get to do the show on KMOX. I've had my power bar, done my workout, I'm feeling ready to go. I walked in there in my 'Hammer clothes' as opposed to my 'Mr. Hyland clothes.' Anyone who knows me knows I always wear a bandana on my head (I had a red one on that day) and my Hammerbodies work out clothes."

The workout clothes were all black with neon pink lettering. He had his clean white sneakers on, his sweatshirt was tucked in neatly. The pair arrived 10 minutes early and Hyland kept them waiting five minutes.

"As soon as we got in the office and I was introduced, Bob Hyland shook my hand," said Hammer. "I could tell he was looking me up and down, trying to figure me out because I could see this hint of a smile

looking down on me. I'm only 5-3, 155 pounds and I look like I'm about nine. I know he was not used to having people like me in his office, but by the long grip he had on my hand I could tell he liked me."

"Liked him" was putting it mildly. Hyland had Hammer in his office for 45 minutes and before they left he was getting fitness advice from the coach himself.

"He asked me a question and I leaned over his big, beautiful, wooden desk and grabbed his yellow pad and one of his fancy Mont Blanc pens and started drawing him a diagram of his linea alba. That was his problem: his linea alba. Pretty soon I had him on the floor doing exercises. He asked me, 'Do you want a job at my radio station?' I looked at Steve because here we were trying to syndicate this show and suddenly I'm getting offered a job. Hyland said, 'Don't look at him. I'm asking if you want to work for me.' Well, needless to say, we never syndicated the show and I worked for KMOX for five years."

Hammer did his fitness segments on the morning show with Bill Wilkerson, Bob Hardy, and Wendy Wiese. Later he was on with Wilkerson and Wiese, then began working in the afternoons.

"One time I was coming out of the studio and I ran into Kevin Horrigan, Dan Dierdorf and Bob Costas. Dierdorf and Costas were real friendly, and we said hello and I reached my hand out to Horrigan to introduce myself and shake his hand. He didn't seem to want to meet me. I said, 'Hi, I'm Coach Hammer.' He just looked at me and said, 'What's a Coach Hammer?' I don't think he wanted much to do with fitness experts at that time."

BOB HARDY

One of St. Louis' most-respected and well-known broadcasters, Bob Hardy was a fixture on KMOX for more than 30 years. He was responsible for many of the station's groundbreaking programs, such as the exchange broadcasts from the Soviet Union, and directed much of the station's political coverage.

"Bob Hardy was outstanding and he was well respected," said former County Executive Gene McNary. "He was very kind and generous. Hardy

was the kind of guy where you could let your guard down. If he called you at home, you did not worry about being set up.

"Politicians learn early on that they have to be cautious about every word they say. You can tell if the reporter has already written the report or has a pre-conceived notion. There are a few people in the media you can let your guard down with, and Bob Hardy was one. He was never really out to say anything bad about anybody."

Having the respect of the people he interviewed was important to Hardy, whether it was during his *Newsmakers* program, on *Total Information AM*, or if he was reporting from a political convention or overseas.

"I went with him to all of the conventions," said his widow, Re. "When you see it on TV and there are all those people in the aisles, those are the delegates. The people in the seats are their guests. People pass their passes to the end of the row and someone goes out with the passes and lets people in. I was actually on the floor of the conventions sitting in a seat. You can't just sit there, though. When everyone is hooting and hollering for their candidates, you have to jump up with them."

In 1968 at the Democratic National Convention in Chicago there were demonstrations outside, and the Hardys were inside.

"Bob used to say, 'Everyone disliked the police because they were taking after the demonstrators, but people didn't see the bags of feces they were throwing at the police or the razor blades they had put in their shoes and were kicking police with,'" Mrs. Hardy said.

Hardy, who joined KMOX in 1960, also was involved in many broadcasts as the Gateway Arch was being constructed. He was fascinated by the project and kept interviewing guests about it. When the final piece was put in place at the top of the Arch, Hardy was there, at the top, reporting live on KMOX.

"As the Arch was being built," said Rita Hardy, "there was this creeper-crawler [creeper derrick] attached to the side. The workmen would go up, and as the Arch got taller, they would move the creeper-crawler. When they moved it, that would be when Bob would do a broadcast. He would do interviews with the head of the Parks Department."

An 80-ton assembly which was a tilt-able platform was mounted on tracks and fastened to the Arch itself and supporting a stiff-legged

derrick. It climbed the Arch and sat at predetermined stations and then lifted the sections with the derrick and put them in place.

The first six sections of each leg (up to 72 feet tall) were put in place by cranes, then the derricks took over.

"Bob was there when they put in the keystone [the last piece of the Arch]," Rita Hardy said. "I remember I took the kids out of school to see them put in the keystone. They sprang the legs of the Arch apart and stuck the keystone in."

When they put the keystone in, there was only a two-foot gap remaining. There were jacks mounted on the top that opened the gap to eight feet to allow the last sections to be inserted. When the jack pressure was released, the natural thrust of the legs clamped the section in place.

The Arch was always a source of interest in the Hardy household. Their daughter, Sandy (Sandra Hardy Chinn who later wrote a book about her famous father and KMOX) worked there.

"I think sometimes people take the Arch for granted," said Re Hardy. "People from out of town tend to go up in it, but some people from St. Louis haven't been to the top. I've been up to the top in the Arch about five times. Sandy worked there when she was in college. She really learned a lot about it. One of the interesting things was that it received funding depending on how many people visited it. If a person was pregnant, she was counted as 'two.'"

Hardy's fascination and interest in the Arch didn't stop when the construction was completed.

"I did a lot of shows with Bob," said Jerry Schober, superintendent for the Jefferson National Expansion Memorial [Arch] starting in 1979. "We'd joke about it; he'd use me when he needed a sure interview. He'd call and say, 'Get over here! I was supposed to have Jack Danforth and something came up.' I'd always help him out in a pinch.

"He told me that on the day the Arch was dedicated Hubert Humphrey came. The president couldn't make it, but the vice-president came. Anyway, it was raining so hard and the water and mud was so deep, there were the vice-president of the United States and Bob Hardy with their pants rolled up above their knees."

Hardy also became quite interested in linking up with broadcasters in Moscow as part of an exchange program.

"The way it got started," said Peggy Cohill Drenkhahn, "was [Soviet leader Mikail] Gorbechev and President Reagan were going to have a summit in May of 1988 in Moscow. A man from a satellite company approached KMOX about buying satellite time to hook up with Radio Moscow."

KMOX did three broadcasts in four days and used different KMOX personalities as the anchors. On May 29, Wendy Wiese, Bob Hardy and Art Fleming hosted the 10 AM (St. Louis time) broadcast. On May 31 Anne Keefe hosted the show in the afternoon and on June 2, Jim White anchored a broadcast from midnight until 2 AM.

"It was so successful that we decided to continue in that manner," said Drenkhahn. "The new idea was to do a joint broadcast, with a Russian host, a Russian guest, an American host, and an American guest."

The negotiations started in May of 1988 and with all of the business details and the programming details the broadcast didn't take place until January 19, 1989.

"Monsanto underwrote the satellite costs and basically sponsored the programs," said Drenkhahn. "We started out dealing with a man named Pavel Kuznetsov, but later Sergei Goryachov became our contact person."

KMOX and USSR Radio Moscow began having an exchange broadcast every Thursday. Hardy was instrumental in this project and he would talk to Sergei Goryachov, who became a good friend of Hardy's.

"I got to work with Bob Hardy on this a little," said Don Corrigan, the editor of the *Webster-Kirkwood Times* and a professor of journalism at Webster University. Corrigan had won a grant to study communications in the Soviet Union.

"Bob Hardy was nice enough to let me get involved," said Corrigan, who also writes for the *St. Louis Journalism Review*. "He let me sit in on the radio show and was very good to me. He set things up so I could talk to Goryachov. I ended up going over to Moscow and through the friendship I'd built up with the help of Bob Hardy, he showed me around and set me up with some radio stations over there."

Hardy had built up a trust with Goryachov and Corrigan knew his friendship with the Russian journalist was because of Hardy.

"When I was over there, Goryachov was so nice to me," said Corrigan. "He took me on a tour of the big shopping area, and he wanted to buy me a soda. There was just one thing, the soda machine just had one cup. Everybody stood in line. You put in your ruble, then you had to drink the soda real fast because you had to leave the glass for the next guy. Sergei said, 'If you are a friend of Russia you'll drink that,' so I drank it."

The way KMOX got such an attachment with Goryachov was when he came to the United States, and that trip started with a broadcast.

On April 20, 1989 Bruce Bradley hosted a show with the topic: Misconceptions We Have About Each Other. The guests included a grocery clerk from the United States and a grocery clerk from Moscow.

The St. Louis guests were Schnucks store checker Karan Kurz and Brian Hahn, a waiter at Ruiz Restaurant. In the studios in Moscow were Olga Vigon, a Moscow food store checker, and Alexander Serov, a Moscow taxi driver. It was just average citizens asking average citizens questions about what it is like to live in their respective countries.

"After that show, Mr. Hyland got a letter from William B. Campey, president of United Food and Commercial Workers Local 655, AFL-CIO," said Cohill Drenkhahn. "It was asking him to forward an invitation to the Russian grocery clerk, Olga Vigon on behalf of Schnucks and the Union. They invited her to be a guest of Local 655 and Schnucks for a week to learn and experience how American supermarket workers live and work. Olga didn't speak any English, so Sergei came as her interpreter."

KMOX had a unique hook-up to make the broadcasts possible. They bounced their signal off of the Stankino Tower and used that facility with a satellite to bounce the signal down.

"That tower turned out to be very important," said Corrigan. "Later, when they tried to overthrow Yeltsin, a big shoot-out took place there [at that tower] with the anti-Yeltsin faction. KMOX used that tower that was right in the middle of the revolution."

The weekly KMOX show was a call-in type of program where people in Moscow could ask people in the United States questions, and Americans could ask people in Moscow questions.

"It was typical of Hardy and Robert Hyland," said Corrigan. "These two men had so much energy for those experiments. It was part of that pioneer spirit that Hyland and Hardy both had to always keep KMOX on the cutting edge. This was the first time anything like this had ever been done in the U.S. It really says something about KMOX because St. Louis was like the 20th city in the country. The people in Moscow could very well have gone with a station in New York or Los Angeles, but they chose St. Louis because of KMOX and Bob Hardy."

Hyland decided Hardy should continue with his international broadcasting, only this time take his act on the road. Hardy and his wife Rita, along with engineer Paul Grundhauser, and KMOX FM personality Kevin McCarthy and his wife went to the Soviet Union and Eastern Bloc countries. McCarthy's wife was from Germany and spoke both German and Russian, so she served as their translator.

"This trip came about because the Wall had come down," said Rita Hardy. "Mr. Hyland figured we could do something by satellite. They had been doing the shows with Sergei. Mr. Hyland thought it would be a good way to celebrate the wall coming down."

"It was a team effort getting everything worked out," said Cohill Drenkhahn. "Our promotions man, Kevin Young, was involved. Kevin McCarthy and his wife had contacts over there. Bob Hardy wrote letters. We all got into it."

The group went to East Berlin, Budapest, Prague, Warsaw, and Moscow. According to Grundhauser it was an engineer's nightmare because he had to set up a different broadcast facility every day in a different country.

"We were given a motorcoach that was provided to President Bush by the Queen of the Netherlands," said Re Hardy. "It had a shower, beds, satellite dish, fax machine and telephone in it."

That was the bus that Kevin McCarthy and the group [minus the Hardy's who had gone ahead to Moscow] were in when they were detained in Poland.

"The most interesting broadcast was in Prague," said Re Hardy. "They did it from an old radio station with old windows all around. It had a mock door to use for sound effects. They had Shirley Temple Black live on the show. She was over there as the Ambassador to Czechoslovakia. One thing I remember was the 'lift' which was what they called

elevators. This particular one was a vertical circle going up and down. It kept going, and never stopped at a floor. You would step on a step and you got on while it was moving. You would go to the floor you wanted and step off as it was moving. It would go all the way up and around a circle and come back.

"Paul had to re-wire that station so we could go on the air. The station was a working station. It was a state-owned station .and they didn't play commercials. In Warsaw we did the broadcast from the only recognized CBS facility over there."

As interesting as the station in Prague was, Rita Hardy said her husband and McCarthy were in for an unexpected surprise in Moscow.

"They did the broadcast from Red Square," she said. "And all of the troops were out there marching, getting ready for the Mayday Celebration. They were all there while Bob was doing his broadcast. They did the broadcast out in the open across from Lenin's tomb. You felt like you were being watched in Moscow. You were very careful about what you said in your room."

Re decided she wanted to buy Bob a shirt made in the Soviet Union so she went to Gumbs Department Store.

"I'll never forget that place," she said. "It was really unique to go in there, the men's shirts were all the same size. I got a shirt off the rack that I liked and I asked the sales person to help me find another size, 'this is the wrong size,' I said. 'Do you have a 151/2?' They told me it would be several months before the shipment arrived and the shipments only came in one size every few months."

As responsible as he was for those groundbreaking broadcasts, Hardy has another legacy at KMOX. He helped launch many broadcasting careers, and among the people he was responsible for bringing to KMOX were Jim White and Ron Jacober.

"Bob Hardy was working so much, he was on all the time," said Elaine Stern, White's producer. "He told Mr. Hyland he needed help. He had heard Jim in Pittsburgh and asked if Mr. Hyland would hire him."

"Bob Hardy is the main reason that I'm not just at KMOX, but in broadcasting," said Jacober "After college and the Army, I went to work for the Auto Club of Missouri (AAA). Eventually I was their public relations director. A couple years into that, I got a part-time weekend job on WIBV in Belleville. I had a journalism degree from SIU-Carbondale and I had taken a few broadcasting courses.

"After a while I got tired of working seven days a week and was about to quit when Bob Hardy called me. He lived in Belleville and had heard me. He asked if I would be interested in a weekend job at KMOX. Well, that was like God calling. I auditioned and got the weekend job. I couldn't wait for the weekends and soon I accepted a full time job as a staff announcer at KMOX. If Bob hadn't made that call, who knows what would have happened."

One of Hardy's strengths was his versatility, which enabled him to conduct interesting interviews about a variety of topics.

"Once when I was on with Bob Hardy, we were talking about prostitution," said attorney Don Wolff. "I had suggested legalization as I had observed in Germany while in the Army. A woman called in and said I should go back to Germany to stay for good!"

All of the people who worked on the early-morning broadcasts became good friends, and often went out for breakfast when the showed ended at 9 AM.

"One of the traditions of the drive-time was going out for breakfast," said John Amann. "We'd get there at 4 AM, and get off the show at 9. Then we'd go down to Fando's for some bacon and eggs or whatever. Ava Ehrlich worked then and so did Barry Birr, and Don Miller would park his helicopter and come in."

"I loved going over to KMOX and having coffee with Bob Hardy," said Miller, the traffic reporter. "After doing the traffic in the morning sometimes I'd go up to the station to have coffee with him. I considered him a friend of mine."

Hardy was always very friendly to the people who worked for or around him, and he enjoyed knowing them.

"Bob invited the newsroom to a barbecue at his house one time," said Stu Esrock who worked in the newsroom in the early 1980s. "We got to go to his home in Highland, Illinois—Dave St. John, Mike Owens, Joan Beuckman, and I. Bob Hardy was a real mentor to me."

"I will never forget being on KMOX with Bob Hardy," said Bob Heil, who has been on KMOX over 40 years talking about electronics. "I was nervous. Bob could speak so well, and here I was this kid with

no radio experience. I was afraid I'd use the wrong word or talk badly being next to this eloquent broadcaster, Bob Hardy.

"After I came out of the first show, Mr. Hyland said, 'Well, kid, how do you feel?' I said, 'I was nervous, I'm fine with crowds, I was Stan Kann's protégé and played at the Fox in front of big crowds, but I feel like my sentences may not be right. I don't sound as professional as Bob Hardy.' He said, 'When I want my sentences perfectly right, I have Bob Hardy. I want you for *your* information. You are the only person who knows all that gobble-dee-gook (Hyland said 'gobble-dee-gook!') about electronics.' So I felt a lot better."

Heil says he was lucky to start with Hardy, who he considered a hero.

"I have Bob Hardy's microphone," said Heil. "He was really close to me. I miss him a lot. He wanted to write a book. I told him, 'Bob, you got to be on the computer. After he got the computer he needed a printer, so I said I'd get him one. I went to Best Buy and was in line with the printer when my cell phone rang. It was my wife. 'Go outside,' she said. 'I have to get the printer,' I told her. 'Don't buy the printer. Go outside.' I went outside and she told me not to buy the printer because he had just died. My wife knew I would fall apart in that store, so she didn't want to tell me when I was inside.

"I loved Bob Hardy like I loved my mother. He was a neat person who changed my life, and I still talk to his wife Rita about him. Forget the radio side, he was just a wonderful person."

Among Hardy's interests outside of work was the Shriners. He was elected 66th Potentate of Ainad Temple, a group of 8,400 Shriners in southern Illinois in 1976. He was a 33rd degree Mason.

"He was terrific, intelligent, and easy to listen to," Jack Buck said. "He had many opportunities to go to New York and work for the network, but he wanted to stay in St. Louis."

Hardy died of a heart attack in 1993.

"Bob Hardy's death was so shocking," said former news director John Angelides. "He had been there over 30 years. He had some heart problems, but they had been corrected. He was working around the house when he had the heart attack. His death really changed things at KMOX. The deaths of Bob Hardy and Jack Carney really changed the

station. I think that ultimately the death of Hardy and Jack Carney brought Rush Limbaugh to KMOX. Carney's shift was up until noon and then Hardy took over. That's the slot Rush fills."

Hardy's daughter, Sandra Hardy Chinn, wrote a wonderful book about her father, and the history of KMOX and the start of *At Your Service.*

KATHE HARTLEY

Kathe Hartley's main job was at the traffic desk. Don Miller would be in the "traffic copter" later to be called "Jet Copter One." She came to KMOX from KSD radio where she was known as "Jody" Hartley.

She would give an overview of the highways and then throw it to Miller for his aerial view. She often did spot reporting when she was needed and was involved in the station's coverage of the VP Fair.

"One of the most fun times I had covering the VP Fair involved Kathe Hartley," said Jim Bafaro, a newsman at the time. "I boarded the Mississippi Queen [riverboat] at the same spot that Kathe got on the Delta Queen in south county. We did 'dueling play-by-play' up the river as the two boats raced toward downtown. They put both of us through the control board at the same time so we were able to gently taunt each other during the course of the race."

CAROL HARTMANN

Carol Hartmann (now Carol Ettman) was secretary to Robert Hyland starting in January 1969, and she worked until February 1971. She handled all secretarial duties in addition to coordinating Hyland's civic involvement.

"She set up for broadcasts, produced them, picked up and entertained 'dignitaries and stars' for such events as the VP Parade, grand opening of the Spanish Pavilion, and the Baseball Writers' Dinner," said co-worker Barb Felt.

Carol Hartmann Ettman also booked guests for and produced *At Your Service* and did additional assignments for KMOX-FM, working in traffic and continuity and music programming.

CLINT HASSE

Now the general sales manager, Clint Hasse started as an account executive in March of 1993.

"I was the first account executive that had been hired in about 10 years," said Hasse. "To join the KMOX radio family was a very big deal. KMOX is a family. Everyone has their place in time and makes their contribution. Robert Hyland built one of the best radio stations on the planet. Rod Zimmerman came in and did some clean up work and put the station back on track as a performer from a ratings and revenue standpoint. Karen Carroll is leading the current generation of KMOXers into the next era."

Hasse is half of the brains behind the *Holiday Radio Show*, which has become so popular on KMOX. He and director of operations, Tom Langmyer, came up with the idea in the car driving back from a trip to Nashville, Tennessee.

"We are both great fans of 'real-live radio' programs like *The Grand Ol Opry* and NPR's *Prairie Home Companion*," said Hasse. "We got our management team together, formed a committee, and talked Kevin Horrigan into writing the first year's show. It was a huge success. Since that time, Kevin Killeen has written the show.

"The reason I like the *Holiday Radio Show* is that it is a true art form bringing great programming and revenue generation together. To create art is one thing, but to have it become successful from a monetary standpoint as well is a rarity. I hope KMOX never loses *The Holiday Radio Show*. It is the one time a year when we do something unique in broadcasting."

BRUCE HAYWARD

Bruce Hayward was on KMOX in the 1950s. Before coming to KMOX he was on KWK for 10 years.

"I started there the same day that Jack Buck did," he said. "Bob Hyland hired me. I did music shows, with easy listening music."

Hayward played music and interviewed musical people. He had

many famous people on his show, but the one he remembers the most is Rosemary Clooney.

"Rosemary Clooney is the most memorable," he said. "The reason for that is she kissed me on the cheek, and my son who was 10 at the time was listening and got very upset! She was just a delightful guest; I interviewed her and we played some of her songs."

Bina Williams was Hayward's producer.

"She was my right arm," said Hayward. "She helped me out so much, producing all of my shows."

At the same time Hayward was working at KMOX, he was also doing the news on Channel 2.

"Jack Buck and I asked right about the same time if we could do television," said Hayward. "Robert Hyland didn't like TV, but he let us do it."

"I worked with Bruce," said Tony Bello. "We were on the air together, I did the news."

"I quit the first day they did *At Your Service* [February 29, 1960]," Hayward said. "I told Hyland, 'It will never work.' See how much I know?"

NANCY HIGGINS

Nancy Higgins worked as public relations director in the 1990s. She was hired by Rod Zimmerman and worked under Karen Carroll. Higgins was instrumental in starting the Voice of Caring Campaign under Zimmerman.

"One broadcast I will always remember," she said, "was the day Mother Theresa died. It was two days before Princess Diana's funeral. *The Rush Limbaugh Show* was on and he kept talking about how people were making such a big deal over Princess Diana that she was practically a saint. He wondered what would happen when Mother Theresa died. Just before he went off the air he said something like 'and by the way Mother Theresa has died.' No one really realized if they had heard it right. It had just come across the wires. All of a sudden I could see the newsroom jump into action!"

Another memory involved actress Cloris Leachman, who was in town to appear in *Showboat* at the Fox. Leachman had appeared on

Charles Brennan's show on the Becky Thatcher to talk about her appearance at the Fox. After one of the performances, she was in her rental car driving back to her hotel. She had KMOX on the radio and heard the overnight announcer talking about her appearance at the Fox and then he said, 'I've got a great Cloris Leachman story; I'll tell you when we get back.'

"Well, she was almost at her hotel and she knew she did not have a radio in her room, so she kept driving around," said Higgins. "She found a spot on the Landing and pulled over. Some police officers saw her pulled over and came up to see if she had a problem. She told them who she was and why she was pulled over. They said, 'Well, that radio station is just right over there,' and showed her how to get to KMOX. She drove over to KMOX and as the announcer started to tell the story about Cloris Leachman, here she was standing in the studio!"

BOB HEIL

Bob Heil, known as "high tech Heil," has been associated with KMOX since 1956. The electronics expert who has designed state of the art innovations used in major stage shows around the world, and has done the sound for such musical groups as the Greatful Dead, Bachman-Turner Overdrive, and The Who, attributes all of his electronic training to an engineer at KMOX a long time ago.

"Larry Burrows was a ham operator. It was around 1956 that I'm talking to him on the ham radio," said Heil. "We had been talking a while and I told him a little about myself. I was taking organ lessons from Stan Kann, and, in fact I was his protégé. My parents owned a clothing store and my mother would drive to St. Louis from our home in Marissa, Illinois, and she would take me and drop me off for my organ lesson, then she would go do her buying for the store. Larry told me he worked at KMOX and said if my mother would drop me off, he would show me around. I saw how he had made this great transformer and asked if he could make me one. He said, 'I'll show you how.' So I started going down to KMOX every Thursday after my organ lesson. Stan Kann would drop me off at KMOX and I watched and learned. I

would follow him around the studio. You couldn't do that today, but I learned so much."

Meanwhile, the Heil family was becoming friends with the Bob Hardy family through a marina they both used.

"This had nothing to do with radio, this was before he was at KMOX," said Heil, "but I was so taken with Bob Hardy, and I thought his wife, Rita, was the most beautiful lady I had ever seen. I was 13 at the time. I really enjoyed them when I would see them when we went water skiing. Bob was like an idol to me at the time."

When Hardy got to KMOX, he decided to do an electronics show. Different people would have Heil on their shows as the resident expert.

"I did some Saturday morning shows that were priceless in my memory," said Heil. "Mary Phelan did a Saturday morning show with Art Fleming. I'd go in once a month to do their show. I have saved all of my tapes from every time I've been on KMOX and I listen to these tapes from time to time."

LINDLEY HINES

Lindley Hines did the 10 PM news in the 1950s. In those days the 10 PM news was a big news show with a big audience as it was before television stations began broadcasting a 10 PM news show. If people wanted to get the news of the day before going to bed, they had to listen to the radio.

JIM HOLDER

Jim Holder did not have the title of sports director at KMOX, but for most of the 17 years he worked there, he ran the day-to-day operations of the sports department. Holder made certain the KMOX roll-a-dex of phone numbers read like a who's who of sports.

The interns in the sports department would often conduct telephone interviews and then write the stories for the on-air talent to read. Holder was very supportive and helpful to the interns, steering many of them into careers in sports.

"Holder was very good to work for," said Steve Overby who started as an intern and then was hired as a sports assistant. "He taught me a lot."

"Jim Holder was very thorough," said Kip Ingle, former public relations director for the Cardinals. "He would call me every morning about 10 AM; he did the morning sports. He always asked what was happening. We'd go over the pitchers, the injuries that were not known publicly. He always wanted to be up-to-date, up to the minute."

Holder did a variety of assignments, anchoring the studio shows, reading the sports news and even doing play-by-play assignments.

"I did the play-by-play of the Steamers in their first year," said Holder. "It started out with Nancy Drew and John Rooney, but Nancy decided she didn't want to do it so I alternated with Rooney. He'd do the first period and I'd do the second. Then we did the MISL All Star Game. Costas got involved with the halftime shows for that."

Jack Carney often gave Holder a hard time when the two were on the air together.

"Jack would have us come into the studio with him just to talk," said Holder. "I normally did the early morning, then Gary Bender came in from 9:30 to noon. Nancy Drew worked from 1-3 and Bill Wilkerson and Bob Costas split the afternoon drive. On the days Gary Bender wasn't there, I'd go in during Carney's show."

Once after Holder's first son, Adam, was born, Carney and Holder were bantering on the air about having sons, and Carney remembered when he used to change his son John's diapers, and was teasing Holder about what happens when little boys are on the changing table and no one lays a towel over them.

"So he started calling Adam, 'dead eye' because of that," said Holder. "because of how they pee when you change them. Well, believe this or not, when Adam was 12, I had the little league basketball team with me and we were walking out of a gym in West County and this guy comes up to me. 'Hey, I know you're Jim Holder. I recognize you.' Then he starts looking at the kids, and says 'which one's 'dead eye'?!'

Gene McNary remembered when he and Holder raced in the Meramec River Raft Races. "Those were fun times," McNary said. "The parks department put them on and there were like 500 floaters. Jim

Holder was with Ron Morgan and I had some of my employees. It was a real good day. We'd float a few hours and end up around Fenton. We did that for several years. There were prizes for most creative and other categories."

Holder was instrumental in starting *The Ottis and Theotis Show*," which was a short radio show done by Ottis Anderson and Theotis Brown.

"The thing about Jim Holder was he was very fast-paced," said Joan Tabash, who worked as an intern in the sports department in 1983. "He was like, 'this needs to get done, that needs to get done.' That's what I remember most about the sports department with Jim Holder in charge, something was always going on. The sports office was a very fast-paced place. Everything was re-active rather than pro-active. He was always going, and he did a great job. There was never a 'normal' day. That was the fun of it."

"When I came to KMOX," said White Sox play-by-play man John Rooney, "Holder was very good to me. He said, 'Come in, work hard, you'll be fine.' I worked closely with him and we've remained friends to this day."

"If it wasn't for Jim Holder," said Mike Claiborne, who worked in the sports department in the 1980s and is now program director for KFNS, "I wouldn't be in this business, so we have him to blame."

Jim Holder now works as the sports director at KTRS.

ROBERT HOLMES

Robert Holmes was a steward and worked in the mailroom. Everyone knew him and he was pleasant and polite to everyone.

"He and Don (Floyd) just did everything," said Wendy Wiese. "After Mr. Hyland died, I saw Robert with tears in his eyes. He had just taken all the things out of the Cavalier. Robert Hyland drove a black Cavalier station wagon. In the later days of his life when he was too sick, the car stayed at KMOX and he had a driver who took him to and from work. Robert had to empty the car. He was carrying a box with Mr. Hyland's sunglasses, his scarf, raincoat, and umbrella. They were packing it up."

BOB HOLT

While Jack Buck did the first hour of the *At Your Service* when it started in 1960, Bob Holt did the second hour. He was known as "the man of 1,000 voices." Holt started at KMOX in 1959 and did a lot of different voices, being a weatherman. He also read the comics from the newspapers on Sunday morning over the radio.

"He was the little 'weather bird,'" said Shirley Bates, who has worked at KMOX for over 40 years. "He worked mostly in the afternoon drive."

"He would come in and kibitz with Jack Buck in his 'weatherbird' voice," said Clarence Nieder, an engineer.

"Bob Holt was so funny," said Taffy Wilbur, who worked on the air during the same years. "He was a tremendous performer. I think of him more as a talent than a radio man. He made a lot of personal appearances and was in great demand."

KEVIN HORRIGAN

Kevin Horrigan was on KMOX as a guest on *Sports Open Line* and for several years as a talk-show host. He had been the *Post-Dispatch* sports columnist before jumping to the *St. Louis Sun*, the ill-fated newspaper that tried to take the *Globe-Democrat*'s place after the *Globe* folded. After the *Sun*'s short life, Horrigan became the co-host of *The Morning Meeting* with Charles Brennan for six years.

"I'll never forget the time I brought Reverend Robert Schuler in to their show," said book publicist Elaine Bly, who has brought some of the best-known authors in the country to KMOX. "Kevin had an incident with him which turned out so badly, he ended up walking out. When Rev. Schuler and I got to the elevator on our way out, we passed a reporter from the *Post-Dispatch* coming in."

The headline in the next day's paper was "KMOX's 'Negative Thinker' Abruptly Leaves Interview With 'Positive' Evangelist." According to the newspaper article "the interview began getting tense when Horrigan questioned Schuler, who has a nationally syndicated television show from Los Angeles, about Schuler's belief that positive

thinking is a powerful remedy for many problems. Horrigan described himself as 'the leading proponent of negative thinking.' Schuler accused Horrigan of 'playing games.'"

The conversation was getting so heated that Charles Brennan tried to step in and Horrigan snapped back at him, "You be quiet! The man has just attacked me."

Rod Zimmerman, the general manager, supported Horrigan.

Horrigan left KMOX with Bill Wilkerson and Wendy Wiese and went to KTRS. He has written several books and is currently working on a novel.

GRANT HORTON

Longtime St. Louis radio personality Grant Horton came to KMOX in 1957 and for the first several years there was the host of the *House-wives Protective League* program. He worked at KMOX until 1969, when he moved to KSD.

Horton, who also went by the name Grant Williams during part of his career, was instrumental in the founding of KSCF in Florissant. He came back to KMOX in 1986 and stayed until his retirement in 1989.

He died of cancer in August 1997 at the age of 73.

RICHARD "ONION" HORTON

Onion Horton was a frequent guest during the late 1970s and early '80s.

"Sometimes Onion was controversial just to be controversial," said Mike Harris, who worked at WIL and sat next to Horton in the pressbox at Busch Stadium.

Horton knew a lot about the local high school and college scene and brought a lot of enthusiasm to the shows he was on. He continues to be active in radio in St. Louis.

RICK HORTON

Former major league pitcher Rick Horton has been filling in on

the Cardinals' broadcasts since 1997, working whenever Mike Shannon misses the broadcast.

"I'm the unofficial fill-in guy," said Horton, who pitched with the Cardinals, White Sox, and Dodgers in the 1980s.

One day in July 2000 this year, Horton learned major league play-by-play is not always the glamorous job it seems to be. He had just run in a charity race in East St. Louis to help promote Jackie Joyner Kersee's athletic club.

"I was driving home from East St. Louis, feeling pretty good after running in the race," said Horton. "I had a tee time set up for that afternoon with my son, Drew; just looking forward to a lazy kind of dad-kid day. I called my wife, Ann, on the cell phone from the car and she said, 'Rick, hang up, Steve Uline is trying to reach you!'"

Steve Uline is the head of Bud Sports and was calling Horton because Mike Shannon had informed him he would have to miss that day's game because of a death in his family.

"He said, 'Can you be here right away?'" said Horton. "I was like 'Sure!' but then I remembered I had the tee-time with Drew. So I called him and he was actually happy for me and said, 'Hey cool!' Suddenly the panic set in. I knew he wanted me right away, but I was all sweaty from the run and I started thinking about the game. Suddenly I'm going, 'Who are we playing?' 'Did we win last night?' 'Who am I doing the game with?' So I raced home, showered and changed and then got to the ballpark about an hour before the game, which is really late for a broadcaster."

Horton looked around for his "ace in the hole."

"I saw Mike Matheny [Cardinal catcher]," said Horton. "I asked him who was pitching for Cincinnati and what he was like and I was going to write it all down. He said, 'I don't know, I'm not playing.' I'm thinking, 'Great, this guy was my lifeline.'"

It ended up that Horton worked with Jack Buck.

"It was actually a good lesson for me," said Horton. "I didn't have anything prepared, so I just had to talk about what I know. I was a little nervous working with Jack Buck and I wasn't prepared, but Jack was great. He is the best there is and he was very helpful and gracious. It didn't help that it was a 10-9 three-hour game and I had to talk more than normal."

DR. DAVID HOY

Dr. Hoy was a frequent and popular guest on Jim White's show and eventually began hosting his own show. Hoy was a self-proclaimed ESP expert. Listeners would call with questions of everything from "Can you tell me where I lost my watch?" to "Who is the man I am going to marry?"

"I always thought the shows with the psychics on them were similar to the trading station," said Bob Costas, who had worked with Hoy. "You really only want to hear what they have to say about your specific problem. A caller might call up and say, 'I misplaced my keys,' and he would say, 'I feel sure that if you looked behind your underwear in your third drawer you will find it; now you'll call me back and let me know when you've found them, won't you?' I always wondered why they didn't hold on until he checked and came back. That would be the true test, wouldn't it?

"Who would want to listen to someone else search for their socks? *With the Trading Station* I always wondered, 'Who in the world could be listening, but the phone lines were always lit up to hear someone from Granite City say, 'Oh, am I on the air? Oh, OK, uh yes, well, I have an old eight-track tape player; a set of golf clubs with only the nine iron, sand wedge and putter missing; and an autographed picture of Kaye Ballard from when she was at the Muny in *Kiss Me Kate*. I'm asking $150 or best offer. My number is…' In the name of God what sort of programming is this? But people listen.

"David Hoy was from Paducah, Kentucky, and was extremely entertaining and amusing. He was a personality. He always got a disproportionate amount of calls. Of course, the phone lines lit up because these people all had their own problems they needed to talk to him about."

Hoy was a very pleasant, jovial man who was well-liked by the listeners. When he was on with White, he was very often doing the shows from his home in Kentucky. In his later years, before he died of a heart attack, Hoy filled in for White when he went on vacation. Always cordial to everyone from the interns to the listeners, Hoy was a successful

fill-in. He once saw a young intern and let her read the weather on the show to give her some on-air experience and help her lose her jitters.

JULIUS HUNTER

In the early 1980s Sunday nights were a free-for-all on KMOX as Robert Hyland tried many different hosts. He spared no expense and flew people in to do it. A bit of stability came when KMOX television news anchor Julius Hunter came upstairs to host the evening programs.

"When Robert Hyland was trying to hire me to do the show," said Hunter, "he used Jack Carney as his 'point man'. He had Carney meet me in Fando's bar next door. We met in this darkened bar for the clandestine meeting. Jack told me to have my boss, John McKay, call Mr. Hyland. I said, 'My boss wouldn't call up there; Mr. Hyland should call him.' Well it took a while because Mr. Hyland thought my boss should call him, but after a while we got the call and it all worked out."

Hunter's popularity with the listeners was a plus as they knew him from television. He could talk about many subjects and the Sunday nights were never dull with Hunter there.

"One of the wildest shows we did was with Sherri Hite, the author of the *Hite Report*, a book she was promoting," said Hunter. "It was one of the most candid sexual interviews I can remember. The fact that it was on KMOX was something because she was saying some very shocking things."

Hite: I don't know why men think their penises are the only thing that satisfies a woman.

Hunter: (Coughs and goes to a commercial break)

Hite: I don't know why a woman can't have five or six or seven orgasms.

Hunter: (Coughs and goes to a commercial break)

"We finally ran out of commercials, but in that interview I used the 'cough and cover' technique as my strategy," Hunter said. "I would cough and cover the microphone."

Hunter said that after working five days at the television station, it was a grueling pace to do the radio show because he prepared so well for it.

"I thought that after the year and a half I did the program I should have earned some kind of a doctorate degree for all the work I put into it," said Hunter. "Every Friday, Peggy Cohill, the producer, would come down to KMOX with books on the subjects I was going to do that Sunday night. We worked together to come up with the topics. I had to bone up on what I was going to talk about. I read so much to prepare for that it was like I was in school."

Hunter realized just how many people listened to KMOX—from all parts of the country and in other countries as well.

"We were heard all over," said Hunter. "I remember I had a guest on talking to us from a hideout in the Ozarks. He was a survivalist talking about how he would be ready for the end of the world. He and his family were prepared. They grew food and practiced weaponry. After he talked a while I opened the phone lines. A guy called from Windsor Ontario Canada and said he thought that was dumb and that we shouldn't be giving this guy the airtime. The guy in the Ozarks shot something back at him and then the guy in Canada said something else. Pretty soon it was just these two going at it, a guy in Canada and a guy in the Ozarks. I interrupted them for a commercial after a while, but that shows you just the far-reaching effects of the station.

"Another show I remember and I thought was funny was the night we had someone on from the Harvard Sleep Clinic talking about sleep disorders. I opened up the phone lines and the first caller said, 'zzzzzzzzzzzz!' He was snoring and the subject was sleep."

Hunter said that after a year and a half he grew tired of all of the research he had to do to prepare for the show.

"It was my sixth day of work," he said. "It was grueling, but I enjoyed it while I was there."

"Julius Hunter could be very funny," said Dr. Armand Brodeur. "I was doing my show, and at KMOX there is glass all around the studio so everyone can see you. Julius just walked in and sat on my lap, which I thought was so funny!"

MATTHEW "MATT" HYLAND

Matt Hyland is the son of Robert Hyland and is in the sports marketing group at KMOX, selling the Cardinals and Saint Louis Uni-

versity basketball. Hyland started at a small station, then came to KMOX in 1986 as a salesman.

Hyland left to work for the St. Louis Blues in 1992 then moved back to KMOX four years later.

Though his famous father could have given him a job at KMOX immediately out of school, both decided that he could get more experience starting at a small station.

"One day we sat down and had a talk about what I was going to do," said Hyland. "Dad said there were two avenues you could take with radio: on-air and sales. He looked at me and said, 'On-air is not for you.' So I started out working at a small radio station in Florida owned by Sam Cook Diggs, an ex-president of CBS Radio."

Hyland was always a sports fan as a youngster.

"I was an avid sports fan, and I still am," said Hyland. When the football Cardinals were still in St. Louis, Hyland served as a ball boy. "It was fun being around the team. I got to know Dan Dierdorf and all the players."

He also got to meet sports greats like Roger Staubach, Sandy Koufax, and many of the St. Louis Cardinal players.

ROBERT HYLAND

Robert Hyland was the general manager of KMOX from 1955 until his death in 1992. He became one of the most well-known and influential citizens in St. Louis during those 37 years. His work schedule was legendary, his demand for quality unmatched, and his desire to make KMOX the best radio station in the country unwavering.

Hyland was known to arrive at work every morning at 3 o'clock and worked through the business day. In the last several years of his life, he came to work earlier and earlier, often arriving before midnight, just six hours after he left after working for 18 hours.

It was suggested by some that he got in a competition with fellow businessman George Capps to see who could get to work earlier.

"He actually got to work at 11:45 PM, at the end of his life," said newsman Bob Hamilton, who would often see Hyland coming in on

his shift. "He worked so hard, he would spend eight hours running the station and eight hours running the city."

Though he was known as a visionary, a genius in radio and a great community leader, Hyland also was a taskmaster. Whenever he called an employee with orders, he would always hang up before saying "good-bye." There was a specific line which directly linked him to the studio, sometimes referred to as the "bat phone." If the bat phone was ringing, an employee really did not want to answer it because he or she knew who was calling and that most likely the subject wasn't good.

"I was the one who came up with the name 'bat phone,'" said Jim White. "That was the line reserved just for Mr. Hyland."

Hyland had the respect not only from his employees, but from CBS Network executives as well. He became a vice president and had the title KMOX General Manager/CBS Regional Vice President for many years.

His approval and blessing was constantly sought from community leaders before they decided to proceed with projects. They knew if Hyland wasn't behind an issue, the chances of it succeeding were not very good.

"He was constantly being asked to get in on things," said Jim Cullen, Hyland's personal lawyer. "Every civic person or entrepreneur who was going into business approached him and he would talk to me about it. He once told me, 'You do me more good by saying no and keeping me from getting into things.'

"Bob Hyland was very sincere in reference to his morals, his religion and his practice of religion. He always had good people working for him. He had an idea of what talent could produce."

Hyland atttended Mass at the Old Cathederal every morning. His Catholic faith was very important to him and he was well connected in the Catholic community. He was so connected that once when Mother Teresa was in town he arranged a late-night radio interview with the nun. He got the phone number where she was staying and the employee who answered the bat phone had to call Mother Teresa at midnight to ask her for an interview.

Hyland was on so many boards of directors that he constantly attended meetings. He was very civic-minded.

He also was a tremendous baseball fan, the love of the game coming from his father, Dr. Robert Hyland, who was the team doctor for the Cardinals and was known as the surgeon general of baseball.

One of Hyland's first moves after being named general manager in 1955 was to acquire the rights to broadcast the Cardinal games from KXOK. The games have remained on KMOX ever since. He knew how important carrying the games would be to the station's success.

"I was a dear friend of Bob Hyland's," said Stan Musial. "He was a dynamo. He meant so much to the city of St. Louis. He was involved in so many things in this town."

When Bob Gibson was being rewarded for his performance in the 1967 World Series, Hyland got in on the act. *Sport* magazine gave Gibson a car and Hyland wanted to show his appreciation to Lou Brock, who had also played splendidly in the series.

"The king of the hill [Gibson] was awarded the Series-decisive automobile by *Sport* magazine," said Bob Broeg in his book, *Redbirds*. "Graciously, Bob Hyland of KMOX told Brock to take his pick of a car, too, at the radio station's expense."

"When I was a kid and he was a kid, I worked at the ballpark," said Cullen. "I knew him first as the son of Dr. Hyland."

Dr. Hyland worked with the Cardinals in the days of Musial, Red Schoendienst, Terry Moore, and Marty Marion. In 1947, Hyland performed surgery on one of St. Louis' most beloved ballplayers.

"[Musial] had got off to a horribly slow start," Broeg said in his book, Redbirds. "In late May, the reason became apparent. He was felled at the old New Yorker Hotel with an attack of appendicitis. Wan and weak, he was rushed back to St. Louis by plane with catcher Del Wilber as escort.

"In St. Louis, Dr. Hyland met the plane with an ambulance, confirmed the diagnosis and suggested that he could freeze the appendix and remove it in the off-season so that Musial could rejoin the ball club."

The young Hyland enjoyed his privilege of getting to go to all of the games because his father worked for the team.

"Bob was a tremendous baseball fan," said Cullen. "He was a good player in those days. He would sit in the same field box every day. He sat by the wagon gate on the first-base side. He was kind of a wild kid back

then. We'd talk during the game, 'How'd this guy look in warm-ups?' and things like that. He was always inquisitive and he loved to talk baseball."

It was only natural, perhaps, that Hyland decided to make radio his career. While attending Saint Louis University, where he was co-captain of the baseball team, he worked at WEW. After graduation, he took a job at WTAD in Quincy, Illnois, making $25 a week. He later said his job there consisted of everything except sweeping the floors.

Hyland moved back to St. Louis to work at WEW, and after serving in the Navy during World War II, joined KXOK. He once again left St. Louis to work for WBBM in Chicago, his start with CBS, and joined KMOX in 1952 as assistant sales manager, moving up to general manager three years later.

As much of a public figure and influential civic leader as he was, Hyland remained a very private man. He shunned publicity, and didn't care if the people who worked for his station were more famous or made more money than he did.

"Hyland promoted personalities," Jack Buck said. "Most radio stations promote their programs. He demanded professionalism and quality. He wasn't just there at 3 AM, he was busy."

When Hyland made a decision, it was tough to change his mind. Very few people could talk him out of something he was determined to do, such as give away KMOX's music library in 1960 and begin talk show programs called *At Your Service.*

Hyland was right about that decision, and he was almost always correct when it came to hiring employees for KMOX, both visible on-the-air talents and important behind-the-scenes staff members as well.

"He was a very good judge of talent and he had very good judgment on impulse," Buck said. "He didn't misfire very often."

When Hyland got behind a project, there was no stopping him until the work was done. Such was the case when he decided to build a new hospital, St. Anthony's.

"He told me one day he had decided to build a hospital," Buck said. "That's like me saying I'm going to go buy a new car. And then he did it. There were so many things like that which really benefited this community."

Hyland never wanted the credit or recognition for any of his good works, however.

When *Post-Dispatch* writer John McGuire went to Hyland and suggested that he would like to write a story about him, Hyland was very stand-offish.

"It was the most interesting and yet challenging story I have ever done," said McGuire. "He was very hard to interview. I went in to interview him several times. He had this absolutely shimmering clean office. His desk was very neat and he had this beautiful crystal collection. He would just say things like, 'Why do you want to do a story on me?'"

After KMOX moved to its present downtown location, Hyland's office was on the third floor of the KMOX building, just around the corner from the newsroom, and with a great view of the Arch and riverfront. The walls of the office were a rich brown wood and he had an expensive Steuben crystal collection on shelves that lined an entire wall.

McGuire ended up spending about two months working on the story and it went from just an article to a two-part feature.

"Robert Hyland was absolutely private about himself," said McGuire. "He was reluctant to talk about anything about his personal life. I had to piece together things that other people said. He was just a difficult interview."

Hyland's assistant, Jeannie Whitworth, would call McGuire occasionally with information for him and he interviewed other people.

"It was unbelievable the response I got for that article," said McGuire. "Word got out that I was doing the article and I got calls from all over the country. What a network KMOX was; people who had worked for him and wanted to express their opinion one way or another. I did a sidebar on that and mentioned that I got 30 calls in all. Some of these people would call me at home on a Saturday morning. It was astonishing. I'd never gotten unsolicited calls when I was doing an article about someone. They would say, 'My name is such and such and I used to work there.' Some had good things to say and some didn't. Some would give me their names and others wouldn't."

Phone calls from Hyland were legendary. He didn't care if he was waking you up at 5 AM, if that was when he needed to find out a piece

of information, that was when he called. Most of the calls also ended very quickly and very abruptly.

"My goal in life was to one time hang up on him before he hung up on me," Buck has said frequently. He never made it.

Most employees would put on their jacket and straighten their ties before going in to see Hyland, who was always impeccably dressed in a dark Brooks Brothers suit, a white shirt, and a plain tie. Almost everyone called him "Mr. Hyland" to his face with the possible exception of one intern who was the son of a friend of the family and called him "Uncle Bobby." One employee was so afraid of Hyland that when he went in to have a private meeting with him he nearly wet his pants. No matter who you were, an audience with Hyland was a big deal, whether it was in the middle of the night or middle of the day.

"The first time Mr. Hyland hired me in 1986 I was 23 years old," said talk show host John Carney. "I was petrified when I went into his office, petrified."

"The only time I ever saw him when he was not dressed up was if he came in on a Saturday," said Rene Servier, former producer. "Mr. Hyland had this orange sweatshirt that he would wear with jeans and deck shoes if he came in on a Saturday, which was rare. It was just an old orange, almost psychedelic, plain sweatshirt like you'd buy anywhere."

Hyland never missed anything that was broadcast on KMOX, either because he was listening or found out about it later. Usually he was listening.

"Bob Costas has told this story and it's true," said Scott St. James, who now works in Los Angeles, but worked at KMOX in the 1970s. "I hadn't been there too long and I was doing the midnight to 3 AM thing. I had no idea Mr. Hyland came to work so early in the morning. I was just doing my show, having fun. I was a boot wearer in those days. I had my boots propped up, my cowboy hat on, my buckskin jacket on, a toothpick in my mouth, and sunglasses on. Remember this is radio, so no one knew what I looked like. I was just having fun."

"Scott liked to dress up like a cowboy and Mr. Hyland didn't like cowboys," said Elaine Stern, St. James' producer at the time.

" Well, unbeknownst to me, Mr. Hyland had seen me through the studio window," St. James said. "The next day the secretary says, 'Mr.

Hyland wants to see you.' So I go in there and he just started talking to me about stuff. Just stuff. At the end, he says, 'Oh, by the way, there was a rumor going around that there was a guy wearing cowboy boots, a cowboy hat, a buckskin jacket, had a toothpick in his mouth, and sunglasses on. If you see this guy would you tell him, 'This is CBS. We don't have any room for midnight cowboys around here.' I said, 'If I ever see anyone like that I'll damn sure tell him.'"

Newsman Robert R. Lynn recalled one similar episode.

"Once I was on with Bob Hardy in the morning," Lynn said. "I swallowed my coffee wrong and I could tell I was going to cough. I got up and ran to the door, but I was a bit too late and started coughing before I could get out the door. After I composed myself, I went back in the studio and Rudy Ruzicka, the engineer, opened the squalk box, 'Mr. Hyland called and said to tell you not to cough on the air.'"

"Then there's the story about Bob Costas trying to see Bob Hyland for a raise," said Jack Buechner. Hyland was always "too busy." Finally Costas spent the night sleeping on the floor outside of Hyland's office. Every morning Hyland went to 6 AM Mass at the old Cathedral. When he came in from Mass, Costas went in to see him whereupon Hyland said, "Not now, can't you see I'm busy?"

Hyland might have acted tough on the outside, but those who were friends or benefited from his acts of kindness knew him on a much different scale.

"He did a lot of things for people that he wanted to do privately," said his son, Matt Hyland. Matt Hyland almost seemed uncomfortable that a chapter in a book would be dedicated to his father, knowing how much he valued his privacy.

"There is not a week that goes by that someone does not come up to me and tell me something my father had done for them," Matt Hyland said. If the elder Hyland were alive today, he would not like the spotlight shining on him personally or on the many good deeds he did to help people, but those deeds are part of the person who helped shape KMOX into the great institution it became.

When Jack Buck's father-in-law became ill on a cruise ship, it was Hyland who came to the rescue using every connection he had to help get him off the ship to where he could receive good medical attention.

Hyland would help people who needed help.

"When Rocky Sickmann came back after being held hostage in Iran," said former news director John Angelides, "Hyland hired him. He had a way of hiring celebrities in one way or another. He also had a soft spot in his heart for people who were down and out."

He has also helped arrange employees wedding receptions or other things that were important to them. At the KMOX-*Post Dispatch* Scholar Athlete Dinners, Hyland would go himself so he could meet the high school recipients.

"I will never forget my first encounters with Mr. Hyland," said Wendy Wiese. "I was sitting in his office, and the first thing that ran through my mind was: 'He is the most powerful man in broadcasting, I've got to get him to respect me. I want him to think I'm a player.' After he offered me the job, I said, 'Could I think about it and call you Monday?' He looked at me and said, 'Do you have any idea what I'm offering you? Do you know how many people would kill for the opportunity to work here?' I actually had another interview scheduled at another station that day and I told him that. He said, 'Are you joking? Is this some kind of a joke?'"

So bright and early Monday morning Wiese called to accept the job.

"When he got on I said, 'Mr. Hyland, hi, this is Wendy Wiese,' and he said, 'Who?' so I said, 'I just talked to you on Saturday and…' then he said, 'I'm just kidding, what did you decide?' I said, 'I'd love to work here if you'll have me' (When I'd told my mother he offered me the job and that I told him I'd tell him on Monday, she said, 'What are you…CRAZY? Call him back and tell him you'll take it now.) He said, 'You'll start in three weeks.'"

It was a coincidence because three weeks later, her grandmother died of a heart attack.

"She was such an important person in my life," said Wiese. "And here I got to spend the last three weeks of her life with her, and she did get to hear me on KMOX. When I found out she died, I got into the car and then KMOX was on, it still gives me chills thinking of it. When Mr. Hyland put me on morning drive, he came up to me after my first show, which I was really nervous to do. 'I'm really proud of you,' he said, 'And you know who else is really proud of you? Your grandmother.'

That was just such a fatherly thing to say. He had a whole other side of him that many people did not get to see."

"He was like a dad to Wendy," said Jim White. "That says something about Mr. Hyland. He had the unique ability of sizing people up and treating them one-on-one. He treated everybody differently. Some he inspired, some he frightened. That was one of his great talents: Treat each person in a way so as to get what he wanted out of them."

"Robert Hyland was responsible for me meeting my wife, " said John Carney. "I was working at KXOK in 1986 and Mr. Hyland hired me, but I had a 'no compete' clause which meant I couldn't work on radio in St. Louis for six months. So he got me on the payroll. Well actually I was on the payroll of some advertising agency. I couldn't go on the air, so I didn't do anything and I got paid. I was getting bored and wanting something to do. One day he calls me in and says, 'I think you're getting a little heavy.' He hands me somebody's card, some gym. He says, 'Go on out here and ask for so and so, he'll be your trainer.' I did that for a little while. Came back after a couple of weeks and said, I'm really bored, I'm getting paid, and working out, but I'm bored.

"The next thing I know, I'm writing for Dick Cavett. Bob Hyland got that for me. Cavett was doing a syndicated radio comedy show that was produced here in St. Louis. I went to New York several times to work with Cavett. So now my 'no-compete' is up and I wanted to get to work. Mr. Hyland says, 'Well, we want to bring you in right and properly promote you. In the meantime, I've got a friend with a station at the Lake of the Ozarks and they need somebody with some personality down there. You go down there three months and it will give us a chance to plan your marketing strategy. I'm 23, I'm still ahead of schedule, so I went to the lake. I went to a country station and he left me there! I was at KLDN in Eldon, Missouri, but I met my wife, Mindy, down there so it turned out OK. I don't look on it as Hyland setting my career back a few years, I look on it as he helped me meet my wife."

Hyland had a way of getting any kind of information he needed whenever he needed it.

"I'll never forget in 1980 when everyone thought there was going to be a baseball strike announced at the deadline of 2 AM," said sportscaster John Rooney. "He called me and told me to go interrupt John

McCormick's show a few minutes before the 2 o'clock network news came on because he knew it would be the lead story and he wanted to scoop the network. McCormick said, 'You better be right." I said, 'God told me', but then I said, 'I better be right.' And it was right, there was no strike, he had gotten it from someone in New York before the networks had it."

In the summer of 1982 St. Louis played host to the Miss Universe pageant. Some of the world's most beautiful and talented women were in the city.

"I'll never forget when Mr. Hyland threw the party for the contestants in the Miss Universe Pageant at KMOX," said Lisa Bedian, a sports producer at the time. "He invited some of the city's most influential businessmen and there they were with all of the contestants from the pageant. I remember trying to go into the bathroom and seeing all these beauty queens who couldn't speak English in there."

Hyland liked to be involved in all aspects of running the station, and that included the mail.

"If you wrote a letter to Mr. Hyland, you can be assured he read it," said former producer Rene Servier. "It wasn't his secretary, it wasn't his program director, or his consultant, it was he who read them. Say a listener would write a letter saying, 'I don't like that *Trading Station* show.' It would not be surprising for Robert Hyland to pick up the phone himself and call the person and say, 'So you don't like the *Trading Station*? I want to clarify some points with you. Is it the time of day or what?'"

"Bob and Robert Hyland were very close," said Re Hardy, the widow of KMOX great Bob Hardy. "He had a healthy respect for Mr. Hyland and called him either the Chief or Mr. Hyland. Mr. Hyland was very protective of the people who worked as hard as he did. He could read people and those were the people who really stood out to him. People like Jack Buck, Bob Costas, Jim White, Jack Carney."

"Mr. Hyland was one of the most influential people in my life," said Costas. "I am sure that many KMOXers would say the same thing. He was tremendously charismatic, a tremendous presence. No one could ever outwork him. He'd come in at 1:30, 2:00, 3:00 in the morning and

stay all day. He never took a vacation. When the boss is like that, it's pretty hard to call in sick with a case of the sniffles."

"He was so difficult to see sometimes if there was an issue you needed to bring to his attention," said Ron Jacober, the sports coordinator, "I used to set the alarm and get up about 2:30 in the morning and call his direct line. He'd answer as if it were the middle of the day with a stern, 'yes.'

"That way I could get maybe a minute or two of his attention. When he would call me at home about something, it was always interesting. He would ask the question and many times as I'm answering I would realize he had apparently heard enough because he had hung up."

"I remember I'd be out with my wife, Mary" said Jim Holder. "We'd be out for a nice night, have a few libations, then I'd get home and suddenly I'd get an idea for an interview or a show and I'd pick up the phone and call him and he would be there. We'd be conducting business just like it was 8:30 in the morning. It never ceased to amaze me. Of course you weren't going to chit-chat with him. It wasn't like, 'Hi boss, let's sit down and chew the fat.' Any meeting you would have with him would be like seven seconds to 22 seconds."

"He liked everyone to do work for charities," said Re Hardy. "Everyone had charities they would support. They would go out and do emcee jobs and donate the money to their favorite charity. Bob Hyland encouraged you to support a charity, and whatever you did he did not disapprove as long as it was for charity. He had a lot of charities he supported. St. Anthony's Hospital, the Zoo, others, because of that the station supported them."

"Bob Hyland was a man of quick decision," said sports executive Bing Devine. "He was very personable, even when he had to be firm. I liked him and thought he was a very fine executive. I'd known him before he worked at KMOX, but not closely. Then I kept hearing how tough and stern he was, but I found him to be very personable."

Bill Bidwill, Jr., knew Hyland personally because his father, Bill Bidwill, the owner of the St. Louis football Cardinals, was a good friend of his. Bidwill went to high school with Hyland's son, Matt.

"Sometimes people would be talking around the office, you know like they do about their boss," said Bidwill, Jr. "One day I was in Mr.

Hyland's office and I could hear a bunch of them in the newsroom. His office was just on the other side of the wall from the newsroom and he could hear every word they were saying. I was thinking, 'oh my gosh, he can hear that stuff!'"

The Bidwills would go to the Hyland's house for backyard bar-b-ques and Bidwill would see another side of Hyland that the employees did not see.

"He could relax," said Bidwill. "On Saturdays he would be sunning himself by the swimming pool. He was really nice, he was great. One night it was funny, though. I had been out with Matt, it was summer vacation, and I was dropping him off at his house. It was about 1 in the morning and I'm dropping Matt off, and we see his dad is about to leave for work. He just smiled at us and said, 'what are you guys doing?'"

Hyland was a very private person and liked to keep his personal life and family life private. His son Matt went into the sales end of broadcasting and his daughter, Molly, worked for Fleishmann-Hillard Public Relations firm, and is now raising her two children. Hyland had two sons from his first marriage, Robert "Rip" Hyland who lives in California and is involved in broadcasting, and William "Clay" Hyland, who passed away in 1988, after receiving a heart transplant.

"One day one of our producers walked in Mr. Hyland's office," said Wiese. "He had his desk drawer open and quickly looked up, 'Oh, you startled me!' he said."

"It was one of the most touching moments of my experience with Mr. Hyland," recalled producer Jeanette Hoag Grider. "He reached into a drawer for something and pulled out a picture of one of his sons [Matt] as a small boy. He said, 'Isn't that a cute little boy?' and passed it over for me to look at."

"I think his love for his children ran deep but he did not discuss it," said Jeanette Hoag Grider. "He was devastated at the death of his son Clay, proud of Rip's and Matt's accomplishments, and of Molly's VP Queen Status."

"Having the name Hyland, my wife, Stacey, sometimes gets asked if she is related to him [Robert Hyland]," said Matt. "People ask her about him, what he was like. I met her after he passed away, so she was never able to meet him. I really wish she could have known him."

One of the legends passed down at KMOX was that Hyland had a radio that just had KMOX on it and you could not change it.

"That rumor was not true," said Matt Hyland with a smile. "We had several radios around the house, and they were all set to KMOX, but he did not have one special radio that only played KMOX."

"Mr. Hyland was known for putting down the worth of television, but we had it on good authority [Harry Hamm] that he loved James Bond movies and would watch them at home," said Grider.

"Mr. Hyland was a hard worker," said Alice English, who wrote his editorials for him. "You couldn't keep up with him. Especially in the early days of the *At Your Service* programs he was very hands on with the programs. He placed great emphasis on quick reaction. He would want us to get a pertinent guest, someone who was in the news."

There was the story passed down that Costas told about the time when someone saw Hyland talking on the telephone. Someone wondered who he was talking to and was told, "He's calling 'dial-a-prayer' to get his messages."

"I got to know Bob Hyland on a personal level," said Taffy Wilbur, who worked on the air from 1960 to 1967. "As a ballplayer's wife, I sat in an area of the ballpark and he was a few rows behind me. His dad was the surgeon general of baseball. Bob loved baseball. We got to know him and I liked his wife, Martha Ann, and his kids."

"He was always on the move," said Jerry Schober, superintendent of the Arch grounds. "If I wanted to talk to him, I would try to just catch up with him. I'd call him and say, 'Tell you what, you're going to that meeting, why don't we meet at the corner and walk over?' Then we'd meet and talk on the way to the meeting. I'd come up with an idea and then decide against it and I'd say, 'I've got this idea; no it probably wouldn't work for KMOX.' Then he'd get curious and say, 'What was it?' And I'd say, 'No, it wouldn't work for KMOX, but KXOK would probably do it. He would run up to me and literally grab me, 'What was it? 'Of course we'll do it!'"

"Many people had heard about Bob Hyland and had preconceived notions about him," said Geri Davison, whose friendship with Hyland led to an internship at KMOX. Davison (and her husband, Kurt), after raising their children in a theatrical family and appearing in movies

including *Bonnie and Clyde* with Warren Beatty, decided to go back to Washington University to get a degree in communications. "I asked Bob if I could be an intern and he said yes. He was a wonderful man and many people did not realize that. They just saw what the public perceived him to be, this hard working tyrant, but he was actually very personable, very spiritual. He was very Catholic and would pray over difficult decisions. He cared about individual people, he was genuine. I would put him in the class with Warren Beatty and I knew them both."

Hyland always was known for his good looks and how he looked was important to him.

"I occasionally saw him wearing his silk KHTR jacket," said Casey Van Allen, the head of production at KMOX. "It was a black silk jacket with 'The Chief'" embroidered on it. Everyone who worked upstairs on the FM side at the time, had those jackets, and I would see him wearing it in the middle of the night."

"He could be casual when he was not working," said Earl Roach of Roach International Hair Salon. Roach cut Hyland's hair. "When he came in for a haircut on a Saturday, he would have khaki pants, a collared shirt, and penny loafers. Once he came in with no socks and I was in a funny mood. I said, 'Mr. Hyland, you don't have any socks on.' He said, 'so.' I said, 'Well, you don't think I'd walk into YOUR office with no socks on, do you?' He got a big kick out of that."

"The most important thing about doing his hair was his 'part.' Every time I'd cut his hair he would talk about his part. He'd say, 'The 'part' is too low,' and I'd have to make it higher. One time he said it and after I moved the part higher, I took a pair of red garters I had gotten just for that occasion out of the drawer. I said, 'Do you trust me?' and he said yes, so I slid those garters up each of his sleeves. I said, 'With these garters and that part I could get you a job at the Red Onion [that was the bar at the Mansion House]!'"

Roach always appreciated Hyland because he felt Hyland had furthered his career. Hyland got him on as the hairstylist at the Muny, enabling him to meet and do the hair of many movie stars and prominent people. He also put Roach on the air.

"Mr. Hyland had a favorite comb," said Roach. "I had a comb that would make his hair look like you just ran your fingers through it. He

liked it, and made it just perfect for what he liked. He had great hair. It was curly at the back of his neck. He couldn't get anyone to control it. The first time I met him was at Musial and Biggie's Restaurant and we got to talking about that. He said he couldn't get anyone to control it without cutting it too short. I said, 'I'll bet I can if you'll give me the chance.' He said, 'Nobody's ever made it lay down in the back without cutting it too short.' I said that with the right cut it would lay down. I knew I could do it. He came to me and he never left."

Rene Servier remembers when Iben Browning, the scientist, predicted the big earthquake in St. Louis in 1990. Hyland told the employees to downplay it.

"He said, 'Don't make too much out of it,'" she said. "'It's not going to happen.' But nonetheless, the night before it was supposed to hit, the Steuben crystal in his office was being packed up just in case."

"It was never put back out in his office after that," said Juli Nieman, who does the financial reports. "I understand it was donated somewhere."

Hyland placed a lot of emphasis on the station winning awards. He had the newsroom do certain stories for the main purpose of winning an award.

"Some people resented the fact that he would not let them keep the awards they won," said Ron Barber who worked in the newsroom. "I won an award for covering the Kansas City skywalk collapse. When word first came across the wire, I said, 'This is big,' and I got our intern at the time, Kent Malinowski, on the phones. We were talking to cops, emergency people, witnesses, etc. As the evening progressed and it got more horrid we realized the magnitude of this thing. Stations all over the country were calling in to KMOX to get our reports and to hook into our coverage. I won the National Journalism Award from San Francisco State University, which is a highly respected journalism program. I didn't get to keep it, though."

Hyland figured if you were working for his station on his payroll at the time, then the station won the award, not the reporter, and the station kept the award. Those who won the awards were able to contact the institution and in many cases get a duplicate award.

He took pride in the awards the station won, and he wanted it known when they won them, but as for his own personal accolades,

Hyland did not like to be in the spotlight. When organizations wanted to honor him, he shied away, and, according to former KMOX newsman Frank Absher, he tried to get out of the Press Club honoring him at one of its dinners because he felt uncomfortable with the spotlight falling on him. If it was his radio station that was fine, but he did not like personally to be in the spotlight.

Hyland was often called a "control freak." He was in control of his radio station, he was in control of his civic committees he served on, and, in the end, it seems he was even in control of his destiny.

Even though lymphoma cancer had ravaged his body, Hyland managed to come to work as much as he could in the last few weeks of his life.

"He would come in to do his editorials," said Wendy Wiese. "Anne Keefe and I saw him about two weeks before he died."

"We knew the end was near," said Bob Hamilton, a newsman whom Hyland held in high regard. "One night Norma [Wallner, Hyland's secretary] came in and put his obituary notice on my desk. 'Don't read it yet,' she said, letting me know that while he hadn't died yet, he would probably die that night."

It was getting late in his shift and Hamilton checked with Wallner. Not yet, she said.

About a half hour before his shift was to end, she came in.

"It's time," she said. "He's gone."

"It was very strange," said Hamilton. "I had to go in and read Mr. Hyland's obituary, and he had wanted me to be the one to read it. Talk about someone who is in control of things in his life. That was unbelievable."

"I wrote the obituary for Mr. Hyland," said John Angelides. "I based it on a file he had. He kept a resume on file and had a bio. We sent it out to the AP and the *Post-Dispatch*.

"Even up to the end he worked even though he had the cancer," said Jerry Schober. "He would still make it to work even though he was taking the treatment and it would make him so tired, and he never missed church. We went to his funeral. It was unbelievable, it was a whopper of a funeral. It was hard to find a seat in the New Cathedral that day."

Wallner, his trusted assistant, sat with the family.

Bill Bidwill, Jr., represented his family and came in from Arizona.

"I was an usher," he said. "There were so many people at the funeral. They packed the New Cathedral. What I thought was interesting was the number of listeners who came. People came up to me and said, 'I listened to the station, is it OK if I come in?' and I ushered them in. It was a very sad time, and a hard time for Matt [Hyland's son] because his mother Pat died six months later."

"The Hyland years were a dynasty," said Jim White. "KMOX was number one in the country for many years. One thing I'll say about Hyland, he was a bastard to work for, but I cried like a baby at his funeral. We all did."

"It was like believing in Santa Claus, that he could beat it [the cancer]," said Wiese. "Sitting there with Bob Hardy, we were having trouble just going on; Bob told me he didn't think he could do it. I told him, 'You know he'd want you to.' We still miss him so much."

CHARLES JACO

Charles Jaco came to KMOX in February of 1995. He was hired by Tom Langmyer, who was then program director, and Rod Zimmerman, who was the general manager.

Jaco has written two novels, been a war correspondent for CNN, a public speaker, columnist, and talk show host. His novels are *Dead Air*, a thriller set during the Gulf War; and *Live Shot*, a novel involving the same character, television correspondent, Peter Dees, who was in the first novel.

Jaco became known worldwide for his live reports from Kuwait, Saudi Arabia, and Iraq on CNN during the Gulf War. It was not the first or last time he has done international broadcasting, and he has won awards for his work.

"The most interesting stories I covered were when I became the first American talk radio host to broadcast live and uncensored from Havana," said Jaco. "This was during the four days of the Pope's trip to Cuba in January 1998. It was groundbreaking radio and I was proud to be part of it.

"The other story involved broadcasting from the Vatican, and from the Pope's plane over the Atlantic and from Mexico City as part of the run up to the Pope's appearance in St. Louis in January 1999. It was the kind of thing you don't expect local commercial radio to do anymore and just reflects KMOX's commitment to go above and beyond what is expected."

Jaco left the network news business and came to KMOX in part because he wanted to move back to his native Missouri to be nearer to his family in Poplar Bluff, and he also liked the reputation of KMOX.

"We spoke with him between six months and a year before we finally had a spot for him," said Tom Langmyer. "Ultimately we were able to get him on board."

Jaco gained fame as a war correspondent for CNN during Desert Storm, so listeners already knew who he was when he came to St. Louis. He hosts *Newsmakers* in the afternoons on KMOX.

Jaco has won many awards for his broadcasting. Recently he won the 2000 Achievement in Radio Award as Best Talk Show Host in St. Louis and Best Newscaster in St. Louis.

"One thing Charles Jaco did was bring cable television to KMOX," said Bob Heil, the KMOX electronics expert. "Robert Hyland would never allow even the word television to be said at KMOX. I remember when Paul Grundhauser called me because Jaco had come aboard and Jaco wanted CNN in the building. Well, there wasn't a decent television set to be found. I went over there and delivered a digital satellite system so Jaco could have CNN in his office. Next thing I knew there were three more television sets in the newsroom."

"Charles is one of the most talented journalists I've ever worked with, and I've worked with many talented journalists here at KMOX," said Peggy Cohill Drenkhahn who produces *Newsmakers*.

Jaco has enjoyed his experiences at KMOX.

"KMOX is to mid-America and St. Louis what CNN is to the globe," he said. "It's a fascinating place to work and I feel very fortunate to be a part of it."

RON JACOBER

Bob Hardy was responsible for Ron Jacober coming to work on KMOX, asking him if he would be interested in a job after hearing him on WIBV in Belleville.

"At that time KMOX and KMOX-FM were in a building on Hampton Avenue," said Jacober. "They assigned me to work mornings on FM. Hampton Avenue was a busy street and it was very difficult to turn into the side street that led to the parking lot behind KMOX during morning drive. One morning I was waiting for an opening in traffic to turn and Bob Hardy was on his way out to get breakfast. Guess what? He turned out. I turned in and we ran head on into each other. So, here's the guy who got me into the business and I ran into him. No injuries, but the cars were not driveable."

Jacober stayed at KMOX for about a year and a half before accepting a job at KSD television.

"I gave Bob Hyland two weeks' notice and he gave me 30 minutes to get out of the building," said Jacober.

Seventeen years later, Hyland hired Jacober back. He had been working at KXOK doing a morning show called *Jacober and Company* as well as doing Blues games with Dan Kelly. Bob Osborne, the KMOX program director, called and told Jacober that Hyland wanted to see him.

"I called him and said, 'I understand you would like to talk to me.' He said, 'And, what about?' The game of cat and mouse continued until an interview finally took place on New Year's Eve, 1986. He all but said he wanted me to come back, but he put me off for over three months. He would say the same thing every time I called, 'Don't have the budget, what's the absolute lowest salary you can live on?' I was always advised not to make any threats or give him a deadline, but on Friday, April 5, 1987 I called him and told him, 'Boss, I must have an answer by Monday, I need work.' He hung up on me. I figured that was it. On Monday morning he called and asked when I could start. I started that day."

Jacober was hired to manage the sports office.

"He asked me to run the sports department, not as the sports director, but as a manager," Jacober said. "I told him I would, but I couldn't be a 'yes' man. He said he didn't want a 'yes' man because he had too many of those already. However, there was never any question as to who was in charge—of everything. I recall making a programming suggestion one time that he didn't like. He looked at me and said, 'Just for the record, I'm the program director, the news director, the sales manager, and the sports director.' I got the message."

Jacober is the host of *Sports on a Sunday Morning*, the traditional and highly popular show that features interviews with many of the executives and coaches of sports teams in the St. Louis area.

He has done play-by-play assignments for the baseball Cardinals, the hockey Blues, the soccer Steamers, and other college and professional sports.

"He has been a constant at the station," said Tom Langmyer. "He's got great organizational skills and he handles all of the day-to-day operations of the sports department. He is a very versatile talent."

STEVE JANKOWSKI

Steve Jankowski worked as a co-host of both *Total Information AM* and *Total Information PM* from 1995 until 1999. He has worked for several radio and television stations in the St. Louis area, beginning his career in 1972 as a sportscaster on WSIE-FM in Edwardsville.

Jankowski now works for KSDK-TV.

COLIN JARRETTE

Colin Jarrette was an engineer for KMOX from 1973 to 1998. He had been working as an engineer on the Montreal Expos broadcasts since the team began play in 1969. Through that he had gotten to know Jack Buck and Mike Shannon, and when an opening for an engineer came up at KMOX, the station contacted Jarrette.

"I did something that made me unique with the Montreal broadcast," said Jarrette. "In those days the engineers did not travel. The visiting club would get an engineer in each town. I did travel because they could not find a French engineer in each town. What I did was I worked on the English broadcast and sat in the English speaking radio broadcast booth with that feed in my left ear. I had the French broadcasters sit in a distant booth and had the French broadcast in my right ear. The commercials for the English broadcast would be played by the station in Montreal [with his direction]. I played the French commercial from a tape recorder in the booth. We worked on a very tight time system. When I was traveling, I was doing it and it was strange to people. Often people would come in to watch me to see how it worked. After a while, the unions in Chicago and St. Louis said I was doing two jobs since it was two broadcasts.

"The unions insisted I had to have a union membership card. There was nothing like that in Montreal. I was forced to join a union and the only one I could find was the pipefitters. You just had to be in a union. I paid my money and they gave me the union card."

When KMOX asked, Jarrette if he wanted to come to work in St. Louis, at first he said no, but about a year later, and after they 'upped the ante and sweetened the pot,' he agreed to come. When he got there he was an engineer.

"I made sure everything worked," said Jarrette. "I would repair the recorders, go to the transmitter, make sure the cart machines worked, do general maintenance."

Apart from that Jarrette did football, baseball, hockey, and some basketball games. If the Cardinals were in town, he might have four days at the ballpark and then he would work three days in the studio. Tom Barton was the engineer on the Cardinal broadcast, and Jarrette would be assigned to the visiting team.

That went on for a number of years and when Jack Carney would go on vacation and Jack Buck filled in, Jarrette often worked on his program. He also filled in wherever needed at the station.

"Colin was very helpful to me," said Anne Keefe. "Especially when I first started."

"I always liked working with Jack [Buck]," said Jarrette. "We had a lot in common. We both liked classical music and show tunes. Jack can sing the words to any song. When Jack would fill in, he would play music, the kind of music we liked."

One day when Clarence Nieder, Carney's regular producer was on vacation, he got in a car accident. He suffered a broken rib. Since Jarrette had experience working on the show, they put him on. When it was time for Nieder to come back, Carney had gotten used to Jarrette and asked that he stay on the show. Jarrette is an artist and he had art in common with Carney.

"I'd started my painting when I was in Montreal," said Jarrette. "Carney liked art and we had that interest in common. My paintings and art were interesting to Carney. We became friends. We would go to Jack's for Thanksgiving. We became friendly, Jack and Clara [Jarrette's wife] and I."

When people think of Jack Carney one of the things they remember are the parades. Jarrette and producer Frank Pawloski were instrumental in getting the first parade started. Jarrette rode a scooter and was a marshal.

Around the time of Carney's death, Barton left KMOX to go to Anheuser-Busch. Jarrette was named to replace him on the Cardinals' broadcasts.

"I started traveling in 1985," he said. "I've known Jack since 1969, I'd see him in spring training and in Montreal. Once I started traveling with the team Jack and I would go to movies and plays. We liked the same types of things."

Jarrette died from a brain aneurism in August 2000. After his retirement, he had worked as a volunteer at the Webster Groves Library and put on shows of his paintings there.

MARY LOU JOHANEK

Mary Lou Johanek Pullen worked as a newswriter in the 1970s before becoming an on-air reporter. She left KMOX to go to the CBS network in New York and eventually went on to work in television. She was an anchor on a station in Columbus, Ohio. She now does an occasional editorial or column in the *Toledo Blade* newspaper and does freelance video.

"I was so surprised to see Mary Lou on the television in Columbus when I was living there getting my masters at Bowling Green," said fellow KMOX newsman Stu Esrock. "I would have lunch with a buddy of mine who was the news director of that station and I'd see her down there."

KEN JONES

A tip from a college instructor that KMOX was looking for writers led Ken Jones to the station in 1945. He was hired as assistant continuity director on the basis of one 30-minute script and was assigned to write *The Land We Live In* weekly broadcasts.

"The show was conceived in 1937 as a public relations vehicle for

Union Electric," Jones said. "It was supposed to talk about the history of Union Electric's service area, which mainly was around St. Louis. We wrote dramatization's of historic events from the area.

"We did stories about Cardinal Glennon Hospital, the Boy Scouts, the YMCA. The show tied in all those things."

The show was a weekly broadcast and was performed live at the KMOX studio in front of about 200 people.

Jones' most memorable show was about Cardinal Glennon. Union Electric brought in actress Maureen O'Hara to star in the show, which was a dramatization of Cardinal Glennon's life as a young boy growing up in Ireland.

"She wasn't able to get through the show," Jones said. "She broke into tears and was crying, because she said the show made her realize how much she missed Ireland. We had to cover it with music at the end of the show. She came up and later apologized and said she didn't know how much it would upset her."

Jones stayed at KMOX, where he also did a variety of other writing assignments, including Saturday at the Chase, until 1948. Union Electric didn't want the show moved to a different time slot, and instead moved the broadcast to KSD, where it remained until going off the air in 1952.

"It went off the air because of television," Jones said. "We attempted to translate it to television but it didn't work."

Jones went on to a successful career in the advertising business, and now is retired and living on a farm in Michigan.

MERLE JONES

Merle Jones was the general manager of KMOX from 1937 to 1944. He succeeded James Shouse, and prior to his appointment he had been working as a sales manager for CBS, based in Chicago.

He resigned in 1944 to become general manager of a station in Washington, DC. He spent 32 years working for CBS, eventually moving into television management. He was appointed vice president of network television in 1956, and served as president of CBS-TV in 1957 and 1958.

Jones died in 1976 at the age of 71.

DR. TIM JORDAN

Dr. Tim Jordan did a show called *Families First* at the end of 1999 and into 2000. The show followed the publication of a book Jordan co-wrote with Sally Tippett Rains, *Keeping Your Kids Grounded When You're Flying By The Seat Of Your Pants.*

Jordan, with his wife Anne, operate a company called Children and Families and is a national speaker. *Families First* was co-hosted by Vicki Atlas. Jordan invited people to call in with problems they were having with their families and he would offer advice. He encouraged teenagers to participate.

GEORGE JUNKIN

After KMOX went on the air on Christmas Eve 1925, the station's investors held a competition to pick the chief announcer. Candidates were given several on-air opportunities to impress a panel of judges and the listening public.

The winner was George Junkin, who had been working as an announcer for S.W. Strauss Co.'s station in Chicago, WSWS. Within a year after moving to St. Louis, he was promoted to managing director of KMOX and later became secretary of the investors' group which owned the station, Voice of St. Louis, Inc.

Junkin was involved in one of the earliest scandals in the station's history. He was divorced in June of 1929, and in November of that year he married Alice Maslin, who was KMOX's director of programs. She had worked at the station since it was founded.

Both Junkin and his new wife resigned from KMOX in 1931 and went to work for a station in Philadelphia.

JACKSON KANE

Jackson Kane was an in-studio newscaster in 1979. He had come from KSD and was known for having a deep and bellowing voice. People tried to imitate him saying "Jackson Kane, KMOX radio news," but they couldn't do it.

"I'll never forget Jackson," said Rick Powers, the sports director at KDNL in St. Louis who was an intern at KMOX in 1979. "He would always send the interns out to get his dinner; we had to go to this Chinese restaurant."

One of the jobs of a newscaster is to know about all of the local news, so it is in the job description to be reading the newspaper every day.

"He had glasses and his eyesight was not very good, so he would be reading the paper holding it up close to his face," said Powers. "He had a great voice."

"When he typed his copy he'd use a lot of abbreviations," said newswriter John Amann. "No one else could read his copy, so when we would want to re-write the stories for a later newscast, we couldn't, we'd have to go get the wire copy and start over."

RANDY KARRAKER

Randy Karraker started his career at KMOX as an intern in 1983 and moved up through the ranks to become the primary host of *Sports Open Line* programs.

He enjoys the programs where special guests appear, such as the broadcasts from Mike Shannon's restaurant during the baseball season.

"It's always fun to have the old Cardinals on at Shannon's," said Karraker. "Having Mike, Bob Gibson, Lou Brock, Tim McCarver, and especially Bob Uecker tell stories about what happened off the field is great. Before one of the 1964 World Series' games, Uecker stole a marching band member's tuba and was catching fly balls with it in the outfield. Even though everybody knows the story by now, whenever Uecker tells it, everyone is rolling with laughter."

And speaking of Mike Shannon's, baseball wasn't the only topic ever discussed there.

"The Rams' ownership and front office came over to Shannon's the night the team announced it was relocating here," said Karraker. "Seeing how thrilled Georgia Frontiere, Stan Kroenke, and all of the front office people were when they finally finished that deal was exciting."

Another highlight for Karraker include covering Brett Hull's record-breaking season for the Blues in 1990-91 and watching how he dealt with the media and fans.

"Every night, it seemed, he would score a goal, and the town buzzed every day about how great he was," Karraker said. "We did a Saturday night show at his restaurant, and he would always bring along teammates for the show. The response was unbelievable. We always had several hundred people lined up out the door, wanting to get in and get his autograph. He's such a great guy for the media to deal with…that was always entertaining radio."

"I think Randy Karraker epitomizes what KMOX is today," said Dan McLaughlin. "He is tremendous and has been so influential in my career. I look at him as being my mentor. I was his reporter for his sportscasts. Along with Mr. Buck he's been the most influential person I've ever met in my life."

Tom Langmyer is impressed not only with Karraker's sports knowledge, but the relationships he has been able to build with players, coaches, and executives on the St. Louis sports scene.

"I think his fairness and his style puts people at ease," Langmyer said. "He is the kind of interviewer who asks the tough questions, but

he does it politely. He gets the answers he needs more so than if he had an in-your-face approach."

Another reason Langmyer is high on both Karraker and Ron Jacober is that their attitude off the air is the same as while they are broadcasting.

"The way they are on the air is not an act," Langmyer said.

"I have a couple of benchmarks when doing a show," said Karraker. "First of all, whenever I'm on, my parents are likely to be listening, and I wouldn't want to offend or embarrass them. Secondly, especially when I'm doing a postgame show, I know that Jack Buck is listening in his car, players' families are listening, and youngsters are listening. I wouldn't ever say anything to disappoint Jack, I wouldn't say anything about a player that I wouldn't say to him in the clubhouse or locker room the next day, and I wouldn't say anything that I wouldn't want my kids hearing in the back seat of my car."

When hosting an *Open Line*, the phones are open and you never know who may call. Once on an *Open Line Show* featured Andy Van Slyke calling from spring training in Florida. One caller identified himself, and he was Andy's dad. "Call home when you get off, we've been trying to reach you,' the elder Van Slyke said. Another surprise caller to Karraker's show one night was Tommy Lasorda.

"Ron Jacober and I were doing an *Open Line*, talking about game six of the 1985 playoffs when Jack Clark hit the dramatic home run that propelled the Cardinals to the National League pennant," said Karraker. "The Dodgers were in town, and lo and behold Tommy Lasorda called in to challenge us as to whether or not he should have pitched to Jack Clark. He was so bold as to ask who we'd rather pitch to, Clark or Andy Van Slyke. Of course, I said Van Slyke. He didn't like that much."

ANNE KEEFE

Anne Keefe could be considered the "Grand Dame" of the KMOX newsroom. She was well respected by co-workers and listeners alike during the 25 years she spent working as a host of *At Your Service* programming.

Keefe had been working in television in Rochester, New York, when she came to KMOX in 1969, almost by accident. On her way from New York to Kansas City, where she was to audition for a new job as an anchorwoman at a Kansas City television station, Keefe stopped to stay with a friend in St. Louis at the Sacred Heart Convent.

Robert Hyland found out who she was and where she was staying. He had been under pressure from the network to hire a woman. He got the number where she was staying and called Keefe at 6 AM. 'What are you doing now?' he asked her, and then invited her to come down to the station, telling her he would send over a car. The car arrived at 6:30.

"My friend Jean Baum had given an audition tape of mine to one of the salesmen at KMOX," Keefe said. "When Robert Hyland called me at 6 AM, I was still in bed. He asked me if I was a good broadcaster and I said, 'I'm the best!' I didn't know who Robert Hyland was quite yet, he was taken aback with that remark. He said he'd send a car over, so I hurried up and got dressed. When the car got there, he had orange juice and coffee in it."

Hyland asked Keefe to do a two-hour audition that night.

"Now you have to realize I was used to being in television, where you have 20 people and a teleprompter to help you and give you signals," she said. "I went in there with one engineer and a producer. I will always remember how much Bob Danko helped me out, he was on the board at the time [as an engineer]."

Hyland liked what he heard and offered her twice what she would make in Kansas City. With this dilemma, she decided to take the radio job. When her first paycheck came it was only half. She marched into his office and asked what that was all about. 'Once you get more experience, you'll get your money,' and she said, 'Match it or I'm out of here.' Hyland found out he had met his match in Anne Keefe.

"It was funny, some of the on-air people at the station were not as helpful," she said. "But the engineers and newsroom people were wonderful. Bobby Danko, Colin Jarrette, all of them, they helped me out so much."

At the time Keefe came to KMOX, she believed she satisfied two big needs that Hyland had.

"Number one, he needed a woman," said Keefe, "and number two, he needed a news director. He had let John Angelides leave for a year to

teach at the University of Missouri in Columbia. With the election coming up soon, he was not going to take long in making his decision."

Keefe was a good editor and writer. With her great success on KMOX and on *Donnybrook*, the television show on KETC in St. Louis, it may surprise listeners to know she was not a career-driven woman.

"[At this point in life] I was not ambitious," she said. "When I did the try-out, I was nervous. Here I was with three kids in college and one in high school I'm bringing with me. I wasn't out to be a star, I needed to make a living. I just wanted a job."

Her first year at KMOX was difficult.

"They picked out all my shows," she said. "I did not have any input in who I was going to interview or what I was going to talk about. I thank God for all the help I got that year. The engineers were great and so were the people in the newsroom. John Angelides came back from Columbia and he was wonderful, also. He ran a great newsroom."

If her first several years at KMOX were difficult, the next ones were very satisfying for her.

"That was when Fred Bodimer came as my producer," said Keefe. "Fred was such a joy in my life. He would give me say-so in my shows. He would say, 'We should set it up with so and so,' and then after we did the show, you would see that same person on the national news. He just had a real feel for the news. Everyone in the newsroom at that time really worked together."

Keefe did approximately three hours a day for 25 years. She interviewed top authors and politicians. KMOX carried a certain power, and if someone was called by KMOX, they rarely said no. Over the years, Keefe felt, the whole purpose of interviews with authors and politicians changed.

"It used to be if you had an author on, you wanted to learn about his book," she said. "With a politician, you wanted to find out more. After a while the interviews changed. With people like [Howard] Stern out there, interviewers have changed to the 'in your face' style of interviewing. Say someone has just written a book about angels. The callers don't seem to want to hear about why he wrote it or learn from it. They want to call up and give their own opinions and say whether they believe in angels or not. And this guy who wrote the book is still on the

line. Somewhere along the line, we've lost our courtesy. I stopped keeping the authors on the line. I would interview them and then I would let them go before I took calls from the listeners. That way the author would not have to hear the comments."

She would do the same with politicians, interview them at the beginning of the show and then open the phone lines.

"Besides the interview, broadcasters began to treat other broadcasters differently," she said. "I was on with Bruce Bradley. He was the funniest guy I ever worked with. In that program we respected each other. We had a lot of gentle kidding going on, but nothing mean. After a while, people wanted to hear that intrusive interview, they wanted negativity. It was an era when people stopped respecting people."

She was known for having her own opinion about the issues and appearing as a strong woman, but she also respected people and tried to do things in a way that would not make a person look bad.

"I got along with Anne Keefe really well," said Gene McNary, who, as the County Executive, was on with her often. "She was talented in asking questions. She's a 'provocateur.' On *Donnybrook* Martin Duggan called himself a provocateur, but to me Anne Keefe really was one. She would frame questions to provoke the person, kind of like Larry King does. It's not like Geraldo where you get mad, it is just sparking someone on and she was good at it."

Keefe said, "I knew most of the politicians personally and could call them if I needed information. The smartest politician I ever knew was Senator Eagleton. He was brilliant and could explain things so well. You asked him something and he would get to the point. I also respected Harriett Woods and Joan Kelly Horn for that reason. They were both absolutely explicit. When I wanted something clarified before I went on the air or when I was on the air, I could ask these people and get good answers."

"That was one of the great things about KMOX," said John Angelides, the news director. "We would try to explain things to the public. Anne would have politicians on and listen to them and let them explain things to the people. You could call these people and say it was KMOX. It was like saying it was *The New York Times*. If KMOX called, people would call back."

Keefe enjoyed talking about politics or items of the news and often would meet up with newspaper reporters or other radio reporters at the Missouri Bar and Grill.

"I liked to meet up with [Roy] Malone or [John] McGuire and just talk about the news," she said.

"Before her shows we would go to lunch," said Joan Beuckman, who worked in the newsroom at the time. "We'd be sitting in the restaurant and she would take one side of an issue and I'd take the other. Before you knew it the whole place would hear us. We argued every day. She was great to work with."

Keefe was a friend to those she worked with. She would make it a point to have lunch with the interns and talk to them about their future.

Keefe realized her star power yet she also realized the unique situation she was in. During the early days of her *At Your Service* shows, women were not put in the position of sounding intelligent and educated very often. Though she had been in television for many years, it was still new for women to be in an authoritarian positon rather than just being the weather girl. Keefe proved to broadcast executives and advertisers as well that people were interested in listening to an educated woman and, in the case of Keefe, a woman with her own views— like them or hate them.

As with any broadcaster doing a live program, however, Keefe never knew exactly what to expect on any given day.

"One time we had on James Watt, the Secretary of the Interior under Reagan," said Keefe. "It was said that he was a Seventh Day Adventist and that he thought the world would be over soon, so he thought it was fine to strip mine and defoliate the forest. I thought I'd ask him about that."

The broadcast began:

Keefe: Good afternoon. We have James Watt, the Secretary of the Interior on with us today. Thanks for joining us. I have heard that you are a Seventh Day Adventist and that you think the world will end soon and that it is OK to strip mine and defoliate the forest.

Watt: That's right.

"I was stunned," said Keefe. "I went to a commercial. Luckily we had a lot of commercials."

Another on-air incident could have turned out a lot worse than it did, thanks to Keefe's quick thinking and that of her producer, Bodimer.

"We were to have a CBS correspondent from the Gulf War on," she said. "After I introduced him, he started telling me how the Iraqis really love Americans and how they want peace. I was thinking this is strange. Then he said one problem they had was no 'petrol.' Fred Bodimer had been giving me signs and looks, and when we heard this we thought, 'Wait, Americans don't say 'petrol,' we say gas.'

"We realized we had a phony. We didn't have a reporter on the line with us at all. The whole thing was wrong and we knew it, but we couldn't quite pinpoint it. Thank God for Fred Bodimer. He was so quick. We went to a break. As it turned out, the CBS correspondent had left the hotel and the message left for him was intercepted by this guy who was an Iraqi."

One of the strangest things Keefe did while on KMOX was go to a wrestling match with Bob Costas and Dan Dierdorf. Keefe wore an evening gown and the men wore tuxes, and they arrived in a limo, later doing reports with the wrestlers. Interviewing Hulk Hogan and then eating White Castles with him is not something you would expect Anne Keefe to have done.

"It was one of those weird things you do," she said. "I took myself quite seriously as a broadcaster. In the long run doing things like that makes you closer to your audiences. It makes people feel they know you. Those funny things you did outside of the norm were what could endear you to people.

"Mr. Hyland liked those strange kinds of things. He felt as though all of us were stars and would have liked to have thought of himself as Cecil B. DeMille. But at the same time he wanted people to know you. He liked it when Bob Hardy would talk about his sausage or about the state fair. Letting the people know we are normal makes them feel they know us. We made dumb mistakes and did silly things and it just made the audiences feel like they knew us. As I look back, I can see what he was doing. He was making us the kind of stars like Art Linkletter. You felt people could come up and say 'hi.' We were real people. That was his genius."

"Anne Keefe is just a fascinating woman," said one-time producer,

Rene Servier. "She has done so much in her life. Every time she spoke, I thought, 'Tell me more, tell me more,' I could sit and listen to her and then listen to her again."

Many people mentioned how Keefe took the time to help them.

"I got that from Dave Kessler, a man I worked for in Rochester," Keefe said. He gave me this advice: 'Don't ever turn away a young person who wants to learn from you.' I've always tried to help young people learn. By heart I'm a teacher. Teaching is what I do best. Not that I think I'm better than anyone or know anything any better. I always thought of my shows as a classroom on the air, but I saw it as 'let's learn together,' 'let's see what this politician or author has to say.'"

"I am now teaching myself," said Keefe, who is retired and still living in St. Louis. She continues to read everything she can get her hands on. "But now I can pick up any book I want. I don't have to read for my kids, the boss, or the audience. I don't have to be accountable."

She does not have any desire to go back into radio and, in fact, she rarely listens to radio.

"During my time I enjoyed it," she said, "but once you're out, you're out of the loop. That's why I left *Donnybrook*. Nan Wyatt is out there, she's right in the middle of it. I love being retired."

DAVID KELLEY

David Kelley was the general sales manager from 1994 until 1997. He left KMOX to become the general manager of KSHE.

BRIAN KELLY

Brian Kelly is a news reporter at KMOX. He was hired in 1997 by news director John Butler.

"I'd been working at WDAF in Kansas City for 12 years," said Kelly. "There was a station ownership change and I'd been doing sports and I could see the new ownership was going in a different direction, so I figured I wouldn't be there long."

Kelly, who was from St. Louis and had always dreamed of working for KMOX, was surprised when a co-worker told him a St. Louis sta-

tion was looking for a news writer. When he asked if it was KMOX, she didn't know. He had done some reports on KMOX about the Kansas City Chiefs and when he saw the phone number he recognized it.

"The whole thing just worked out so well," he said. "I called the number and it was John Butler. Several days later I flew to St. Louis for my interview. I will never forget that day because my wife had been going through an illness and on that morning we were told she was doing great and that afternoon we flew to St. Louis for the interview and I ended up getting the job."

Kelly has done several *Sports Open Lines*, including some Blues open lines, but primarily he does news.

"I don't know which I like better," he said. "The one thing I know is I like being in the middle of the action. My favorite thing to do is be in the middle of a big fire or the highway shutdown and giving the play-by-play.

"My most memorable broadcast was during the Pope coverage. I thought we did a great job with Fred Bodimer and Charles Jaco. It was just really special being in the Trans World Dome and seeing how they changed it into a church. They did a great job of converting it. They covered all the scoreboards and advertising boards with gold and white alternating material. When the Popemobile came in, there were so many flash bulbs and the light was bouncing off of the glass, I described it like a 'drummer doing a drum solo with strobe lights on him.'"

Another big moment for Kelly was when I-70 was shut down by protesters.

"I was right in the middle of it," he said. "I was walking down the ramp with the protesters. People wondered if they would really be able to shut down traffic. I had my cell phone. I said, 'Put me on! They're doing it! Three guys are on the highway, another just got on, they're blocking the highway.' You knew at that time the people in the cars were listening and many others were listening. I was the point man, getting the information out."

He also covered an event the day Steve Fossetts took off in his balloon from Busch Stadium on his attempt to fly around the world.

"It was great live radio," said Kelly. "Kevin Killeen was at Busch and I was called out to cover a plane crash near highway 40. Kevin does his

report and then they go live to me out at this plane crash. The pilot had tried to land on the highway, but he had hit the median and crashed. To be covering two live stories at once, I just thought it was something."

Live coverage of breaking news story played a major role in building the reputation of KMOX.

"When I first got the job, we were moving here from Kansas City," Kelly said. "We had just pulled in after a four-hour drive. We sat down at the dinner table for some pizza and I just popped the top off a beer when I got beeped. The Admiral had been hit by that barge. I left my food where it was and said good-bye to my wife and headed down to the riverfront. I love it, though, I really do.

"It's really exciting to be there and be part of the great tradition and to try to keep the tradition up. Ever since I was a kid growing up in Florissant, I listened to KMOX. Jack Buck and Dan Kelly were my favorites and Bob Costas on the St. Louis Spirits."

DAN KELLY

Dan Kelly was considered by many to be the finest hockey announcer who ever lived. His distinctive voice, his knowledge of the game, and his passion for it transcended his broadcasts and turned many people into hockey fans.

He was as instrumental in the success and popularity of the Blues, an expansion team, as were any of the players and front-office personnel. He really enjoyed the challenge of educating the audience about hockey, and accepted it as his responsibility.

"He knew the finer points about hockey the way I knew baseball," said Jack Buck. "He occasionally broadcast baseball games with me, and he would say, 'How did you know that was a slider?' and I would ask in return, 'How did you know the shot hit the post?' He knew hockey the way I knew baseball."

On those cold winter nights when a radio signal, especially one going out on a 50,000-watt station, could travel a far distance, Kelly became the link for hockey fans to St. Louis, the Blues, and KMOX.

"I was a huge hockey fan, and I used to listen to the Blues' games on KMOX because of Dan Kelly," said Tom Langmyer, who grew up

outside of Buffalo, New York. "I knew KMOX because of Dan Kelly and Jack Buck and the Blues and the Cardinals. It was one of the stations I knew I wanted to work at some day."

Kelly became the play-by-play announcer for the Blues in their second season, 1968. He stayed with the team for 20 years, also working many national broadcasts in the United States and Canada.

He died of cancer in 1989 at the age of 52, eight months before he was inducted into the broadcasters' wing of the Hockey Hall of Fame.

"When Dan started doing the play-by-play for the Blues," said Susie Mathieu, the team's longtime public relations director, "there was no broadcast booth, so Dan did the announcing from the pressbox. The entire pressbox could hear him with his booming voice. The visiting press were always so interested in hearing what he had to say. He was so intelligent."

Kelly worked with many color analysts. To name a few, Gus Kyle, E.J. Holub, Ely Gold, Rick Francis, Nancy Drew, Bill Wilkerson, Jim Holder, and Joe Micheletti.

"I remember I did less than half a dozen games with Dan," said Jim Holder.

That year Holder went to Port Huron, Michigan, the training camp of the Blues. He did interviews and reports for the sportscasts.

"When I was up there, I had an experience I challenge anyone to do," said Holder. "People all know Bobby Plager and Noel Picard. On successive nights in Port Huron, we closed the Port Huron Bowling Alley bar. One of them was a ladies' night. I needed a week's vacation to recuperate from that."

"Dan Kelly really didn't need a color analyst," said Mathieu. "Every year there was a parade of analysts he had to work with. It was like if you drew the short straw at KMOX, you would be the Blues analyst. He always had to help train the person."

Kelly was a perfectionist. After games he called in a report on the game for KMOX to use in the midnight sportscast, and also use the next morning. He was known for being someone who could do the "voicers" on the first or second try. He would always begin his voice report to the producer at KMOX with "Blues hockey game coming your

way in 3,2,1…" and then he'd say, "Last night the Blues defeated the Maple Leafs…"

"There was one night I remember that shows what a perfectionist he was and also how much he liked his fans," said Mathieu. "He was getting frustrated because he was having more trouble with the voice report after the game. There was an electrician working in the arena, he had nothing to do with the broadcast equipment, he was just doing his own work nearby. Suddenly Dan just went off on the guy, 'It shouldn't take this long for me to do this thing! I've got to get down to the Arena Club!'"

Every night after home games Kelly would retreat to his regular table at the Arena club and have his usual: a juicy steak and a glass of B & B.

"He would eat at the Arena Club and talk to the fans," said Mathieu. "It was incredible how open and cordial he always was with the fans. Everyone knew him and liked him."

Mathieu remembered one episode which shows how connected Kelly was in the hockey world and the type of friends he had everywhere.

"It was when the Blues came back to KMOX after being on another station," she said. "Dan Kelly wanted to really get a good interview to please Mr. Hyland. He told me, 'I have a great guest, could you pick him up at his hotel and bring him down to KMOX?'

"I said, 'Sure, Dan, who's the guest?' and it turned out to be Wayne Gretzky. So I had to pick up the greatest hockey player in the history of the game and here I was driving my station wagon. I'm driving down highway 40 at the last Missouri exit and Wayne looked at a car next to us and sees this little kid with his hands on his father's shoulders. Here's this 22-year-old hockey player and he said to me, 'That's just absolutely disgusting, that kid should be in a car seat!'

"Dan Kelly did so much for the Blues' franchise. He really put the Blues on the map. Because of KMOX's reach, people all over the country could pick up the Blues' broadcasts. People would always say the Blues were their second favorite team if they were from out of town because they listened so much to Dan Kelly on the games. And he was a great speaker at dinners. You could hand him a script a half hour before dinner and he would add jokes and personalize, it and it would be great."

Kelly was known for his love of a good restaurant and his sports

colleagues kidded him about his quirky pronunciation of the word potato, which he called a "poday'duh." Everyone who worked with or for Kelly liked him; he was nice to everybody. Though he had a quick Irish temper, he treated people nicely. Later in Kelly's career, the on-air talent started to do some of the engineering tasks. The phones were put into the studio so the hosts could punch the buttons themselves. That was something Kelly just did not want to do. He did not know how to operate the machinery and he was not going to do it. It was never a problem; the producers always operated the equipment and answered the phones for him and it worked out fine.

Kelly also was a quality football announcer, working on both the Missouri games and the Cardinals' broadcasts. He worked with Bill Wilkerson on the Missouri games, and the most difficult part of the assignment on Saturday afternoons usually was trying to get back to St. Louis in time for the hockey broadcast that night.

Greg Maracek, owner of KFNS, held the Missouri broadcast rights from 1978 to 1982 with his SNI Sports Network. Maracek, along with Jim Bakken and Ron Jacober, did the television broadcast and Wilkerson and Kelly did the radio. They always traveled together.

"Mr. Hyland was always so concerned that Dan Kelly get back in time for the hockey games on Saturday nights," said Maracek. "I would always get the travel schedules set up and he would call me back and change the travel plans. Some weeks he would have a private plane from Ralston Purina, Emerson Electric, or somewhere. Kelly hated to travel in small planes. I'll never forget this one trip in Stillwater, Oklahoma. They sent two little planes for us and one was a four-seater. We all knew about it and we knew Kelly would hate it, so we were in cahoots playing a trick on him.

"On our way to the airport, Bakken says he needs to stop at a liquor store. So he comes out with this bag. We knew Kelly had to get back early, so we waited until the last minute and the little four-seater is warming up. Kelly's looking around, 'Who's getting that one?' We say 'you.' He says, 'I'm not going.' Bakken says, 'Mr. Hyland said you're in that plane, you gotta get back, it's going.' So we walk him on and Jim pulls out two six packs of Bud and hands them to him. 'You're gonna need these!'"

Buck also remembered how much Kelly hated to fly.

"One night we were landing in Houston, and it was a routine, normal landing," Buck said. "Kelly was sitting next to me, and I noticed how clinched his fists were. When he opened his hands, the water just poured out. He was sweating that much. He really hated it."

"I used to listen to Dan Kelly when I was growing up," said Brian Kelly, a newsman at KMOX (no relation). "Even when he died, I'll never forget I sat in the room and cried. My wife said, 'You didn't even know the guy,' and I said, 'You don't even know how much I knew the guy.' I taped the tribute they did to him when he was in the hospital. I still have it."

DAN KELLY, JR.

Just like Joe Buck and John Carney, Dan Kelly, Jr., followed in the footsteps of his famous father onto the airwaves of KMOX. He worked as the play-by-play announcer for the Blues for two seasons, 1998 to 2000. He left to become the voice of the expansion team in Columbus, Ohio, much as his father had left Canada to become the voice of the Blues in 1968.

"I have a funny Dan Kelly story," said Susie Mathieu, the longtime public relations director for the Blues. "I've known Danny since he was a little kid. I was at the NHL broadcasters meeting two years ago and it was after the whole Marv Albert thing. I said, 'You think Marv Albert was the first broadcaster to bite a woman, well you're wrong. Dan Kelly was the first—he bit me. The Blues were having a Christmas party and he was about four years old and he bit me."

JOHN KELLY

Before Dan Kelly Jr. could become the voice of the Blues, he saw his older brother John assume the job for several seasons.

John Kelly used to hang around the Arena on nights when his dad, Dan Kelly, did the Blues' games. He always loved hockey and was there in the press cafeteria eating dinner and always knew his way around

the Arena. It was only natural that he found his way into becoming an NHL announcer.

"John Kelly is just a delight," said former Blues executive Susie Mathieu. "He interned at the Blues when he was very young. John spent a lot of time doing his apprenticeship. He went to Kansas and did sales, then the Adirondack Red Wings, and then he had the internship at the Blues. He really earned his stripes because of it."

According to Mathieu, when John Kelly was hired by the Blues, his contract called for him to do two periods of play-by-play. The unfortunate thing was Ken Wilson's contract also called for two periods of play-by-play, and there are only three periods in a hockey game. On nights when the games were not televised, there were many tense moments in their relationship, which according to Mathieu was, for the most part, friendly.

"There was one game where they were at the Arena and Kenny and John were about to do a broadcast," she said. "They were saying, 'I'll do these two periods,' and the other one would say, 'No, I'll do these two.'" It got pretty heated. They picked up the phone and called Jack Quinn who said, 'Figure it out.'

"It was just better for John to leave and go somewhere else. John had always been around the Blues and under the tutelage of his father and when his dad died, he felt a bit lost. It was just a bad situation. While you always wanted a Kelly to be in the broadcast booth, I think it was better for him in the long run. He's a really great person and is having much success now."

Kelly left St. Louis to become the play-by-play announcer for the Colorado Avalanche, and has since moved to Florida to become the voice of the Tampa Bay Lightning for the past several years.

MIKE KELLY

Mike Kelly was hired in the mid-1980s to work as a reporter in the sports office and as a frequent host of *Sports Open Lines*. His goal was to become a play-by-play announcer, and he was later hired to do the University of Missouri football and basketball games. Before getting that assignment, he did a variety of assignments. On one Saturday morning while at home, he was listening to another radio station when

Hyland called. After their conversation was finished, Hyland added, "By the way, that music is terrible." When Missouri decided to combine the play-by-play job with a position in the athletic department, Kelly and his family moved to Columbia.

KEVIN KILLEEN

Kevin Killeen is a news reporter and is the writer of the KMOX Christmas specials.

"He is so funny," said Vicki Atlas, who has worked in the newsroom with Killeen. "He comes up with such funny twists in his stories. They are human interest, like he once went to a Christmas tree lot and just started talking to people, asking them why they pick the tree they do. He got such crazy answers, like 'I look for one that stands up.'"

NELSON KIRKWOOD

Nelson Kirkwood worked in the newsroom in the late 1960s.

KITTY

"Kitty" was listed in an ad for KMOX in 1958. There were 17 male employees listed with their pictures and Kitty was the only female. Everyone's picture included a first and last name, except for Kitty.

Kitty was the host of a children's show called "A visit with Kitty." The show included music and stories for children and the last 15 minutes were French lessons with "Mademoiselle Jeanette."

GUS KYLE

Gus Kyle was the longtime analyst on the Blues' hockey games, working with Dan Kelly. His first assignment in the team's inaugural year was to work with Jack Buck. He may have been best known for his use of the phrase "barnburner" whenever the team was locked in an exciting game.

"One time some fan sent up a wooden barn to the pressbox," said Susie Mathieu, former public relations director for the Blues. "Gus says [on the air], 'OK, so we're gonna have a barnburner' and he proceeds to light the thing on fire. They were on the air having a real 'barnburner.' The pressbox all saw it and were cracking up."

"I'll never forget the late great Gus Kyle, a warm and good-natured man," said Bob Costas, who did fill-in play-by-play for the Blues in the late 1970s and worked with Kyle. "Somebody fires a blast from the blue line. Mike Liut, who is in goal, gets hit in the face. He's down on the ice. A trickle of blood is coming from his mask. Kyle says, 'Bob, it's probably nothing serious, probably just a broken nose,' although how he could tell that from way up in the booth I'm not sure. Then he says, 'The trainers are trying to make sure that the blood from his nose doesn't run down his face and get into his eyes,' which displayed, I thought, a curious grasp of anatomy."

Kyle also was known for informing listeners at home whether the Blues would be skating left to right or right to left on their radio dial.

"He used to say a player was 'agile, mobile, and hostile,'" said Jack Buck. "He said things that drove me crazy, like 'Toronto are at Montreal' and 'Minnesota are a good team. That was Canadian grammar, and it used to make me shudder."

TOM LANGMYER

Tom Langmyer was hired as the program director shortly after Rod Zimmerman became the general manager. He still is in charge of programming on KMOX, but now has the title of operations manager.

Langmyer was a self-described radio nut growing up outside Buffalo, New York, where he used to sit in his room at night and listen to far-reaching stations from across the country, including KMOX.

He also was an avid hockey fan, so many of his early memories of KMOX feature listening to Dan Kelly broadcasting the Blues' games.

"I would listen to the games on KMOX, then call the Buffalo stations and give them the scores," Langmyer said, "especially if there was a playoff race going on."

Langmyer's radio career took him to Pittsburgh, Buffalo, and Syracuse, New York, before he made the move to St. Louis. One of his earliest jobs was serving as a traffic pilot in Buffalo in addition to serving as program director, news announcer and an on-air personality.

He arrived in St. Louis at a time when changes were occurring on many of the station's shows. Langmyer was able to make most of the decisions about hiring the new on-air talent, a job he definitely enjoys.

Langmyer views himself as something of a scout, and frequently will take trips specifically to listen to the announcers working in different markets to see if they are good enough to come work at KMOX.

He discovered Carol Daniel working in Cape Girardeau, Missouri. He went to Omaha, Nebraska, and stayed at an airport hotel so he could

listen to McGraw Milhaven. Sometimes he takes trips and doesn't come back with any new candidates.

"I think it's a better way to do it than just listen to tapes that people send in," Langmyer said.

Langmyer has developed a good relationship with the KMOX staff.

"Tom Langmyer really cares about his employees," said Mike Miller. "When I got sick on the air and had to go to the hospital, Tom Langmyer came down to the hospital. He was there almost as soon as I got there. He has provided a tremendous amount of insight and guidance. He's taken the time to sit down with me. There was never a time when he was too busy."

Traffic reporter Megan Lynch also appreciates Langmyer's attitude toward his employees.

"Tom Langmyer has a way of saying, 'Maybe you could try it this way, instead of saying, 'That sounded stupid!'" she said. "He is gentle in his criticism and very positive."

FRANCE LAUX

France Laux was the first of the great sports announcers to work at KMOX, beginning his career in 1929.

His career did not begin in a normal way. Laux was a 29-year-old high school coach and a referee in Bristow, Oklahoma, in 1927 when his break came. It was the opening day of the World Series between the Pirates and the Yankees, and station KVOO in Tulsa found itself without an announcer to translate the Western Union tickertape of the game. The owner of the station knew of Laux and his sports background, and he hurriedly drove to Bristow. When he arrived, it was 50 minutes before the game was to begin.

The owner quickly explained the situation to Laux, and both got in the car and raced back to Tulsa, 45 minutes away. Laux arrived at the station literally 90 seconds before he had to go on the air.

"I had never seen the symbols of the ticker before," Laux recalled in an interview years later. "They just said, 'let's go,' and I went. It worked out all right."

The owner was impressed enough to hire Laux to a $30-a-week

job as the station's sports broadcaster. Laux worked there for a year, until he received a telegram from KMOX in the spring of 1929 offering him a 30-day trial as the station's sports broadcaster. He accepted the offer by telephone, was on a train headed to St. Louis that evening, and the next afternoon was behind the microphone at Sportsman's Park, broadcasting a Cardinals' game.

Laux' 30-day trail lasted until 1953.

He was the play-by-play announcer for the Cardinals and Browns, broadcast football games, hockey games, wrestling matches, basketball games and fights. He also was the host of a nightly broadcast, *Sports Review*, sponsored by Hyde Park Breweries, Inc.

Laux was named the national sportscaster of the year by *The Sporting News* in 1937, the first year that award was given. He was the play-by-play broadcaster of the World Series from 1933 to 1938 and did the play-by-play of the All-Star Game from 1934 to 1941.

He said his two greatest thrills in broadcasting both came in the same year, 1934, the All-Star Game and the World Series. It was in that All-Star Game when Carl Hubbell of the New York Giants struck out Babe Ruth, Lou Gehrig, Jimmie Foxx, Al Simmons, and Joe Cronin in succession, a feat that is still talked about today. It was more remarkable for Laux, because Hubbell was also from Oklahoma and had actually played semi-pro ball against him.

"You can imagine my thrill when I told them [his listeners], 'Now Hubbell has struck out Ruth, he put another third strike over on Gehrig and so on down the line... What a day it was for us Oklahomans."

The 1934 World Series between the Cardinals and Tigers was memorable for Laux, but not because of anything that happened on the field.

"This was more intimate, and personal," Laux said. "The late Will Rogers, a great fan and our most famous Oklahoman, was attending the games at Detroit and I managed to get him to the mike. Maybe I had mentioned to him that I was an Oklahoma boy. Anyway, with the whole nation listening in, he asked, 'You don't happen to know Judge Laux out in Oklahoma, do you?' I replied, 'Just slightly, he's only my dad.'"

Laux had fans all over the country because of those national broadcasts, but his biggest fans were in St. Louis.

"France was very good," said Adelle Burnes, widow of *Globe-Democrat* sports editor Bob Burnes. "Bob knew him well and thought he was very enthusiastic about the game. He was very well liked."

"I really used to enjoy listening to France Laux on the radio," said Gordon Barham, a longtime KMOX listener. "He never got too excited, he was just calm through everything he said."

"France was a very straightforward broadcaster," said Jim Toomey, former Cardinals public relations director. "He told it like it was. Ball one, strike one, ball two. No chatter, no interviews. He just told where the ball went, who caught it. That's how it was done back then. He just gave the facts, ma'am. In those days he was the best.

"There were three or four stations broadcasting the baseball games. Dizzy Dean was on one station, Bart Slattery and Bill Durney were on one, and Thomas Patrick was on another. It wasn't until Cardinal owner Sam Breadon sold the exclusive rights to the Griesedieck Brothers that the Cardinals went with one station. That was when Griesedieck hired Harry Caray to do the games and they were first on KXOK. Mr. Hyland brought them back to KMOX, but in the early days of the broadcasts, it was France Laux on KMOX."

The broadcasters also did not travel to away games in those days, doing the live play-by-play only on home games. In addition to his sports show and play-by-play broadcasts, Laux worked as the chief announcer at KMOX.

One of his more memorable broadcasts came as the result of a suggestion from Sammy West, the Browns' center fielder. During a visit to Laux' home, West was impressed with the baseball knowledge of Laux' two sons, France Jr., who was seven, and Roger, who was six. West suggested that Laux put the two boys on the air with him, and he did, having them answer numerous questions about the Cardinals and Browns.

After leaving KMOX in 1953, Laux remained popular in St. Louis as a leading bowling promoter. He died in 1978 at the age of 80.

DEAN LEWIS

Dean Lewis came to KMOX from the NBC network in New York in June of 1978 and left the station nine months later. While he was

there, John Angelides was promoted to executive news director and Lewis became news director.

KAY LINDBERGH

Kay Lindbergh was a traffic reporter on KMOX.

IRV LITVAG

Irv Litvag worked as a staff news writer from 1950 to 1957. He did newswriting, interviews, and was an editor.

"In those days the people on the air were separate from those not on the air," he said. "We covered the stories and wrote them, they read them."

One of the biggest stories Litvag covered while working in the newsroom was the Greenlease kidnapping. Six-year-old Bobby Greenlease, the son of a wealthy car dealer in Kansas City, had been kidnapped.

"The two kidnappers had been living together. They were Carl Austin Hall and Bonnie Heady. She was an alcoholic, he was an ex-con," said Litvag. "They kidnapped him from his Catholic private school. She told them she was his aunt to get him out. They killed him in Kansas City and buried him somewhere. They gave a ransom note and got the money."

The story takes on a St. Louis angle when Carl Hall went to the Coral Courts Motel with a prostitute and was caught there. The police who arrested him turned in $300,000 of the $600,000 ransom money and the other half was never found. The police officers were charged with stealing it. There was always the question of where the money went and local folklore had the money hidden in cushions at the Coral Courts Motel, but it was never found.

Litvag is retired and living in St. Louis.

LAWRENCE LUDWIG

Larry Ludwig was an engineer who used to work on the transmitter.

"When I started working there the transmitter was so big, and now it is a completely different one," said Ludwig. "The transmitter at that

time had close to 100 tubes in it. It was built before transistors. It was very complex. Our 50,000-watt transmitter was 60 feet long and in four-foot square cubicles, boxes like cells all hooked together.

"The whole transmitter now would fit in two of those boxes. It was very complicated to fix the transmitter."

Ludwig worked all shifts but at one time he worked on Jim White's show.

"I'll never forget seeing the sales information on one of our biggest sales spectacular," he said. "It was Carol House Furniture. Somebody sold them a package for the whole night shift. This was back when nobody advertised after midnight. They didn't think anyone was listening. It turned out to be a great buy for them. Nat Dubman, the owner, had an old lumberyard in Valley Park where he was selling furniture and he started advertising on Jim White's show and it was so successful that his business expanded. It really said a lot about KMOX and about Jim White."

MEGAN LYNCH

Megan Lynch came to KMOX in 1996 when the station decided to add another aircraft for traffic reports. After years with a helicopter, they were looking for variety and added "Airborne One" which is a single-engine plane. Lynch, who holds a master's degree in Public Affairs Reporting, started as a bureau reporter in Springfield, Illinois, covering the Illinois Capital; and then worked in Carbondale for a public radio station and was promoted to the assistant news director.

"Rodger [Brand, who flies Jet Copter One] and I divide up the metropolitan area," Lynch said. "Our program director, Tom Langmyer, thought if we each did an area, then the people would get used to hearing the same person. They could tune into that voice to help them through their traffic."

Being above the city, they see things happening as soon as they take place.

"One day I was up there," she said. "And it was just the luck of the draw that day that Rodger wasn't up, I saw that 79-car pileup on Interstate 70. I had only been working at KMOX a year and a half at that time."

The traffic reporters all fly out of Parks Airport in Cahokia. Lynch, who lives in Granite City, remembers one of her first days with KMOX.

"It was the day after Christmas in 1996," she said. "We'd just had one heck of a storm overnight. I figured, 'It's going to take me a half hour at the most to get to the airport, and I was supposed to go up with Rodger Brand so he could show me how it all works. Well, the highways were iced over and I was about a mile from the Cahokia Exit and we were stuck. First I hear the promo on KMOX that I'm going to be starting on KMOX, and then a few minutes later I see Rodger's helicopter take off. It took me two hours to get there and I missed my first day up with Rodger. Fortunately, I still had a day and a half to learn, and Rodger was so nice."

In the airplane, Lynch has several radios which she listens to for reports of accidents or traffic jams. She also has the radio which has KMOX on and she is listening to it live as they throw it to her, with her only cue being the "and now up to Megan Lynch in Airborne One" that she hears on her regular radio. They have to be sure they are not in "delay" (the format they use during the *At Your Service* shows to insure nothing questionable gets on the air) or she will hear it seven seconds after they say it.

"One time they had it in 'delay,'" said Lynch. "I did my report and then I could hear myself after I was actually saying it. I don't think Nan Wyatt will forget that, it sounded so weird that all I could do was do my report very slowly."

Because of her background in news, Lynch likes going into the station and working in the newsroom.

"Tom Langmyer and John Butler have been so nice about letting me do news and fill-ins," she said. "I'm also on *Total Information AM* on Saturday mornings with Bill Reker, and I like that because we talk about current events and do interviews on current topics."

ROBERT R. LYNN

Robert R. Lynn achieved his fame in St. Louis as the newsman on KXOK in the 1960s and 1970s, the days of AM music stations. KXOK was one of the most popular radio stations in the area, and, for the

teenagers at times it was the biggest station. He came to KMOX as a fill in and worked off and on for 16 months from 1979 to 1981.

"I remember back when KMOX was on Hampton, Jim Butler called and asked if I'd be interested in working there," said Lynn. "Even though we were a music station, I think I became recognized as a newsman when President Kennedy was assassinated and for four days we didn't play a song. We went to all news. They lost a lot of money, but it was the right thing to do. There were only four of us in the newsroom and we worked long hours using the network feeds, calling people for interviews, and doing 'man in the street' interviews. So Jim Butler asked me to come over to the station."

Lynn went over to KMOX and ended up having an interview with Robert Hyland.

"He told me KMOX was the only station worth working at," said Lynn. "I said, 'KXOK was not a bad place to work, a happy ship with a happy crew.' He said, 'Then why are you looking for work?' I said, 'I'm not; you called me.' And that was that. I stayed at KXOK, but Mr. Hyland kept in touch and 20 years later when I quit KXOK, he called me."

Lynn filled in for Bob Hardy and Rex Davis on some Saturdays and Sundays.

"I remember I had been out of town and then I went in for my interview the day I got back," said Lynn. "Mr. Hyland said, 'If you hadn't been out of town, you could have started yesterday?' I was thinking, 'If I hadn't have gotten back, then I couldn't start tomorrow!'"

On his first day at KMOX, he had been back from an overseas trip for only two days. Lynn did not realize the jet lag would set in because he had been so excited about the job the day before.

"They told me to report to work at 5:15 the next morning and Bob Hardy would meet me outside the garage to let me in, because I didn't have a parking pass," he said. "My jet lag kept me up a little late and I realized I wasn't going to make it at 5:15, so I called and said I'd be there at 5:25. I was supposed to go on the air at 5:30.

"They said somebody will be there to let you in at 5:25. Somebody was there at 5:25; it was Bob Hyland. I said, 'I'm very sorry; I got jet lag. It won't happen again.' He looked at me and said, 'I know.' Everything turned out fine. I had fun working there as a fill-in."

He remembers being sent to the County Government Center one election night to await the returns.

"It was in 1980," Lynn said. " That was the most boring night. There was absolutely no information until midnight because their computers were down. Everybody else was filing reports and going to victory parties, and I was sitting at the Government Center doing nothing. I remember I got my information at midnight and then went back to the station and worked all night. I hadn't worked all night in a long time."

Another story he covered that stood out in his mind was when the Annex next to the Arena burned.

"I remember I took the KMOX newscar," said Lynn. "It had a phone in it at the time, but it wasn't a very good one. I remember I had a heck of a time being connected and I finally gave my report. I had interviewed the assistant fire chief and I had to send the interview to the station through alligator clips over the phone."

Lynn lives in St. Louis and does commercials and is semi-retired.

ED MACAULEY

The former Saint Louis University All-American returned to broadcast the Billikens' games on KMOX in the early 1960s after the end of his NBA career. He provided the analysis while Jack Buck did the play-by-play.

"I think I was making $50 a game, something like $1,000 a year," Macauley said. "I got an offer from KSD-TV to become their sports broadcaster making $15,000 a year. I went in to tell Mr. Hyland that I was going to take the job, knowing that he didn't believe television existed.

"He told me, 'Ed, I think you're making a big mistake.' I spent the next 12 years there, so I think it worked out OK."

BILL MACK

Bill Mack was a sportscaster in the 1920s. He started at KMOX in 1927. Mack was the original founder of the "Hot Stove League" which is the term for baseball talk in the middle of the winter. (It's cold, gather around the hot stove and talk about spring training and baseball and that will warm you up) Mack would go to the St. Louis Browns and the St. Louis Cardinals spring training camps and send back detailed reports.

Mack was the first sports reporter to report from spring training.

He did it by telegraph. Mack would telegraph the information back and they'd read it on the 10 PM news. KMOX was the only broadcast station who assigned a report to cover spring training.

TED MANGNER

Ted Mangner joined KMOX as the station's farm editor in 1944. He did two broadcasts each morning, one at 5:30 AM and the other at 6:45 AM.

What was unusual about his reports is that he often included notes from farmers who were looking for either a husband of a wife. He reported in 1963 that in the previous 11 years he had been responsible for the marriages of 16 farm couples.

In each case, Manger acted as a go-between, with one person asking for his help, and if he received any replies, he then would forward them to the person who asked for help. He usually received a letter or postcard when the couples decided to get married.

Part of Manger's show also included reporting on strange and unusual events going on in the farming community of Missouri and Illinois. He once reported on acres of roses being grown under glass in Pana, Illinois, and another time filed a report on a cow with false teeth.

"Part of my job was to market his show," said salesman Bob Canepa. "If he was doing a promotion with blue ribbon pigs, I would go out and be involved in it. They did a lot of promotions for the farm show."

MARGIE MANNING

Now a reporter with the *St. Louis Business Journal*, Margie Manning began her reporting career at KMOX in 1981 and worked there until 1990. She worked the overnight shift before becoming an on-air reporter. Since there were so few employees in the station at the time of night Manning worked, she was able to do a lot of different things.

"That was a wonderful time to be in the newsroom," said Manning. "I worked with some great people. There was Joan Beuckman, Steve Shomaker, Steve Houston, Jim Bafaro, Jeff McKinney, Eric Thomas, Kent Martins, and Jeff Rainford. Of those people, one is now a news director at a radio station, three are television reporters, and several of them have gone into business. They were very qualified people.

"We worked so well as a team. Everybody clicked. Everyone had their own sort of stories they were good at. If something was going on, you didn't even have to call people, they just came in. It was like our job was more than a job, it was a lifestyle."

Manning remembered a specific time when they were meeting on Friday after work at McGuirk's. It had become a regular weekly ritual, for the news reporters to go to McGuirk's and talk about the week's happenings.

"Suddenly Bob Hamilton called us there to tell us about FBI agent Doug Abrams being killed," she said. "We all went back to work. Steve Shomaker went to the scene where the news people were gathering. We all went to work on the story. That was just how it was. We all worked together as a team."

They also worked as a team during the Anthony Daniele hostage situation over Labor Day in 1988.

"Tony Daniele was a former St. Louis police officer who held Police Commissioner John J. Frank prisoner in his downtown law offices," said newsman Bob Hamilton. "I was on the desk and they were calling in their reports to me."

"We did round the clock coverage," said Jim Bafaro, a news reporter at the time. "We were even reporting in at times like 2 AM and 3 AM."

The 25-hour standoff took place in a downtown law office. Donald Wolff, Daniele's attorney, told the *Post-Dispatch* that Daniele had taken a pistol from Frank when he took him prisoner. According to Wolff, he gave it back and said, 'Here's your gun back. If you want to use it against me, go ahead.'

The day before the hostage situation, Daniele was sentenced after being convicted of fraud, extortion, and conspiracy in a plot to defraud the St. Louis police pension fund. Frank was the police commissioner and though the two had been friends in the past, Daniele resented having become a target of an investigation. Incidentally, Wolff, Daniele's attorney, later went on to moonlight at KMOX on the weekends with a music show.

"In those days cell phones were not used much," said Manning. "I remember being outside the building waiting, because we couldn't go inside, for word of what was happening. Whenever I would do my report, I would run across the street to Ruth's Chris Steakhouse and keep borrowing their phone. There was a lot of standing and waiting. Really, it was pretty boring just standing around waiting for the news."

The news sometimes sounds more glamorous as it is being reported than it really is while being covered.

GREG MARACEK

Greg Maracek, owner of all-sports station KFNS, was involved with the University of Missouri broadcasts in the 1980s.

"The Missouri Net had the broadcasts from 1977 to 1981," said John Rooney, who did play-by-play for the football and basketball teams. "In 1981, Maracek and his Sports Network (SNI) got the contract, and they did the games until 1984. They kept Bob Costas and Wayne Larrivee on the basketball broadcasts as well as Rod Kelly and Bill Wilkerson for football. I picked up some games for them. When Bob Costas left for NBC, I came back and worked for them."

MARTY MARION

Cardinal shortstop great Marty Marion was a regular guest on Wednesday nights on *Sports Open Line*. The white haired, handsome Marion was quite a presence in the KMOX studio. His smooth southern drawl provided fun for the callers. Most of the time his show was moderated by Bob Costas or Bill Wilkerson.

Costas referred to Marion as "the greatest shortstop that ever lived" at the time. He, of course, did not know that in a few years he would be watching Ozzie Smith, but he was very respectful to Marion and enjoyed having him on as a guest.

GARNETT MARKS

Garnett Marks was one of the first sports announcers at KMOX, and broadcast the home games of the Cardinals and Browns in 1927 and 1928. Broadcasters did not travel to the road games, but Marks often did recreations not only of games involving the Cardinals and Browns but other games as well.

A native of St. Louis, born in 1899, Marks enlisted in the Army shortly after his graduation from Soldan High School and served as an ambulance driver in France during World War I. After returning to the United States, he moved to Los Angeles, where he first got into radio working for station KFI as a "song plugger." He returned to St. Louis in the fall of 1926 and joined the staff of KMOX.

A newspaper profile in 1932 reported that Marks "was without a peer" in his baseball broadcasts. As a reward for his work, Marks was added to the CBS broadcast crew for the 1928 World Series between the Cardinals and Yankees.

Marks moved back to Los Angeles in 1929, then to Chicago before returning to St. Louis in 1931. He worked again at KMOX as an announcer, before moving to WIL as host of that station's morning program.

DON MARSH

Don Marsh, best known as an anchorman on St. Louis television, has had shows on KMOX at several times, starting in the summer of 1994.

"I was at Channel 2 in those days," said Marsh. "They called the promotions department and wanted someone to fill in in the mornings. They were going to do cross promotion with the radio station and the television station. I went on KMOX and then ironically I ended up leaving Channel 2 a week later. I worked for KMOX at that time for about a year."

He did drive time in the mornings and also often worked at night.

"One day that stands out was the day we found out we got the Rams," said Marsh, who now owns his own company [In The Line Of Duty Videos] with fellow newsman, Ron Barber. "I got to do a little broadcasting with Jack Buck. That was one of the highlights of my career. Word got out in the middle of the afternoon that we got the Rams and I was doing the afternoon drive."

As was the custom at the time, everything shut down at KMOX except coverage of the breaking story. Everyone turned their attentions and efforts toward the story of the Rams coming to St. Louis.

"The programming was dedicated to the Rams," he said. "We had Tom Eagleton on, and Al Kearth from Civic Progress. Lots of people came in. It was fast-paced, like a revolving door. The thing that was finally cleared up was how Georgia Frontiere pronounced her name; Jim Holder got that."

"I have a high regard for Don Marsh," said Gene McNary. "He is in a rare group of reporters you can talk to and let your guard down with. I think he has a good reputation and people like him. He's an outstanding community leader and donates much of his time to emcee events where he does a great job. He may not have the list of jokes that Jack Buck has, but he does a really good job."

"Of all the days I've been on KMOX, the day that stands out was one day after Thanksgiving. I was doing the *Newsmakers* show [before Charles Jaco came]," said Marsh. "Now cell phones weren't as prevalent back then and people were all out and about the day after Thanksgiving. They may have been listening in their cars, but they weren't near the phones. Anyway, no one called. There I was doing an open line and no one was calling. It was awful. I was there by myself, just me and my microphone. Finally Peggy Cohill, the producer, called Jay Nixon and he was more than happy to come on. It was unnerving thinking I'd be on there by myself for two hours!"

If that was a bad day at the office for Marsh, then this would have been considered a good day.

"I was doing an *Open Line*, and I look up and there's Denise Brown, from the O.J. Simpson trial," said Marsh. "She came in unexpectedly because she was here in town with a group associated with victims of violence. She came in and was on the air, and as it turned out she got word that she had to leave because the jury was very close to a verdict, and that was the day the jury came to their verdict. That was really a timely interview."

KENT MARTIN

Kent Martin was a news reporter in the 1980s. He was involved in covering anything that came across the police radios or the wire service, as well as community events such as the VP Fair.

Two particular stories stand out in his mind, coverage of the Times Beach dioxin story and the Farm-Aid concert in Champaign, Illinois.

"Covering the dioxin crisis in Times Beach, Missouri, was something none of us who worked the newsroom at the time will ever forget," Martin said. "It was the perfect story: An environmental disaster over a chemical that had not been fully studied, researchers being asked to come up with conclusive facts against their will, a politically embattled politician at the head of the government agency in charge of the cleanup, and, in the middle, the residents of a little Missouri river town who wanted nothing more than go back home. They just wanted their lives back! Human tragedy, scientific research, and classic bureaucracy were all rolled into one horribly complicated story.

"I remember covering news conference after news conference and seeing the frustration on scientists' faces as the media demanded answers that the researchers were hard-pressed to give. Shouting matches between reporters and scientists from the Centers for Disease Control were not unusual. Questions were plentiful. Answers weren't.

"It seemed as though any researcher who had done even the most minor study on dioxin was able to attract all the media for a news conference. Even the media themselves got involved. I remember coordinating a meeting, at the townspeople's request, with the regional administrator for the EPA. We held the meeting in a downtown motel, residents packed the room, the EPA official tried to offer answers (though he couldn't answer everything), and in the end, not much was cleared up. Eventually, the people of Times Beach were scattered to new homes across the region and, in some cases, across the country. Today, dioxin's effects are still uncertain."

Martin was able to convince Hyland and news director John Angelides of the importance of the Farm-Aid concert in 1984 in Champaign, Illinois, and he, Jim Bafaro, and Jeff Rainford were assigned to cover the event.

"Family farms were going out of business in record numbers, a drought had shattered countless farmers' crop hopes, and Congress was trying to come up with a new farm bill to deal with the future of agriculture," Martin said. "We had produced a yearlong series of reports and documentaries to explain to our listeners what the crisis meant to them and the future of the American farmer. Farm-Aid came smack in the

middle of it all and brought some of the country's greatest entertainers, and more than a few area politicians, to the University of Illinois campus, all led by Willie Nelson's call to arms to save the family farm.

"We provided 'round-the-clock reports back to the KMOX audience on Farm-Aid. Covering a concert for a a talk station might have seemed an odd fit, but we tried to give our listeners a feel for the atmosphere of this nationwide event in their backyard. Farm-Aid was full of memories: The tour bus that pulled up, out of nowhere, it seemed, in a field outside the stadium, and a rumpled bus driver climbed down and asked, 'Is this where this concert's being held?' 'Sure, this is Farm-Aid.' 'Great. I got Bon Jovi in here. We just wanted to make sure we got the right place.' Then there was the time I boarded an elevator in the stadium and there, inside, was the cutest little lady you'd ever want to meet, the legendary Brenda Lee, who was hosting the festivities for The Nashville Network. She was grinning ear to ear, clutching a Farm-Aid program that was filled with autographs from every performer at the concert. She looked like a little kid who had just collected the autographs from her favorite Cardinals. Cute as a button."

Martin's other two memories of his days at KMOX are more personal—watching the fireworks on the Fourth of July from the station's balcony, and the night his wife brought their children, in costumes, to KMOX on Halloween.

"What we didn't expect was to run into Mr. Hyland in the hallway outside his office," Martin said. "Mr. Hyland could be tough as nails, but around children, he was like a grandfather. He invited us into his office and let my son hold a ball. It was a baseball, signed by all the Cardinal greats. My son blinked a little, not quite understanding, but my wife and I were stunned. Here was Robert Hyland, one of the most powerful men in broadcasting, playing with a child. It was unforgettable."

Martin currently heads up marketing and communications for Numerof & Associates, a management and consulting firm in St. Louis.

SUSIE MATHIEU

Susie Mathieu worked at KMOX as the public relations director in 1998 and 1999. She was hired by Tom Langmyer. Before coming to

KMOX, she was well known in St. Louis as an executive with the St. Louis Blues.

"One thing I'll always remember was the Jim White retirement bash," she said. The on-air party was held at The Summit Restaurant. "Bob Costas was late and he couldn't find the restaurant, so I left the party and went outside. I flagged him down in the street and sent him right in to be on the air with Jim White while I parked his car. What a hot car!

"I also remember working late into the John Carney overnight shift. The station takes on a whole different 'aura' at that time of night."

She learned about the immediacy of radio and the importance of news on KMOX.

"We were doing our fourth-quarter charity campaign," she said. We had a 'live' auction planned at Plaza Frontenac and we had lined up all of our weekend specialty hosts to anchor their shows and raise funds for Edgewood Children's Center. However all the planning, scheduling, and effort went for naught due to news coverage of the Clinton impeachment."

Mathieu is currently doing independent work with hockey and is working on a book.

SUE MATHEIS

Sue Matheis was the in-studio traffic reporter. Don Miller would file reports from the helicopter and then they would throw it to Sue Matheis who would use her cheerful delivery to point out how "traffic is moving at a brisk clip!" or whatever was happening.

"Sue Matheis was the first one to come in as a desk person on the traffic with me," said Miller, "The way we got her was that she was friends with the people who owned the helicopter. She was Miss Perfection."

Later Matheis became St. Louis' first airborne woman traffic reporter and was the first woman to earn a Missouri Commercial Helicopter rating.

BOB MAYHALL

Bob Mayhall went from traffic and sports reporter on Magic 108 FM (currently known as Z107.7) to KMOX in 1982.

"I worked there until 1988," said Mayhall, who currently works in the research department for *The Sporting News*. "I did the baseball show after the games with Bob Gibson."

After Cardinal games Hall-of-Fame pitcher Bob Gibson and Mayhall took calls from listeners and re-hashed the games. He also did sportscasting, reporting, and other open lines.

"Mayhall was a great guy to work with," said Duane Davison, who produced the Gibson show with Mayhall. "He was not a self promoter. Even though he was an on-air talent, he was down to earth, a real genuine person."

"Back then, I remember going to spring training and seeing Joe Buck, still a teenager running around playing video games in the hotel," said Mayhall.

"I remember KMOX being very corporate back then. Everyone had to wear shirt and tie, and most wore suits or sport coats, especially if you were going in to see Mr. Hyland."

One of his most memorable days on the air was the day Jack Carney died.

"I will never forget that day," said Mayhall. "Word came over about 9:30 that night and everybody came in."

Many of the KMOX regulars came in to pay tribute and talk about the popular Carney, who died unexpectedly of a heart attack after a scuba diving lesson.

"There was Jim White, all the big names, even Mr. Hyland came in," he said. "I'll never forget it. After they did an hour on the air talking about Jack, we broke for the CBS news, and then had the local news, weather, and sports like they always do on KMOX.

"After the news, I was reading the scores, and I remember I was doing the basketball scores and I looked up and there was Mr. Hyland. He was sitting in the studio kind of leaning back and looking at me like 'Get on with it; let's get back to the real story.'"

EMMETT McAULIFFE

Emmett McAuliffe has hosted the Friday night 2 AM-5 AM shift for more than four years. By day he is a lawyer downtown, but his real interest lies in talking about politics and St. Louis. He has appeared on *Donnybrook* a dozen times and worked at KJSL doing a political show before coming to KMOX.

His listeners know him for his "donut meetings" which take place at the Krispy Kreme Donut store in South County from 5:30 to 6 o'clock on Saturday mornings after he gets off work. There is even a framed picture of McAuliffe next to the Mark McGwire signed bat in the trophy case at the Krispy Kreme store.

"When I get off the air, I am always too keyed up to just go to bed, so I was trying to think of something to do," said McAuliffe. "One night I announced I would be at the First Donut House on Morganford at Siebert at 5:15 buying donuts for my family and if anyone wanted to meet me there to continue our discussions, I'd love to see them. The first time one person showed up, the next week, three and now we have a pretty good group. When the Donut House sold out, I moved it to Krispy Kreme.

"Everybody is pretty mellow at that hour and we have great discussions over coffee and a hot donut."

McAuliffe talks a lot about St. Louis history so many of the listeners bring him "show and tell" items about St. Louis.

"I've got one guy who is a poet," he said. "Sometimes he'll bring a poem. One is an artist and sometimes brings pictures. It's a great way to get to know my listeners."

Overnight shows bring opportunities for all kinds of callers.

"Once I got a cell-phone call from a guy who was a veteran horse-racing writer for one of the Chicago papers and he was traveling to Louisville for the Derby," said McAuliffe. "He was really interesting talking about the history of horse racing and about the Derby. That's what I like about doing late-night radio. Here is a guy driving from Indiana to Kentucky and radio is keeping him between the lines."

One of his callers really surprised him.

"It was the night John Goodman called the station," McAuliffe said. "Goodman is from St. Louis, so he is used to listening to the station and knows it has long-distance capabilities.

"I got a call from 'John in Toronto.' We had been talking about the football Cardinals. He called in and started talking about the Big Red.

At the end of the call I said, 'Is this John Goodman?' He said, 'You are right, sir!' He was in Toronto and he was taking a break from filming the *Blues Brothers* movie. You never know who is listening to you."

KEVIN McCARTHY

For years Kevin McCarthy worked on the FM side of KMOX as a disc-jockey. He was involved in some monumental broadcasts on KMOX, including the day the Berlin Wall came down. Another story he was involved in was a hijacking in Poland.

KMOX had sent Bob Hardy and Kevin McCarthy to Eastern Europe and Russia. It was at the end of the Cold War. They rented a bus from a cigarette company and while driving through Poland the bus was hijacked. Hardy had gone on ahead to their next destination, but McCarthy was on the bus when it got stopped in a small town by a rebellion of Polish potato farmers.

"Kevin called us on a cell phone to tell us the bus was surrounded by Polish potato farmers," said news anchor Bob Hamilton. "He said they were drunk and they would not let the bus pass. I took the call and then Mr. Hyland got on the phone."

Hyland talked to McCarthy and got all of the facts, and then according to Hamilton, he said "oh!" and had a sparkle in his eye. The wheels were turning in Hyland's head.

"We had a big story here," said Hamilton. "All night we had this story—the KMOX bus was hijacked. Every hour Kevin was calling and we were reporting what was the latest. We had contact with Kevin and he was even able to talk to his wife. Pretty soon it was getting late and I was due to go home in half an hour. I got this great idea and we actually called the CIA station chief in Warsaw to find out how serious this situation really was. We got a call back in a few minutes saying they would let the bus go in a little while. I called Mr. Hyland to tell him."

Hamilton was surprised at the reaction he got when he informed his general manager that the drama was almost over.

"He got a bit angry," said Hamilton. "He was angry because now the story wasn't exciting anymore. After I hung up from Mr. Hyland a few minutes later the CIA in Poland called me back and said, 'What's going on there? We just got a call from Washington. I've been told to go out there to where the bus is.' I said, 'I don't understand what's going on.'"

As it turned out, Hamilton's high contacts at the CIA in Poland were not quite as high as Hyland's.

"Who is higher up than the CIA chief in Poland?" said Hamilton. "William Webster, who was from St. Louis, was the head of the CIA in Washington at that time. Robert Hyland called William Webster in the middle of the night. That's how powerful Mr. Hyland was. That was an amazing story."

J. ROY McCARTHY

It was J. Roy McCarthy's programs on a smaller St. Louis station which gave Robert Hyland the idea to begin talk radio and *At Your Service*.

He had worked at WTMV using the name of Byron Scott before going to KXOK. At KXOK he used the name Roger Bell and it was Roger Bell on KXOK who did the first talk program.

"J. Roy McCarthy was one of the first talk show hosts," said C.J. Nieder, longtime engineer. "He was a history teacher so he had a lot to talk about."

Jack Buck was one of the people who told Hyland he didn't think talk radio would be successful.

"I was taught going to college that the average education of your audience in radio was the eighth grade," Buck said. "I didn't think people would call."

On some of the early programs, Buck was right. Nobody called, forcing station employees to fake calls so the host and guest would have something to talk about. As soon as the proper lineup of guests was established, however, including shows such as *Ask the Doctor*, or *Ask the Vet*, or *Ask the Gardener*, the calls started pouring in.

"The program that McCarthy did got it all started," Buck said. "Hyland was the first to commit everything to it, and it worked."

McCarthy screened and paraphrased the phoned-in questions and comments in the early days of *At Your Service* and was later on the air. He also served as the public relations director.

One of the things McCarthy is remembered for was writing a play which involved many of the people at the station.

"He wrote the KMOX Playhouse," said Shirley (Jacoby) Bates, who has worked at KMOX for more than 40 years. "We were all in it, whether you were an on-air person or a behind-the-scenes person. We put it on in the fall. I remember it so well because we had a cast party over at my house afterwards. It was really great and with the good feedback from it we considered making it an annual event. As it turned out we only did it that once because it was so much work to get it done."

"My first appearance on KMOX was on J. Roy McCarthy's show," said Dr. Armand Brodeur, who has been with KMOX for 41 years. "He wanted to interview me so he had Jeanne Bonner, contact me."

McCarthy had asked Brodeur to appear as a guest, but according to Brodeur, three minutes into the show the door flew open and Robert Hyland offered him a job.

"I thought J. Roy was going to go into shock," said Brodeur.

JOHN McCORMICK

John McCormick was the self proclaimed "man who walks and talks at midnight." He was the voice during the overnight hours on KMOX for 31 years, from 1958 until he retired in 1989.

"You always knew what you would get on his show—he was a good talker, a good thinker, a profound person, very accomplished," said Jack Buck when McCormick died in 1994 at the age of 80.

"He had the greatest set of pipes in the business," said Jim White. "He had a voice that if broadcasters could ever get a voice transplant, his would be it."

The listeners knew McCormick primarily by his voice, but the staff of KMOX also knew him for the eccentric mannerisms he repeated nightly during his show.

During his shift, he would turn all of the lights in the studio off except one little gooseneck lamp which he brought from home.

"He would lay a cloth on the counter," said one of his producers, Rene Servier. "He would put this here, and put that there, everything had

to be 'just so,' Everything had to be absolutely perfect just how he liked it. He marked his copy with notes for what he was going to say.

"And he would have me bring him his coffee. He always wanted half coffee and half water because you wouldn't want to be jittery all night. We had a little china cup for John. He liked his coffee in that little china cup."

"McCormick was like the voice of God," said Joe Sonderman, KMOX traffic reporter, who once produced McCormick's show. "He terrified me when I was a kid, especially late at night huddled in the basement while the thunder rolled and the lightning crashed, coming in through KMOX on the night of a storm. He made it sound as if the world was coming to an end. He never just gave the temperature, it was always something like, 'On bustling Peachtree Street in Atlanta, Georgia, it's...or at the Caterpillar Plant in Peoria, it's a sultry 81 degrees. He worked by the light of that tiny desk lamp, everything else was darkness. It added to the mood."

He ad-libbed all of his sportscasts, and the weather reports, adding catchy phrases like "at the Wrigley Building in Chicago," or "on the frozen pond of the National Hockey League."

His broadcasts always ended with the playing of the National Anthem and the phrase, "the night has separated from the day." His most famous phrase, however, came at the end of a news story: "And now you know, via radio."

McCormick, who smoked a pack of Camels a night while on the air, knew he was broadcasting to a different audience than someone working in the day, and he treated his show that way. He liked talking to "his people" during the early-morning hours.

"Half of the world is up at night," he said in a *Post-Dispatch* interview in 1971. "The other half thinks that everything shuts off at 5 PM but this isn't so. Night radio reaches a wide variety of people, in our case, in 44 states. It might be a lawyer working on a brief, a taxi driver waiting for a call, or a woman whose husband works nights so she does her housework then."

One of his best-remembered nights on the air came in 1968, the night Robert Kennedy was assassinated after winning the California primary. All music plans for that night were immediately scraped, and

McCormick talked for more than an hour about his own memories and knowledge of the Kennedy family before KMOX switched to the network coverage.

"He had a magnificent voice," said Gene McNary. "John McCormick was one of my favorite people on KMOX. I heard he was incredibly prepared, but he sounded informal, like it came off the top of his head."

"I'll never forget when he was first coming to KMOX," said Tinker Reilley, who worked there in the mid-1960s. "They did all this pre-publicity on him, made a big deal out of him. Then when I saw a picture of him I thought, 'Why he couldn't fight his way out of a paper bag!' He was a really nice guy, very nice. His wife worked with him back then. She would pull the records for him."

"He was one of my favorites," said Emmett McAuliffe, who now does the overnight shift on Friday nights. "When I was a kid on those nights, I could stay up late or get up early, I'd listen to John McCormick. I was a kid who kept the radio by my nightstand. I liked the way he read the weather in foreign cities. He also did it with giving the scores.

"Maybe subconsciously I was imitating him when I started doing my free association baseball scores. I get a lot of compliments because it is different. I may say, 'The Diamondbacks bit the Braves,' or 'The Twins defeated the Indians 2-4; that's one run per twin.' I probably picked it up from McCormick. He had a real style about him."

McCormick was from Chicago and his first job was as a copy boy at the *Chicago Tribune*. He got his pilot's license when he was 16 and joined the British Royal Air Force in 1939, before switching to the Army when the U.S. entered World War II. He was the pilot of B-24 bombers during the war.

He wanted to be a newspaperman but journalism veterans encouraged him to enter the new field of radio. Six months after going to work for WGN, he became an announcer. He also worked at WBBM after the war, went to the West Coast, then back to Chicago and to New Orleans. He was thinking about going back to California when he received a call and a job offer from Robert Hyland.

"I liked it when he would get on the 'red hot thermometer' in the mornings and give the weather in other countries," said Servier. "He would say the temperature in the City of Light or the Eternal City. He was very elegant. It was elegant when Mac spoke."

McCormick once told a *Post-Dispatch* reporter that he considered the radio almost a source of magic.

"You're never alone," he said. "You can be locked in a vault at Mercantile Trust, but if you have a radio with you, you're not alone."

ROSCOE McCREARY

Roscoe McCreary mixed two things that every sports fan loves—barbecue and sports. McCreary was the owner of McCreary's Ribs and he frequently brought samples in when he was a guest on *Sports Open Line*. Built like a person who liked to eat the ribs, McCreary was quite a character. He was well liked by many and well-known by even more.

"I used to love it when Roscoe would send over those ribs," said high school reporter Jim Baer. "I'd come in late at night to do my high school report at midnight and Bob Costas would be there. Roscoe would have the ribs sent over by cab and we'd be chowing down on ribs at 11:30 at night. Man, they were hotter than hot."

Costas was the emcee of the MS (Multiple Sclerosis) Dinner, a big sports dinner held every year in St. Louis. McCreary came up to the microphone to give out an award when he was suddenly stricken with a heart attack.

"He was talking and all of a sudden it was 'lights out,'" said Costas. "His eyes are closed and we all think he's dead. He looks dead. Now I'm not a coroner, but he looks dead. He's a big man. Knowing him as I did, I was not surprised that he was having a heart attack. His cholesterol level must have been higher than Ty Cobb's lifetime batting average. In fact, earlier in the evening I remember he was eating pats of butter. Just stabbing them with a fork like it was an hors d'oeuvres. He actually did not die that night, though many people thought he had. Somehow they revived him."

McCreary died several years later.

MARK McDONOUGH

Mark McDonough was a news writer and reporter who also worked as a producer while at KMOX. He later went into public relations and worked as a producer for ABC News. He was killed in a helicopter accident while on the job.

McDonough was a quiet, mild-mannered person who got along with everyone. He was very knowledgeable about the news events he was covering.

"On New Year's Eve in 1980 there was a big ice storm," said Joan Beuckman, news director at KTRS who worked at KMOX for many years. "The newsroom was going crazy with phone calls and I needed another reporter to come in. Somehow we found Mark and he came in to help out."

"Mark McDonough had a little more interest in being out in the street than in the newsroom," said Tom Dehner, who also worked in the news department. "He liked doing the reporting. He never aspired to be on the air. He once said to me, 'I'm not a broadcaster, I'm a reporter.' And he was a good writer and reporter."

"I'll never forget that terrible day we found out about the helicopter crash," Beuckman said. "I was one of the first people to realize it was Mark's helicopter. It was early in the morning and he was covering a story. When the story came across the wire and it said it was the ABC News team from Chicago, I knew right then it was probably them. I knew he was based in Chicago; we'd kept in touch after he left. It was a really tragic day."

DOUG McELVEIN

Doug McElvein is a host on *At Your Service* programs. He came to KMOX from WHAS in Louisville, Kentucky, and his arrival was a little unusual.

"He happened to be passing through town with his family and wanted to get a tour of the station," said Tom Langmyer. "I talked to him and we ended up hiring him."

McElvein always provides many possible topics for his shows and works well with his producers.

"He was great to produce for," said Chris Mihill, the producer for *The Morning Meeting* show on KMOX, who began producing McKelvin's show when he first came to St. Louis. "There are some hosts

who would prefer to do the show like 'what are we doing today?' but Doug had a lot of input in the shows."

McElvein liked to do a lot of "bits" in his shows. He would go out and do segments on tape and then use them in his shows.

"A funny one was driving the Zamboni at Queeny Park," said Mihill. "One of us had read a story about the Zamboni machine having its 50th anniversary. It was named after a guy named Zamboni. We went out to Queeny Park one day and he got to drive the Zamboni and he did a segment from up on it. We did it into a tape recorder and then he inserted it into the show that afternoon."

DAN McLAUGHLIN

Dan McLaughlin started producing on KMOX in 1994 when he was 18 years old. He had gone to Lindenwood College, where one of his teachers was Casey Van Allen.

"I was at KMOX because Casey was holding the class in the studio," said McLaughlin. "Program Director Tom Langmyer saw me and pulled me out of the studio. He talked to me about working at KMOX and I started. At first I would do anything. I produced *Sports Open Line, Ask the Lawyer*, gardening show, I cut tape, took phone calls, anything."

He also produced Cardinal baseball games, working the board, inserting commercials for KMOX and the Cardinal baseball network.

"I tell people that board experience was the most important I could get," he said. "It forced me to sit there and listen to the games. I would listen to the broadcasters and learn from them."

He left and went to KTRS for one year, returning in an on-air position, handling sports open lines and sportscasts. McLaughlin decided he wanted to get into television so he approached FOX Sports Midwest and they were impressed with his abilities and hired him to produce features for their pre-game show in a try-out.

"I did my first feature on Mr. [Jack] Buck and it was nominated for a local Emmy," McLaughlin said. "They were happy with that and that started my career in television. I was lucky that KMOX allowed me to work in television as well as on radio."

His first play-by-play assignment on KMOX was a Saint Louis Uni-

versity basketball game in 1998 with Earl Austin, Jr. That led to him doing play by play for 30 Cardinal games on Fox in 1999. The next year (2000) he did 85 on Fox.

One day he was driving on Interstate 270 listening to the ballgame when he got lucky.

"I was listening to the game and it was in a rain delay," he said. "I checked my cell phone messages and one was from Steve Uline. I called him and he said, 'Can you do me a big favor and fill in on the radio and do some play-by-play? Shannon's got his Night at the Races CBC Fundraiser. He has to leave early. Can you come down as quickly as possible?'"

McLaughlin was thrilled. He got to do his first Cardinal game on KMOX with Jack Buck.

"My mom was out doing errands and she turned on the game. She said, 'Oh my gosh, that's Dan!' she ran home and threw in a tape and I'm glad I have a tape of that game," he said. "It was a dream come true doing the game with Jack. He was so helpful. He would talk to me between innings and calm me down. He was great."

GENE MCNARY

When he was the St. Louis County Executive, Gene McNary made frequent appearances on KMOX and he has continued to be a guest over the years. It was during the early years, however that McNary joined a group of only a few mayors and county executives around the country hosting their own call-in show. McNary's public relations assistant, Pam Grant, arranged for his first appearances on KMOX

"I'd seen in *The New York Times* that Governor Cuomo was doing a radio show out of New York and doing it without any help," she said. "We started it with Gene and right away he got on the front page of the *Post-Dispatch*, being a government official sitting at a microphone with no co-host."

"I handled my own calls," said McNary. "After several times of being on the air taking calls from listeners, I started doing it myself with no host. I was the only one in the studio. We were one of the first in the country.

"Pam is very knowledgeable. She knows a lot about KMOX and she knows a lot about the media. She was instrumental in starting the Press Club's Person of the Year Award. She also knew John Angelides real well."

Said Grant, "John Angelides kept us on our toes as news director. I worked with him from the outside, representing government. He always wanted to be first with anything. He was hard driving. KMOX was strong in what they wanted to accomplish. I like people who are not afraid to try new things, that's why I like Gene McNary. Very few people are like that, willing to take a chance. KMOX was always willing to try something new."

One of the events McNary was involved in was the annual broadcast of the Memorial Day Riverboat Race between the County Executive and St. Louis mayor Vince Schoemehl. It was a media event set up by the Convention Bureau to kick off the tourism season in the St. Louis area. McNary's boat won seven out of the eight years they raced. This was not due entirely to McNary's skill as a riverboat captain.

"There were two boats, the Huck Finn and the Tom Sawyer," said McNary. "The Huck Finn was the fastest; it was just a fact. Schoemehl and I would flip a coin to see who would get which boat and believe it or not I won seven times. If my luck was always that good, I would be in Las Vegas right now."

McNary used to get embarrassed that he was always ahead even though it was a friendly competition. One year, the mayor decided he would pull a fast one on McNary and he turned his boat around a little before they reached the halfway point, and ended up winning.

"He cheated," McNary joked, "but at least he could say he won that year."

Schoemehl and McNary had a great relationship and during their tenure, St. Louis city and county made great strides working together. They were involved with the Convention and Visitors Bureau, the regional Arts Council, Bi-State and Regional Hospital.

"Speaking of KMOX, Bob Hyland was instrumental in starting that hospital," said McNary. "He was a major player along with Vince Schoemehl, Lee Lieberman, and myself. All four of us exerted leadership in that. Hyland didn't sleep much. He was really a community leader."

JON McSWEENEY

Jon McSweeney worked for years in the KMOX newsroom in the 1970s and 1980s. McSweeney was born blind, but didn't stop his interest in sports and his ambition to work in broadcasting.

Jack Buck heard about McSweeney's interest in baseball and broadcasting, and invited him to attend a Cardinals' game and sit in the KMOX booth. That led to an interview with Robert Hyland and McSweeney's job at KMOX.

His primary job was to write features and transcribe interviews, many for the *To Your Health* segment hosted by Buck.

CHARLIE MENEES

The Big Band Sounds of Charlie Menees was a regular feature on KMOX on Saturday nights from 1987 until his death in 1993.

Menees was a well-known jazz scholar, lecturer, journalist, and disc jockey in St. Louis for almost 50 years. He played big-band and jazz recordings from his vast personal collection.

Menees moved to KMOX from KWMU-FM, a public radio station, where his show was the most highly rated show on the station for most of the 1970s.

Robert Hyland learned of Menees from several friends who were with Hyland in a limo on their way to a black-tie dinner in 1978. Hyland never listened to any station but KMOX, but these friends overruled him on this night and switched the limo's radio to Menees' show. Three days later, Hyland hired Menees for KMOX.

Menees' show reached listeners in some far-flung places, as did other KMOX programs.

"He had listeners call in from as far away as the Atlantic Ocean and 30 miles below the Arctic Circle," said his wife of 49 years, Mary, who helped her husband with the show every Saturday night. "One night, a taxi driver called him from New York and said he was listening to him from the middle of Times Square."

His son estimated Menees' collection at 30,000 albums, not including the 78s. The foundation of his home in Kirkwood had to be reinforced with steel to accommodate the weight of the records.

JASON MERRILL

Jason Merrill was the producer of *Total Information AM* with Nan Wyatt and Doug McElvein until October 2000.

"He's a very 'gung ho' guy," said Wyatt. "He keeps all the trains of the morning running. We decide who we want on, and he calls people to book them for the shows. Sometimes he books people on a dime. Something might break and he would have to wake someone up at 7 in the morning. He's a real sensitive guy and he hates to wake people up."

"I grew up in one of those houses that always had KMOX on," said Merrill. "So when I got a chance to intern there in 1994, I was excited. I interned in sports in 1994 and that led to a part-time job as a sports producer. I ran the Cardinal baseball network and did some weekend/nighttime/vacation fill-in as an online producer for about a year."

Merrill was moved to the morning drive in 1995.

"I was moved to board-op [hitting all of the buttons] for *Total Information AM*," said Merrill. "I did that until Bill, Wendy, and their producer Jeanette Grider packed their bags for Belleville. With no one around who really knew the show as well as I did, I became the executive producer of *Total Information AM* soon after their departure."

DONNA MICHAELS

Donna Michaels, who for years has been the voice of the Schnucks' radio commercials as well as many other commercials, got her start working on KMOX and KMOX FM. On the FM side Michaels spun records and had a music show, but on KMOX she was a newscaster.

Michaels had a distinctive, clear style and was comfortable behind the microphone in any situation. She was a host, did commercials, and read the news.

"We even had her doing the traffic at the traffic desk," said Don Miller.

CHRIS MIHILL

Chris Mihill, who Charles Brennan calls "the hardest working man in broadcasting" is Brennan's producer on *The Morning Meeting*. He came to KMOX as a summer intern on KHTR (the FM side), and then came to the AM side in 1987 as an engineer for the morning show. Brennan credits Mihill often on the air for all of the work he has done in setting up the guests and producing the broadcasts.

"I started in March of 1996 producing *The Morning Meeting* with Charlie," said Mihill. "It's a unique show. I can't think of any show that would start off with a comment line at the beginning and most of the calls are pretty mean."

MCGRAW MILHAVEN

McGraw Milhaven joined KMOX on August 2, 1999. He came from KFAB in Omaha, Nebraska, where he was a sportscaster. He has been the host of programs in different time periods and the co-host of *The Morning Meeting* with Charles Brennan.

The Morning Meeting takes its show on the road and doing a remote broadcast can be a nerve-wracking situation because you never know what will happen.

"I am always apprehensive on remotes," said Milhaven. "Every single remote is a challenge. One time we were doing a show in Kiener Plaza and we were going to have Jackie Joyner Kersee on. I got there a few hours early. Well, it looked like rain, it looked terrible. We were trying to decide what to do. There was a truck we could use, but how would that be interviewing Jackie Joyner Kersee in a truck. Finally at the last minute we decided to move it into the Bank of America building. We moved as quickly as possible to get set up in there and we were ready about 20 seconds before we went on the air. Jackie Joyner Kersee was there inside the lobby and the show went fine."

Besides the uncertainties of the remotes, Milhaven feels more comfortable in the studio because there is no audience that he can see.

"It's weird," he said. "When you're doing a show on the radio you can't see the people who are listening to you. I know I'm doing a radio show, but I can forget it and it's like I'm just talking to the callers and to Charlie. It's just like a conversation. When you're on a remote and you have a live audience, it's a little like stage fright."

On one remote, Brennan and Milhaven took their show to the Loretto Hilton Theater at Webster University. Bob Costas was to be their guest to talk about his new book. As time for the show approached their special guest was no where to be found.

"Costas had had a landscaper on his street and the street was blocked so he was delayed," said *Morning Meeting* producer, Chris Mihill.

In typical Costas fashion, he came in with such a funny story the listeners soon forgot he was late. Was Milhaven nervous Costas wouldn't show?

"I was nervous the whole show," he said. But why would he be nervous the whole show, Costas showed up? "Then I had to interview him!"

Being somewhat new to the St. Louis scene, Milhaven hadn't interviewed Costas.

"I was excited to interview Bob Costas, wouldn't you be?" he said.

Milhaven's interest in baseball, and his having read the book helped him ask some good questions. Brennan joined in and the audience asked good questions making it a successful show.

Milhaven likes working with Brennan.

"Charlie has been wonderful," he said. "He is easy to work with. He gives you room to work. We have a chemistry together. I appreciate Charlie, and I really appreciate the producers. They are worth their weight in gold. Chris Mihill is great. Fred Bodimer is good and so is Peggy Cohill. Whenever I have a question about anything, they are so great in helping me out."

"I like McGraw," said Nancy Newton, a regular listener who enjoys going to the remote broadcasts. "He's quite young, I think from listening to him. He's a single person and you realize that from listening. You get a different perspective from him. Charlie and McGraw really compliment each other, with Charlie being married with a child and McGraw single. He knows a lot about things, especially sports. I like those two together."

Carol Daniel has worked with Milhaven on the afternoon drive show.

"I love doing afternoon drive, especially since McGraw came along," she said. "He's a breath of fresh air in my professional life here. I hope to keep working with him a long time."

DON MILLER

Don Miller came to KMOX from KSD, where he was known on the air as "Officer Don Miller." He was a police officer and had been assigned to work at KSD. When he came to KMOX, he quit the force, and had a long successful career guiding drivers through the streets of St. Louis.

"Robert Hyland made me an offer to come to KMOX," said Miller. "I told him I would have to quit the police force and before I'd been paid by KSD and the police department. If I went to KMOX they would have to make up for it. He made up for it and then some."

The helicopters he flew were leased from a private company, and even though Miller is a licensed pilot, CBS rules prohibited him from piloting while he was on official CBS business, meaning doing his traffic reports or visiting schools. Miller came up with the term "gaper block" meaning people were stopping to look at something and it was clogging up the traffic. This term plus the LMD ("In bad weather I'd say we're flying the LMD…Large Metal Disk") were included in a proclamation he received from the mayor's office.

"I really enjoyed working with Don Miller," said Scott St. James, a former talk show host who now works in Los Angeles. "Before I left for California, the station out there was trying their best to impress me when they flew me out there. They took me up in a helicopter and I just thought to myself, 'They think this is good, you should see the one Don Miller has! I've been on dates in Don Miller's helicopter!' They were doing their best, but it couldn't compare to Miller's."

St. James really did go on a date in Don Miller's helicopter.

"I came up with this idea to do the mother of all birthdays for my girlfriend's birthday and Don Miller helped me with it," St. James remembered. "In cahoots with Miller we told her to drive to a certain place. There out of the sky came Don and me. We picked her up and took her to a boat and landed on the boat where we ate dinner. After that we went somewhere else for drinks."

Miller used the helicopter for other tasks, including running errands that needed to be done quickly.

"Occasionally on an emergency basis," said Miller, "I would fly to Mr. Hyland's house to pick up some important papers and bring them downtown."

He also served as a taxicab to at least one employee.

"I picked up Mary Phelan sometimes when she was doing the afternoon shift at KMOX," said Miller. "One time she was joking around about how it would save her a lot of time on the highway if I picked her up, so I did. I would pick her up at the heliport at St. John's Hospital so she wouldn't have to put up with the traffic."

Though he was supposed to be reporting the traffic, several times he actually became the news when the jet copter crashed.

"There were only three bad crashes," said Miller. "By a bad crash I mean the kind where you don't walk away from them. Broken bones. Once we collided with another helicopter at the heliport and once we ran out of gas over Highway 55 and we crashed near the brewery at the Arsenal exit. I suffered a broken back in that crash."

There were times when he was doing the traffic reports and he came upon a news story.

"I saw the car bombing on Interstate 55," said Miller. "Just seconds after Jimmy Michaels' car exploded I arrived. It was the most monumental traffic jam in the history of St. Louis because they had to shut down the highway at rush hour."

Even though he was not on the police force, Miller carried a police radio.

"Once we saw a stolen car with the police in hot pursuit," he said. "He was headed east on Interstate 70 and stopped on the 70 eastbound side. The guy got out of the car and ran across the westbound lanes nearly killing himself. He ran into a neighborhood and I was able to pinpoint the house he ran into. It was around Lillian and Riverview. We watched him run into the house then he tried to hide himself in a crowd and was sitting in a group of people on the porch. I saw the whole thing."

The late Alan Barkledge was his pilot at times.

"I learned a lot about flying from Alan Barkledge," said Miller. "He was my pilot on traffic for many years. Rich Barkledge, who is flying now for a radio station, is his brother."

Miller did the traffic for the morning and evening drive time, but he also came in for special events such as baseball games or the VP Fair.

"It was a pretty good service," said Miller. "I was up there and I could spot parking spaces and I'd tell the drivers where to park. One time during the World Series, I noticed the levy had parking spaces open. I told the folks, 'If you're having trouble finding a parking space, there's plenty of room on the riverfront and it's free parking.' Pretty soon we had McDonalds and the Robert E. Lee complaining to KMOX that too many people were blocking their spots! I flooded the riverfront with cars!"

Miller retired January 1, 1993 and remained in St. Louis. He is planning to move to Michigan to be with his daughter and her family.

"I've been talking it over with my daughter," he said. "I'm going to build a home on their property. There's good fishing up there and the weather's great."

MIKE MILLER

Mike Miller is the gardening expert on KMOX. He started as a guest for four years and then got his own show on Sunday afternoons and celebrated his seventh anniversary in August of 2000.

"One day after I'd been there as a guest expert on horticulture, Rod Zimmerman came in and said he wanted to change the format," said Miller. "They had been rotating six horticulturists and I was one of the six. He hired me to do the horticulture shows and I started doing them with Charlie Brown and then with Dave Dugan."

One of the most well-known episodes was when his listeners were surprised to know he got sick on the air.

"I actually had epilepsy and didn't know it," he said. "The previous year I'd been having some symptoms and I knew something was going on, but I wasn't sure what. On that day Tracy and I took one of our walks like I always do before I go on the air, we went to Carondolet Park. I was feeling kind of strange, but I went ahead and went to work."

Bill Reker was running the board and realized something was wrong. He sent an assistant out to get a glass of water for Miller.

"I remember drinking the water, then a caller asked a question about

a peachtree and a borer in the peach tree," Miller said. "I went lights out, fell out of the chair, and woke up just as they were putting me in the ambulance. Luckily Bill Reker's wife is a nurse and he knew something about seizures. He knew to leave me alone, but he just tried to make sure I didn't swallow my tongue or hurt myself."

The chaos that ensued as Reker tried to help Miller caused a few minutes of dead air on KMOX, leaving the listeners to wonder what was going on.

"They real quick found some Don Wolff jazz show tapes and put that on the air," said Miller. "The next week the husband of the woman who had asked the question about peach borers' husband called. He said, 'Hope my wife didn't cause the seizure.' There had been a story about a fan who had said Mary Hart's voice [Mary Hart from *Entertainment Tonight*] caused her to have a seizure. I felt bad that she felt so bad, she was afraid to call. I said no, I had epilepsy. So many of the fans sent me flowers and cards. I'd say 90 percent of all the cards and flowers I got were from people I didn't know."

Working at KMOX has given Miller much exposure and he has many loyal fans. He led a trip of listeners to Belgium and Holland in September of 1999.

"It was springtime when the tulips were out," said Miller. "There were 36 people on the trip."

Miller has written two books (*Missouri Gardener's Guide* and *My Missouri Garden: A Gardener's Journal*) and is the Horticultural editor for *St. Louis Garden Magazine*. He served as emcee for the Soulard Family Center walk which took place the day Mark McGwire hit his 69th and 70th home runs in 1998. As part of the festivities, Miller was in a hospital bed race and won.

He recognizes groups or individuals who go above the call of duty in the gardening area with his Tip of the Trowel on-air award.

"I give it to someone who's impressed me—Boy Scouts who have been planting plants, people who have helped with Forest Park, Volunteers with the Granite City Parks Department, anybody, really who I see doing something extra," Miller said.

On his show he always talks about his wife, Tracy.

"People always come up to her and think she knows a lot about gardening," said Miller. "They ask her questions about their plants. When we do our remotes, she comes with me and it's sort of funny to see these people asking her about their gardens.

"My show is for everybody and I tell the listeners. I make sure that every time I'm on the air I thank the audience for listening. I really appreciate all of my listeners. If it were not for them, I would not be there."

STRETCH MILLER

Stretch Miller was broadcasting minor league baseball in Springfield, Illinois, in 1946 when he received a call from an advertising agency in St. Louis asking him to audition for a spot on the Cardinals' broadcasts, working with Harry Caray and Gabby Street.

Miller got the job, and remained on the broadcasts for eight years, also working with Gus Mancuso. He was moved out of that spot in 1954 when Jack Buck was brought in from Rochester, New York.

In addition to baseball, Miller broadcast Saint Louis University football and basketball, Washington University football and basketball, wrestling matches, hockey games, and high school sports.

Miller moved back to Peoria, Illinois, in 1955 and later died of Lou Gehrig's disease.

GARY MOORE

"Gary Moore was from St. Louis," said Jim "Peanuts" Zagarri. "His real name was Gary Morfit and I was friends with him. We went to dances all over town. He was on KMOX. Later he went on into television and became famous. He ended up doing a show with Jimmy Durante."

RON MORGAN

Ron Morgan had been a popular St. Louis radio personality before he came to work at KMOX as a co-host of afternoon drive in 1985.

ELLEN MORPHONIUS

Ellen Morphonius was a judge in Florida who came to KMOX as a guest. When Mr. Hyland heard her, he hired her. She was like the modern-day Judge Judy, tough on crime. On KMOX she was known as Lady Ellen or Judge Ellen. She did shows on crime and punishment and politics. She even filled in for other hosts, including Jim White, on occasion.

SCOTT MOSBY

Scott Mosby is the host of the *Home Improvements Show* on Saturdays from 10 AM until noon.

"It originally started with True Value as the sponsor and they had Al Schroeder who was called 'Mr. Tinker.' When Central Hardware went out of business, there was no more 'Mr. Tinker'; but Al stayed on for about six years and then the Home Builders Association got hold of me and told me KMOX was looking for seven people to audition for it."

As it turned out he was called in when the American League playoff games were cut short and they had an evening to fill.

"I came in there prepared to send the callers to this hardware store or that," said Mosby. "But I took eight calls and none of them were from St. Louis. They were all from out of town."

Once he became a regular on the *Home Improvements Show* on Saturdays he was on the air for two hours followed by Mike Miller's *Gardening Show*. When the baseball games are on Saturdays, they would cut Miller's show because it is the second show.

"One time I said, 'Hey, Mike hasn't been on in a while, couldn't we split the time when there's a game?' and that worked out well," said Mosby. "The listeners like to be able to hear both shows."

Mosby remembers his funnniest call, which was really a serious call.

"He said, 'Hi, this is Melvin [not his real name] from Washington, Missouri, I-44 and 100.' Luckily I knew what he was talking about, Interstate 44 and 100 since it was near Washington, Missouri," Mosby said. "I've got a problem. Toby's been out playin' in the yard and he's covered with all this slimy stuff and I can't tell if the smell is coming from the septic tank because my truck's broke and I haven't been able to get to the dump in a month.' Well I knew he had a problem and I had to walk him through it. I knew he had a septic tank problem and that he hadn't emptied his trash in a while. It was just a funny call to me and I couldn't let on like it was funny while I was on the air.

"The other kinds of calls I always get are the ones 'My husband says it can't be done and I say it can, what do you think?' I always say 'I think I'm not answering that question.'"

Mosby is the owner of a home remodeling construction company, Mosby Building Arts Center, in Kirkwood.

MIKE MURPHY

Mike Murphy was the first broadcaster who tried to take the place of the late Jack Carney. He had been working in Kansas City when he was hired by Robert Hyland and Tim Dorsey.

He was only on the air for a couple of weeks before he resigned.

DAVE MURRAY

Dave Murray, the chief meteorologist for KTVI-TV, also provided weather reports for KMOX for many years in addition to his television work.

JANICE SETTLE MURRAY

Janice Settle Murray, who started her career in broadcasting at KSDK-TV as Janice Settle before marrying meteorologist Dave Murray, has done fill-in work on KMOX. She has appeared with Charles Brennan and in other capacities. Though Murray got out of full-time news reporting, she has remained in the public eye, doing many reports (mostly about gardening) with her husband on KTVI-TV.

"I really liked it when she was on with Charles Brennan," said *Morning Meeting* listener Margie Tippett. "She is really funny and is enjoyable to listen to."

STAN MUSIAL

The exploits of Stan "The Man" Musial were followed by listeners on KMOX throughout the years. He was always being interviewed by KMOX, but once when the *Globe-Democrat* and *Post-Dispatch* newspapers were on strike, Musial did a little broadcasting himself.

"The newspapers were on strike and we did a lot more news coverage," said Jim White. "Mr. Hyland wanted the people to be able to hear the funnies, so who better to read them than Stan 'The Man'."

"I went down to the station and read the funnies," Musial recalled..

"It was good," said White. "He'd go, 'And then in the next frame, Popeye takes off his hat and says….' He was funny."

"I remember when he did that," said Lil Musial, Stan's wife. "It was every Sunday during the strike. It was kind of funny because I was the one who read the funnies. Stan didn't even read the funnies."

Musial's career was full of exciting moments and KMOX covered them all.

"I remember they covered the 3,000th hit," said Lil Musial. "We have this wonderful picture of us getting off the train after we came home that reminds me of that day. And we got such good coverage when he went into the Hall of Fame. Every year when you go to the Hall of Fame you see how emotional the new inductees get. That's how it was for us. It was just such an emotional time, with your family and your friends. The people from KMOX were there.

"I'll never forget we were flying home from the Hall of Fame on a special Ozark private plane. Casey Stengel was riding along because it would be faster for him to go though St. Louis to get to his home in California. We were having a party on the plane, you know just getting really 'happy,' when we realized something was wrong with the plane. The pressure in the plane was getting bad. We had trouble flying and actually had to go to Syracuse to land. They did a little work on the plane and we started for St. Louis. There was more trouble with the pressure in the plane, but we made it home safely. I was really scared and light-headed when we got off. Casey said, 'It took me two days to get back to my home in California and I was taking the short cut!'"

Lil Musial remembers a special gift that Robert Hyland gave Stan after he made an appearance for him.

"Stan had done an appearance and Bob Hyland gave him a $500 gift certificate to Sax Fifth Avenue, but instead of giving it to Stan, he gave it to me," said Lil. " My birthday is in October and it's opal so I bought myself a mosiac opal pendant. It's very beautiful. Bob Hyland said, 'It's for the woman behind the man.' I thought that was nice of him."

Jack Buck has long had a friendship with Stan Musial. He often mentions Lil on the air and over the years KMOX listeners have gotten to know her as well as her famous husband.

"When I started having trouble walking," said Lil, "people started sending me canes. One man gave me a real nice one with a redbird on it. When I meet Stan's fans, many people call me Lil. I always say, 'I know you're a great fan because you know my first name.'"

JUAN NAJARA

Juan Najara was an engineer at the station. Producer Rene Servier remembered a story involving Juan and Jim White. Najara was engineering White's show at the time.

"A lady called in from North Carolina and said, 'Jim, I just love listening to your show, but I'm having a terrible time getting you in tonight. It's all fuzzy.' So Jim White says, 'Well, I'll get our engineer on it. I'll have Juan go out and move that transmitter.' As he's talking, Juan just leaned back, crossing his arms [the transmitter is in Illinois and it is huge so it would be impossible for Juan to move it]. 'Juan,' White said, 'this lady needs to be able to hear us better, so could you move the transmitter?' 'Now, ma'am you'll have to tell us how it sounds as he moves it, how's that?' and she says, 'A little too much,' so he then says, 'How's that?' as Juan is just still sitting there grinning. We were all cracking up, this lady was actually believing it. What was funny was I'll be darned if there weren't several callers later complaining that now that Juan moved the transmitter, their reception was messed up!"

MISS NANETTE

Miss Nanette was the fashion expert who appeared frequently on the early *At Your Service* shows in the 1960s.

DOUG NEWMAN

Doug Newman was a staff announcer on KMOX from 1956 to 1974. One of the things that was interesting about Newman was that his wife was an astrologer, and often brought the subject into his conversation.

"He'd say, 'Oh, that's OK, Shirley,' said fellow worker, Shirley Bates, "'you couldn't help it, you're a Leo.' He and his wife lived in Kimmswick and they grew grapes. He would not do anything, paint or anything, if it wasn't right in the stars."

One of Newman's duties over the years was to write the news for Rex Davis.

CLARENCE NIEDER

Clarence Nieder grew to become a recognizable name to many St. Louisians as Jack Carney's producer, although in his 35 years at KMOX he completed a variety of assignments.

Carney was always talking to Nieder on the radio. The listeners could not hear Nieder's end of the conversation, but they could hear Carney say, "Clarence let's get Joe Sullivan on the phone." Joe Sullivan was the football Cardinals' vice president and he and his wife were good friends of Carney and his wife. Though Sullivan seemed to be disliked in the sports world, Carney would make him seem pleasant and humanize him to the public.

Nieder came up with so many different creative ideas that, coupled with the genius of Carney, created a show that remained a broadcasting standard even after Carney's death. He was always ready with a sound effect and it was as if Nieder and Carney knew each other's mind. Carney would say something and instantly a sound effect would be played as if Nieder knew what his host was going to say before he actually said it.

"It was fun then. I would get recognized because he mentioned me so much on the radio," said Nieder. "Jack was very good to me. One Christmas he had a private party and invited my wife Dolores and me. He had Harry Fender dressed up in a Santa suit and he presented me with a very nice television set. He was always doing nice things for me, once he bought me a VCR."

One of the best things Carney did was take Nieder and his wife with him on a trip. "He took Dolores and me on a trip to Las Vegas," Nieder said. "He got us into some great shows, including Frank Sinatra. That was a great trip."

Known to many as "C.J.", Nieder was a friend to everybody.

"When you would get stressed out, like if an *Open Line Show* was not going well, he would always cheer you up," said Lisa Bedian who worked with him. "He would say, 'Kid, don't worry about it, the money is still the same. If it goes great or not so great, the money's still the same. I still say that today."

Nieder did so many different things at KMOX. He produced Harry Fender and he did a lot of sports remotes including the St. Louis Hawks' basketball games.

"I remember Ben Kerner [the Hawks' owner] was trying to increase attendance," said Nieder. "They had big band remotes on the stage at Kiel Auditorium after the Hawks' games. They had really good acts like Lionel Hampton and Harry James at those concerts."

"Clarence was always a hoot," said former producer Rene Sevier. "He always had eight projects going. They were always wonderful projects, he was always up to something. And he was always reading and trying to improve himself. He would take notes and make underlines in his books."

JULI NIEMAN

Juli Nieman has done the financial reports since 1988. Nieman, who works for R.J. Jones Capital Equity, first came to KMOX when Ruth Jacobson of Flieshman-Hillard recommended her to Anne Keefe.

"I came down and did Anne's show and we had so much fun," Nieman said. "Afterward, someone came in and said, 'Mr. Hyland would like to talk to you. I thought, 'Uh-oh, we had a little too much fun.'"

Hyland offered her a job doing the financial reports every day.

"Aside from doing the financial reports I work on Thursday afternoons with Charles Jaco on *Total Information PM*," she said.

Nieman coined a new term to save herself some trouble.

"I started saying 'Steens' instead of sixteenths," she said. "The market started going with 16ths and 32nds and I only had a certain amount of time so I started saying 'steens.' Everyone gave me trouble. 'What's a steen?' I could have used teeny or weeny, in the industry 16ths are called teenies and 32nds are called weenies, but I thought that would be too much for KMOX."

One of her all-time memories in her years on KMOX was the brief time that announcer J.C. Corcoran was on.

"J.C. hated business," she said. "He said, 'It's totally boring,' and he felt it would bring down his show. They made him use me. I'm sure he was thinking ,'Oh great, we have to stop the show for a report from Juli Nieman.' Well, I decided to be creative. Once when I was about to do the closing markets, he had had a hockey player for a guest so I did the report in hockey lingo. Then the next day he had an entertainer and I did it in show biz lingo. Once Joe Edwards was on from Blueberry Hill and I did it all in rock and roll lingo. J.C. really liked it and we ended up getting along really well."

TONY OREN

Tony Oren was the host of an overnight talk show on KMOX. He had an interesting life, living in Australia as a young man where he appeared as an actor in motion pictures. He traveled in Europe and moved to St. Louis in 1957.

"Tony would bring a suitcase in with him," said Rene Servier, one of his producers. "He had his stuff in his suitcase. Tony had a miniature paper cutter and would slice up the wire copy and put it in a binder. He'd write in the columns what it was. 'Man bites dog story' or 'wedding' or whatever. Say he played a song called "Eternal Love," he would real quick turn to the section on weddings and read an article about something that pertained to the song."

"Tony would come in and empty this little coin purse on the desk," said newswriter John Amann. "We would use that money all night for snacks. I'd go to the second floor, the television station snack room because it was better than KMOX's. Tony would give me his key and I'd keep making trips; we lived on coffee and Oreos all night.

"Tony had a deep voice that women must have liked. He would have women calling him all night. I'd take the calls for him, they would say, 'Come over and I'll fix you breakfast.' They didn't even know him, they just liked his voice."

"For years, Tony hosted the overnight on the weekends while I was with the station in the 1970s," said Barb Felt. "Bob Osborne told me this story and I have no reason to question it. There was a middle-aged woman living on the east side who became addicted to Tony Oren's voice on the weekends, but it was a love/hate relationship on her part. She would call him on the off-air line during the breaks and accuse him of reading her mind. She claimed she would be thinking a thought and then Tony would instantly bring that subject matter up in the on-air dialogue."

According to Osborne, Oren began to question her sanity and also his safety as she called him so often at the station.

"One night after his show, Tony went to his car, [which was parked on the street in front of the station] and while he was unlocking the car door, a frenzied woman jumped up from behind the car and sprayed Tony with mace," Felt said. "She screamed obscenities while threatening him that if he ever 'read her mind' again, she would take more drastic actions. She then disappeared into the shadows."

Oren worked in St. Louis radio for 22 years before retiring in 1994. He died in 1998 at the age of 75.

BOB OSBORNE

Bob Osborne worked on several stations, including WIL before coming to KMOX. He was on KMOX from 1969 to 1996, starting on the FM side before Hyland moved him to the AM station and eventually named him program director.

"He was really a music man," said traffic director Shirley Bates. "They brought him to the AM side. Bob Osborne really knew radio. He knew programming inside and out, and he was an all-round good person."

"Ossie [Osborne's nickname] had the best music ears in the business," said Barb Felt, who worked with him at KMOX and became good friends with him. "He could tell if something was going to be a hit. It was a big deal for disc jockeys in those days to 'break' a record, play it for the first time and it would become a hit. I'll bet he broke more hits than most disk jockeys. He should have stayed in music, I thought. He was so creative."

One of his duties was hosting the *Trading Station* show on Saturday mornings. Rene Servier was his producer for a time.

"He was a real happy-go-lucky kind of guy," said Servier. "But when it came to the *Trading Station*, he took that show so seriously. To some people it was just people calling up to buy or sell something, but to him it was serious and it was important. He was always worried that I take the calls in a fair order. He wanted me to really keep an ear out to make sure we did not get repeat callers."

"I'll never forget the first time I met Bob Osborne," said Wendy Wiese. "I was the morning news person at KWTO in Springfield, Missouri. One day I got a message that a 'Bob Osmore' called from a radio station in St. Louis. I called him back, wondering who Bob Osmore was. I called the number on the paper and said, 'Is Bob Osmore there?' and he said, 'Wendy, it's Bob Osborne from KMOX radio.' I said, 'Bob! This is Wendy from the newsroom in 1983,' when I'd been an intern. I said, 'I'm the tall one.' Then I thought, 'like he'd really remember me.' We set up an interview and when I got to KMOX, I remember exactly what I was wearing. It was a purple silk blouse and purple skirt. I remember that because I was so nervous I had to keep my hands to my sides so the sweat wouldn't show. The first thing he said to me was, 'I remember you.'"

Osborne was the program director at that time.

"He was a great friend to have," said Wiese. "He took a lot from Mr. Hyland so that those who worked under him would not have to. One time I was talking outside Mr. Hyland's office and I heard some loud conversation going on between Mr. Hyland and Ossie. Mr. Hyland was yelling and Ossie was just taking it. He was saying, 'I don't know why she needs a vacation!' And Bob [Osborne] is saying, 'Well, I think she should be able to.' I said to someone, 'Man, he's really hot! Who's he yelling about?' and she said, 'You.' He was in there defending me."

"Bob Osborne was one of the people they tried at Jack Carney's spot after Carney died," said Felt. "He did not do well there. As much as I liked him, I knew it and I felt for him. He was so brilliant in music, but he just didn't do well with interviews. He knew it too, and the callers were so cruel. He was a very sensitive person and I think when people started calling the station and criticizing him, it really hurt him. I think that may have contributed to him getting sick."

Osborne put in many hours at KMOX. He did whatever Hyland asked him to do, whether it was play records, do the news, conduct interviews, or be the program director. While doing a show on KMOX, he got sick and left the program to go to the hospital. He was in the hospital about three weeks before he died.

"There was just such a short time between the day he got sick in the trashcan at work to the day he died," said Wiese. "He was so sick when he was at the hospital, we knew we couldn't visit him because he was so sick. I got married when he was in the hospital and he would have surely come to the wedding. We brought one of the floral bouquets from the pews to his room. He was the kind of person who would do anything for you."

"I set up a phone line in my home," said Felt. "We called it the Ossie Get Well Hot Line and people called it 24 hours a day with messages that I would take down to the hospital and give him. Messages would be like, 'Hey, get well Ossie!' or 'That's a hell of a way to get out of Christmas shopping!' KMOX was like a family to him and he really appreciated those tapes. Bob Osborne had a big heart, he was just a really good man. For the first tape, I took the messages and mixed it with music and produced a special tape to give him. His son let me in the hospital room, he was so sick with pancreatitis that they would only let in family, but he was so happy to get those tapes. When I took the third tape up to him, I got there and there was a curtain closed over his door, and I knew he was gone. He was a dear person."

BILL OTT

Bill Ott has been an engineer for 32 years at KMOX and in that time span he has performed a wide variety of jobs, working on studio shows, remotes, and maintenance work. If the cart machines needed repair or if there was trouble with the transmitter, Ott wore a beeper and would be called to help fix the problem.

"I first came to KMOX in 1967 for six months as vacation relief," said Ott. "That was the same year Charlie Domourous came. I went to work for KATZ for a year and a half and then came back to KMOX to stay."

Ott's life as an engineer has never been dull, that's for sure. Shortly after he started at KMOX, Robert Hyland told him about an opening at Lindenwood College.

"Mr. Hyland's wife had a connection to Lindenwood through Martha Boyer, who was a teacher out there and was the head of the communications department. They were looking for a chief engineer at their college station, KCLC, so I worked full-time at KMOX and was KCLC's chief engineer for 25 years. When I got there it was a 10 watt station. At the beginning it was not much bigger than a CB set. You were lucky if you could hear it from the highway, then we raised it to 2,500 watts and finally to 25,000.

Ott ended up working two full-time jobs for 25 year. Just to be sure he wasn't bored, Ott decided to start his own radio station in 1982.

"I put an FM radio station on the air in Vandalia, Missouri," said Ott. "I started KMWR. Here's a trivia question for you. Where did Randy Karracker get his first experience in play-by-play? Vandalia, working for KMWR. He did our high school games."

As an engineer, it was Ott's job to do in-studio work as well as remotes. He has worked many baseball and football games for KMOX.

"I remember doing the football Cardinals," said Ott. "It was so cold this one day; the chill factor was 10 below zero with the wind. It was so cold we had cardboard on the floor to keep our feet off the cement. We had insulated clothes and thick gloves. There was a little bitty heater. It was the coldest I've ever been. The broadcasters were Jack Buck and Bob Starr. We had hot coffee and hot chocolate but the restroom was so far from the broadcast booth that the only way we could go was to have a real long commercial break and we'd have to run down there with a stopwatch in our hands."

Ott's first day of work was the same week Skip Caray, Harry's son, started at KMOX.

"I had to record something with Skip and I was so nervous because it was Harry's son," he said. "I was pushing the wrong buttons on the recorder. There were all these clicks on the tape. I really thought I'd get in trouble because it was Harry's son, but I was able to edit it and it sounded fine.

"I did some of the Spirits' games with Bob Costas. I did his first game. Bob would come in at the last minute. He was never at any broadcast until the last second, but he was never upset. We love Bob, he was such a nice young man. Everybody thought the world of him. He was a pro with everything except being on time."

STEVE OVERBY

Steve Overby was a sports assistant in the late 1970s to early 1980s. He did many of the interviews that were run in the sportscasts as well as wrote sportscasts, gathered scores, and produced shows.

"One of the funny interview situations happened at the airport," said Overyby. "We went out to interview a manager after he was fired. He was coming in on a plane. When we got there, we noticed that waiting for him was not his wife and children, but someone else. That was actually more of a scoop than the interview about his firing."

Overby worked with Bob Costas on a daily basis when Costas was doing the Missouri basketball games. Occasionally Costas would invite him to go up to Columbia with him.

"We would ride up there with Sam Stipanovich and his wife [parents of M.U. standout Steve Stipanovich]," said Overby. "We always stopped at Gasper's Truck Stop in Kingdom City for dinner. I'll never forget the time Bob Costas almost got beat up by a bunch of truckers.

"There was a section marked 'for Truckers only' and Bob went and sat down at one of the tables. He started talking to some of these big burly guys saying, '10-4 good buddy' and 'What's your 10-20?' He was just joking around, but these guys were getting mad. I'm like, 'Bob, these guys don't care if you're the voice of the Mizzou basketball team, they're about to beat you up, let's get out of here.' Here was Costas and Overby, we were like these two little hoods about to get beat up by a dozen truckers.

"We had a lot of fun in that sports office," said Overby. "I'll never forget the time we asked one of the reporters to bring us back a souvenir from the Streak [the Women's Professional Basketball Team] and she brought us back the nameplate from Jane Ellen Cook's locker. We put it up in the office. Just a little souvenir of the Streak."

MIKE OWENS

Mike Owens, who later went on to work for KSDK, started at KMOX as a producer for Jim White. Owens had been an intern at KMOX before getting experience at stations in Wichita, Kansas, and Sedalia, Missouri. He is originally from St. Louis and wanted to get back to St. Louis.

"KMOX was the place to be back then," said Owens. "When I got there on my first day I looked out the window at the Arch and said 'Man, this is the big time! This is cool.' I had been working in radio stations that were literally surrounded by cornfields and beanfields.

Owens was put on White's show as producer. Pat White, Jim's wife, did the booking of the guests, and Owens screened the calls, working from 8 PM to 3 AM.

"Jim White was so easy to work with," said Owens. "He was laid back, calm, collected, always in charge. He knew where he was going and how to get there. I remember we would have different guests on like Rev. Bill Little, [psychic] David Hoy, [ghost chaser psychic] Gordon Hoehner, and Bevvy Jagers. Bill Little had been very successful during the day on Anne Keefe's show and Jim wanted to try him at night. He was a big success on Jim's show."

Owens screened the calls and signaled to White when to go to a commercial break. If a news story happened on his shift, Owens would be in charge of calling up people to get them on the air to talk about it.

"I'll never forget the show we did the night Jim Jones killed all those people in Guyana," said Owens. "They had all been found dead in the afternoon and then they learned that one of them was a congressman. The story was unfolding and by the time it was our shift, everyone was interested in it. We made a lot of calls that night. We called the embassy in Guyanna. It was great to be able to have a radio station that would spend that kind of money. Back in those days there wasn't the directory assistance there is today and it was harder to make an overseas call. It cost $35 a minute to talk to them. Not many radio stations would do that.

"I loved working on Jim's show, but I wanted out of those hours. When Mary Lou Johanek left the newsroom to go to the network, an opening came and I was moved over to news."

"I knew he was interested in doing news," said former news director John Angelides, "He had worked in news in Sedalia, and then came to work for Jim. When an opening came in news, we moved him over."

"I covered City Hall, working a normal 8-5 day," said Owens. "I was already interested in politics and I knew a lot about it. During that time Jim Conway was the mayor, and the comptroller was Paul Berra. I worked at KMOX for six years and I really liked it."

Owens left in 1983 to go to KSDK-TV, where he is an investigative reporter.

FRANK PAWLOSKI

Frank Pawloski was a producer at KMOX for 23 years, from 1973 until 1996. At times he worked in the sports department, sometimes for Jack Carney and also for Jim White.

"I started producing *Sports on a Sunday Morning*, then did *Sports Open Lines*," said Pawloski, who was always more interested in sports. He spent several years as Carney's producer with Clarence Nieder at the controls.

"I worked for Jack from 1976 to 1984," said Pawloski. "He was so wild, and Clarence and he worked so well together. People used to love to listen to Jack's show and they would especially love to hear the monologue."

Pawloski did all of the highlights for the station. Each week on *Sports on a Sunday Morning* they would run a re-cap of all of the sports happenings and he would have written the script and pulled the cuts from the tapes.

"Our highlight tapes were like 15 minutes long," Pawloski said. "We put everything that happened in St. Louis on it, but we also put other big events. Say Reggie Jackson hit his 50th home run for the Yankees, we'd throw that in. When I first came to KMOX, one of my jobs was to go back and catalog all of the big sports plays. As I went on, I added each week's highlights and at the end of the year we'd have a yearly highlight show that I'd put together."

Besides the Carney show and the sports highlights, Pawloski also produced White's show.

"Frank was there the day Jim White had his heart attack," said Elaine Stern, who later became White's producer.

"Frank Pawloski was one of those great KMOX guys perfectly suited to the whole culture of KMOX," said NBC's Bob Costas, who worked around Pawloski in his days at KMOX. "He was a keeper of archives, a keeper of secrets, and would do anything to help people like Jack Buck or me. I think he got lost in the shuffle of the change over. He was an indispensable guy, always cheerful, very capable; an old style radio man."

LOU PAYNE

Lou Payne was a female disc jockey who worked for KMOX in the 1950s.

MARY PHELAN

Before Mary Phelan became a recognizable face in St. Louis as a news reporter for KMOV-TV, she was on KMOX radio in the mornings with Bill Wilkerson, Bob Hardy, and Wendy Wiese. Phelan came aboard as a young newscaster fresh out of school and her quick wit and confidence soon won her the morning spot.

"She was good in the morning," said Chris Mihill, the producer for *Total Information AM* at the time. "She also co-hosted the midday with Art Fleming."

"I loved Mary Phelan," said Bob Heil, who has been associated with KMOX for over 40 years as an electronics expert. "I did some shows with her and Art Fleming. They did a show together and I was on once a month.

"I remember one specific show with Mary," he said. "We were talking about the latest thing which was satellite television. I was on a test team for this RCA satellite and it was a 13-year project, so I knew it was coming. The listeners were fascinated and the phones were lit up. Just then the red phone rings and it's Mr. Hyland.

"You're talking too much about television! Talk about radio!" he said.

Phelan had resigned her job at KMOV-TV and had been married for only three weeks when she was killed in a car accident in 1998.

NOEL PICARD

Blues Noel Picard worked with Dan Kelly as a color commentator for a while.

"He was always interesting to listen to," said former Blues executive Susie Mathieu. "Because of his French accent, 'Sid Soloman the Third' came out 'Sid the turd,' and if he were going to say a player 'suffered a concussion,' he would say 'had a commotion in his head.' It was priceless to watch Dan during these broadcasts."

JOE POLLACK

Joe Pollack was involved with the football Cardinals in many capacities, including as a newspaper reporter, as the team's public relations director and for two years, in 1972-73, as the analyst on the games for KMOX.

He has also hosted *Open Line* programs over the years on the station, in addition to providing music, theater, and restaurant reviews for years.

Even though he remained on the air, Pollack said he never quite forgave Hyland for firing him from the radio broadcasts. He didn't even find out he had been fired until a week before the 1974 season was to begin.

"I was at the Cardinals' office and one of the secretaries told me I wasn't on the traveling party for that week," Pollack said. "That's when I discovered I had been replaced. I talked to [owner Bill] Bidwill and he blamed Hyland, and Hyland always blamed Bidwill."

RICK POWERS

Rick Powers, who is now a television sportscaster for KDNL-TV, got his broadcasting start as an intern at KMOX in1979.

"It was really a great place to start," said Powers. "They gave you lots of opportunities. I remember the interns really wanted to be on the air, so it was a big thrill to us to be able to record the KMOX *Sportsline*. Then you could call it up and hear that it was your voice on the *Sportsline*."

Football Cardinal owner Bill Bidwill's son was also an intern at the same time Powers was there.

"I remember working with Billy Bidwill," said Powers. "He could have been a spoiled rich kid because he had everything, but he was really a nice kid."

Bidwill now lives in Scottsdale, Arizona, with his wife and children and helps his father run the Arizona Cardinals. When reminded of his days at KMOX, Bidwill looked back on them fondly and said that he enjoyed working there.

"One of the biggest thrills I had while working at KMOX," Powers remembered, "was getting to cover Lou Brock's 3,000[th] hit. I wanted to see it so bad so I said, 'Can I take a tape recorder over there and interview the fans?' They said yes and I grabbed my tape recorder and ran over to the stadium. Right when I got there he hit it and I got the chance to be there and see it. I interviewed the fans about how they felt being able to be there, and we ran those interviews on the news."

ROY QUEEN

Roy Queen was a musician and an emcee who was responsible for the success of many country western singers. He started on KMOX in 1929 and worked off and on until the 1950s. He achieved much attention with his successful *Uncle Dick Slack's Barn Dance Show.*

When Queen was 16, he played for his first audience in Peckerwood Holler near Ironton, Missouri. It was such a success he loved the feeling of the audience's enthusiasm.

"After that dance I was in demand," said Queen. "Because people had heard me pick and sing. I told my dad, 'I think I hear the big city ah calling me! So I went in to Arcadia, Missouri, and got a job at Harry Clay's garage. He was the only place in town who had a radio! I heard them say on KMOX radio that they were lookin' for talent and holding auditions on Saturday morning."

Queen ended up going to St. Louis for the audition. His father was proud of him and wanted to give him a good send-off.

"My dad said, 'I don't want you to be ah ridin' that freight train either, I'm gonna buy you a ticket!' Dad sold the only pig he had to a neighbor for $8. He sent me off and said, 'May God help ye!'"

KMOX's studios were in the Mayfair Hotel at Eighth and St. Charles Street at the time. Queen, being the free spirit he was, decided to hop a freight train anyway, so he could have the $8 to spend when he got to the "big city."

"Back in 1929, a woman named Katherine McEntire was the manager," Queen said in his home in Bixby, Missouri. "I went in to do my audition. The announcer for the show was France Laux. I sang the first Hillbilly song ever sang on radio in St. Louis, my old favorite, 'Can't Give Up My Good Old Rough and Rowdy Ways.' I played my guitar and yodeled. Katherine McEntire was listening in another room. She came in and said, 'Who was that a yodelin'?" She had never heard such a sound. France Laux pointed to me. She said, 'That's something new. I believe I can sell it.'"

He started on a 15-minute feature show called *Roy Queen, The Lone Singer*, Mondays through Saturdays from 9 AM to 9:15. In the 1930s wild west films started becoming popular with such stars as Roy Rogers and Gene Autry.

"Back in those days we had no records," Queen said. "We had to make our own music. We had three organists, Ruth Hulse Nelson, Margot Clark and Ken Wright. We'd also have the Benny Fells Orchestra come in, they were very popular at the time. Singers would come in and sing popular songs of the day with the piano. They wouldn't be famous singers, they just sang popular songs. Another thing was you could not touch the microphone if you were an on-air person. They had strict engineer union rules that prohibited you from touching your mike, even just to adjust it to get it closer, the engineer had to come over and move it."

Queen started the *Farm Hour* on KMOX at 5:30 AM. Every Saturday they would feature bands from the area to give them their start. He also started *The Country Fair Show* on Saturday nights. Queen called his music 'hillbilly music,' but it eventually became known as country music. At that time, no one was playing that type of music on St. Louis radio. He was a pioneer in that area.

After about a year he started having throat problems and decided to quit the radio business and go to Texas. About a year later and after he had his tonsils removed, he came back to KMOX. KMOX had just moved to the Mart Building at 12th and Spruce.

At one point he bought a bar (the late 1930s) and named it "Roy Queen's Cow Barn."

"Eddie Arnold was ah playin' honkytonks before he got famous," said Queen. "I hired him to play for us."

Queen had what he calls "the ramblin' fever," and after a stint at KMOX, he would go on the road and perform, but he would always come back to KMOX. In 1936, Queen was in Texas when he got a call from KMOX.

"They said they were building a big show with Pappy Cheshire, who was big in Vaudeville, and from Wichita, Kansas," said Queen. "They said they wanted to build it around me and Pappy, so I came back and we started the *Uncle Dick Slack's Barn Dance Shows*. Pappy got so great they called him to Hollywood."

This was in the 1940s when radio barn dances became popular.

Uncle Dick Slack was a pitchman for his furniture store and he was the sponsor of the show. Once Cheshire left, Queen became emcee of the show. It became quite successful, but his situation soon changed.

KMOX newsman Guy Runyan, who was very popular at the time, decided to leave KMOX to start a new radio station and he asked his friend Queen to help him.

"I helped him start KXLW in Clayton," said Queen. "I said I don't want to take my *Barn Dance* show over there because they've been so good to me at KMOX, I've got to come up with something else. No one was playing hillbilly records, so I decided I'd become the first hillbilly disc jockey in St. Louis."

Since country music records were a new thing, Queen got the idea that since he was promoting them on his show, why not open a record store and then sell them, too.

"I had St. Louis right where I wanted them," he said. "I'd play the records then say, 'If you liked that song, come on down to Roy Queen's Record Shop and buy it. The *Post-Dispatch* called me every week to ask what was the top selling record that week."

Queen, whose show had launched many country western singers careers, had many famous singers come in his store.

"Roy Rogers, Tex Ritter, Eddie Arnold, they all came in my record store and signed albums."

Rogers and his Sons of the Pioneers were on Queen's show. If they weren't on his show, Queen would discover talent playing in bars.

"I found Ferlin Husky at Vandeventer and Olive," said Queen. "He was playing in a dive called 'The Juke Box.' I put him on and he never forgot it. He still sees me in Branson and remembers that."

Queen used Barbara Fairchild as an extra because union rules at the Khorrasan Room at the Chase required a 12-piece band.

"She was just a cotton picker then," said Queen. "It was hard to find 12 hillbillies with union cards back in those days."

Another person he happened on was Elvis Presley. Presley was still relatively unknown.

"His advance man from Nashville came in," Queen remembered. "'I'm bringing a kid into town, his name's Elvis Presley.' I said, 'Elvis who?' He bought a lot of time on my show and said I'd like for you to put him on and I did."

Afterwards, Presley and Queen were talking and Presley said, 'Where can I go tonight to let my hair down?' Queen was performing at the New Lindy Ballroom in Clayton and he told him to go there.

"The manager of the place was there," said Queen. "He called me over and said, 'You can't bring him in there. You have a country show, he's vulgar! I could have gotten Elvis for nothing!'"

Queen had become a big name in St. Louis. The Mizerany Brothers came to him and said they wanted to sign him to an exclusive contract, but they didn't want to have him on KXLW. They first wanted him on WIL.

"I said 'for X amount of dollars, I'll do it,'" said Queen. "I was under contract to the Mizerany Brothers at the time and was on WIL in the mornings and then on KMOX in the evenings. On Saturdays we did a show on KMOX."

He became in high demand and was very successful and popular. His show was broadcast just before Bob Burnes' nightly sports show. He had just built a ranch in Warrenton, Missouri, and was planning to move there with his family as soon as his oldest son graduated from Ritenour High School.

"I was gonna commute back and forth doing the radio," he said, "And we were going to run a 'Dude Ranch,' it was going to be called the RQ Ranch."

Tragedy struck and changed his life.

"My wife and I had just been out to the ranch and had just put up curtains," he said. "When some old boy doing 90 MPH with a big old Buick hit us head on. It sent my wife through the windshield. Killed

her outright. Bless the Lord, though, my youngest son, who was three years old at the time and was lying on the back seat [no seat belts in those days] never broke a bone."

Queen had to be cut from the car. He suffered numerous injuries, and was in traction at St. Joseph Hospital for 19 months.

"They were so good to me," said Queen. "Mr. Hyland said I could come back any time and Joe Mizerany visited me in the hospital. I got my check every week."

After about a week, they brought a microphone to the hospital and taped Queen doing commercials from his hospital bed. They played his songs and used his commercials. When word got out about his accident many aspiring disk jockeys contacted WIL to get his job.

"The general manager waited until I got a little better and he said, 'You can clean out your desk,' and he gave me all of the hillbilly records from the station. He said, 'Now, that Roy Queen's gone, you'll never hear another hillbilly record on this station,' and they changed their format to rock and roll. Well, now you can look at it and see it's a country and western station."

KWRE radio in Warrenton made Queen an offer he couldn't refuse, as he had braces on his legs and was recuperating at home with the children. The station installed a telephone line in his house so he could do a show from his bed.

"That way I didn't have to drive," he said. "I called Mr. Hyland and said, 'I'm sorry I can't be back,' and then I called the Mizeranys.'"

Queen spent 25 years on KWRE and ran the RQ Ranch. They raised animals as well as had a dude ranch.

"I had a workin' ranch," he said. "We had hayrides, horseback ridin', blue grass fesivals, and auctions."

Queen had gone to auctioneering school and on Saturdays people would bring their things out to sell and he'd have an auction.

"Jack Carney would come to my auctions," said Queen. "He said he wanted me to come down there and be on his show, but shortly after that he died. I never got the chance to be on his show."

Another similar thing happened with Hyland.

"Bob Hyland called me on a Sunday morning," Queen said. "He told me about the big KMOX Day he wanted to have. He said he wanted

to have this big dinner with lots of old KMOX people. 'I don't know where we'll hold it yet, but it will take a big hall,' he said. He told me 'you're gonna be in it.' I sent him some pictures of me at KMOX. He said, 'We'll have to get you to do some promos'. Well, he never got to do that show because he died."

Queen is semi-retired and lives in Bixby with his wife, Sylvia. He has memorabilia from his old radio days, including certificates of recognition from people including congressmen and mayors. Former St. Louis Mayor Freeman Bosley proclaimed him to be the one who started country music in St. Louis.

Two years ago he wrote a book called *The Grand Daddy of Country Music* chronicling his life and his influence on country music. (To order the book, send $10 payable to Roy Queen to Roy Queen HC82 Box 460, Bixby, MO 65439 . For an hour-long cassette of 20 songs and jokes from the *Uncle Dick Slack Show*, add $7.)

His wife Sylvia has the distinction of being the first clogger ever to perform at Silver Dollar City. "So we have something in common," he said. "I had a first [first country western DJ in St. Louis] and she had a first. We still entertain. I play guitar and sing, and she clogs, at nursing homes and special events. Every year we still perform at Silver Dollar City."

The three year old in the back seat of the car is now grown.

"My son, Jimmy Queen, is a musician, and he worked at KWRE, too," said Queen proudly. "He plays all over especially at the Lake of the Ozarks. He was on the KUSA Road Show and the WIL Road Show with his band, the Jimmy Queen Band.

"I still have my tapes of Pappy Cheshire and the old Barn Dance Show. I'm the only one still alive and I'm only 88. With all the things I've done, I've really had a fun life and I still do."

JEFF RAINFORD

Jeff Rainford was a news reporter in the 1980s. He later opened a public relations company, Rainford Angelides with former KMOX news director John Angelides.

BOB RAMSEY

Sportscaster Bob Ramsey got his start on KMOX in 1979 providing interviews for the high school reports. "Jim Baer had been doing these weekly high school reports and I had just gotten out of college, and didn't have a job yet, so I asked if I could help. I wanted to do interviews from the high school football games and then Jim could use them in his reports," Ramsey said.

Baer thought it was a great idea and soon Ramsey and others were stringing for Baer, who was very knowledgeable about the high school scene and had his own column in the *Suburban Journals*. The high school reports were a standard on KMOX with Baer covering Missouri and Bob Emig providing coverage of Illinois schools.

"The stringing job for Jim Baer actually gave me my first on-air experience," said Ramsey, who now is a co-host of a daily show on KFNS and the play-by-play announcer for the Saint Louis University. basketball team. "It was the State Championships for high school football (The Show Me Bowl at Busch Stadium in 1979). They needed more reporters at the ballpark so I was called. One of the games ended and Baer was in the locker room interviewing people from the previous game and suddenly they needed someone on to do a live shot, a report on the game. It should have been Jim Baer, but in live radio, you can't wait. The sports reporter in charge told me to go on and I went on with about a minute's warning."

Ramsey had met Baer at the St. Louis Hummers' games. The Hummers were the St. Louis Women's Professional Softball Team. At the time the Hummers were playing, the St. Louis Streak was also playing . The Streak was the Women's Professional Basketball entry from the St. Louis area. Ramsey did the play-by-play for the Hummers on KCLC, the Lindenwood College station, and he did the public address announcing for the Streak. KMOX was very supportive of both women's teams.

"KMOX has had a long time connection to KCLC and continues it today," said Ramsey. "Randy Karraker, Earl Austin, Jr., and Dan McLaughlin were all at KCLC. I got a lot of my early experience doing those Hummers games on KCLC. They tried to do it up as much like a professional sports league as their finances would afford. They flew us to games. It was really fun because they were in the World Series twice. They didn't win, but they were in it and I got the experience of covering it."

Ramsey used his stringing of high school games as a springboard to start producing broadcasts of DeSmet High School basketball. Television sportscaster Frank Cusumano was one of the DeSmet ballplayers Ramsey was covering. After doing other things and progressing in his radio career, Ramsey found himself back on KMOX in 1988 doing a few Billikens games when they were in the NIT.

"I've been doing the Billiken's ever since," said Ramsey. "It's been 15 years of doing the broadcasts. They moved to KMOX during Charlie Spoonhauer's reign. The team got so popular when Spoon was the coach that when the broadcast rights were up, KMOX went after them."

There are times when Ramsey can be heard on two competing radio stations. He has a radio show on KFNS (all sports 590 AM) and he can be heard doing play-by-play on KMOX.

"I have been really lucky," said Ramsey. "There have never been any conflicts. KMOX and KFNS have a great relationship. I give a lot

of credit to Greg Maracek and Karen Carroll. They have developed a good working relationship between the two stations."

One broadcast on KMOX that stands out in Ramsey's mind involved his wife, Jen. Jen played basketball for the Saint Louis University women's team. Charlie Brennan challenged three of the players to a three-on-three game with him and two others from KMOX. They played it on the parking lot of the Old Cathedral.

"I did the play-by-play for the game," said Ramsey. "Charlie still teases us about it, about how Jen dominated him in the game. This was when Jen and I had just started dating. It is funny to think about it because Jen actually played a basketball game on KMOX and I broadcast it."

Ramsey says working at KMOX gives a person the feeling that they have "made it" in broadcasting, especially someone from St. Louis.

"I remember the first time I saw my picture on the wall at KMOX, it was really exciting," said Ramsey. "Coming from St. Louis and listening to the station all my life, working there was something for a broadcaster to aspire to. They have this hall with pictures of on-air people and when I started doing the baseball games, they put my picture up there. It was a kick to see it, it was a big moment. Someone from another town may not understand, but I felt very lucky to be up there."

JAY RANDOLPH

Jay Randolph's long broadcasting career in St. Louis began in 1966 at KMOX doing the play-by-play for the football Cardinals' games. He also called Saint Louis University Billikens basketball games before moving into the baseball booth, on radio and television.

He found out about the KMOX job almost by accident. He was working at KRLD in Dallas, broadcasting the Cowboys and SMU games. He also was covering college basketball, and was in Oklahoma City to broadcast a game between SMU and Oklahoma. The game was part of a doubleheader, and the other game matched Saint Louis U. and Oklahoma State. Doing the play-by-play of that game was Jack Buck.

"I had met Jack before in Dallas, and we were at the hotel after the games having a drink," Randolph said. "He asked me if I knew any good football announcers in Texas. I gave him a couple of names, and then asked why he wanted to know. He told me there was going to be an opening for the Cardinals' games the next year. I asked him what the job paid, and I found out it was $5,000 a year more than I was making in Dallas.

"Three weeks later I was in St. Louis interviewing with Mr. Hyland and Bill Bidwill and a month later I had the job."

Randolph quickly learned he would have other assignments, however. His first job was to replace Buck as the host of a nightly show at Musial and Biggie's Restaurant, where he conducted interviews and spun records after the baseball games. His first major assignment came when Hyland called and told him he was going to anchor KMOX's coverage of the Fourth of July activities on the Riverfront.

"I really thought I had come a long way in my career," Randolph said. "I was describing fireworks on the radio. There's a blue one; this one's green. Luckily, Harry Caray and Jack were with me and we had a good time."

Randolph also broadcast games of the St. Louis Stars in the NASL, basketball games, and hosted *At Your Service* programming. He was the television voice of the Blues in their first season, and Buck did the radio play-by-play.

"Neither of us knew a thing about hockey," Randolph said

Randolph had been at KMOX for 28 months when he got another television job offer, to do the nightly sportscasts on KSDK-TV. "They offered me nearly twice as much money as I was making at KMOX, and I didn't know what I should do," Randolph said. "I asked Jack and Jack told me I should take it.

"I went in to tell Mr. Hyland I was going to leave, and he said, 'You can't leave.' I said my wife is pregnant with our first child; it's a much bigger contract and I want to see if I can do TV on a regular basis. He threw a chair at me. He was very upset.

"It was nearly10 years before he spoke to me again. We did make up, shortly before he died, and I was glad we were able to do that."

CURT RAY

Curt Ray joined KMOX in 1947 as a disc jockey host of *The Clockwatcher* and other musical programs. For 10 years he was host of the morning program on KMOX-TV, which also featured his wife, singer Dottye Bennett. After the show was canceled, Ray remained an announcer for the station for eight years before retiring in 1976.

Ray died at age 61 in 1981 of complications from emphysema.

OLLIE RAYMAND

Ollie Raymand was a broadcaster in the 1950s. He was a musician and went on to become the weathercaster for KMOX-TV.

"Ollie was always a character," said Irv Litvag, who wrote the news in the 1950s for KMOX. "He was a trumpet player and had a band. He was very active around town playing music with his band. Ollie did some live music shows on KMOX including *Saturday at the Chase.*"

Saturday at the Chase was a Saturday afternoon show which was fed to the entire CBS network. It was a 30-minute show which featured the top entertainment that was playing at the Chase.

BOB REHG

Bob Rehg was in the promotions department when the station had its headquarters on Hampton Avenue. One of the things he did was write the scripts for John McCormick to read when he did his dramatic readings.

"He took *The Robe*," said Shirley Bates, 40-plus year employee at KMOX. "It had been written for television, but he took the story and adapted it for radio. He got the music and helped with all the production."

TINKER REILLEY

Tinker Reilley worked at KMOX from 1961 until 1965. She started as a writer for the sales presentations and worked into doing many other things, including merchandising and writing commercials for such clients as Famous-Barr.

"I was 18 years old and working at the Saint Louis University radio station," Reilley said. "I used to ask anyone and everyone to come on my show and once I had Bob Goddard [who wrote a column for the *Globe-Democrat* and also had a show on KMOX] on my show and then he asked me to be on his. I got on there and made some pithy remark about the role of women in broadcasting among other things, and when Mr. Hyland called right after the broadcast ended, I was wondering what I did wrong. He said, 'Can you be in here tomorrow morning?' He wanted to hire me and I started two weeks later."

Reilley was in her last year of college (she graduated two years early) and had always dreamed of moving to Europe after graduation.

"I told Mr. Hyland I was planning to live in Paris or Rome," said Reilley. "I don't think he believed me until I actually left. He asked me to stay but I said, 'I would always feel like I missed an opportunity.' He was very nice about it and got on the phone to Edward R. Murrow to see if he could help get me a job with the Voice of America. When I left I gave him an itinerary of my trip and I gave one to my mother. I went to Ireland, London, Italy, and when I got to Spain I received a telegram.

"Well I am one of six girls, and getting a telegram scared me to death. I was sure something was the matter. I panicked, I just sat there and shook for a few minutes before opening it. It said, 'Please call me at your earliest convenience during station hours, Robert Hyland.'"

She waited until it was the right time to call and reached Hyland.

He basically asked if she wanted to come back to KMOX, but she said she wanted to stay in Europe.

"Then he called me in Paris. He asked me about my trip and then put Aline [Surmeyer] on the phone. After she asked me how I was, I asked her how she was and she said, 'To tell you the truth, it's taking two people to do the job you used to do.'" said Reilley.

Since things weren't looking up in the job department, she called back and decided to return to KMOX.

"He said, 'When can you be here and what do you need in the way of money?' I got a price of an airline ticket and he sent me the money. I went back and was there another four years."

One of Reilley's jobs was to write the commercials for Famous-Barr. She would take the ads from the newspaper and use them to write the radio spots.

"I'd get the approval on the copy and take it to Famous. Then I

would book the time in the studio to record the commercials. Bob [Anthony] was doing the commercials at that time."

Once when Reilley was speaking to a group of journalism students at Lindenwood College, she spoke about the role of promotion in broadcasting.

"I talked about how it all looks so 'glamorous' but it really isn't," she said. "Now it sounds so glamorous, but believe me when you're on your knees hand-lettering a sign because someone forgot to do it, that's not glamorous."

Another time she remembered that it was not as glamorous as it seemed was when she was helping get ready for a parade.

"I think it was the Easter Seals Parade," she said. "We had a camel in the parade and I was trying to throw this drape over the camel that said 'KMOX radio' on both sides. The camel was smelly and it was nasty and then it threw up. I had to go home and change clothes before I could go back to the office. Ever since then I've had a slight hatred of camels!"

Reilley later married KMOX personality, Bob Anthony, and together they started E.M.Reilley and Associates Advertising Agency. They ran that until shortly before his death in 1998. Anthony had encouraged her to get her pilot's license and she continues to enjoy flying. In the year 2000 she started training to be a broker for Edward Jones.

BILL REKER

Bill Reker is the co-host of *Total Information AM* on the weekends as well as many other things at KMOX. This is his second stint at KMOX.

"I started in 1984 after working at KOMO in Seattle," said Reker. "I came to St. Louis when Bob Osborne was program director and Mr. Hyland was the general manager. I was originally hired to do just news. Back then it was like if you're news, that's it. It was the 'old school'. I worked evenings, weekends, afternoon drive."

He left in 1988 to help start radio station WRYT in Edwardsville, Illinois. He became the program director and worked there for three years before going to WIBV.

"When I was at WIBV, I had Holly White working for me," said Reker. "Holly is Jim White's daughter."

"I'll never forget the day Bill Reker helped our daughter, Holly," said White. "It was an icy day and she'd locked her keys in her car. We took another set out there and Bill went across this ice to help her."

"It was one of the worst day you could imagine, just so icy," said Reker.

At that time WIBV had Rush Limbaugh, Dr. Laura, and was almost all satellite talk. They were building the station around the Limbaugh show. When KMOX acquired the rights to Rush Limbaugh the station began moving in a different direction and so did Reker. He headed back to KMOX.

"I came back in 1995," he said. "They brought me back to take Charlie Brown's place when he left for Guam."

Now he is doing news, commercials, *The Trading Station*, and two weekend shows, and has more expanded duties.

"One of my most memorable moments was the day I cut Ronald Reagan off the radio," said Reker. "This was under Robert Hyland. We were taking a press conference and then we had a hockey game. My news director, John Angelides, told me we had to break from the press conference because we were obligated to hockey. He said all you can do is do it gently. So Reagan talked for a good half hour and they were getting to the part where the reporters are joking around with him, it was winding down. I thought this won't be a problem, so I cut him off and said, 'You've been listening to President Reagan's press conference, now let's go to Blues hockey.' Clarence Nieder, the engineer just stared at me with a red face and the phone rang. He picked it up and gave it to me. It was Robert Hyland.

"'Why did you cut off the president?' he asked. I said, 'Well, Mr. Hyland I was told I was obligated to take Blues hockey. He said, 'Hold on,' and he put me on hold for at least eight minutes. When he came back, he said, 'You screwed up that time,' and then he hung up. I was really upset, but Clarence said, 'You should take that as good news, because he didn't fire you!'"

"I really enjoyed working with Bill Reker," said Vicki Atlas, who worked with Reker on *Total Information AM* on Saturdays. "He is a riot."

EARL ROACH

Earl Roach has appeared on KMOX many times with many different hosts. Roach first met Robert Hyland through mutual friends at Musial and Biggie's Restaurant. Hyland began talking about the problems he had with his curly hair and how he couldn't seem to find a barber who could cut it the way he wanted. Roach suggested he could and after one trip to Roach International, Hyland was sold on Earl Roach.

"I think Mr. Hyland liked me because I told it like it is," said Roach who has been heard on KMOX for 26 years. "If someone would say something about KMOX good or bad, I'd talk to him about it. A lot of times Tim Dorsey would call me after I'd told him something. Once I was at the Johnny Mathis concert and someone was introducing me to Tim Dorsey. 'Do you know Earl Roach?' they said and Tim said, 'Yes, you're the assistant manager of KMOX.' He was kidding me of course."

When Roach was on KMOX he talked about men and women's good grooming.

"I was on with everybody, even Bob Burnes," said Roach. "We talked about ballplayers and their haircuts."

One time Roach was in Pittsburgh to accept the 'Men's Hairstylist of the Year Award'. Hyland knew about it and wanted him interviewed.

"They sent me over to KDKA," said Roach. "When I got there, Jack Buck was there waiting for me."

When Hyland was in charge of the Muny Opera, he hired Roach as the hairstylist. Hyland had planned to pay him, but Roach was so grateful to him for all he had done and said he wanted to give something back to the community; so he was never paid and he did it for years.

"One time Archie Bunker [the actor, Carroll O'Connor who played Archie Bunker on the television show, *All In The Family*] was coming to St. Louis and Mr. Hyland set it up for me to cut his hair," said Roach. "I flew to New York, and Jerry Berger, who worked for the Muny at the time, went also. I took all my hair cutting tools with me and we went to his hotel. It ended up that we had to wait four hours because he was doing a charity event; he was very big in charity events. We knew he was coming, they told us, but we didn't know it would be four hours. So we waited outside his room, and when he got there, he said, 'Where the hell you been? You're late!' He was joking and so friendly. His wife was there with him. We talked to him while I cut his hair and it was real fun."

Roach ended up cutting the hair of many famous people, including Shirley Jones, Gene Kelly, and Senator Ted Kennedy. He did many local celebrities as well, including Trish Brown from KMOV-TV.

"I did Bill Wilkerson's hair," said Roach. "The thing about him was he has such big hands. My daughter gave him a manicure and she said his hands totally and completely enveloped hers. Bill enjoyed my cutting his hair."

Roach appreciated what Hyland did to help further his career so he wanted to do something for Hyland when he was in New York once.

"I knew he had a Steuben Crystal collection," he said. "I called his secretary and told her I wanted to buy a piece of Steubenware. I was right by the store. I asked her what he didn't have. She thought and then said, 'A penguin.' I bought it with my wife. We had it shipped to arrive two days before Christmas. Well, two days before Christmas, I get this phone call and it's him. He's ranting and raving and talking to me like he's never done before. 'You're not supposed to be doing this!' he was saying. I said, 'Are you through? Doesn't your mouth open wide enough to say 'thank you'? and I hung up on him. He called me right back and said, 'Thank you! But we're not going to be doing that anymore.'"

JOHN ROONEY

CBS Radio sportscaster John Rooney enjoyed two stints at KMOX, doing play-by-play, on-air sports reporting, sportscasts, and also some producing. Rooney, who had come from the Missouri Net, a statewide news service, soon showed a talent for play-by-play and left to do minor league baseball. He returned to KMOX before leaving again to work for the CBS network. He currently also does play-by-play for the Chicago White Sox.

"In 1981 I was out of work because I was laid off from the Missouri Net," said Rooney. "I had a tryout for KSD and was doing a show on the air. Hyland heard it and called me, 'What are you doing over

there?' He knew me because I'd worked with Costas on the Missouri basketball broadcasts."

His first appearance on KMOX was in the morning drive with Rex Davis and Bob Hardy.

"I walk in and they both go, 'Boss talk to you?' And they're both laughing," said Rooney. "I said no, they said, 'He will.' I thought, 'Oh, what have I done?' So sure enough he calls me up and says, 'John, this is Robert Hyland.' I said, 'What can I do for you, Boss?' He said, 'We're one big happy family here, and we don't have to say "thank you" on the air (like if someone says, 'Here's John Rooney with the sports,' and I say, 'Thank you, the Cardinals won today). Now would you pass that on to Buck and Bender?' I said, 'Sure Boss,' then he said, 'Thank you,' and hung up!"

Among other duties during his shift from 4 PM until 2 or 3 AM was doing the midnight sports and the Calendar with Jim White. In those days the midnight sports was an expanded sportscast which included highlights and actualities from games all over the country. He got along so well with Jim White that White would have him stay after the sports to go over the Calendar.

"He'd also have me do the birthdays," said Rooney. "He'd throw out a person's name who was having a birthday that day and I'd have to guess how old they were. I loved working with Jim White. He had an unbelievable sense of humor."

Rooney did the University of Missouri basketball games and some football games. He worked with Costas on the basketball games and Costas would often be on the road and have to fly in for the games.

"I used to pick Costas up at the airport in Kansas City to go to the games, Columbia, Lawrence, wherever," said Rooney. "Costas would be reading the press guides on the way over to the game. He could memorize a press guide in an hour, just looking over it in the car.

"At that time Mizzou had this really hot guard named Steve Wallace. This was before the three point shots. I'll never forget the time Costas was doing the play-by-play and he goes, 'Wallace from the point for two—Bang! From the corner for two—Bang! From the corner for two— No Bang, it rimmed off.' I said, 'NO BANG'?"

After Rooney left KMOX, he was still heard on the station through his broadcasts for CBS radio network.

"That station [KMOX] had so many stars back then when I started there," said Rooney. "At first I didn't feel like I fit in, there were some heavy hitters with Buck, Costas, Dierdorf, and the rest, but everybody was so nice, and they didn't let their egos get in the way."

Rooney had a big weekend as a young sportscaster in the fall of 1984. He was the voice of the Triple-A Louisville Redbirds, who had just won their division.

"On Thursday night the Redbirds won their division and drew their one millionth fan, which was a huge deal," said Rooney. "Then they called me to do a game with Jack Buck in Cincinnati, so Friday I drove to Cincy and did the games with him Saturday and Sunday. I was so nervous and keyed up to be doing my first game with Jack Buck."

Rooney was filling in for Dan Kelly, who was doing a hockey feature in Canada.

"Someone bunted the ball up the first-base line, and the throw hit the runner," said Rooney. "Jack saw the play one way and I saw it another. He thought it was interference and I said, 'No, Jack I think he was hit by the ball.' It was just reaction that I said that. I would never try to correct Jack Buck and when I realized what I'd done, I thought, 'Oh, I better be right.' So Jack checked with the Reds and they said, 'Yeah, he was hit in the back by the ball.'"

STEVE ROWAN

Steve Rowan was one of the outstanding reporters who worked at KMOX, and his work caught the attention of the CBS network. He left KMOX in the early 1960s to become a network correspondent, and covered the war in Vietnam, among other assignments.

He also was assigned to the coverage of the space program, which led to a memorable exchange with anchor Walter Cronkite.

"There was a missing spacecraft, and Walter was being very serious and dramatic and saying something about the people in Houston working 24 hours a day to try to find the missing capsule, and about the lights in the building being on all night," Jack Buck said. "Rowan told him 'that building is always lit up all night' and Cronkite said something about 'thanks for pointing that out.'

"I don't know what happened to him after that."

FATHER GEORGE RUBEL

Father George Rubel played religious records on KMOX.

"It's a trivia question," said former KMOX personality Roy Queen. "Who was the first disc jockey in St. Louis? It was Father George Rubel. He played lots of religious records."

GUY RUNYON

Guy Runyon was on KMOX from 1941 to 1942. "He was a clean-cut gentleman," said Roy Queen, who worked at KMOX at the same time. "He did the news, I have nothing but good things to say about Guy."

Runyon left KMOX to start a new radio station, KXLW in Clayton.

RED RUSH

The third spot on the Cardinals' broadcast with Jack Buck and Mike Shannon was hard to fill in the 1970s and 1980s. Among those who moved in and out of the booth were Jim Woods, Bob Starr, Dan Kelly, and Red Rush.

"Red Rush was a wonderful guy," said Tom Barton, who was the producer/engineer on the Cardinal games. "St. Louisians are so used to Jack Buck, it was just hard for them to accept Red Rush."

Rush came from the Oakland Athletics and listeners probably remember he would occasionally say, "This is the Oakland A's network," rather than the St. Louis Cardinals'. He also used sayings such as, "He's 0-for-2 and overdue."

"One day we were in Los Angeles and he showed up at the booth," Barton said. "'I'm working here tonight,' he said. We had no clue. He said, 'Bob Hyland hired me.' It was an interesting experience. He really was a wonderful guy, but probably did not live up to St. Louis' expectations."

MARK RUSSELL

Mark Russell represented Arthur Godfrey. "Godfrey was in New York, but he had stringers throughout the various stations," said Bob

Canepa. "Russell's job was to find guests for the *Arthur Godfrey Show.* Godfrey visited KMOX, and we got to meet him."

RUDY RUZICA

Rudy Ruzica was an engineer. He started at KMOX-FM in 1970 and then moved to the AM side. He produced the morning show with Bob Hardy, Rex Davis, and Wendy Wiese.

"Later when Rex got out, I produced Hardy, Wendy, and Art Fleming," said Ruzica. "Art Fleming was a prince to work with."

Hardy would always mention Ruzica on the radio.

"We got along beautifully," Ruzica said. "I used to help them. They didn't have to worry about the commercials. I let them know when to run the commercials. I helped produce and engineer. I also liked working with Wendy. She was nice to work with and very broad minded."

Ruzicka took early retirement in 1988 and lives in St. Louis.

"I'm taking life easy, cutting the grass, repairing things around the house and traveling," he said. "We've gone to Jamaica and Cancun. It's nice not to take orders from anyone anymore."

ZIP RZEPPA

Zip Rzeppa was the popular sports director of KMOV-TV when he decided to step down and work only part-time to expand into radio. He did a three-hour syndicated radio show, one hour of which was broadcast on KMOX every week

"We gave away a lot of prizes," said Rzeppa. "It was a lot of fun to do, but I doubt it was very important in KMOX's illustrious and successful history."

JOHN SABIN

John Sabin worked in the newsroom starting in 1950 and stayed at KMOX full-time for 25 years. He remained working part-time at the station into the 1980s in a position that amounted to weekend news director. He wrote questions to give to the hosts in the early days of *At Your Service*. Later he was in charge of the overnight news.

"In the early days," said Alice English, a producer of *At Your Service*, "we did it differently. We would write out the questions and show them to the guest so he would be prepared. We would also do a lot of research to provide it to the hosts. It was aimed at informing the people, so there was a lot of preparation."

Sabin would get the information from the producers about what the topics were and would then do the research and write the questions. He also did a lot of newswriting and later on worked in the newsroom over night.

"He worked primarily for the morning drive," said his news director, John Angelides.

"He was a good one," said former newsman Robert R. Lynn. "He had the most incredible address book with phone numbers of anybody and everybody. He could find anybody. I'll never forget when he would call someone who did not know him he would say, 'This is John Sabin, S-A-B as in Boston-I-N.' He always said that."

Sabin taught writing classes and Lynn was always pleased to know that every year he would use a tape of Lynn's to teach the students a lesson.

"One time a guy called the station with a news story," said Lynn. "John saw me take the call. The guy said he'd just parachuted from the Arch and wanted to get interviewed on the radio. I asked him his name and he did not want to give it. I could tell it was a hoax, but wanted to make sure and check it out. He called several times and finally gave me a name and phone number, which turned out to be phony when I tried to call him back. He just wanted to get his voice on the air.

"John Sabin was impressed with my work on that and asked if he could keep the tape of the call to use in his classes to teach the students how important it was to check out the facts. John was a teacher in more ways than just in the classroom. He had an impact on young interns or new reporters. If you talked to some people who were learning under him, I'm sure they would say he was invaluable."

Sabin was 86 years old when he died in 1997.

SCOTT ST. JAMES

Scott St. James worked at KMOX from 1977 to 1979. He started by filling-in for other hosts and working on KMOX-FM.

"The big break I got, unfortunate as it was, was when Jim White had his heart attack," St. James said. "He had called me to come in and shoot the breeze with him on the air. It was not a big thing. He just asked if I wanted to come in. I was listening as I was driving in and he was on with Bob Costas. Suddenly Costas was on by himself. I didn't think anything of that, I was just driving along.

"When I got there everyone in the newsroom was coming up to me saying, 'Did Mr. Hyland call you?' 'What are you doing here?' It was really weird and I had no idea what was going on. Soon enough I found out that Jim had had a heart attack while he was on the air. I found out later that as he was laying on the studio floor, Jim could see my reflection in the studio window. He said, 'What the hell is HE doing here?' In the state he was in he had forgotten that he invited me down and I guess he thought the vultures were circling. He went off to the hospital and I did the rest of the show."

When White was coming back, Pete Rahn from the *Globe-Democrat* wrote, "now everyone wants to know what will happen to Scott St. James."

"No one wanted to know more than I," said St. James.

At the time White was doing a split shift, coming in the afternoons and returning in the evenings. Hyland determined that was too much for White after he came back from his heart attack, so he put Jack Buck on in the afternoons.

"Mr. Hyland teamed me as an alleged co-host with Jack Buck," St. James said. "I say 'alleged' because I idolized Jack Buck. I got the thrill of working with the icon of icons. I was young and he was a hero of mine and here I was working with the man. It would never have worked without Buck's blessing and he was great about it. As it turned out he started doing *Monday Night Football* and suddenly his schedule was overloaded so I started doing the shift alone."

St. James had worked at other radio stations in St. Louis, including KSD. He says he thoroughly enjoyed KMOX and liked all of the people there.

"How bad could it be for me? I had Bob Costas doing my sports sometimes, Dan Kelly doing my sports sometimes, or Gary Bender or Bob Starr, it was great. I didn't leave because I didn't like it," he said. "As it turned out I just wanted to go to Los Angeles. One night I was doing my show on KMOX and Kenny Rogers [the singer] was over at the National Association of Broadcasters Convention which was being held down the street. I found out he was there and I got the producer to contact him. He was in the middle of a press conference, but he thought he knew me so he interrupted it to come on my show. He really didn't know me, but he thought he did and I didn't blow his cover because it made me look pretty good. He came on my show like my long-lost friend. He said, 'Why don't you come over?' and I did. I ran into Michael O'Shea, the program director from a station in Los Angeles and it turns out Michael (who did know me) had been listening to my show and he started asking me if I wanted to go to Los Angeles and work for him. I really liked my job at KMOX, so it took a while for them to persuade me, but I finally went. I still look back on St. Louis as my favorite city in the United States."

After St. James decided to leave, he told the station he would need plenty of time before he got there.

"I told Mr. Hyland I'll work as long as you need me," said St. James. "I remember on my last show, people were asking my why I was leaving and I said the best way to explain it would be to play the old Elvis Presley record, 'Follow That Dream,' and I've been following that dream ever since. I have such great memories of KMOX, though. I learned more in those two years at KMOX than I have ever learned in my broadcast life. I listened to what Mr. Hyland had to say. Sometimes he had a different curve and corner in the road before he got to where he was going, but I found most of what he said to be very compelling."

DAVID ST. JOHN

David St. John started as an intern, as did many of the KMOX reporters. He interned in 1979 and then was hired to do writing, interviewing, and features. St. John now lives in the Washington, DC, area and has been a speechwriter and worked for Senator Fritz Hollings of South Carolina and for the Labor Department.

DON SARNO

Don Sarno, a commodities broker, was the pilot of the KMOX hot air balloon for more than 20 years. He was one of the organizers of the Great Forest Park Balloon Race.

Sarno died in 1998 of complications from a blood infection. He was 57.

CHRIS SARROS

Chris Sarros was the chief engineer at KMOX.

Besides his interest in electronics, Sarros was a licensed pilot and owned several planes.

"He used to fly all over the country collecting airplane frames and he re-built them," said Tinker Reilley, who was the wife of Bob Anthony, a good friend of Sarros. "He was quite a pilot. Bob and he were friends and they would go flying quite often."

TOM SCHILLER

Tom Schiller is the sales manager at KMOX. He manages the local sales force.

VINCE SCHOEMEHL

The former mayor of St. Louis was the host of a Sunday afternoon show on KMOX from 1993 to 1997.

"I had anybody and everybody on that show," said Schoemehl, who remains civically active in St. Louis and is involved in businesses, including a publishing company. "During the Bosnian crisis, we had Don Schlaffly, Jr., who was a professor at Saint Louis University who specialized in that. We also had Clayton Mudd on. He was the last minister from the State Department in the old Yugoslavian Embassy. We'd have something like that, and then we'd do a show on health care."

Schoemehl, both from his perspective as mayor and as a business leader, knows how important KMOX has been to the community.

"If I were on KMOX news, I would hear about it more than if I were on television," said Schoemehl. "Part of that is because they run the news every hour, so if you are interviewed in the morning, they may run portions of that interview throughout the day and night.

"KMOX radio was, and remains the most dominant news medium in the area," he said.

Schoemehl has been a long time listener of the station.

"Everybody remembers the Harry Caray days," he said. "I really enjoyed listening to him. And then of course there was Jack Carney. He was one of the funniest people I've every heard. He could really get you laughing."

JIM SCOTT

Jim Scott was an engineer. He worked the maintenance. It was his job to repair the transmitter, although they had a backup transmitter, so the station usually stayed on the air if there was a transmitter problem. He wore a beeper in case someone needed to reach him in a hurry.

"We hired him to do a show for KMOX FM," said engineer Bill Ott. "It was done from a restaurant in Clayton. We'd tape the show live and then air it the next day. Jim Scott did that and then he started working at the transmitter. He wasn't a technical person at first, but he caught on really well and became the transmitter supervisor."

JOHN SCULLY

John Scully was the announcer at Fairmont Park, the racetrack in Illinois. Each night during the midnight sportscast, the sportscaster would give the winners of the races at Fairmont. Scully would call and a producer would tape it. The race results usually came in late because they had to wait until the last race. It always made it exciting for the producer to try to get it recorded and put onto a cart in time to go on the air. Many times the producer would come running in at the last moment and hand it to the engineer.

BILL SEIBEL

The former outdoors editor for the *Globe-Democrat*, Bill Seibel has been the host of the outdoors program on KMOX for years. He usually worked with Tony Albright as they gave out information regarding hunting, fishing, and other outdoor activities.

Seibel also works for the Missouri Department of Conservation's St. Louis office.

RENE SERVIER

Rene Servier worked for 10 years as a producer, starting as an intern on the Jim White Friday night program, *Dateline*, and then being hired to help with that show and produce in other areas.

"We got so many calls on that show," said Servier. "It was really a successful show for a while and then it just played itself out. Towards the end we started getting the same callers, and we started getting people who wanted to be matched up with the same sex. It was just too difficult to try to do heterosexual relationships and same sex relationships.

After a while, we just dropped the show, but it was hugely popular when it started out."

She also produced Bruce Bradley and Anne Keefe in the afternoon.

"They were great together," said Servier. "They had such a great chemistry and good rapport. They were both so wonderful in their own way."

After a while it seemed to some of the listeners that Keefe and Bradley's relationship had gone sour.

"Really, it was a lot of things," said Servier of the two talk show hosts parting ways. "Bruce was the type of person who took things very personally. It was a bad time around the station, because Robert Hyland was very sick with cancer. For all of us it was a tough time, really devastating. It was like your father was really sick and there was no mother figure to tell you everything would be all right. Anyway, Bruce had some other problems going on in his life as well as his own health problems. He began to misunderstand a few things with Anne and took a few things personally and one day he just decided he did not want to do the show. It was a great show when they did it, though."

JACK SEXTON

Jack Sexton worked at KMOX in 1941. He was program director and also acted in several of *The Land We Live In* programs. He later went on to a career in television under the name of Jack Sterling in the *Big Top Show*.

MIKE SHANNON

When he was named to join Jack Buck on the Cardinals' broadcast team in 1972, Mike Shannon had no idea how long he would be there. His plan was to try it for a year and see what happened.

Nearly 30 years later, he is still there, spreading his love of the game and his knowledge to fans not only on KMOX but throughout the Midwest on the Cardinals' 100-plus station network.

"Mike Shannon is bigger than life," said Tom Barton who used to produce and engineer the Cardinal broadcasts. "He is the perfect color

analyst and people person for the Midwest. He always somehow inte-
grates the audience into the broadcast. He talks about how high the
corn is, or he will talk about the pig farmers. He manages to be one
with the audience. People feel they know him.

"Jack sounds cultured. They're a great 1-2 combination. Mike is
'one of us.' Jack's a little more polished. You get the feeling listening to
Mike that you'd be comfortable drinking at the bar with him. When
Jack comes in, you might stand up."

Shannon had been an outstanding player for the Cardinals, whose
career was cut short because of a life-threatening kidney disease. He
spent a year working in the front office, turning down offers to coach
or manage in the minor leagues, before he was asked about becoming a
broadcaster.

One thing he never professed to be was an expert at broadcasting,
but he is an expert and fan of the game, and that is what he tries to pass
along to his listeners.

Joe Castellano was a reporter covering the Cardinals when Shannon made the move to the broadcast booth. One story illustrated
Shannon's lack of understanding about his new position.

"I was doing an article on Shannon," Castellano said. "My favorite
story was one Jack Buck told me about Mike's first year as a broadcaster with the Cardinals. Jack said they were down in spring training
and getting ready to do the first broadcast. Jack says to Mike, 'You got
the umpires?' and Mike says no so Jack tells him to get them. Shannon
leaves and in a few minutes Jack looks up to see what all the commotion is, and Mike had gone down to the field and dragged the umpires
up to the pressbox."

Because of his naiveté, Shannon also was being victimized by practical jokes. Engineer Mike Breitenstein recalled one time when Shannon was working at KMOX and was in the studio doing a sportscast.

"Buck came into the studio and lit Shannon's paper on fire,"
Breitenstein said. "He took his lighter and set the copy paper on fire
while Shannon was reading it. Shannon lost it. I don't remember what
he said, but I know Jack was doing it just as a joke."

Usually when listeners remember something Shannon has said, it's
because he got a couple of words confused.

"Shannonisms" don't have the reputation that statements by Yogi Berra have earned, but they have earned their own place in the lore of the Cardinals.

Some of the bext examples:

Commenting on Whitey Herzog's managerial ability: "The key thing is he has that photogenic mind."

Talking about the Cardinals-Cubs rivalry: "It doesn't matter if they're home or away, or vice versa."

Giving the scores of an interleague game between the Mets and Yankees: "New York is ahead 4-2."

When people recall those lines, they do it for fun. That's why everyone has such a great love and respect for Shannon, include the people who have worked with him over the years.

"One of the things I always tell people is how generous a broadcast partner Mike Shannon is," said Bob Ramsey, who has worked with him on the broadcasts. "Mike's worked with a handful of people filling in for Jack and I've just never had a more generous partner. He was always asking, 'What can I do to help you?' He does more than just be professional; he goes out of his way to make you feel comfortable. This business is so ego-driven and people can get very territorial, but that is not how Mike is."

Shannon frequently mentions people's names on the radio. He might wish someone a happy birthday who wrote to him or tell the fans someone is visiting at the ballpark.

"I grew up about four hours from St. Louis," said Lynn Busby, classified ad manager for *USA Today's Baseball Weekly*. "I wanted Mike Shannon to say my name, so once when my friends and I went to St. Louis we came up with a plan. We took the stadium tour and taped up an index card in the KMOX radio booth hours before the game. It worked!"

Before coming to *Baseball Weekly*, Busby worked at *Baseball America*.

"I worked on our Radio-TV guide as an assistant editor since I knew my baseball radio stations so well, especially the Cardinal network. As a kid I used to listen to KMOX while I was out in my back yard pitching to my 'pitch back' [training device]. I really looked forward to listening to Mike Shannon, Jack Buck, and Bob Starr."

In addition to his work on the baseball broadcasts, Shannon hosts an interview program on Friday and Saturday nights after home games at his restaurant a couple of blocks from the ballpark.

His guests usually are managers or coaches from the opposing team, or former players or scouts who are in town. The listener gets the impression that it's a bunch of friends sitting around having a good time, and they are part of it, and that is exactly what the program is supposed to be.

"It's like when ballplayers get together or army buddies get together," Shannon once said. "You really can only tell some of those stories with your buddies. You can't go home and tell your mother or wife or anyone who wasn't there."

Perhaps the most significant moment in Shannon's broadcast career came when he happened to be calling the play-by-play when Mark McGwire hit his 62nd home run in 1998, breaking Roger Maris' record.

Shannon, Buck, and Joe Buck had decided ahead of time that they would keep their regular rotation of innings so whoever happened to be there when McGwire reached that magical moment would make that call. It turned out to be Shannon, and perhaps it was fitting. He had played with Maris and was a very close friend with him.

Shannon also ended up making the radio calls of McGwire's last two homers of the season, number 69 and 70, on the final day of the season.

What he said on all of those moments really was no different than a routine call in the middle of the season, and that's exactly how it should have been. It wasn't pre-rehearsed, it wasn't planned or stilted. It was entirely natural, the way Shannon broadcasts all of the games.

"I have a great love, a great appreciation, and a great respect for the game, and for the people who play the game and for the fans," Shannon once said. "I know what a guy feels like when a ball goes through him and a run scores and you lose a ballgame or you have to put another pitcher in. You try to relate that to the fan so that he understands that. Hopefully, through the years, I've educated the fan to some of that. And that's what it's all about.

"Plus, the elation that a player feels, the satisfaction that a player feels, the team feels, the manager feels—I hopefully bring that in there as well."

Grant Horton (center) interviews actors Larry Storch (Agarn, from *F-Troop*) and Marian Ross. *Courtesy of KMOX Radio*

Jack Carney (1980). *Courtesy of the Tippett family*

Harry Fender and Charlie Menees ride in the Jack Carney Parade. *Courtesy of the Tippett family*

Miss Blue at Jack Carney's Parade (1980). *Courtesy of the Tippett family*

Bob Hardy at the microphone (1970s). *Courtesy of KMOX Radio*

Charles Brennan interviews BobKeeshan (Captain Kangaroo) and John Ferrara
Courtesy of Charles Brennan

Jack Buck, Mike Shannon
Courtesy of St. Louis Cardinals Baseball Hall of Fame

John McCormick, the man who walked and talked at midnight for 31 years, from 1958-1989. *Courtesy of KMOX Radio*

Dan Dierdorf, Bob Costas, Harry Caray, and Bill Wilkerson with the "Friday Frank Forecast."

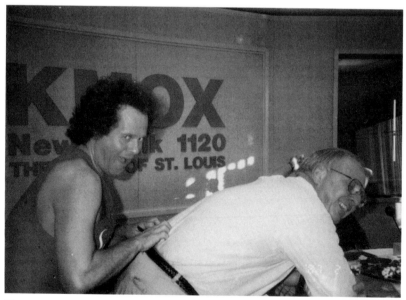

Fitness guru, Richard Simmons in the studio clowning around with Sports Coordinator Ron Jacober. *Courtesy of Ron Jacober*

Anne Keefe and Jeff Rainford. *Courtesy of KMOX Radio*

Anne Keefe in evening gown. *Courtesy of KMOX Radio*

The Steubenware collection. *Courtesy of the Hyland family*

Robert Hyland. *Courtesy of the Hyland family*

Jasper Giardino (of Jasper's Fruit Baskets and the Radio Museum) poses with one of his old radios and Jim White. *Courtesy of the White family*

Dr. Armand Brodeur, Jim White, and Ralph Graczak. *Courtesy of the White family*

Jim and Pat White. White's wife used to book guests on his show. *Courtesy of the White family*

Dan Kelly. *Courtesy of St. Louis Blues*

Bill Wilkerson, Wendy Wiese, and Bob Hardy (1980s). *Courtesy of KMOX Radio*

Bill Wilkerson, Wendy Wiese, and Bob Hardy celebrate Hardy's birthday. *Courtesy of Jeanette Grider*

Roy Queen looks over newspaper clippings of himself as he prepares to come to St. Louis for the KMOX 75th Anniversary Gala. *Courtesy of Roy Queen*

Roy Queen still has his microphone from his days on KMOX. *Courtesy of Roy Queen*

Jack Buck chats with Dick Vermeil on the air, as Randy Karraker looks on. *Courtesy of Missouri Athletic Club*

Joe Buck emceeing an auction for Rainbows for Kids. Buck as well as his famous father, Jack, do a lot of charity work.

Charles Brennan and former Senator John Danforth.

John Carney, playing drums with his band, The Carn Dawgs. *Photo by Bill Greenblatt*

Karen Carroll, General Manager of KMOX.

Carol Daniel, host of *Total Information PM*, with former mayor, Freeman Bosley, Jr. *Courtesy of Carol Daniel*

Robert Hyland celebrates with his family after his daughter Molly was crowned Veiled Prophet Queen. To the left is his son, Matt, and to the right of Molly is Robert's wife, Pat. *Courtesy of the Hyland Family*

ELLEN SHERBERG

Ellen Sherberg was a newswriter at KMOX in the 1970s. She is now the publisher of *The St. Louis Business Journal.*

"She was really helpful when I was an intern," said Stuart Esrock. "She took the time to help me script out my reports when I was sent out on a story."

STEVE SHOMAKER

Steve Shoemaker worked in the newsroom in the 1980s. He earned a reputation as a hard worker and a diligent reporter, whose primary beat was the St. Louis County government.

ROB SILVERSTEIN

Rob Silverstein was a producer and sports coordinator in the mid–1980s.

"He was sort of like Bernie Fox," said Bob Mayhall, who worked in the sports department. "He was in charge of sports operations. He had a lot of responsibilities. Jim Holder had been doing it, but Holder switched to afternoons and then was doing the Saturday and Sunday night open lines."

Silverstein left KMOX to go to CBS network in New York, and eventually moved on to the FOX Network in Los Angeles.

UNCLE DICK SLACK

"Uncle Dick" Slack was a retail business owner who sponsored a show in the 1940s. He ran a furniture store, and was the pitch man for his business.

"I used to wake up in the morning in Collinsville, Illinois, and hear the *Uncle Dick Slack Show,*" said Jack Tippett, who now lives in St. Louis. "It used to drive me crazy because I was not a big fan of country music. My uncle used to turn it on at 6 o'clock in the morning and it woke us all up."

The show featured live country music as well as music played from records.

"They would play this great country music and they'd also tell lots of jokes," said Margie Tippett, his wife. "I was a kid living in Farmington, Missouri, and country music was really 'it.' We loved it."

The *Uncle Dick Slack Show* ran from 6 AM until 8 AM and had a big following.

"Oh, I remember listening to The *Uncle Dick Slack Show*," said Adelle Burnes, widow of KMOX *Sports Open Line* host Bob Burnes. "It was a big show."

"Morning radio shows were a lot different back then," said Tippett. "They were not as as well packaged as they are now. There really wasn't that much traffic, so we didn't need the traffic reports. There were not as many news or weathercasts either."

"The *Uncle Dick Slack Show* helped me get ready in the morning," said Margie Tippett. "KMOX has been helping me start my day for a long time. It's gotten all my children through school. Bob Hardy and Rex Davis were on in the morning when my children were growing up. They knew they were up early if they heard *The Morning March* and I tried to get certain ones up in time to hear the "thought for the day" because I thought that was always a good thing for them to hear."

"We always heard Uncle Dick Slack on the radio," said Babe Barham, a longtime KMOX listener. "He was a little like Steve Mizerany, a real colorful guy. He did a lot of commercials."

"I got to meet him," said Doug Sleade who lived in St. Louis at the time. "I remember that after I met him I found out he came to my neighbor's house regularly to buy goat's milk. Both of my neighbors had a barn full of goats and our area was sometimes referred to as Billy Goat Hill."

JEFF SLEADE

Jeff Sleade was a sports producer in the 1980s.

"He was a real nice guy," said Mike Harris, a WIL sportscaster who saw Sleade at various sporting events in the pressbox. "He would do interviews, produce open lines, things like that. Jeff wound up going

with Bob Costas to NBC and being a producer there for *Show Time* that Costas did with Julius Erving."

CHARLIE SLOES

Charlie Sloes was said by some to sound a bit like Bob Costas in his delivery. Sloes did sports reporting and sportscasting in the 1980s. His stay at KMOX was fairly short as he became one of the many who left and went on to play-by-play jobs. Sloes worked in Washington, DC, broadcasting the Washington Bullets (now the Wizards), and then moved on to the Tampa Bay Devil Rays where he does play-by-play.

"He had an agenda when he came here," said Mike Harris, of WIL at the time, who knew Sloes from the pressbox. "Every time I talked to him he would say, 'I'm going to do it, I'm going to do play-by-play. He never hurt anybody or anything, he just knew what he wanted to do and he worked to do it. Working at KMOX there were so many good play-by-play men and he knew he would never make it if he stayed there, so he just got the experience and then moved on."

"KMOX was a proving ground for Charlie," said former Cardinal public relations director Kip Ingle. "He, along with Randy Karraker and Joe Buck, took great advantage of it and they would go in one of the broadcast booths not being used and do mock broadcasts. They knew they could further their careers by being at KMOX."

JOE SONDERMAN

Joe Sonderman started as an intern for KHTR (when it was the FM side of KMOX) in 1985 and then ended up on KMOX running the board for Jim White and John McCormick.

"When I came to KMOX," said Sonderman, "I could not even believe I was in the same room with those two greats. I grew up listening to Jack Buck, Jack Carney, and the others. My one goal was to work in the 'Temple of Sound' as John McCormick referred to One Memorial Drive."

After that, he went back to the FM side as music director, leaving for a while and then coming back to KMOX. He has been doing traffic reports for KMOX for three years.

"Tom Langmyer and John Butler were gracious enough to allow me to do some part-time work as well," said Sonderman. "Even if it's 3 o'clock in the morning I still get a thrill every time I say those call letters. There is no radio station in the country that has become as much of a fixture in the community as KMOX has. It truly is the 'Voice of St. Louis.'"

BOB STARR

Bob Starr came to St. Louis from Boston in 1972 to do the play-by-play for the football Cardinals. He also was the play-by-play announcer on the Missouri football games and worked on the baseball Cardinals' broadcasts.

His versatility and durability were two of his strengths. Especially when the baseball and football seasons overlapped, he was extremely busy. On one particular weekend in September 1975, for example, Starr's schedule had him broadcast a baseball game in New York on Friday night, fly to Minneapolis for the football Cardinals' exhibition game on Saturday night, return to New York for the baseball game on Sunday afternoon, then fly to Birmingham, Alabama, to broadcast Missouri's upset of Alabama on Monday night.

In addition to the play-by-play assignments, Starr anchored sportscasts on KMOX and frequently was involved in skits on the Jack Carney show. It's not surprising that Starr was involved in many humorous incidents during his broadcasting career.

Perhaps the most famous was the "Miss Cheesecake" story, which occurred one day in the baseball booth.

"Each year at Busch Stadium a group of area bakers get together for a night at the ballpark," Starr told Curt Smith in the book, *The Storytellers*. "They come upstairs to our booth—large, double-level, with a three-step stairway down to where we were. On the far left was producer Tommy Barton. Jack [Buck] sat next to him, Mike Shannon in the middle, and I'm to the right. If Mike wasn't involved, he'd get up and let the person interviewed sit in his chair. That's what he did as the head of the retail bakers came upstairs with goodies and a young lady in a nice little outfit with a sash across her that said 'Miss Cheesecake.'

She was, I suppose, 17 or 18 years old. Miss Cheesecake sat down, and Jack talked to her for a few minutes while doing play-by-play. After a few minutes, she was excused.

"Keep in mind the great distance between Jack and me—he's to the far left, I'm far right—and that we usually kept a hand over our ear and worked without headsets, which were uncomfortable. There also was a retail baker guy over my left shoulder, holding a box of cheesecake. Jack says, 'Do you like cheesecake, Bob?' And I said, 'Jack, I haven't had any yet, but it looks good enough to eat.'"

"With that, Jack chokes his way through the last hitter in the lineup. I noticed Tommy Barton was turning his face to the wall in hysterics. Jack finished the half inning, we break for the spot, and he says, 'Do you know what you said?' I said, 'Yea, you asked me if I liked cheesecake. I said yes, and you asked me if I liked this cheesecake." He said, 'No, no, I asked how you liked Miss Cheesecake?' We went from there. I got home that night, and my wife Brenda's waiting for me. 'Tell me I didn't hear what I think I heard on the air tonight in the first inning.'"

Another well-documented incident with Starr occurred when the Cardinals were playing in Pittsburgh. Starr also talked about that night in *The Storytellers*.

"The Cardinals were in Pittsburgh about 1978 when a game was called at 5 o'clock—rain," Starr said. "We head back to the Hilton Hotel from the ballpark and enter a friendly tap. I was keeping Napa Valley in the black at the time with my consumption of burgundy, but at about 11 o'clock I excuse myself and go upstairs to try to get some sleep. We have a golf game the next morning.

"Somewhere between 1 and 2, nature calls. Now, understand that I'm sleeping in the same uniform that I had on when I came into the world. I get up, half asleep, and take a left, walk from my bed to the bathroom, relieve myself, come out and take another left and walk out the front door of my room. The door slams shut behind me, and as I hear that noise I am wide awake and I am absolutely without any clothes on. I'm standing outside the room totally nude and now trying to figure what the hell to do.

"I know my only hope is to go down the hallway and put my ear up to each door. If I hear noise, I'll knock, and if someone approaches I'll

say, 'Don't open'—just ask 'em to call downstairs and send somebody up with a key. I'm about to start on this maneuver when I hear commotion down the hallway. I think, 'Good Lord, someone's coming out of a room and I'm standing outside my door without any clothes on." Instead, it's a bellman who looks at me in absolute disbelief. I say, 'I have a little problem here.' Some later asked if I was referring to a psychological notation. He says, 'I see that'. I continue, 'Do you have a pass key?' He says, 'No, but I'll get one.' He leaves without giving me his frock coat—goes about mid-thigh, would have worked fine—while he pursues the key. In about 40 seconds he comes back with a raincoat that doesn't fit, to wrap around me. Then he leaves again, comes back with a key, lets me back in the room, and bids me an affectionate good night.

"The next morning, I get my wake-up call, and I'm laying in bed thinking, did that really happen? I came to the realization that it did. I go downstairs, and there are our broadcasters, Jack Buck and Mike Shannon, producer Tom Barton, our traveling secretary, Lee Thomas, plus Dick Kaegel of the *St. Louis Post-Dispatch*. We have breakfast and I tell this story and it wipes 'em out. Before long, we're disturbing the coffee shop. I don't think anything about it as Jack says, 'Excuse me, I've got to run upstairs and get my golf shoes. I'll meet you guys at the cab out in front.' We play golf, I come back, shower and shave, and call my wife. Brenda says, like in the Cheesecake Story, 'Tell me that I didn't hear Jack Carney say what he said this morning after talking with Jack Buck.'

"What Jack had done when he got his shoes upstairs was call the late Jack Carney, a terrific KMOX on-air talent, and tell about me locking myself out of my room without any clothes on. If the 50,000 watts of clear channel KMOX weren't bad enough, that afternoon Dick Kaegel supplied the coup de grace. Ever been stripped naked in the paper?"

"I'll never forget the Miss Cheesecake story," said Frank Cusumano of KSDK and KFNS. "It's just one of those stories you laugh every time you hear it."

Another incident also involved Carney.

"One day when Bob Starr was doing the news," said Rudy Ruzicka, the engineer on the show. "Jack Carney played a trick on him. Bob Starr was the type of person you just could not crack up. No matter what you did, you could not break him up. I was running the board. Carney came walking in cutting through the studio, and saw Bob Starr reading a long list of scores from the night before. He walked in about two or three feet from Starr's face and pulled his pants down and mooned Starr while he was doing the sports. Starr just paused one second and looked up at them and then went back to work as if nothing happened. It was so funny to watch."

Most of the time, however, Starr was serious about his work.

"He always looked like he was so relaxed but really he did his homework," said Joe Pollack, who worked with Starr on the football Cardinals' games. "He worked totally form having a numerical roster in front of him, not even a depth chart. He never missed anything."

"Bob Starr was an outstanding football announcer," said former news director John Angelides. "He had a good cadence when he did football, but he was known for his baseball."

Said Barton, "Starr was a phenomenal football broadcaster. He was probably better than anybody I've ever witnessed. And he was pretty good at baseball. "

Starr left St. Louis in 1980 to move to Los Angeles. He was the play-by-play announcer for the California Angels for 15 years and also did the Los Angeles Rams' games from 1980 to 1989 and again in 1993.

Starr died in 1998 from lung disease. He was 65.

JILL STEIN

Jill Stein worked as a newswriter in the 1970s. Under the direction of John Angelides, Stein was assigned stories and went out to get the interviews and write the stories and features. One of her big responsibilities was to write the "Jack Buck, To Your Health" features.

Stein became interested in health issues and concentrated on being a medical reporter, and has continued in that field.

"She works in Paris as a freelancer for medical news," said Angelides. "Drug companies send her all over the world to attend conferences and cover stories about new drugs that come out on the market."

ELAINE STERN

Elaine Stern has been a producer at KMOX for many years, most of them on Jim White's show.

"They were a good match," said Emmett McAuliffe. His show on Friday nights is now produced by Stern. "Both Jim White and Elaine had a lot of experience. They didn't let the crazies affect them. They took everything with a grain of salt and could distinguish the crazy people from the regular callers. At that hour of the night that's important. She didn't over-produce Jim White's show which would have been a disaster for him. They worked very well together."

"I'll never forget when I first started working at KMOX," said Stern. "I walk in and hear all these voices I'd been hearing since I was a little kid on the radio. They didn't look like they sounded. Well, Bob Hardy did, but the rest of them didn't."

"Elaine was so good with Jim White," said fellow producer Rene Servier. "He would only use me if Elaine was not there. When she would go on vacation, Jim would always say, 'Elaine's on her honeymoon,' so it looked like she got married a lot and went on her honeymoon every year. He looked to her a lot to gauge how the show was going. Some producers just go about the motions. Elaine listened to his show and gave him her feedback. He trusted her."

PHIL STEVENS

Phil Stevens was the emcee of the *Housewives Protective League Show*. Lee Adams started out as emcee, and Stevens took over after he left.

"He had a low voice," said former salesman Bob Canepa. "He would tell interesting things such as you might find in the *Reader's Digest*. He would use the HPL packet sent by the network and take out any stories he wanted. He could talk about anything or just read the stories."

CHARLEY STOOKEY

Charley Stookey was the host of *The Farm Folks Hour*, a program that was broadcast from 5:30 AM until 7 AM. The program begin in 1932 only when Stookey was able to convince his bosses that people were up and listening to the radio at that hour.

"In the early days of radio the permanence of a program was determined by the amount of mail it pulled," Stookey wrote in a magazine article in 1969. "During the first broadcast I urged listeners to write if they liked what we offered and wanted it continued. The afternoon mail that day brought 130 letters and cards as a result of that first program."

The mail was entirely from St. Louis, and the next day the total was at 500 cards and letters. By the end of the week, mail had been received from 15 states. The program was set, and in the month of December 1934, the show received more than 50,000 pieces of mail.

KMOX provided a staff organist, Ken Wright, and a hillbilly band, The Ozark Mountaineers, for the program.

"One day the mail brought a letter from the captain of an oil tanker, the SS Yorba Linda, in which he requested that a musical selection be played for him and his crew," Stookey wrote. "The band complied, and within two hours we had a radiogram from Captain Jack Jacobsen thanking us for the music. He reported the position of his ship as being off Dry Tortugas in the Gulf of Mexico."

Stookey later met Captain Jacobsen and sailed on his ship.

DAVID STRAUSS

David Strauss started out as a guest on Jim White's show and then eventually became a regular and went on to have his own show with former *Jeopardy* host Art Fleming. He worked at KMOX for almost 18 years.

"I was working part-time for *St. Louis Magazine* in the fall of 1977," said Strauss. "I wrote an article which was a trivia quiz. The quiz was so hard that even my friend who was really good at trivia only got about 38 out of 100. The average listener only got 7 out of 100. *St. Louis Magazine* got some publicity for the trivia quiz and John Auble of *Newsbeat* came out and did a feature on me. I casually joked to the folks at *St. Louis Magazine*, 'you should get me on KMOX.'"

That night Strauss was surprised to get a call from KMOX.

"They'd had a cancellation of a guest on the Jim White Show," said Strauss. "It was a Monday night, a school night and I was a school teacher, it was snowy and the show was at 11 o'clock at night. I was thrilled to do it."

Bob Costas was doing the midnight sports in those days and he would come in and banter with Jim White. When he saw the topic was trivia, he went in the studio.

"We started going at it," said Strauss. "I knew he was a good guy when I heard him singing the theme songs from Warner Brothers' westerns on his way out."

The trivia show was a success and soon he became a regular on White's show. In 1980 KMOX hired Art Fleming and the ex-*Jeopardy* host and the trivia expert seemed like a perfect match.

"We worked as a team from 1980 to 1992," said Strauss. *The Trivia Show* became a regular fixture on Sunday nights. Sunday nights before that had been so hard to fill. We'd had various people come in like Julius Hunter, Patrick Emory, but nothing seemed to stick. I went to Mr. Hyland and asked him to try it and he did and it worked."

One of Strauss' claims to fame is he helped name the Ted Drewes' "All Shook Up" Concrete.

"I used to see David since he taught at the high school next door to one of my stores," said Ted Drewes. "Well, one day I saw him at the Chippewa store and we had been trying to add some new flavors. I said, 'Jim White pestered me into adding some peanut butter in a concrete and I finally did. Dave said, 'If you add bananas, you would have Elvis Presley's favorite combination, and you could call it the 'All Shook Up.'"

"Elvis used to eat peanut butter and fried banana, sandwiches," said Strauss. "His print ad guy was there and we were talking and I just came up with that idea. Dottie thought it was a great idea. They gave me a $20 gift certificate to Ted Drewes for coming up with that idea. I wish I'd gotten one percent of all the people who have ordered it over the years."

Strauss does a trivia show on KTRS in St. Louis and continues to teach at Cleveland Jr. Naval ROTC.

GABBY STREET

Gabby Street was the baseball catcher known for catching a ball dropped from the Washington, Monument, and he did color commentary on the St. Louis Cardinals' games in the 1940s.

"Gabby Street was the famous catcher who caught Walter Johnson," said Bea Higgins, who worked at the advertising agency that hired the broadcast team at the time (Ruth, Rouff, and Ryan). "Gabby added a lot of color to the games. He was like a mentor to Harry Caray. He told a lot of stories and Harry learned a lot from him."

"Bob thought he was a very nice guy," said Adelle Burnes, widow of longtime *Globe-Democrat* sports editor Bob Burnes. "He had a high regard for Gabby. He was a very casual person. He played on the Cardinals when Bob covered them for the *Globe* so he knew him real well and thoroughly enjoyed him."

"Gabby told the most interesting stories," said listener Doug Sleade from Decatur, Illinois. "I still remember some of his stories. I used to look forward to rain delays when Harry Caray and Gabby would talk baseball and 'the old times.'"

"The thing I always remember about Gabby," said Jim "Peanuts" Zaggari, "was he had all the fingers on his right hand broken from being a catcher."

JOE SULLIVAN

Joe Sullivan was the vice president of the St. Louis football Cardinals for years. To some, he was the man you loved to hate. Disgruntled Big Red fans blamed Sullivan for many of the football team's woeful seasons. Though he was often written about negatively in the media, the KMOX listening audience got to see another side of him on the *Jack Carney Show*.

Joe and his wife Joan were best friends with Carney and his wife, Jody. Carney often had Joe on just to chat about anything. The Joe Sullivan who was on the *Carney Show* was far from the ogre he was often painted out to be by the media. The Carneys and Sullivans would often go to the Muny or the Fox or other cultural events and Jack and Joe would talk about it or Jack would merely relay a story involving Joe and Joan.

"Joe and Joan Sullivan were among the Carney's best friends," said Carney's producer, Frank Pawloski. "Joe Sullivan would come in and if the Cardinals were traveling to Philadelphia, he might be at the airport

and call in. Jack would say, 'OK, Joe, what we gonna lose by, 40 or 50?' and Joe would say, 'Now wait a minute, Jack'. Jack would get the other side of a general manager with a lousy team. He would talk about the arts and where they went with their wives to eat."

ALINE SURMEYER

Aline Surmeyer was in sales in the 1960s and 1970s.

"Aline was Alice English's assistant," said Tinker Reilley. "She worked more in terms of sales promotion, and Alice was more involved in civic activities and major accounts."

SALLY TIPPETT

Sally Tippett Rains started as an intern in 1979, and was hired when her internship was over. Her main jobs were gathering and writing the sports for Bill Wilkerson and Bob Costas.

"I was majoring in horticulture at the University of Missouri and I realized I was in the wrong major," said Tippett. "I started working at an ad agency in Columbia and going to a radio station every day because it interested me. I'd gotten to know Coach [Warren] Powers [the Missouri football coach] and one day he just said, 'Why are you majoring in horticulture? You should be in public relations!' He arranged for a job interview with the Kansas City Chiefs, which I didn't get, but it got me thinking I might like to go into a career in sports and in radio. My dad said, 'Why don't you write a letter to Bill Wilkerson from KMOX?' I did and he called me up and met me for lunch and before I got home from that lunch Mr. Hyland had called my house twice."

There was never a dull day working in the sports office with Costas and Wilkerson.

"They were hilarious; they were both funny. It was just always a happy, fun atmosphere when either of those two were around," said Tippett. "During the day before they got there, Jim Holder, who was my boss, would give me assignments and tell me who I was going to interview that day. Holder treated me the same as he treated Steve Overby, the other sports assistant, which I appreciated. I was a little more nervous during the day because things were more serious

because you were working hard to get the drive time sportscasts ready. If Hale Irwin was one of the leaders of a golf tournament, Holder would have you call him. If there was a new player on a team, he would send you out. I remember going over to Busch to interview Andy Van Slyke when he first got there.

"Sometimes players would hang up on me because I was a female, and other times I would be waiting with the players' wives until the halls were practically empty until a player would shave, get dressed, and then come out to let me interview him."

Those were the days when female sports reporters were just that. They were "female" sports reporters. Some of the men in media saw them as threats, and some of the players would refuse to be interviewed by them.

"Even the *Post-Dispatch* got in on the act," said Tippett. "The football Cardinals were trying a new 'interview room' so there would be equal access. Of course, it is a lot quicker to get the quotes if you can run in the locker room right after a game while they are changing. To wait until the players come out to the interview room was an inconvenience to the newspaper reporters since they were on deadlines. Anyway, on the first day they tried it, Jim Holder said, 'Why don't you come in and just watch so you can see how to do the interviews.' I was still an intern at the time and he thought it would be helpful."

One of the reporters from the *Post* came up to her and started talking, which was normal she thought because at every event she covered, the reporters would talk to each other. She did not realize he was "interviewing" her for a story. He asked her what she was majoring in and she said "horticulture."

"Now this is before I got hired by KMOX and went on to get my degree in journalism," said Tippett. "The next day on the *Post-Dispatch* sports page I see this headline: 'Horticulture Student is Plant in Cardinal Locker Room.' The article was about this mysterious female in the interview room. 'She didn't have a tape recorder and she didn't have a notebook,' it said. The silliest thing the article said was that [kicker] Mike Wood came out in a towel, insinuating I saw him that way. Believe me I would have remembered if I saw him in a towel and I never even remembered seeing him.

"Well I was devastated. It still hurts me today when I think how young and gullible I was to let that happen. Mr. Hyland called me up and was furious at me. He said, 'Here at KMOX we report the news, we don't make it!' The strange part of it was all my friends were calling me up, 'Hey cool, you're in the newspaper!' I was afraid I was not going to be hired as my internship was almost over. I talked to Jack Carney and Bob Costas, both of whom went to Mr. Hyland on my behalf. The next day he called me and offered me a job and I worked there for three years. I found out years later from the reporter who wrote the story, the newspaper had an agenda and he was assigned to do that to me. He apologized and I accepted it, and consider him to be a friend today, but I remember glaring at him for years!"

Being female, everyone just assumed Tippett was interested in the women's sports teams.

"I became the 'beat reporter for the women's sports teams,'" said Tippett. "At least I could go in their locker rooms. In those days there were the 'Streak,' the basketball team, and the 'Hummers,' the softball team. I also got to do all of the things no one else wanted to do. I really liked going out and doing things no matter what they were. Once I gave a pep talk on behalf of KMOX and sent the runners off on the 'KMOX Fun Run.' Another time I was the KMOX Easter Bunny at a function. Once I went with Mr. Hyland to the KMOX/Post-Dispatch Scholar Athlete Dinner. I got to go to the airport each week after the football Cardinals lost and interview the players, and I got to talk to O.J. Anderson and Theotis Brown each week when we were setting up *The Ottis and Theotis Show.* I had a blast working there."

One time Jim Holder had Tippett call Missouri basketball coach Norm Stewart, for an interview before the upcoming Kansas game in Lawrence.

"I called him and started to do the interview and then Coach Stewart said something strange and hung up on me," said Tippett. "I felt bad, but I knew Holder wanted that interview so I called him back and he hung up on me again. I talked to Costas and he talked to Stewart and it seemed he didn't believe I worked for KMOX. He thought I was a spy for the Jayhawks. Once he realized what he'd done, he sent me a nice note saying he was sorry."

Tippett left KMOX to run SportsRadio, a regional radio network, for three years and is now an author.

JOHN TOLER

John Toler was an engineer at KMOX.

"He was great," said Rene Servier, who produced many shows with him. "He went to high school at SLUH with Robert Hyland. He would never call him 'Mr. Hyland.' He was like 'he was a classmate of mine and I'm not going to call a classmate "Mr."' He called him Bob. Everyone else called him 'Mr.'"

Toler was from the old school and had worked as an engineer for many years. For such a long time, the engineers were the only ones who could touch the equipment and even when the rules changed, he wanted to hang on to the old ways.

"He was very much like 'I will cue up the cart,'" said Servier. "'I will put them in, I will adjust that.' The engineers began losing their power and this had been his job. He wanted to keep it that way. Other engineers were easier to change."

Toler always got along well with the people he worked with. Even though he wanted to do the engineering, people understood and usually let him. He had a lot of respect from everyone he worked with.

TORCHY

In its first year on the air, KMOX ran a contest to determine the most popular artist on the station. A young piano player and singer who went by the name of Torchy received more than 58,000 votes.

For winning the contest, Torchy, whose real name was Honorine LaPee, received an all-expenses paid trip to Havana, Cuba. On her way, she was featured on radio stations in Tennessee and Florida.

According to a newspaper feature story in 1953, Torchy was accompanied by a motion picture cameraman and pictures of her tour were screened on weekly newsreels.

"A candy bar was named for her," the newspaper said, "and requests for repeat numbers reached such a height at one time that she was given an additional spot on the schedule during the noon hour."

She soon abandoned her radio career and began playing with her own band.

LAURENT TORNO

Laurent Torno was on KMOX from 1958 to 1976. He played classical music on Sunday nights.

"He was like Don Wolff is today, only Don Wolff plays jazz," said Shirley Bates a longtime KMOX employee. "Mr. Hyland loved good music so he put Laurent on."

"Laurent was one of us who came over from KXOK in the late 1940s," said Clarence Nieder, a longtime engineer at KMOX. "Laurent Torno was originally a musician with the St. Louis Symphony. In those days radio had 'platter men' which meant turntable operators. He was a platter man. He ended up doing the Sunday night show playing light classical music because he knew so much about it."

Torno died in 1992 at age 89.

STEVE TRENKMAN

Steve Trenkman, who went on to become a television reporter for KMOX-TV, started at KMOX radio. Ron Barber, who worked with Trenkman at KMOX, had the terrible task of reading the wire copy that came in when Trenkman and two of his sons were killed in a car accident on a St. Louis highway in 1980.

"It is a very difficult task in this business," Barber began, "to have to report the death of a colleague and a friend, which is what I have to do right now."

While at KMOX, Trenkman and John Terry won a Peabody Award for the writing and production of a series titled, "Sleeping Watchdogs."

CASEY VAN ALLEN

Many people think Casey Van Allen is a genius in radio production. For years whenever a spectacular production was spliced together it was Van Allen who did it. He started as a disc jockey in the early days on KMOX-FM and continued to work on KMOX-AM, putting together sports shows, commercials, musical montages, and anything else they asked him to do until October 2000.

Van Allen was a popular disc jockey in St. Louis having worked at KXOK, KADI, KSHE, KKSS, WGNU, and even KGRV ("Music for 'groovy grown-ups.'" He built the Florissant Valley College station in 1970 (KCFV). While he was on KMOX-FM as a disc jockey, the format was changed to hit radio (KHTR). He drew many listeners.

"We made KHTR the number-two station in St. Louis, just below KMOX," said Van Allen. "Between KMOX and KHTR we had nearly 50 percent of the market at that time slot." (He worked 7 PM until midnight.)

Tim Dorsey, who had been the general manager of KHTR, went to work in the same capacity for KMOX when Robert Hyland became a CBS vice president. He knew about Van Allen's production techniques and wanted to bring him downstairs. Van Allen also was doing a television show on KMOX-TV at 10 PM on the weekends called *Hot Hit Videos.*

"I was riding pretty high at that time," said Van Allen. "My ratings were high on the radio and I had the television show, and then Tim

330

Dorsey asks me if I want to go to KMOX. I said, 'I don't think I'm suited for 'talk.' I'm a music guy."

One night just before his shift was about to end, he looked up and saw Robert Hyland looking in the studio at him.

"He came up to my studio," said Van Allen. "He had come in to work an hour early to see me. He said, 'When you get off the air, come down to my office.' So I went down there and he was wearing a satin KHTR jacket. It was odd to see this dignified man in the satin jacket. All of us at KHTR had the jackets. His was embroidered with his name and 'The Chief" over the pocket. He said, 'I really need your help down here.' I said, 'I want to see where I would work," and he took me back to this antiquated studio that looked like it was made by Marconi. 'I'd like to come down here, but I can't work in this studio. I can't create in a studio that looks like its from the 1930s.'"

Hyland told him to make a list of what it would take to get him down there. Van Allen really did not want to leave his music job, so he put everything he could think of on the list. He would not have to turn Hyland down, he thought; Hyland would turn him down.

"I got the broadcasting equipment catalog and put every single piece of equipment I could ever possibly want, and some I would probably never use," Van Allen said. "It totaled up to be $500,000. That was a humongous amount of money. I show it to him and he looks at it, sets the paper down, puts his hand on top and says, 'When can you start?'"

The studio took several months to build and Van Allen supervised the project, including the wiring and design.

"The guy who did sound for the Steve Miller Band put it in," he said. "We had probably one of the first Corian counters in the country. It was my private studio, I had a lock on it and no one really used it."

Van Allen changed the overall texture of the station. Where there had been one-second pauses between commercials, he tightened it up. He began putting music behind the commercials for the first time.

"That was the next evolution for the station," said Van Allen. "We had had some of the worst sounding commercials in relation to what was going on. It really hadn't made a difference though, the station has such an incredible selling power. I think the commercials sound a lot tighter, but people listen to them for the information. It's a lot different

than I experienced as an FM disc jockey. People change the station when the commercial comes on, they want music. On KMOX, people want to hear the commercials."

"I really enjoyed working with Casey Van Allen," said Elaine Viets, who did a show on KMOX in the 1980s. "Whenever I do radio, I like the behind-the-scenes, the production aspect. Casey was very good at what he did."

He got started doing the production on several songs with baseball highlights in them and soon he was requested to do others. He donated his time to compose a special song for the St. Louis Pinch-Hitters at their charity Ball-B-Que one year.

"I got started in those songs by accident," said Van Allen. "It was 1982 and Hyland had just built me my studio. I was still very connected to FM. My heart was still in music, but I was getting off on this news-talk thing. The Cardinals were hot and it looked like they would make it to the World Series. My friend Terry Fox from the FM was there and we were talking and he said, 'That new song by Glen Frye, "The Heat Is On," is really a good song.' We started playing it. It just so happened Bob Gibson was there and I asked him would he say, 'The Cards are Hot' into the microphone and I taped it. I accidentally recorded it in the middle of the lyrics of the song. I meant to do it at the beginning, but I liked what I heard.

"Then I saw Kelly Peach, our intern, the daughter of George Peach the prosecutor. I said, 'Kelly, come in here and say, "The Cards are hot." She said it in between the lyrics of the song and I said, 'Hmmm, I may have something here.' So I started listening to old highlights and then I'd put it in the song. I tried to match the lyric with the highlight. For example 'The Heat is On,' 'There's a high fly into left field.' I started getting cold chills down my back I was so excited. I took it up to Terry Fox who said it's great. After working until 3 AM on it (at least eight hours) I took it to Mr. Hyland who let me play it on the air. It was such a success that Mr. Hyland let us play it on KHTR and he was very protective of his highlights. He never let any other radio station play the baseball highlights. "Let's let 'em know we're proud of our Cardinals," he said. It became the number-one most requested song on KHTR in three hours."

Van Allen slept until 1 PM the next day and awoke to the television cameras from four stations wanting to interview him. He would update the song as new plays were made during the World Series.

"I've done tons of those types of songs now," he said. "I did 'Shake Down, Sold on St. Louis,' and then during the home run season I did 'Calling Air Traffic Control' for Mark McGwire."

For the 2000 season he chose the Thin Lizzy song, 'The Boys are Back' and changed the words to 'The Birds Are Back.'

Van Allen owns several radio stations at the Lake of the Ozarks, and he left KMOX to devote more time to those stations.

ELAINE VIETS

Elaine Viets was a *Post-Dispatch* columnist for years, who specialized in writing about the quirkiness of south St. Louis natives, pink flamingos and all. She went on to become a successful author, syndicated columnist, and radio contributor. After Jack Carney's death, Arnie Warren took over his show and one of the new things he brought to the time slot was Viets and her comments on life in St. Louis, especially on the south side.

"Mr. Hyland paid my AFTRA fees," said Viets. "I actually had two stints on KMOX. The first was with Arnie Warren, then I went on to do some commentaries in the afternoon."

The second show was a three-minute show, formatted with a sponsor. She did a commentary on a specific topic, very much like her columns in the *Post*. Viets decided that since she was going to have a regular show, she should take some voice lessons.

"I went to New York to take voice lessons from Ruth Franklin at AFTRA," said Viets. "She is very successful and does a lot of voiceovers. My agent thought I needed some voice training and we wanted to go to New York to get the best. It's paid off, though, because, thanks to my background at KMOX, I now have a segment on NPR (KWMU in St. Louis) during the *All Things Considered* show.

"When I did that afternoon show, I would come into the studio and tape the shows," she said. "I worked with Casey Van Allen. He was great. In fact, the great thing about KMOX is that they have so many talented people who work behind the scenes."

Viets, who now lives in Florida, comes to St. Louis occasionally to do book signings. On a recent trip, she was happy to hear a familiar voice on KMOX.

"I heard John Carney," she said. "He sounds so much like his dad. I was so glad to hear him. He really does a good show. Only in St. Louis could a son succeed his father and have such success."

J.L. VAN VOLKENBURG

J.L. Van Volkenburg joined KMOX in 1932 as sales manager. He was promoted to general manager in 1933 and kept that job until 1936. He also was an executive with WBBM in Chicago.

Later, he became the first president of the CBS television network in 1951, retiring five years later. Van Volkenburg was only 29 years old when he was named GM of KMOX, becoming the youngest head of any major broadcasting station in the country.

Van Volkenburg died of a heart attack in 1963 at the age of 59.

HARVEY VOSS

Harvey Voss was an engineer at KMOX for 40 years. He retired in 1978. He was involved in a first for KMOX, when Arthur Fiedler conducted the St. Louis Symphony from the Khorassan Room. Voss engineered the show and it was the first time the symphony had ever been broadcast in stereo.

BARBARA WAGMAN

Barbara Wagman was the executive producer for *At Your Service* in the early 1970s.

NORMA WALLNER

Norma Wallner was Robert Hyland's administrative assistant from 1981 until his death in 1992.

"She was his right hand for many years," said Bob Hamilton.

Many transactions took place within earshot of Wallner in Hyland's office and she felt a loyalty to him even after his death. In doing this book, many stories were related with the tag, "Ask Norma, she'll tell you." When she was contacted, however, she politely declined to be interviewed.

JACK WARNICK

Jack Warnick was a staff announcer for KMOX.

"I worked with Jack Warnick," said Jim White. "Jack did sports and sat in with me on my shows."

"Jack Warnick was of the old school," said Robert R. Lynn, who worked at KMOX for a year and a half after 20 years in news at KXOK. "He was a newsman the way it was when I broke in. He had a sonorous, deep voice with authoritarian tone. He was fairly laid back."

Warnick was a big sports fan who covered four Olympics while working in Europe for the Voice of America, the BBC, and the Armed Forces radio network.

Warnick died in 1989 of complications after surgery. He was 64.

ARNIE WARREN

Arnie Warren was one of the hosts who tried to replace Jack Carney after Carney's death in 1984.

"Arnie was a very nice person who was sort of a sacrificial lamb in the situation he was in," said author Elaine Viets, who appeared frequently on his show. "I have seen him since the days at KMOX."

Warren joined KMOX in February 1985 and resigned from the station in November of that year. His family had remained in Florida, and he said the strain of commuting between St. Louis and Florida was proving to be too difficult for him.

Viets lives in Hollywood, Florida, and has a lucrative novel writing career with a radio show on NPR and a syndicated column. "I saw him down here at a book signing," she said. "He has become an author himself and has written inspirational and self-help books. He looks great."

JIM WHITE

Jim White did almost every assignment possible during his 30 years with KMOX. He worked mornings, he worked afternoons, he worked nights. At one time he was the news director, the program director, and the host of his own show.

It was no wonder White was honored with the Achievement In Radio Lifetime Achievement Award shortly after his retirement in 1999.

"The only shift I didn't work was the 9 AM to noon, the Jack Carney hours," said White.

White had been working at KDKA in Pittsburgh before moving to KMOX in 1969. Bob Hardy was being overburdened with work and he wanted some relief. He went to Robert Hyland, who told him, "Find someone yourself." Hardy had heard White in Pittsburgh, and had him come in for a tryout.

"I was hired on St. Patrick's Day in 1969," said White. "I started as an assignment editor and on-air news and street reporter. I worked 9 to 5. That only lasted for two days."

The first week White was in town, CBS had a stockholders' meeting. Mr. Hyland wanted to send Hardy to the meeting, so White was assigned to fill Hardy's shift on *At Your Service*. After only one show it was evident White was a talk-show host.

"I immediately became a talk show host," said White. "I alternated with Bob Hardy. One of us was on every other hour, and then we did the 4 o'clock hour together."

At the beginning, White was used so much and his schedule changed so much that at one time he was the news director, program director, and an on-air talent all at the same time.

"Mr. Hyland asked me what I wanted to do and I picked talk show," said White.

When they were working together, Jack Buck dubbed Hardy and White "the babbling bookends."

It wasn't long before White found a home working the nighttime hours. He called his listeners "creatures of the night" and said the topics for the show were "things that go bump in the night." That earned him his nickname of "the big bumper" and quickly earned many loyal fans.

"We've been in our house 26 years," said listener Mary Stark. "My son was 10 or 11 when we moved in. He always used to listen to Jim White every night when he went to bed. It would always take us by surprise when he would get up and tell us these things he'd heard. I'll never forget the night he told us Jim White had the Happy Hooker on."

"Mr. Hyland almost went nuts on that one," said White.

"Eddie said the reason he always did so well in school was that he listened to Jim White every night," said Stark.

"One good story," said White, "was the night I was doing a promo for Charles Kuralt. He was doing a weekend series on radio. He had that motor home and traveled around the country. It sounded like a great job and I said on the air, 'There's a guy I'd kill for his job.' Not one minute later the phone rings in the studio. I pick it up and it's Charles Kuralt in his deep voice, 'This is Charles Kuralt and I'm in a phone booth in a blizzard in Nebraska. If you want this damn job, you can have it!' He had been listening to my show and heard me say that."

Another surprise for White came when he was doing a political show.

"It was one of those boring political shows," he said. "Suddenly the door flew open. I mean it flew open, and in comes this gigantic black man shouting, 'I am the greatest!' It was Muhammed Ali. He was there and they sent him down to the studio. He went into his 'I am the greatest' and 'float like a butterfly' schtick.

"I said, 'Ah come on, you don't look so tough to me,' and he said 'Come on stand up!' Then he threw about 10 punches past my ears. He was very mild mannered and a very nice guy when the mike was turned off, but when it went on…!

"One night John Goodman called the show. He was filming a show in Toronto, Canada. Later when I was about to retire, someone asked me on the air, if there was anyone I wish I could have interviewed or was there anyone I wish I could have met in my career and I said probably John Goodman. I always liked his acting. A few minutes later, in comes John Goodman walking through the door. He is from St. Louis, and his mom still lives here. He had been listening to the show and was driving from the airport to his mom's home. He took a detour and came down to the station to meet me. He came in and did about two hours with me."

White's wife, Pat, booked guests for the show. She worked out of their home using her maiden name so no one would know she was his wife.

Mike Owens produced White's show in the late 1970s. Owens worked in the studio, screening the calls and instructing White on when to go to a commercial.

"I remember one time when President Jimmy Carter was running for re-election," said Owens. "He was going down the Mississippi on a riverboat, and Jim had his connections on the river. We were able to make contact with the boat on the show."

White's show hours were dependent on what sports were being broadcast that night. During the winter when there was no baseball, he would start as early as 8 PM. He would usually have guests on when he started that early.

Even though most of his shows were lighthearted, with people coming on the air and talking about what they wanted to talk about, there were times when White realized the responsibility involved in letting people come on the airwaves.

"One night Jim was on the air," said Pat White. "Some guy called and said he had a nuclear device."

"The call came in near the end of the show," said White. "He claimed he'd stolen a nuclear warhead from Whiteman Air Force Base in Knob Noster, Missouri."

Because of KMOX's wide reach at night, the story gained international attention. According to the Kayhan International Newspaper in India, the caller started out by saying, 'Would you like to buy an atomic weapon? I've got one in my garage.'

He said he was a security guard from the Air Force. He said five people got together and took the warhead to prove a point. The man gave specific details of a 20-megatron warhead and said he and his cohorts had stolen it and pulled the stunt to emphasize lax security at the base.

"He said they have real ones and they have dummy ones and they have different markings on them. According to him they had painted a real one to look like a dummy one and driven it right out the gate. I doubted the story at first, but after a while he was saying things that made me question it. I'd been in missiles when I was in the service and knew a little about the terminology. On the other line we called the FBI, while I kept him on the air."

Soon Whiteman officials were on another line, giving White specific questions to ask the caller.

"The FBI was trying to trace the call," said White. "And back then it took a lot longer to do. I had to keep him on the air for five and a half hours. We went off the air and I was still on the phone with him. The FBI found out who he was and went to his house. They followed clues around the house that led to his car in the garage. His feet were sticking out from under it and they thought he was dead. Turns out he was drunk and was hiding. It all turned out to be a hoax. He had some mental problems and had been listening to his brother and his brother's friends talking and decided to call KMOX. They didn't press charges because he agreed to seek professional help."

Besides the studio shows, White occasionally reported from his boat. On the Fourth of July he would park it at the riverfront and broadcast from it. Once he was doing some reporting of flooding in 1973 from his boat, when Hyland called and changed his assignment.

"He had me wired for sound," said White. "I had a beeper on so they could contact me. He called and said he had heard about a secret meeting of the country's top Democrats out at Sid Solomon's house in Gray Summit, Missouri. He said he'd send a helicopter out to the marina to get me to go out there. That in itself was pretty funny because I'd put on a coat and tie, and then the helicopter comes down stirring up all this wind and dust.

"Mr. Hyland told me the way to find Sid Solomon's house was that his swimming pool was shaped like the emblem of the Blues. Everybody out there had pools, there were big estates, but we looked for the Blues' emblem. We finally found it, but no one was there. The copter pilot said, 'Let's go down by these woods,' to try to get a look.

Well as we approached a group of trees, here comes a bunch of men scattering everywhere, and papers are flying from the wind we were creating with the helicopter. The Democrats were meeting in the trees. They were not happy with us."

White's stories about his boat and traveling on the river have become legendary to his listeners. He also is an avid ham radio fan and has been very active in ham activities and has even been involved in life-saving situations using the amateur radios.

"In this part of the country you have to have the number '0' in your ham license number," said Bob Hamilton. "Jim has the highest license you can have and recently he was able to get the letters KM and then the number 0 and then X for his license, so he has KMOX."

"I always liked to talk to the engineers about the ham radio," said White. "That was my background, ham radio and electronics. I liked to talk to Charlie Domorous, John Toler, and the others. When I started at KMOX there were 22 or 23 engineers on staff and only four salespeople. Now there are three engineers and about 25 salespeople."

Because of his heavy work schedule, which often included working the afternoon hours of *At Your Service* then coming back to host the nighttime show, White was under a lot of stress. It wasn't all that surprising one night that he suffered a heart attack.

"It was definitely a stress-related heart attack," said his wife, Pat.

Bob Costas had just come in to do the midnight sportscast when White began to realize what was happening.

"It was a classic heart attack," said White. "I knew what was happening. I asked Bob, on the air, if he would stick around after the news for a few minutes since it was such a big night in sports. Then when the news came on, I called 911. At first I couldn't get through to 911 so I called our contact at the police department and he came over and took me to the hospital."

Adds Costas, "I stayed on the air until Scott St. James took over. I told the audience that Jim wasn't feeling well, and we thought it was best for him to leave."

St. James was in his car on the way to the station when he realized White was not on and Costas was on alone. When he got there he found out what had happened, and he ended up filling in for White until he came back. When White came back, he started working only on the nighttime show and remained there until he retired.

"That was when I stopped booking the guests for Jim's show," said Pat White. "It had just become too much. The haven that your home is supposed to be had disappeared. From the moment he woke up, we were talking about the show. It was just too much stress."

After that, White said he really enjoyed his hours and his life.

"I would get home at 3 o'clock or so and then go to bed until 11 or 12," he said. "Pat could do whatever she wanted to get done in the morning, and the kids were at school. After I got up, we had the whole afternoon and evening. It was great."

"It was a big thrill to follow Jim White's show for several years," said Emmett McAuliffe, who did the 2 to 5 AM slot on Friday nights. "I had always listened to him, having grown up here in St. Louis. He's a talk show genius. As a listener I would get mad at him like anyone else if I didn't agree with him, but once I got to know him I instantly liked him.

"One story I remember about his show was the night Princess Diana was buried. He hated talking about that, but that was all anyone would want to talk about that night and he knew it. As I remember it, he started his show out by saying, 'This is the last place I want to be tonight, but I'm here and I will go through with it.'"

First caller: "Hey, Jimbo, how you doing?"

Jim White: "Don't call me Jimbo or I won't let you call here again."

Caller: "OK, Jim don't you think Prince Charles tried to have Diana killed because of that woman. [Camilla Parker Bowles] Don't you think…" (and he proceeded to give his big conspiracy theory, which White wanted no part of).

Jim White: (after he cut the caller off) "On second thought, call me Jimbo, but don't call this station again."

Elaine Stern was White's longtime producer and she was involved in setting up special shows. One idea which turned out to be very popular was the *Dateline St. Louis* shows.

"Martha Roper did it with me," said White. "She is a sex educator and she helped get the show started."

It required two producers because there was the complication of matching people who called and not getting their phone numbers said on the air. Rene Servier helped Stern with the producing duties.

"We estimated we had about 1,000 marriages from the show," said White. "We asked them to send us announcements if they were getting married and we got several announcements a week."

One of the couples who got a lot of publicity for being married were Norman Hinrichs and Sharon Leutzinger.

A yearly show White originated was the Halloween night show.

"The Halloween shows were always really popular," said Stern. "Sometimes we would stay in the studio and Jim would play spooky music or read the story of the Piasa Bird or something and people would call in with ghost stories. Several times we went out to haunted houses, those were some wild shows.

"Dr. Brodeur went with us. He was like the resident skeptic. We brought him and Dr. John Oldani, professor of folklore and superstition at SIU-Edwardsville. Dr. Oldani was always a little scared to come, but we got him to come. Psychic Bevvy Jagers would come and bring her ghost hunters. People called us to tell us about places where they felt they had ghosts."

One particularly scary trip was to the Three Mile House. It was a restaurant, which has since burned down.

"It used to be part of the Underground Railroad for slaves," said

Stern. It was three miles to the next town, that's why the name Three Mile House. Bill Ott was our engineer that night so he knows this, but all of the off switches suddenly became on switches and the on switches became off switches. At the end of the show they switched back. That was so eerie."

Stern said they would bring cameras with infrared detection to look for ghosts.

"Dr. Brodeur got something on the camera that night," she said. "Another place we broadcast from was the Lemp Brewery, that was the last place we went. It was really creepy, like a cave. It got so cold that we went back to the studios and did the last two hours from the studio. I put the guests in the car and left early to go back. Jim stayed until they did the news and then he left. We made it in time."

Joe Sonderman also worked as a producer for White. "He was wonderful to work for," Sonderman said. "He has this image as a curmudgeon, but I never met anyone who was so patient and helpful. I'll never forget how he took me to his home and gave me several antique radios. I treasure them."

"One thing about Jim White," said Stern. "He really was not interested in having, say, an author on and read his book and interview him, and he didn't care much about politicians. He was more interested in his callers. He had certain people who were his 'regular guests' and he liked to have them on. There for a while Rev. Bill Little was on giving out advice on families. He also had Bob Heil, the electronics expert. He would talk about electronics and new high tech things. Jim called him High Tech Heil."

Listeners, as well as those who worked with White over the years, have their own special memories of particular broadcasts.

"One time a caller had heard Jim tell a recipe for stuffing a turkey with popcorn," said newswoman Vicki Atlas, who had heard the story. "She had not realized his recipe called for cooked popcorn and she put in uncooked popcorn and it popped in the turkey. She called the station complaining that her turkey was ruined. Mr. Hyland sent her a turkey with all the trimmings."

"It was a joke," said Jim White. "I said you make your regular stuffing and stuff the turkey, then add a cup of uncooked popcorn and when

the tail blows up, the turkey is done. I was just making a joke. This lady did it. She had turkey all over her kitchen! She was threatening to sue KMOX. Mr. Hyland got involved and had one of the nice restaurants in town cater her Thanksgiving dinner and she lived in Herculaneum."

"I remember working with Jim White in what he calls the real radio days," said Don Wolff, St. Louis attorney and host of the *Jazz Show* on KMOX on Saturday nights. "I remember sometimes when I would be on with Jim White talking about 'hot' issues and afterward we would go across the street to Bulls and Bears [an old restaurant/bar, now the site of the Adams Mark Hotel] for a drink. Jim had his regular—a peanut butter jar was waiting for him served up by a client of mine who was the bartender."

"Jim White used to talk about my radio museum on the air [the museum is at 2022 Cherokee]," said Jasper Giardina, the owner of the museum and Jasper's Tropical Gift Fruit Baskets. "People would call and ask where they can get an old radio repaired and he'd talk about my radio museum. I have the largest collection of radios in the world, over 10,000 radios. Jim would joke about mixing the fruit with the radios. Jim was always interested in old radios."

"I loved working with Jim White," said David Strauss, known on KMOX as "Mr. Trivia." "He was one of those guys who, when he was working, made it all seem so easy. He was very relaxed, was having a good time. I thought he was a great interviewer. And he helped me out so much. I ended up doing about 85 shows with him and became good friends. We went out socially a few times. Just a great guy."

"When Jim retired, I contacted him, by e-mail," said Stuart Esrock, who had worked with him. "When I worked there, I worked sometimes on the overnight and talked to him, then when he was in the afternoons I produced a little for him. He knew my parents had a cabin and boat at the Lake of the Ozarks because we'd talked about it. He knew I loved the water. One time he said, 'You ought to come out on the boat.' I said, 'Just ask me,' and he did. He took me out on his boat."

On White's last day KMOX had a day long party at the Summit Restaurant.

"I was kind of unhappy that they had me on the air the whole time," said White. "I didn't get to schmooze and visit with all the people

who came in to surprise me because I was on the air. So many people came. It was a blur because we were there on the air the whole time.

"I remember Bob Costas came in with a sack full of White Castles and tossed them out into the crowd. I still have the 'big bumper' that Dave Sinclair gave me along with all of the things I got that day."

White has a web page and welcomes anyone to check it out. It is *www.bigbumper.com*.

White enjoys his retirement and does not regret ever leaving his job at KMOX. He celebrated his retirement by taking a several month journey aboard his boat with his wife and dog. They traveled down the Mississippi River, across the Gulf of Mexico, around Florida, up the East Coast, up the Hudson River to the Great Lakes, and back home.

"I found I was doing too many tributes and it was time to leave while I still could," he said. "In my time at KMOX I was involved in tributes to Milt Peters, Jack Warnick, Bob Hardy, Bob Osborne, Jack Carney, Dan Kelly, Bob Hyland, and there were others I saw who died like Steve Trenkman and Mary Phelan.

"It was a great run. I was number one in my timeslot for 30 years. They asked me to stay, but after all those tributes, the trip with my wife was always something we dreamed about."

PAT WHITE

Pat White, Jim White's wife, booked the guests for his shows for four years. She used her maiden name because she didn't want the people to know she was Jim's wife.

"Working from home, there were a few times you couldn't keep from letting it out," she said. "One time, Holly [our daughter] came in the room bleeding. I was in the middle of a phone call and she sat on the floor and was very quiet even though she was crying. As soon as I saw her come in, I hung up and took care of her."

The way she got started was the producer at the station who was assigned to book White's guests found it difficult to book guests in the middle of the night. Jim and Pat were talking and Pat said she thought it could be done.

"So I made a proposal to Mr. Hyland," she said. "I booked people

in different time zones. Jerry Berger helped me out a lot with contacts he had on the West Coast, like agents. You could book though 1 o'clock in the morning and it worked out real well."

The downside to the arrangement was the White home became the office.

"As soon as Jim would get up, we'd start talking about it," she said. "It was fun, but then it became like washing dishes. You would get up and then start filling in the holes. After Jim had his heart attack, which was stress-related, we decided he needed to relax at home. Our home which had been a refuge was suddenly becoming 'KMOX South.' He could never get away from work as long as we were constantly talking about the show. After the heart attack, I stopped being his producer, and he slowed down a little."

As it turned out, White did not need to book as many guests because he began doing more *Open Line* programs.

"Mr. Hyland finally accepted that the *Open Line* format would work," said Pat White. "Jim proved to him that he could make it work. He would rather talk to his listeners and they responded by calling."

"I was the first person to do *Open Line*," said Jim White. "Mr. Hyland didn't want to do it. He said, 'You have 30 days to try it.' The ratings were out in 30 days. There had been *Open Lines*, but they were directed *Open Lines*. I started the true *Open Lines* where anyone could call up and talk about any topic"

WENDY WIESE

Wendy Wiese joined the morning team of Bob Hardy and Bill Wilkerson in 1986. She was hired as a newswriter, and had only worked at the station for six weeks when Robert Hyland gave her the new assignment.

"He called me into his office after only two weeks on the morning show," said Wiese. "He said, 'Bill's going on vacation, I want you to fill in for him.' I was terrified. I was scared to death to work with Bob in Bill's place."

Once the word got out that Wiese would be taking Wilkerson's place while he was on his vacation, Hardy set about helping her get prepared.

"He had his bifocals on," she said. "And he said, 'I want you to bring a legal pad, take notes, write everything down. You have to do everything he does, you have to be Bill Wilkerson.'

"So I get a legal pad—now you have to remember I was still a kid at the time [24]. I have my little ponytail and ribbon on, and my note pad. OK, '7:14 Bill scratches his nose, 7:17, Bill clears his throat...' I got totally prepared and the big day got there."

At that time KMOX would air the long version of CBS news. There would be about 10 minutes of national news, then Hardy and Wilkerson would do about 15 minutes of an expanded newscast.

"So here I was sitting with Bob Hardy," said Wiese. "Absolutely fearful. I kept thinking, 'This is where I crash and burn'. Actually I was doing OK. I started noticing things were going well, I hadn't stumbled over the news or anything. We got all the way through it, and Bob Hardy says, 'I'm Bob Hardy,' and I say, 'And I'm Bill Wilkerson, oh my God!' I looked up and could only see our engineer Rudy Ruzicka's feet, he'd fallen over from laughing so hard. Bob Hardy was laughing so hard I could only see the top of his mouth. I'd been told early once, that if you make a mistake, don't point it out and maybe no one will notice. Maybe no one would notice I just called myself Bill Wilkerson on KMOX radio, so I just threw it to Kay Lindbergh for the traffic report. Kay said, 'Thanks Bill.'"

Wiese was so distraught when she got off the air, she thought she'd just ruined her chances for any type of career, much less at KMOX. She tried to hide but ran right into Hyland.

"He said, 'You're looking lovely today, Bill,'" said Wiese. "I think that was a turning point for me. Everybody was able to laugh it off. If they could laugh at a mistake like that I thought, maybe I'll fit in. They knew I was scared, it was pretty obvious, but they were all so nice about it. Of course, then when Bill got back from his vacation, he said somebody asked him at the airport, 'Did you hear what she said?'

"We just had so many wonderful times back then. And there were so many sad, horrendous moments, like when someone would die. We were like a family. We went through so many things, weddings, babies. Looking back on it, to be there at such a young age was just unbelievable."

There was never a dull moment on the morning show. It was a tradition that the senior members of the show, Wilkerson and Hardy at the time, would divide the news stories.

"If there was ever a story about a homicidal cross-dressing maniac, they would give it to the other person," Wiese said. "Whoever was dividing the stories would give the bizarre ones to the other person. So one day they were dividing the stories and Bill started laughing. 'No, I can't do that to you,' he said. I said, 'Do what?' He shook his head smiling. I started being sarcastic and said, 'I'm a professional, whatever it is I can handle,' and Bill said, 'OK, you got it.' I said, 'No problem at all, I'm a professional.'

"Well the story was about 'Skippy the Rat Terrier' who had commandeered his owner's car. They'd left it idling, and Skippy had somehow popped the car into drive and sent it crashing through a window. All I could think of was Toonces the Cat from *Saturday Night Live*. It made me laugh so hard. I was hysterical, in tears, I kept saying, 'no, no, I can do this!' but I laughed all the way through it."

Hardy and Wilkerson became almost like father figures to Wiese, who felt so green and new at the time. She formed a special relationship with both of them, and when she was about to get married, she chose them to be in the wedding party as ushers.

Several weeks before the wedding, Wiese started getting strange mail. It began to worry her when the sender sent a lock of his hair in an envelope and then when he said, 'Could you love your fiancé if he was in a wheel chair?' She finally told Hyland about it, and Hyland called the Secret Service. They put a detective on the case and eventually tracked him down. But before they'd caught him, Hardy and Wilkerson knew he was out there somewhere and they were determined not to let him ruin their friend's wedding.

"So here they are at the wedding, and we have this on the wedding videos," she said. "They're in the background and you can see they've got a guy they're talking to. They see this strange guy, by himself, and they don't want to spook me so they go over to him. You can see them signaling each other and kind of giving each other the eye, pointing to this guy on the video. Finally they kind of get him in the corner and start asking, 'Who are you? What are you doing here?' He pulls out his

badge and it was the detective! Here they thought they were being Starsky and Hutch!"

One day on the way to work, a raccoon got in the way of her tires and she unavoidably ran over it.

"I felt horrible," she said. "It was this gigantic raccoon and it had crawled out of a drain pipe in my subdivision and wiggled in front of my car. When I realized I'd hit it, I screamed. I saw these little beady eyes and then there was this thud and I realized I'd hit it! Well, I was pregnant at the time and just one big nerve ending anyway so I got to work and was still all shook up. I mentioned it on the air that morning."

Little did she know, one of the afternoon producers [at the time], Fred Zielonko, had heard her say it while he was still at home.

"So later that day, I'm doing the news," said Wiese. "I'm sitting in the studio doing the news and I look up and there behind the glass is this big stuffed raccoon with a sign on it that said, 'You Killed My Mother!' I almost lost it. I was doing this real serious story about a murderer and here Fred had set that up there."

Zielonko is now the general manager at KTRS. After Hyland died, Tim Dorsey, who had worked at KMOX under Hyland, decided to start a radio station and hired Wiese, Wilkerson, and several other people away from KMOX in 1996. They started in Belleville at station WIBV and after several investment changes, Dorsey and his crew moved to their Westport location.

"When we left, we weren't running from our co-workers and I hope they know that," said Wiese. "It was a hard decision to leave. That was a truly amazing time. Looking back on it you can appreciate it."

She left with the respect of her co-workers,

"Wendy Wiese is the funniest person in the world," said Anne Keefe. "She can do stand up comedy. We haven't seen her at her best yet."

TAFFY WILBUR

Taffy Wilbur was on KMOX from 1960 to 1967. The wife of Cardinal baseball player Del Wilbur, Taffy did interviews for the news and the sports department.

"I was the first woman who didn't just do cooking," said Wilbur,

who had five children and managed to do her interviews when they were at school or when she made other arrangements. Wilbur, who was a groundbreaker for women at the time, was instrumental in starting the charitable organization St. Louis Pinch Hitters, which originally consisted of baseball players' and sportswriters' wives.

"I got started at the Pinch-Hitters' first fundraiser, which at the time was a fashion show," said Wilbur. "Now this was before the Ball-B-Que got started. We had a fashion show at the Chase and Robert Hyland wanted me to do interviews with some of the people who were doing the modeling. Shortly after that, Mary Devine called me. She is so nice she wanted me to know about it ahead of time. 'I've told Bing to call you,' she said to me, 'because Bob Hyland is going to call you about a job.'"

Wilbur had been working in radio since she was five years old living in Texas. The manager of a radio station in San Antonio heard her read a poem as part of a school visit to the station and asked her to come on each week and do monologues.

Besides her radio experience, it was partly due to the fact that she was a baseball player's wife and partly due to the novelty that she was a woman that landed the task of interviewing many famous people.

"I'll never forget the day Senator Symington gave me 'ups' in line at the airport when I was there to interview Barry Goldwater," said Wilbur. "In those days, the 'press' did not always get to barge right up there like they do today. When someone was coming in on a plane, everyone would go out there and line up. I was at the back of the line and Senator Symington saw me, 'Come on up here, Taffy. You can be up here,' he said."

Hyland promoted Taffy as a celebrity and nothing let her know that as much as a giant cut-out he had made of her and set it up at the Post Office, where she was to do interviews. "That was really embarrassing," she said. "He had me get Jules Pierlow pictures taken. Anybody who is old enough to remember those knows they were very glamorous pictures. He had the picture made into a life-size cut-out and when I was doing these weekly interviews at the Post Office, I would always see this glamorous life-size shot of myself. It was bigger than life."

Wilbur is a very down-to-earth person and really enjoyed her job of interviewing people like Carol Channing, A newspaper photographer took a picture of the interview.

"My favorite picture was with a chimpanzee," she said. "We were at 8th and Olive for Old Newsboys Day. They always did something special to draw attention to 'celebrity corner' and that year they had a chimp and I got to hold him."

"My sister knew Taffy Wilbur real well," said listener Babe Barham. "She lived in Kirkwood and her husband was a ballplayer. I used to enjoy listening to her do her interviews."

Besides the movie stars, politicians, and newsmakers, Wilbur got to interview baseball players, including her husband. When her husband found out she would be interviewing certain ballplayers, he teased her about it.

"When Maris and Mantle came to town," said Wilbur, "my husband said, 'I wouldn't interview them.' They had reputations. He thought they'd be a little hard to handle, but they turned out to be charming and they were fine."

She went on the field to do her interviews.

"I was always dressed up back then," she said. "I wore dresses and you had to be well groomed. You would not wear the casual clothes I wear today in that situation back then."

EMIL WILDE

Longtime listeners to KMOX will remember Emil Wilde. He was a staple in local radio in the 1960s and 1970s. Wilde read the news, mostly from the studio, and did not do a lot of on the street reporting. He worked for eight years in the regular 9 AM until 5 PM hours, and the last year he worked the overnight.

He had a crisp delivery and good command of the news. Near the end of his broadcasting career he was put on midnights and he did not mind, helping the news interns learn as he read the wires and called police stations to see if there was any news.

"When Mr. Hyland hired me," said Wilde, "he went straight from hearing a broadcast I had done on KSD. He had me in and he said, 'Do

351

you like KMOX?" I said, 'I sure do,' and he said, 'You're hired.' I always had a real good relationship with Mr. Hyland."

"The thing I remember about Emil," said Rick Powers, who works in television sports on a St. Louis station, "was that he liked jazzy leads. We would write the stories for him and he would always change the leads. No matter who wrote the stories he would always change it to suit his particular style."

"Mr. Hyland asked me to take the midnight to 7 AM slot to write the news for Rex Davis and Bob Hardy," Wilde said. "I had a lot of experience and Mark McDonough, who had been doing it, left the station.

"I remember when it snowed, I helped Bob Hardy and Rex Davis with the school closings. There were so many school closings in bad weather. As an announcer we didn't mind reading them because we were going to be reading something anyway. We would take turns reading them. It was a chore, but not that bad for those of us on the air. It was the listeners who did not like it. The school closings were a pain in the neck for those who did not care about them."

"Emil was the first person I met on my first night at KMOX," said former producer Rene Servier. "He was doing the overnight news desk. We introduced ourselves, then he said, 'I'm going to show you the most important thing you will ever have to know,' and then he led me out into the hall. I was picturing all sorts of things, but he took me into the little room and showed me how to make coffee.

"One thing about Emil," said Servier, "was that he did not want any of his newscasts to sound like another. He would not use the same cut or copy during his shift. If the mayor said, 'I'm firing the entire city council,' then Emil would use that cut once, and rewrite the story several different ways."

BILL WILKERSON

Bill Wilkerson was not planning a career in radio when he graduated from Southern Illinois University at Carbondale with a degree in journalism, majoring in advertising.

He was working two jobs, in the public relations department at

SIU-Edwardsville and selling suits at the J.C. Penney store in Over-land, when Robert Hyland offered him an internship in 1969.

Wilkerson's first job was to write the news for overnight host John McCormick.

"I had never written news under pressure before," Wilkerson said. "The woman who was supposed to train me was talking to her boy-friend the first night I was there and never showed me what to do. An ice storm hit the second night and she didn't show up.

"I was alone when McCormick came into the newsroom and asked for his news. So I nervously wrote it. That's how I got indoctrinated into radio news."

His first on-air experience came one Saturday morning when the sports reporter didn't show up and Wilkerson read the sports. He also read news on the FM station, and in 1970 he was hired as a full-time reporter.

He remained in news for several years. His first assignment was to cover an appearance at the airport by Vice President Spiro T. Agnew. Among other stories he covered were the 1972 Republican and Demo-cratic national conventions. He regularly reported on area elections and the St. Louis Board of Aldermen.

He was getting restless in news, however, and convinced Hyland to move him into the sports department.

"Bill Wilkerson was my first partner on the Spirits," said Bob Costas, who started his KMOX career as the play-by-play announcer for the Spirits of St. Louis games in the American Basketball Association in 1974. "He did the color and I always enjoyed being with him. He was very professional and even a bit reserved on air, but off the air he was funny as hell."

Wilkerson was primarily known for his football announcing, how-ever. He did the play-by-play for the Missouri Tigers and Cardinals for many years. He became the first African-American to work as a play-by-play announcer in the NFL, and also doing NFL games on NBC, and the first African-American color commentator in the National Hockey League when he worked with Dan Kelly on Blues broadcasts.

He also was a regular host of *Sports Open Lines*, where his jovial personality caused all of the callers to feel as though he was a personal friend. Wilkerson even wrote a book about football which was tar-

geted to women, teaching them what to look for when they were watching a game.

As play-by-play man for the football Cardinals, Wilkerson spent a great deal of time at Lindenwood College, the site of the team's training camp for many of its years in St. Louis. On a normal practice day in 1980, the football field became eerily quiet and the team was huddled around a teammate, J.V.Cain, who collapsed and later died. Wilkerson had been in the pressbox.

"I remember it was a Sunday," said Jim Holder. "I was at a barbecue and I got the call. I went immediately to the hospital and Wilkerson went to the station with Costas to anchor an *Open Line*."

Wilkerson and Costas fielded calls and kept in constant contact with Holder to get reports on Cain's condition.

"I was with Bing Devine, who was working for the Big Red back then," said Holder. "Bill was at the mike and would throw it to me for updates. Bing Devine came out and made the announcement [that Cain had died]. It was just really sad.

"One thing I remember about that day was how Bill Bidwill [Cardinals owner] stayed in the dorm with the players after they announced that J.V. had passed. I went back to the dorm to interview them. I think he showed a different side to him that maybe the players had never seen by sitting out there with them."

In 1982, Wilkerson changed the focus of his career again, moving into a new assignment as the co-host of the KMOX morning show. He worked with Bob Hardy, taking the place of Rex Davis, who had retired. In 1986, the program added a third partner when Wendy Wiese was hired.

That trio remained intact and proved to be extremely popular with the listeners until Hardy died of a heart attack in 1994. Two years later, Wilkerson and Wiese were part of a group of employees who left KMOX to work for a rival station, KTRS.

GENE WILKEY

Gene Wilkey became general manager in 1952, succeeding John Akerman, who was promoted to a sales job with the CBS network in

New York. Wilkey had been the general manager of WCCO in Minneapolis.

Wilkey served as GM until 1955, when Robert Hyland was named to the position. Wilkey eventually was reassigned by CBS to set up the new television station, KMOX-TV.

PAUL WILLS

Paul Wills was an announcer on KMOX from 1958 to 1959.

KEN WILSON

Ken Wilson came on the St. Louis scene in the fall of 1984 when Sportstime Cable was in business.

"They hired me to do Cincinatti Reds, St. Louis Blues hockey, and Big Eight basketball," said Wilson. "After Sportstime had hired me to do the Blues, they were told by the Blues to have Dan Kelly [Sr.] on the broadcast, so it ended up that we worked together and simulcast it on Sportstime and KMOX."

In April of 1985 Wilson did his first Cardinal baseball game on KMOX.

"I remember it was Opening Day and we were playing the Mets at Shea Stadium," said Wilson. "Bob Costas came on with me because he was in New York."

Besides the play-by-play duties, Wilson began doing *Sports Open Lines* and he started doing a regular Blues' *Open Line* on Friday nights which he did for 10 years. He now is the television voice of the Blues.

"One of the strangest memories I have of being on KMOX was the last day of the season one year in the mid-1980s," said Wilson. "I'd just done a recap and was in the middle of the wrapup when I heard the phone ring. The engineer, Colin Jarrette, answered the phone and tapped me on the shoulder. I was still talking but I could see it was important. He was being animated trying to get my attention. I was planning to wrap it up and thank the producer, engineer, cameramen for all their help all year like they do at the season-end broadcast. Colin gets close and says, 'This is important. Mr. Hyland says get off the air,

the season's over, nobody cares.' I just said, 'So long from Wrigley.' I never thanked anybody, never wrapped it up, that was just it, the season was over and nobody cared."

Wilson, who had broadcast baseball for many years before coming to St. Louis, wanted to stay in baseball, but no positions opened up.

"When I saw that was not happening, I decided to combine my love for baseball with my love for the St. Louis area and start a team," Wilson said.

He started the River City Rascals, an independent minor league team in the Frontier League. The team, which plays at the Ozzie Smith Field in the T.R. Hughes Complex in O'Fallon, Missouri, has broken league attendance records in each of its first two seasons. For more information on the River City Rascals, their web site is *www.rivercityrascals.com.*

JEANNIE WHITWORTH

Those who knew Jeannie Whitworth at the time she was the public relations director will never forget her. She was the first and only woman who was allowed into the Knights of the Cauliflower Ear dinners for many years. This intelligent lady who knew a lot about promotions also knew a lot about turning the heads of the males she worked for or around with her plunging necklines and deep sexy voice.

"Jeannie Whitworth was a very amusing, fun loving person," said Bob Costas. "She worked for Bob Hyland, who was a very 'button down' guy but she could always find the fun, or see the absurdity in the situation. I remember we got on this silly kick where in order for her to let me in to see Hyland, I would have to do a limerick for her. One day Hyland hears me reciting a bawdy limerick for Jeannie Whitworth and he calls, 'What are you doing? Come in here!' The next day I gave her this one:

> Said Hyland to Bob and to Jean,
> "What I'm hearing out there is obscene,
> So I'll issue this warning,
> Stop these limericks each morning
> Or your next jobs will be in Moline!"

Whitworth worked with the football Cardinals to start the "Big Red Line." "She started it," said Jan Fox, who eventually took it over. "Before the Big Red Line, Mr. Hyland would pay to have the Golden Girls from Mizzou come in for the football games. Jeannie had the brainstorm 'why don't we hold auditions and have our own girls?' It was a big success.

"He (Hyland) always wanted the 'biggest' or the 'best' of anything we had. So he decided we should have a 'Little Red Line.' He had Jeannie put together a group of little girls to do the same types of dancing."

She sought the help of Yvonne Cole, the sponsor of the always first-place award-winning Lindbergh High School Pom squad. Cole came in and coordinated the numbers for the Little Red Line while Whitworth directed the Big Red Line.

Whitworth had many clever ideas, including the KMOX Easter Bunny, who showed up at the "I've Always Wanted To Be In A Parade But Nobody's Ever Asked Me" parade that was originated by Jack Carney. Whitworth worked with Carney to make that Forest Park parade a success.

One of the things Whitworth was most proud of was that she was one of the only women who attended the early Knights of the Cauliflower Ear dinners. Actually she was the only female who sat out with the males.

"I went," said Jan Fox, "but I sat with the Big Red Line, eating our steak dinners back by the kitchen."

KMOX broadcast the dinners each year. The Knights of the Cauliflower Ear dinners were exclusive, private dinners.

"They were big community leaders," said Fox. "Advertising sponsors of the team and the station and guests of the Cauliflower Ear members. A lot of the same men belonged to the MAC [Missouri Athletic Club]. They'd have a cocktail party and then during the dinner, there would be a master of ceremonies who would introduce the team members. [The Cardinals' dinner was often at the Baurnhoff at Grant's Farm and the football Cardinals' one was often at a hangar at the airport. This was before the Blues had a Cauliflower Ear dinner.] Then people got the opportunity to ask questions of the players. They could ask sports questions or personal questions. This was a no-holds-barred event. When KMOX broadcast it there were bleeps every two minutes. Good thing we were on delay!"

Whitworth was right out there with the men acting as hostess, and later for the entertainment she would bring out the Big Red Line and there might be a comedian to entertain the men. One time at Grant's Farm, Fox remembers Gallagher [the Watermelon smashing comedian] was there.

"I was sitting next to Gussie Busch, and just as Gallagher was getting up to perform, Gussie took his fork and knife and very loudly started pounding them on the table, 'Bring on the Dancing Girls! Bring on the Dancing Girls!' he yelled."

DON WOLFF

St. Louis attorney Don Wolff started doing his music show on KMOX in January 1993 after the death of Charlie Menees, who did a jazz and big band show on Saturday nights. He does the Saturday night *Entertainment St. Louis Show* from 8 PM to 10 PM and the *Jazz Show* after that until 2 AM. He also does *At Your Service* if needed and serves as a legal expert at times.

"Doing the only jazz show on a talk-sports station presents some interesting feedback from callers all over the country and in Canada," said Wolff. "Almost all of the listeners love the music, including very young listeners and very old ones. I had one caller that said he loved the music I played but would not listen to my show because I had defended President Clinton's positions in the impeachment process on an earlier talk show!"

Since KMOX is an information station, they often break into a show with a major news story and sometimes programming is changed due to the news.

"When Princess Diana died, we interrupted my show for updates," said Wolff. "On the spot, I changed the content of the program to sad and quiet music, soft jazz."

"The most rewarding aspect is the callers who call in on this non-talk show to say how much they love the show and the music. Some are sad, some happy because of the memories attached to the music or the feelings of the mood."

JIM WOODS

Jim Woods worked on the baseball Cardinals' broadcasts in 1970 and 1971. He was the announcer who replaced Harry Caray, and when he left his place was filled by Mike Shannon.

Woods was a veteran broadcaster who had worked for the Giants, Yankees, and Pirates before coming to St. Louis. He took a job broadcasting for the Oakland A's after he left St. Louis.

NAN WYATT

Nan Wyatt was hired by Robert Hyland in the fall of 1990 after Mary Phelan left the station to go to KMOV-TV. She was excited to work at KMOX after coming from WILM in Wilmington, Delaware, because she was originally from the Midwest and her mother had moved to St. Louis.

"I was the last on-air person that Mr. Hyland hired," she said. "I felt like I had one foot in the past. I sounded the way the women he hired sounded. Wendy [Wiese], Anne [Keefe], and I all had a similar quality in the way we did things. When Rod Zimmerman came, I felt like I put my other foot in the door to the future, so I felt like I fit in both camps."

Wyatt likes the excitement of the newsroom when it springs into action to cover a developing story.

"I'll never forget this one story," she said. "It was a slow day in news, we were basically sitting around the newsroom, nothing was going on. Suddenly the phone lines just lit up. Listeners were calling in to report of a tornado touching down at Page and 270. Carol House Furniture is right near there at Page and Lindbergh and they had gotten some damage from the storm."

"We got a million and a half dollars worth of damage," said Carol House owner Brook Dubman. "We were just working like any other day and it happened. There were no sirens or warnings. Luckily it was after 4 PM and most of the warehouse people had gone home for the day because it peeled our warehouse wall off. We had one guy who was up on a forklift and he could have been blown away but he didn't get hurt, nobody got hurt, thankfully, but the damage was bad."

"So many people calling," said Wyatt. "It was a perfect example of the community getting involved in a news story."

"Our store is right out there in the open, so people see it," said Dubman. "If I had a choice, I would have rather not had it happen, but as it did, we got some publicity out of it by having it broadcast on the radio and television. We tried to make the best of it."

"I remember hearing Brook being interviewed on the radio," said Cindy Lennox, the KMOX salesperson on the account. "They've had a fire and a flood, and he was interviewed about both. I remember with the fire, the agency that handles the spots, Weintraub Creative, called me at home because they wanted to pull the spot."

Working in news, you never know when a big story is going to break.

"In the newsroom, it is 90 percent tedium, and 10 percent action," said Wyatt. "At that time, you know you're a service. You feel a responsibility. KMOX is who the people turn to in an emergency. Sirens ring, a president gets shot, an earthquake happens, people turn to KMOX."

Wyatt left KMOX in 1994 to spend two years in Chicago at radio station WBBM.

"I wanted to stretch my wings and try a bigger market," she said. "But I love the St. Louis community, so I was glad to come back."

Program director Tom Langmyer contacted her to come back after Bill Wilkerson, Wendy Wiese, and Kevin Horrigan announced they were leaving KMOX to go to a new station being started by Tim Dorsey.

She hosts *Total Information AM*, the morning drive show, with Doug McElvein.

"Every morning when we get dressed, we listen to Nan Wyatt and Doug McElvein on KMOX," said listener Bill Hepper. "We have a radio in the bathroom. I don't have to look at the time I just listen to the radio and I know what time it is."

"Nan Wyatt calls me occasionally to have me on," said Charlie Hoessle, director of the St. Louis Zoo. "She'll call about the Children's Zoofari or the Zoo-A-Do event we had, just trying to get the word out about what's going on at the zoo."

"She is a very down-to-earth person," said Dr. Armand Brodeur. "The first time I met Nan, I knew who she was. I was just about to start

my show and I saw her in the hall, so I went out to meet her. She is not at all aloof like someone in her position might be. She's low-key, gracious, and charming, and she's very capable."

"Nan has been such a mentor to me," said Megan Lynch, who does traffic and works in the newsroom. "You always think when coming to a station like KMOX, 'Oh this is a big market, people are going to be brutal, back-stabbing.' Nan was nothing like that, she is just a great example to so many people."

SKEETS YANEY

Skeets Yaney came to St. Louis with a group of traveling hillbilly music makers. He sang on the air for nothing until he was discovered, making his living doing construction work.

Within three weeks after starting his radio appearances, his programs had a sponsor, Uncle Dick Slack's furniture store. Slack remained Yaney's sponsor for 19 years, from 1931 to 1950.

FRED ZIELONKO

Fred Zielonko joined KMOX as an intern while going to Southern Illinois University at Edwardsville. After Frank Pawloski left the Jack Carney show to go into the sports department, Zielonko took over as Carney's producer. The two formed a relationship that lasted until Carney's death. The red-headed fresh faced kid, who started just helping out, soon became invaluable to Carney and to the show.

After Carney's death, Zielonko progressed into administrative duties at the station eventually becoming the assistant to program director Bob Osborne. He is now the program director at KTRS.

"I was an intern in the sports department writing the sports for Bob Costas and Bill Wilkerson," said Zielonko. "When my internship was over, they went to Mr. Hyland and asked him to hire me. I was still going to school and I'd come in on the weekends and produce *The Dierdorf and Hart Show.*"

He eventually took on more duties at the station. He lightened his load of college classes and began producing the Carney show.

"I worked for Jack on the weekends," said Zielonko. "I put together the comedy shows and biographies. When I watch those A & E biographies I think 'we were doing those on radio years ago.' I'd go out and interview Kenny Rogers and write a script and give it to Jack. Then on his birthday we'd have a special for Jack to use on the air."

When it was time for Pawloski to come back to the Carney show,

Carney took Zielonko and Clarence Nieder, his engineer, to a Cardinal game.

"He said, 'You know they're moving Frank back, what are you go-ing to do?' Zielonko said. "I said, 'Finish school.' And he hired me to work at the studio he had at his house."

So Zielonko was working part-time for KMOX and full-time for Carney.

"He had this two-story apartment in the Chase on the 17th floor with this great view of Forest Park," said Zielonko. "Down the hall from that was a little room he used as a studio. I had a key to that room and that's where I went every day for six months. One day I saw all these teenagers outside of the Chase on my way to work. I didn't know what it was. When I was leaving, I got on the elevator and there was Stevie Nicks and Mick Fleetwood and the whole Fleetwood Mac band! The elevator operator dropped me off at the first floor and took them down to the garage. As I walked outside, all those screaming kids were coming up to me and I said, 'You just missed them.' Another day I rode in the elevator with Sammy Hagar."

Carney moved into a mansion on Lindell when he married his wife, Jody, yet he kept the studio for a while and Zielonko continued to work there.

"One day he called me," said Zielonko. "He was at the station. I was listening to the show and I knew he'd gone to a commercial to call me. He said, 'Have you got a drinking glass?' I was wondering why he would ask that, but I looked around and found one. 'Yes,' I said. Go to my old apartment and listen through the drinking glass and I'll call you back.' Well, I thought it was pretty strange, but he was my boss so I did it. I didn't hear anything. He called me back and I asked him, 'Why did you want me to do that, Jack?' He said, 'I just found out that the sex therapists, Masters and Johnson, just rented my apartment and I wanted to know if there was any heavy breathing going on.' He was always doing things like that."

After a while, Zielonko moved into the carriage house behind Carney's home. It was a seven-room sprawling apartment and he lived in part of it and the other part was converted into a production studio.

"One day Jack called me at the studio [he was at the station] and said, 'The Smothers Brothers are staying at the Park Plaza, could you go pick them up?'" said Zielonko. "I was like 22 years old and drove a little Datson pick-up truck. I told him they wouldn't fit in my truck and he said, 'Take the Mercedes.' Well, I'd never driven this car. So I went to the hotel lobby and picked them up.

"Tommy sat in the front seat with me and Dickie, who at that time was driving Indy Light Cars, sat in the back. They could tell I didn't know what I was doing. When we got to the station and I tried to parallel park, they said, 'No, it's OK, we'll just get out here.' So they did an hour show. I remember they were talking about this bit they used to do that their dad didn't like. It was with this song they sang called 'My Old Man's A Refrigerator Repairman, What Do You Think Of That?'"

Zielonko became very close with Carney. When he did the week of shows at the Fox Theater just after it re-opened, Carney took him to dinner with the celebrities.

"We had Eddie Fisher, Jimmy Dean, Phyllis Diller," Zielonko said. "We picked all the people up at the airport. I remember Eddie Fisher saying to me, 'You're such a nice young man, you should meet my daughter, maybe you saw her in Star Wars.' Well it was Carrie Fisher. That was something being with those people and it happened all the time."

On the night Carney died, while the rest of the employees were at the station talking about how shocked they were, Zielonko was holed up in the home studio by himself preparing a special for the next morning. He worked feverishly for three days putting together tributes.

"One day Jody [his wife] came in and I quickly turned down the sound because it was his voice and I didn't want to upset her anymore," he said. "She said, 'No, no, it's OK, you keep it on,' and we listened to it a little. Then she said, 'They're cremating his body right now,'. That was such a chilling moment. People were in the house downstairs and here she was upstairs listening to Jack's voice at that moment."

Zielonko was devastated at the death of his friend, but he also had other problems.

"When Jack died, I lost half of my income," said Zielonko. "I went in to Mr. Hyland and asked him if he had more work. He hired me back full-time and I worked at the station and continued doing the *Comedy Show*. We had trouble finding a host for the show, so one time Mr.

Hyland wanted me to fly up to Chicago to try to talk Milton Berle into doing it.

"So I flew up there with Al Schotin [a friend of Jack's] and we went to the Westin Hotel to talk to Milton Berle. It soon became apparent he was not going to work for what we were willing to pay him, so we left and flew back to St. Louis the same day."

ROD ZIMMERMAN

Rod Zimmerman was brought into KMOX by CBS as general manager after the death of Robert Hyland. They knew he would not be able to replace Hyland, but that wasn't to be his job. The network gave him a budget and some goals. Zimmerman worked hard to achieve those goals.

"It was a hard act to follow," said Bob Hamilton. "He knew it, too. Rod Zimmerman kept the station going. Robert Hyland had been able to call his own shots, he had carte blanche with the network, but he was the last of the line of that. Rod Zimmerman came in with a job to do and he did it."

"I got along great with Rod," said Jim White. "When I retired, he called to wish me well. I think he got a bad rap. It was a losing situation to take over after Robert Hyland, especially when he wasn't from St. Louis and was ignorant of all that Hyland was. He was just told by the network to come in and do a job."

Zimmerman was originally from the Midwest, having grown up in Elgin, Illinois, and graduated from Southern Illinois University-Carbondale.

"One of the things Rod Zimmerman started was the Voice of Caring Campaign," said former public relations director Nancy Higgins. "Rod wanted to get the air personalities involved in charity in a community outreach, so we had a meeting about it and came up with the Voice of Caring Campaign, since the station is the Voice of St. Louis."

Each month would be dedicated to one of the on-air personalities personal charities. They would voice public service announcements and have the freedom to do shows on the organization.

"We tried to do it when it would best benefit the charity," said Higgins. "For example, October is Domestic Violence Awareness

Month, so Nan Wyatt featured ALIVE which is a support charity for victims of violence. Charles Jaco did Habitat for Humanity. He recorded a set of PSAs and then he devoted a show to Habitat for Humanity."

They kicked the program off with a radio-a-thon at Chesterfield Mall, raising $53,000 in 24 hours. It was for Ron Jacober's charity, the American Cancer Society.

"Of course, we earned the most money when Jack Buck and Randy Karraker did *Sports Open Line* from it," said Higgins. "There were several very sweet stories to come out of that telethon involving Jack Buck. They were broadcasting from a stage with a fish bowl in front for people to stop by and drop off their money. These two little girls came up with baggies full of change. Someone told Jack about them giving their money in a plastic bag. Jack got them on the air and asked them how long they had been saving their money and if they knew what it was for. After that he gave them each $100 to let them know that if you give to charity you will get twice as much back. He then matched their donations and added more to it.

"Another story involved a little boy who was disabled. He had 'I love [heart] Jack Buck' written on his face. Jack saw him and it just broke him up. Bob Rowe was our sales manager at the time and we got involved in cancer with three types: breast, prostate, and lymphoma. Bob's son had had Hodgkins' lymphoma, so it started as KMOX helping our own. His son is doing great and plays football for the University of Missouri."

"Shortly after Rod Zimmerman came, he and Tom Langmyer held separate meetings with each department," said Margie Manning, who worked in the newsroom. "They brought flip charts and all sorts of information to explain to us what our demographics were, things we should know about our market share, and just generally information about our listeners. It had never been explained to us like this before."

"He said, 'This is the audience we are going after,' and it was a much younger audience. He had a different style than we had been used to. He told us this was one of the goals of the radio station."

In the past, employees did what was expected of them and most of them were not included in the target audience. Most of the time, the

newsroom people and sports people did not really think of who they were aiming at. They went about doing the stories in the best manner they could. Suddenly with Zimmerman, there were shorter highlights, new music, young hosts. It seemed like KMOX wanted to portray itself as a snappier, more hip radio station.

"There was no doubt they were going for a younger audience," said Anne Keefe, longtime newswoman and afternoon talk show host. "They said the sponsors wanted to go after the 20-40-year-old group, maybe even younger."

"Here they are today, making more money than ever before at that radio station," said Jim White. "It all started with Rod Zimmerman and the financial constraints he was under. Times have changed and though in the past, the station may have had higher ratings, it is true that Rod had to make a lot of cuts and they paid off for him financially."

"I remember when Rod Zimmerman first got here," said Bob Heil, KMOX electronics expert. "I knew he did not know me and I went in to meet him. Here he was leaning against the door of the office that had been Mr. Hyland's—the office which was so revered to me as I had gone in and talked to him so many times. Rod Zimmerman was more casual and as I handed him a folder with something I'd written down about myself, I said something like, 'Hi, Mr. Zimmerman, I just wanted to introduce myself and give you some information about myself.' He flipped through the papers and spotted one where I had been inter-viewed in the paper for being the sound director for the Grateful Dead tour."

"He said, 'Greateful Dead? You worked for the Greatful Dead? Did Jerry Garcia really take all those drugs? Did you work for The Who? What was Pete Townsend really like?' I could tell he was so much dif-ferent from Mr. Hyland just in that first encounter. It seemed strange talking to the general manager in this casual manner in the same office I had seen Robert Hyland in."

Jim White had a dealing with Zimmerman which he appreciated, although it surprised him.

"The only contract I had ever had with KMOX was with Rod," said White. "CBS offered a buyout of your contract. I did the math and the pension could be greater than if I waited, so I accepted it. Zimmerman

came to me and said, 'We don't want you to retire.' I said, 'Well then, make me an offer I can't refuse'. He said, 'You come up with a contract,' so I had my accountant do that and I sent it to Rod. My accountant said, 'We've got a counter offer.' I said, 'How bad is it?' He said, 'They offered you more than you asked for!' So I signed a three-year contract. That really floored me."

Zimmerman left KMOX to become general manager of WBBM in Chicago.

EPILOGUE

Throughout different parts of the book, KMOX Radio staffers past and present talked about their memories of the KMOX newsroom springing into action whenever a big story happened. When President Kennedy was assassinated, one employee remembered hearing the news as she ate french fries at the Parkmoor and then headed right down to the station. When President Reagan was shot, newsroom staffers recalled the various jobs they had. When the floods came, Jack Carney died, and anytime a major news story was breaking, the people banded together and the KMOX newsroom snapped into action.

The same was true in the late hours of October 16, 2000 when word reached the station that a light plane licensed to Missouri governor Mel Carnahan went down in Jefferson County. It was after 11:30 in the evening and Charles Jaco came in and anchored the coverage. Within a few minutes of the story breaking, Nan Wyatt was on her way to Jefferson City, McGraw Milhaven was at the Carnahan campaign headquarters in University City. For additional information they went to Phil Brooks in Jefferson City. Though Brooks is employed by the Missouri Net, he has provided coverage from Missouri's capital for many years, as has Bob Priddy. Charles Jaco referred to others who were working the phones getting more information.

As it became apparent that the governor, his son, and a co-worker had been killed, KMOX Radio provided stunned listeners with details

and interviews. It was the night before the third presidential debate set to be held at Washington University in St. Louis, and the night the Cardinals had lost the National League Pennant to the New York Mets. It was also the night King Dodge (a local car dealership) went up in flames and someone drove their car through Ted Drewes' Frozen Custard store (a local landmark), all of which would have been the major news story of the day.

This book was already to the printer by that date. A listener who knew the authors had written the book commented that she had stayed up all night listening to the coverage. She'd heard the tragic news after the baseball game and could not sleep. She just wanted more information. As in so many times in the past, KMOX Radio proved to be a light in the darkness of the night for those who could not seem to get to sleep and just needed to know more.

BIBLIOGRAPHY

BOOKS:

At Your Service, KMOX and Bob Hardy: Pioneers of Talk Radio; Virginia Publishing Co.—Sandra Hardy Chinn (For more information on this book contact Virginia Publishing Co. 4814 Washington Blvd., Suite 120; St. Louis, MO 63108, (314) 367-6612.)

Voices of The Game: The First Full-Scale Overview of Baseball Broadcasting, 1921 to the Present, by Curt Smith, Diamond Communications Inc., South Bend, IN, 1987.

Historical Dictionary of American Radio, Edited by Donald G. Godfrey and Frederic A. Leigh.

A History of Missouri, Volume V 1919-1953, By Richard S. Kirkendall.

World Book Encyclopedia Book Q-R, Field Enterprises Educational Corporation, Chicago, London, Rome, Sydney, Toronto.

The Gateway Arch, Gateway To The West; Dedication Program, May 25, 1968.

The Storytellers; Curt Smith, MacMillan, 1995.

Holy Cow!; Harry Caray, with Bob Verdi, Villard Books; NY, 1989.

THE MIGHTY 'MOX

Baseball From A Different Angle; Bob Broeg and William J. Miller, Jr., Diamond Communications, South Bend, IN 1988.

Under The Influence; Peter Hernon and Terry Ganey; Simon and Schuster 1991.

This Date In St. Louis Cardinals History; John Leptich and Dave Baranowski, Stein & Day Publishers, 1983.

The Broadcasters; Red Barber, Dial Press, 1970.

Redbirds, A Century of Cardinals' Baseball; Bob Broeg, River City Publishers, 1987.

INTERNET:

Stlouisradio.com edited by Frank Absher
Oldtimeradio.com

ABOUT THE AUTHORS

Rob Rains and Sally Tippett Rains are the authors or co-authors of a combined 20 books. This is the second book they have written together. Both also are alums of KMOX Radio, where Sally worked for three years in the sports office and Rob was a frequent co-host of *Sports Open Line* programs and also a regular contributor to *Sports on a Sunday Morning*. In fact, the couple believes they owe their marriage to KMOX. Sally was working at KMOX and Rob at United Press International when they met in the pressbox at Busch Stadium in 1980.